Jewish and Christian Self-Definition
Volume Three

JEWISH AND CHRISTIAN SELF-DEFINITION

Volume Three
Self-Definition in the
Greco-Roman World

EDITED BY BEN F. MEYER
AND E. P. SANDERS

FORTRESS PRESS   PHILADELPHIA

Published in the United Kingdom by SCM Press, Ltd., London
First Fortress Press Edition 1983

Library of Congress Cataloging in Publication Data (Revised)

Main entry under title:

Jewish and Christian self-definition.

    Vol. 3 edited by Ben F. Meyer and E. P. Sanders
    Includes bibliographies and indexes.
    Contents: v. 1. The shaping of Christianity in the second and third centuries.   — v. 3. Self-definition in the Greco-Roman world.
    1. Church history — Primitive and early church, ca. 30–600 — Addresses, essays, lectures. 2. Judaism — History — Talmudic period — 10-425 — Addresses, essays, lectures. 3. Rome — Religion — Addresses, essays, lectures. 4. Philosophy, Ancient — History — Addresses, essays, lectures. 5. Identification (Religion) — Addresses, essays, lectures.
BR165.J53 1980   270.1   79-7390
ISBN 0-8006-0578-0 (v.1)   AACR2
ISBN 0-8006-0660-4 (v.2)
ISBN 0-8006-0690-6 (v.3)

9606J82   Printed in the United States of America   1-690

Contents

Contents

Contributors

Hans Dieter Betz
Professor of New Testament, The Divinity School and The Division of the Humanities, University of Chicago

G. W. Bowersock
Professor in the School of Historical Studies, Institute for Advanced Study, Princeton

Walter Burkert
Professor of Classics, University of Zürich

John M. Dillon
Regius Professor of Greek, Trinity College, Dublin

Albert Henrichs
Professor of Greek and Latin, Harvard University

Howard C. Kee
Professor of New Testament in the School of Theology, Boston University

Abraham J. Malherbe
Buckingham Professor of New Testament Criticism and Interpretation, Yale Divinity School

John M. Rist
Regius Professor of Classics, University of Aberdeen

Tran tam Tinh
Professor of Classical Archaeology, Université Laval, Québec

Contributors

Heinrich von Staden
Associate Professor of Classics and Comparative Literature; Master of Ezra Stiles College, Yale University

Preface

The essays presented here – on Graeco-Roman philosophical schools and medical schools, on religious cults and magic – treat these various institutions of the ancient world under the formality of social self-definition. Within this framework they are all expert answers to their own questions. But it should be noted from the outset that they were commissioned with the ulterior purpose of finding the answer to a question that none of them poses. To make this question clear and so to set these essays in their intended context, we must step back and survey the larger research project to which they belong.

This project is an inquiry, undertaken in recent years at McMaster University, into the historic movement towards normative self-definition both in Judaism and in Christianity during the first centuries of the common era. Judaism was an old religion, Christianity a young religion. Still, both came of age at approximately the same time; that is, by about the middle of the third century both had found the features that would make them recognizable for centuries to come. But until that time each was engaged in its own drama of decision among competing options.

For whatever reasons neither Judaism nor Christianity willingly settled for pluralism. On the contrary, both drove towards a self-definition – comprehensive, flexible, normative – fashioned for the long haul of history. A main stream had formed. An option that had been normative in intent now established itself as normative in fact and determined what set of suppositions, values and practices would henceforward inform the corporate life of the group. Judaism had become Rabbinic and Christianity Catholic.

The question, 'How and why did these developments take shape?' fundamentally defines the McMaster Project. The first volume in the series *Jewish and Christian Self-Definition* applied this question to second- and third-century Christianity; the second

ix

volume applied it to Judaism from the Maccabees to Judah ha-Nasi. In the present volume the 'how and why?' question appears in a new form. When Judaism and Christianity were moving towards the mature normativeness epitomized respectively in Mishnah and rabbinate and in New Testament and episcopate, were they moving with the general tide of Hellenistic and Roman history, or were they moving against it? Was the direction of their development typical or idiosyncratic? That is, was its explanation to be found in the sphere of comprehensive social causes? Are there persuasive analogies in the history of the institutions of the Graeco-Roman world to this Jewish and Christian drive towards normative self-definition? Or is its explanation to be found in the native traits and self-orienting tendencies of these religions?

These questions, which have concerned the McMaster research group almost from the start, may be formulated as the issue of the self-definition of institutions in the Graeco-Roman world. When first proposed to the scholars whose work is presented here, the issue was received as a 'new' and 'challenging' question, and the symposium on 'Self-Definition in the Graeco-Roman world', held in June 1980 at McMaster University, confirmed that response. The quest for analogous developments, to be sure, yielded an almost entirely negative result. But the world of ancient schools and cults came alive in exchanges that are now largely incorporated in the revised form of the papers. Those of us who are primarily engaged in biblical and post-biblical Jewish and Christian studies found ourselves brought into living contact with classical scholarship at its finest. The symposium was a happy experiment in interdisciplinary inquiry.

These essays have a richness that goes beyond the bounds of the McMaster Project. The collection assuredly does not pretend to deal with all schools of philosophy in the Graeco-Roman world nor, much less, with all that world's religious cults. But from the opening to the final essay – or from Pythagorean craftsmen in the sacred to the evolution of Roman imperial cult – they shed broad, bright, and often new light on the intellectual and religious life of the classical and, especially, later classical world. It is accordingly with great pride that we present this collection as the third volume of our four-volume series on Jewish and Christian self-definition.

The editor wishes to express heartfelt thanks for generous help before, during, and after the symposium. Dr Benno Przbylski was principally responsible for the practical arrangements of the symposium and shared in the hunt for typographical errors and

Preface

in the checking of references. Dr William J. Slater checked the
bibliographical entries and indexes. Dr E. P. Sanders cooperated
in the original planning of the symposium and, most important,
in the final preparation of the volume for the press. Ms Phyllis
DeRosa Koetting did all the secretarial tasks, including not only
typing but also the checking of references and the initial compi-
lation of bibliography and indices.

McMaster University   *Ben F. Meyer*
Hamilton, Canada

Abbreviations

Abst.	Porphyry, *De Abstinentia*
Acad. post.	Cicero, *Academica Posteriora*
Ach.	Aristophanes, *Acharnenses*
Adv. Col.	Plutarch, *Adversus Colotem*
Adv. Math.	Sextus Empiricus, *Adversus mathematicos*
Adv. Galil.	Julian, *Adversus Galileos*
Agr.	Tacitus, *Agricola*
AJ	Josephus, *Antiquitates Judaicae*
AJA	*American Journal of Archaeology*
AJP	*American Journal of Philology*
Alc.	Euripides, *Alcestis*
Alex.	Lucian, *Alexander*
Amor.	Ovid, *Amores*
Anat. admin.	Galen, *De anatomicis administrationibus*
ANET	*Ancient Near Eastern Texts* (ed. J. Pritchard), Princeton² 1955
Ann.	Tacitus, *Annales*
An. proc.	Plutarch, *De animae procreatione in Timaeo*
ANRW	*Aufstieg und Niedergang der römischen Welt*
Ant.	Plutarch, *Antonius*, Sophocles, *Antigone*
Antr.	Porphyry, *De antro nympharum*
AP	*Anthologia Palatina*
Apol.	Apuleius, *Apologia*, Justin, *Apologia pro Christianis*, Tertullian, *Apologeticum*
APAW	Abhandlungen der Preussischen Akademie der Wissenschaften zu Berlin, Phil.-hist Classe
ArchDelt	*Archaiologikon Deltion*
ARW	*Archiv für Religionswissenschaft*
Ath.	Aristotle, *Constitution of the Athenians*
Att.	Cicero, *Epistulae ad Atticum*
Ba.	Euripides, *Bacchae*

Abbreviations

bAZ	Babylonian Talmud, Abodah Zarah
BCH	*Bulletin de Correspondance Hellénique*
Bibl.	Apollodorus, *Bibliotheca*
Bis Acc.	Lucian, *Bis Accusatus*
BJ	Josephus, *Bellum Judaicum*
Bull. épig.	*Bulletin épigraphique*
CAF	*Comicorum Atticorum Fragmenta*, ed. T. Kock, 3 vols., Leipzig 1880–8
CAH	*Cambridge Ancient History*
Cal.	Lucian, *Calumniae non temere credendum*
CC	Origen, *Contra Celsum*
Char.	Theophrastus, *Characteres*
CIG	A. Boeckh, *Corpus Inscriptionum Graecarum*, Berlin 1827–77
CIL	*Corpus Inscriptionum Latinarum*, Berlin 1862–
CMG	*Corpus Medicorum Graecorum*, Leipzig 1908–
CML	*Corpus Medicorum Latinorum*, Leipzig 1915–
CN	Plutarch, *De communibus notitiis adversus Stoicos*
Cod. Iust.	*Codex Iustinianus*
Cod. Theod.	*Codex Theodosianus*
Coh. ira.	Plutarch, *De cohibenda ira*
Collect. Alex.	*Collectanea Alexandrina*, ed. J. U. Powell, 1925
Comm. math.	Iamblichus, *De communi mathematica scientia*
Comp. med. per genera	Galen, *De compositione medicamentorum per genera*
Comp. med. sec. locos	Galen, *De compositione medicamentorum secundum locos*
Comp. verb.	Dionysius of Halicarnassus, *De compositione verborum*
Cons. ad ux.	Plutarch, *Consolatio ad uxorem*
Conv.	Lucian, *Convivium*
CP	*Classical Philology*
Crat.	Plato, *Cratylus*
Cup. div.	Plutarch, *De cupiditate divitiarum*
Def.	Pseudo-Galen, *Definitiones medicae*
Def. or.	Plutarch, *De defectu oraculorum*
Dem.	Plutarch, *Demosthenes*
Demetr.	Plutarch, *Demetrius*
Demon.	Lucian, *Demonax*
Dial.	Justin, *Dialogus cum Tryphone Judaeo*
Didasc.	*Didascalia apostolorum*
Didask.	Albinus, *Didaskalikos*

Dig.	Digesta
Diog.	Diogenes Cynicus
Dion.	Nonnos, Dionysiaca
Disc.	Epictetus, Discourses
Div.	Cicero, De divinatione
D.L.	Diogenes Laertius
Dox. Gr.	Doxographi Graeci, ed. H. Diels, 1879
Ecl.	Stobaeus, Eclogae, Virgil, Eclogues
Enn.	Plotinus, The Enneads
Ep(p).	Augustine, Basil, Crates, Diogenes Cynicus, Fronto, Heraclitus, Hippocrates, Pliny, Socrates, Epistula(e)
Epp. fam.	Cicero, Epistulae ad familiares
EPRO	Études préliminaires aux religions orientales dans l'Empire Romain
Err. prof.	Firmicus Maternus, De errore profanarum religionum
Essays	A. D. Nock, Essays on Religion and the Ancient World, 2 vols., 1972
ET	English translation
Eun.	Lucian, Eunuchus
Expos.	Theon of Smyrna, Expositio rerum mathematicarum ad legendum Platonem utilium
FGrH	F. Jacoby, Fragmente der Griechischen Historiker, Berlin 1923–
Fin.	Cicero, De finibus
F, Fr(r).	Fragment(s)
Frag. Scaen.	Ennius, Fragmenta scaenica, ed. J. Vahlen, 1903
FT	French translation
Fug.	Lucian, Fugitivi
Gaur.	Porphyry, Ad Gaurum
GCS	Die Griechischen Christlichen Schriftsteller
GdH	U. v. Wilamowitz-Moellendorff, Der Glaube der Hellenen, 2 vols., Berlin 1932
Geor.	Virgil, Georgics
Gp.	Geoponica
GRBS	Greek, Roman and Byzantine Studies
GT	German translation
Haer.	Hippolytus, Refutatio omnium haeresium
HE	Eusebius, Historia ecclesiastica
Her.	Philostratus, Heroicus
Herm.	Lucian, Hermotimus

Abbreviations

Hipp. et Plat.	Galen, *De placitis Hippocratis et Platonis*
Hist.	Tacitus, *Historiae*
Hist. phil.	Pseudo-Galen, *De historia philosophiae*
HN	Pliny, *Historia naturalis*
Hom. h. Cer.	*Hymnus Homericus ad Cererem*
HSCP	*Harvard Studies in Classical Philology*
HTR	*Harvard Theological Review*
Icar.	Lucian, *Icaromenippus*
IEJ	*Israel Exploration Journal*
IG	*Inscriptiones Graecae*, 14 vols., 1873–
IGBulg.	*Inscriptiones Graecae in Bulgaria repertae*, ed. G. Mihailov, Serdica 1956–
IMagn.	*Die Inschriften von Magnesia am Maeander*, ed. O. Kern, Berlin 1900
IGRom.	*Inscriptiones Graecae ad res Romanas pertinentes*, ed. R. Cagnat et al., 4 vols., Paris 1906–
Il.	Homer, *Iliad*
ILS	H. Dessau, *Inscriptiones Latinae Selectae*, 1892–1916
Im.	Philostratus, *Imagines*
In. Hp. De artic.	Apollonius Citiensis, *In Hippocratis de Articulis commentarius*
In Hp. Epid.	Galen, *In Hippocratis Epidemiarum librum primum commentarius*
In Phd.	Olympiodorus, *In Platonis Phaedonem commentaria*
In Ti.	Proclus, *In Platonis Timaeum commentarii*
Intr. Arat.	Achilles Tatius, *Introductio in Aratum*
Introd.	Pseudo-Galen, *Introductio sive medicus*
Is. et Os.	Plutarch, *De Iside et Osiride*
JbAC	*Jahrbuch für Antike und Christentum*
JCPh	*Jahrbücher für Classische Philologie*
JEH	*Journal of Ecclesiastical History*
JHI	*Journal of the History of Ideas*
JHS	*Journal of Hellenic Studies*
JRS	*Journal of Roman Studies*
Lac. apophth.	Plutarch, *Apophthegmata Laconica*
Lat. viv.	Plutarch, *De Latenter Vivendo*
LCL	Loeb Classical Library
Legat.	Philo, *Legatio ad Gaium*
Lg.	Plato, *Leges*
Libr. propr.	Galen, *De libris propriis*

Abbreviations

LSCG	F. Sokolowski, *Lois sacrées des cités grecques*, 1955
LSJ	H. G. Liddell and R. Scott, *A Greek-English Lexicon* (rev. H. S. Jones), Oxford⁹ 1925–40 (reprinted with supplement 1960)
Luc.	Cicero, *Lucullus* (= *Academica Priora*)
Lys.	Aristophanes, *Lysistrata*
MAMA	*Monumenta Asiae Minoris Antiqua*, ed. W. M. Calder et al., 6 vols., Manchester 1928–39
Med.	Marcus Aurelius, *Meditations*
Mens.	Lydus, *De mensibus*
MH	*Museum Helveticum*
Metam.	Apuleius, Ovid, *Metamorphoses*
Meth. med.	Galen, *Methodus medendi*
MNAW.L	*Mededelingen der Koninklijke Nederlandse Akademie van Wetenschappen, Afd. Letterkunde*
Mnem.	*Mnemosyne*
Mor.	Plutarch, *Moralia*
Mort. pers.	Lactantius, *De mortibus persecutorum*
Mul. virt.	Plutarch, *Mulierum virtutes*
Mus.	Aristides Quintilianus, Philodemus, Plutarch, *De musica*
Myst.	Iamblichus, *De mysteriis*
NA	A. Gellius, *Noctes Atticae*
ND	Cicero, *De natura deorum*
Nigr.	Lucian, *Nigrinus*
NJA	*Neue Jahrbücher für das klassische Altertum*
Non posse	Plutarch, *Non posse suaviter vivi secundum Epicurum*
NovT	*Novum Testamentum*
Od.	Homer, *Odyssey*, Horace, *Odes*
Oec.	Xenophon, *Oeconomicus*
Oed.	Seneca, *Oedipus*
Olymp.	Pindar, *Olympian Odes*
Onom.	Pollux, *Onomasticon*
Op.	Hesiod, *Opera et Dies*
OpAth	*Opuscula Atheniensia*
Opusc.	Dionysius of Halicarnassus, *Opuscula*, ed. H. Usener and L. Radermacher, 2 vols., 1909
Opusc. Sel.	M. P. Nilsson, *Opuscula Selecta* I–III, 1951–60
Or.	Aelius Aristides, Isocrates, Julian, Libanius, *Orationes*

Orph. Fr.	*Orphicorum Fragmenta*, ed. O. Kern, Berlin 1922
OT	Sophocles, *Oedipus Tyrannus*
Pan. Lat.	*Panegyrici Latini*
pAZ	Palestinian Talmud, Abodah Zarah
PBSR	*Papers of the British School at Rome*
PCPS	*Proceedings of the Cambridge Philological Society*
PE	Eusebius, *Praeparatio evangelica*
PG	*Patrologia Graeca* (ed. J. P. Migne), Paris
PGM	*Papyri Graecae Magicae*, ed. K. Preisendanz, Stuttgart² 1973–4
Ph.	Euripides, *Phoenissae*
Phd.	Plato, *Phaedo*
Phdr.	Plato, *Phaedrus*
PhilosQ	*The Philosophical Quarterly*
Piet.	Philodemus, *De pietate*
Pisc.	Lucian, *Piscator*
Plac.	Aetius (Pseudo-Plutarch), *Placita*
Plant.	Philo, *De plantatione*
Poem.	Philodemus, *Peri poiēmatōn*
POxy	*Oxyrhynchus Papyri*
PP	*La Parola del Passato*
Prim. frig.	Plutarch, *De primo frigido*
Protr.	Clement of Alexandria, *Protrepticus*
Prt.	Plato, *Protagoras*
Puls. diff.	Galen, *De pulsuum differentiis*
PW	Pauly-Wissowa, *Realencyclopädie der classischen Altertumswissenschaft*, Stuttgart 1894–1978
Pyrrh.	Sextus Empiricus, *Pyrrhoneioi hypotypōseis*
Pyth.	Pindar, *Pythian Odes*
Quaest. conviv.	Plutarch, *Quaestionum convivialium libri*
Quo. adul.	Plutarch, *Quomodo adulator ab amico internoscitur*
Ra.	Aristophanes, *Ranae*
RA	*Revue Archéologique*
RAC	*Reallexikon für Antike und Christentum* (ed. T. Klauser), Stuttgart 1950–
RB	*Revue Biblique*
REA	*Revue des Études anciennes*
REG	*Revue des Études grecques*
REL	*Revue des Études latines*
Resp.	Plato, *Respublica*
RGG	*Religion in Geschichte und Gegenwart*, 6 vols.,

Abbreviations

	(ed. K. Galling), Tübingen[3] 1957–62
RGVV	Religionsgeschichtliche Versuche und Vorarbeiten
Rh.	Aristotle, *Rhetorica*
RhM	*Rheinisches Museum*
RHR	*Revue de l'histoire des religions*
RPh	*Revue de philologie, d'histoire et de littérature anciennes*
RSR	*Religious Studies Review*
RR	Varro, *Res rusticae*, Cato, Columella, *De re rustica*
RTP	*Revue de Théologie et de Philosophie*
Salt.	Lucian, *De saltatione*
Sammelb.	*Sammelbuch griechischer Urkunden aus Ägypten*
Sat.	Juvenal, *Satires*
SBAW	*Sitzungsberichte der Bayerischen Akademie der Wissenschaften zu München*, Phil.-hist. Classe
Sch. E.	Scholia in Euripidem
Sch. Luc.	Scholia in Lucianum
Scr. Min.	Galen, *Scripta Minora*, ed. J. Marquadt et al., 1884–93
SEG	*Supplementum epigraphicum Graecum*
SHA	*Scriptores historiae Augustae*
SIRIS	*Sylloge Inscriptionum Religionis Isiacae et Sarapiacae*, ed. L. Vidman, 1969
SHAW	Sitzungsberichte der Heidelberger Akademie der Wissenschaften
Smp.	Plato, *Symposium*
SMSR	*Studi e Materiali di Storia delle Religioni*
Sol.	Plutarch, *Solon*
SPAW	*Sitzungsberichte der Preussischen Akademie der Wissenschaften zu Berlin*, Phil.-hist. Classe
SR	Plutarch, *De Stoicorum Repugnantiis*
Strom.	Clement of Alexandria, *Stromateis*
SVF	*Stoicorum Veterum Fragmenta*, ed. H. von Arnim, Leipzig 1903–24
TAPA	*Transactions of the American Philological Association*
tAZ	Tosefta, Abodah Zarah
TDNT	*Theological Dictionary of the New Testament*, ed. G. Kittel and G. Friedrich, 10 vols., ET ed. G. W. Bromiley, 1964–75

Abbreviations

Tetr.	Ptolemaeus, *Tetrabiblos*
TGF(N)	*Tragicorum Graecorum Fragmenta*, ed. A. Nauck, Leipzig² 1889
TGF I, IV	*Tragicorum Graecorum Fragmenta* I, ed. B. Snell, Göttingen 1971; vol. IV, ed.S. Radt, 1977
Tranq.	Seneca, *De tranquillitate*
VA	Philostratus, *Vita Apollonii*
VH	Aelianus, *Varia historia*
	Lucian, *Verae historiae*
Vit. Auct.	Lucian, *Vitarum auctio*
Vit. Const.	Eusebius, *Vita Constantini*
Vit. contempl.	Philo, *De vita contemplativa*
Vit. Hippocr.	Soranus, *Vita Hippocratis*
Voc. Hp.	Erotian, *Vocum Hippocraticarum collectio*
VP	Porphyry, *Vita Pythagorae*
	Iamblichus, *De Vita Pythagorica*
VS	Philostratus, *Vitae sophistarum*
WS	*Wiener Studien*
WZHalle	*Wissenschaftliche Zeitschrift der Martin-Luther-Univ. Halle-Wittenberg*, Gesellschaftsreihe
ZPE	*Zeitschrift für Papyrologie und Epigraphik*

1

Craft Versus Sect:
The Problem of Orphics and
Pythagoreans

WALTER BURKERT

It is the advantage of interdisciplinary studies to raise questions
that are not yet assimilated or domesticated within a specific field
of research. The historian of ancient, 'pagan' religions is wont to
look at traditional rituals and myths from the outside, surveying
their functions and varying adaptations and interpretations, and
any attempt to arrive at an inside view becomes a kind of
psychoanalytic diagnosis or rather guess: It is stated in ancient
sources that the worshippers did not really know why they did
what they were doing, nor did they take very seriously what they
were saying in the form of myth. In so far as this holds true, the
problem of 'normative self-definition' is non-existent. Still there
were, even within the static traditional societies and their religious
practice, what we used to call 'movements' or, in a more modern
vein, 'alternative groups', forms of protest or deviance, and it is
to these that the question of self-definition is justly applied in this
symposium. Among the oldest of these 'movements', still rooted
in the archaic age, are Orphism and Pythagoreanism; the following reflections will concentrate on the pre-Hellenistic materials.

It is true that the state of the evidence might discourage any
study of this kind from the start. There is nothing even remotely
resembling the extensive documentation of Jewish or Christian
theology and party politics. The dearth of reliable sources on early
Pythagoreanism has often been deplored; as to Orphism, there
have occurred spectacular discoveries recently – the Derveni
papyrus with a Presocratic commentary on the theogony of
'Orpheus',[1] the bone plates from fifth-century Olbia with one
graffito '*Orphikoi*'[2] – but one may still speak, in the words of Albert

1

Henrichs,[3] of a 'jigsaw puzzle' with 'isolated pieces, or at best some matching colorations which suggest possible combinations; but no complete picture, not even in its broadest outlines, seems to emerge'. It is easy to dwell on the motives that have dominated the scholarly controversies about Orphism: on the one side the craving for a more spiritual, quasi-Christian religion with a 'church' and a saviour god; on the other, the irritated reaction of the 'pure' Hellenists against this 'drop of foreign blood'.[4] But how are we to get a view of the phenomenon itself, let alone an insider's view that would enable us to ask a question such as that of self-definition?

One possibility of overcoming the deadlock seems to be provided by structuralism, i.e., by establishing systematic relations between those isolated pieces. Marcel Detienne[5] has shown that we may see the Bacchic, the Orphic, and the Pythagorean movements or 'sects' as a system of alternatives to the dominating life-form of the time, the Greek *polis*. They were different *'chemins de la déviance'*. And in fact Detienne succeeds in integrating practically all the transmitted details of customs and values, of rites and myths into the picture. This is highly instructive; and still it may fail to do justice to the multidimensional complexity of historical facts. There are obvious overlaps in what is called by the sources Bacchic or Orphic, Orphic or Pythagorean – overlaps not accounted for in the structural system. The fact that Dionysus is a god, Orpheus a mythical singer and Pythagoras a historical personality suggests that we are dealing with different dimensions that cannot be divided as 'ways of deviance' on a single plane.[6]

In the following pages another approach will be tried which resolutely starts from the outside, adopting the concept of 'sect' as a well-defined sociological model. In fact the expression 'sect' has long been used with reference to both Orphism and Pythagoreanism,[7] usually without reflection, though often in a deprecatory sense. But is is in connection with church history, phenomenology of religion and, last but not least, present-day phenomena that the concept of the 'sect' has been more fully elaborated. This may give us a reference system with regard to which even fragmentary evidence can be seen either to agree or to disagree; and this in turn will provide a framework within which it can be decided whether the problem of self-defintion does exist.

The following characteristics of 'sects' are taken from the

empirical case studies of Bryan Wilson and from the remarks of Arnaldo Momigliano:[8] A sect is a minority protest group with (1) an alternative life style, (2) an organization providing (2.1) regular group meetings and (2.2) some sort of communal or co-operative property, and (3) a high level of spiritual integration, agreement on beliefs and practices, (3.1) based on authority, be it a charismatic leader or a sacred scripture with special interpretation, (3.2) making the distinction of 'we' versus 'they' the primary reference system, and (3.3) taking action on apostates. The historian will add (4.1) the perspective of diachronic stability (some religious sects have by now survived for more than two thousand years) and (4.2) local mobility (many sectarian groups have been migrating through continents without losing their identity). It is evidently the integration of family reproduction into the sectarian life, with the resulting indoctrination of the infants according to the rules of the group that makes such organizations virtually indestructible. In contrast to this, an 'order' of the monastic type remains dependent on symbiosis with a 'normal' society outside to refill their ranks, though these organizations, too, may persist through millennia. One might further distinguish an 'order' whose members have dedicated their lives to the common cause from a 'club' whose members remain integrated into the outside society. The difference between 'sect' and 'church'[9] will be mainly quantitative, minority versus majority, whereas a 'sect' is distinct from a 'religion' in so far it remains within a more comprehensive spiritual unity. There are Christian, Jewish, Islamic sects within Christianity, Judaism, or Islam. The one surviving Gnostic sect, on the other hand, Mandaeism, isolated in an Islamic environment, may conveniently be termed a 'religion'.

1. Orphism

Orphikoi

Wilamowitz – moved by the 'pure Hellenist's' animosity – was the first to pose sharply the problem whether there was anything like an Orphic sect in the classical age.[10] There was Orphic literature, no doubt, but were there any 'Orphics'? Wilamowitz put his finger on the fact that the ancient evidence for *Orphikoi* is scarce indeed. What is more, three meanings of the term are to be distinguished: it designates (1) the putative authors of Orphic poems; this use is attested since Apollodorus,[11] equivalent is *hoi*

3

amphi Orphea in Plato (*Crat.* 400C). The plural is an indication of scepticism, implying 'Orpheus, Musaeus or whoever wrote those books'. Close to this is meaning (2) of *Orphikoi*, a designation for the priests who perform initiations according to the teachings of Orpheus, *hoi ta Orphika mystēria telountes*; both expressions occur in the doxographic account of Achilles Tatius.[12] Synonymous is the term *Orpheotelestēs* which is attested three times;[13] Plato paraphrases the concept mentioning 'mendicant seers' who 'present a throng of books of Orpheus and Musaeus . . . according to which they perform their sacrifices . . . which they call *teletai*' (*Resp.* 364BE). Of course the believers would say that Orpheus himself instituted the initiations, and the sceptics that the Orpheotelests forged the Orphic writings. The problem, however, is that there is no incontrovertible attestation of meaning (3), 'Orphics' in the sense used in modern scholarship, 'members of a community founded on the authority of Orpheus'.[14] The only exception to this statement may now be found, possibly, in the Olbia graffito (n. 2).

Telestai

Apart from marginal Olbia, away in Scythia, the tangible reality behind the phenomenon of Orphism is the existence of itinerant initiation priests, the *Orpheotelestai*. One might be inclined to think that a priest, even a *'Winkelpriester'* (hedge-priest) as the Orpheotelests have often been called, implies the existence of a community. But this is not the case. It is precisely the phenomenon of a priest without a community that, though often overlooked, stands out in the figure of a *telestēs*.

Plato, in that passage of the *Republic* which is basic for our understanding of Orpheotelests (364B–365A), gives the following details; these are wandering people making money (*agyrtai*), wherefore they go to the 'doors of the rich'; they perform 'purifications' (*katharmoi*) and 'initiations' (*teletai*); they claim these are effective for the living as well as for the dead, and refer to terrible sufferings awaiting the uninitiated after death; they can make amends for an evil deed committed by a person or his ancestors; they can as well bring evil upon an enemy by 'binding' him or raising a demon against him; they use sacrifice and magical formulae (*epōidai*). Additional information on *katharmoi* and *teletai* comes from the *Phaedrus*, though Plato does not name Orpheus there, but Dionysus as the Lord of 'telestic madness':

4

Moreover, when diseases and terrible sufferings have been visited upon certain families through some ancient guilt (*palaia mēnimata*), madness has entered in and by oracular power has found a way of release for those in need, taking refuge in prayers and the service of the gods, and so, by purifications and sacred rites, he who has this madness is made safe for the present and the after time, and for him who is rightly possessed of madness a release from present ills is found.[15]

This account is more sympathetic than that of the *Republic*, since the blessings of madness loom large in the *Phaedrus*; but we find the same ritual means, the same reference to ancestral guilt and to this life and another in both passages; we are on the same track. In addition, the *Phaedrus* realistically indicates the occasions that make people turn to these *teletai*: these are 'present ills', 'terrible sufferings' such as occur in 'certain families', especially 'disease'; in modern terms, these are situations of individual crisis, somatic, psychosomatic, psychic and social disturbances. The 'Orphics', in Plato's view, are practitioners of magical healing.

This is not just Plato's view. As Wilamowitz pointed out, Euripides concurs: according to the chorus in *Alcestis*, there is no medicine (*pharmakon*) against necessity either in the 'Thracian tablets' written by the 'voice of Orpheus' or in the pharmacy of the Asclepiads;[16] this is setting magical and Hippocratic medicine side by side. The satyrs in *Cyclops*, on the other hand, boast they know a magical formula (*epōidē*) of Orpheus which will automatically burn the eye of the ogre (646) – in Plato's words, if somebody wants to harm an enemy, Orpheus is there. New corroboration comes from the Derveni papyrus:[17] the philosophically minded commentator embarks on an invective against people who 'make a craft of the holy rites', *hoi technēn poioumenoi ta hiera*, who just take the money (*dapanē*) of their clients and do not give any explanation while they make them 'see the holy things' – an expression equivalent to 'initiation'. But, like the commentator, they evidently make use of the books of Orpheus, though in a very different way. We may add a remark of Strabo,[18] speaking about enthusiasm, mantics, and mendicant charlatans (*to agyrtikon kai goēteia*): 'of this kind are the arts used in the crafts of Dionysus and Orpheus', *to philotechnon to peri tas Dionysiakas technas kai tas Orphikas*. Here 'Dionysiac' and 'Orphic' are set side by side, as the *Republic* and the *Phaedrus* passages of Plato proved to be mutually explicative. It is the 'craftsmanship' employed by

5

the migrating specialists that is suggestively expressed in Strabo's term *philotechnon* as in the phrase of the Derveni author.

Religious craftsmanship

This type of religious 'craft' is amply documented even outside what we call 'Orphic'. We know the names of some *kathartai* of the seventh and sixth centuries: Thaletas established the healing song, the Cretan *paian* at Sparta on occasion of a plague about 675 BCE;[19] Epimenides purified Athens from the 'Kylonian pollution' about 600;[20] similar feats are ascribed to the semi-mythical 'Hyperborean Abaris'.[21] We even get an insider's view in the middle of the fifth century from the *Katharmoi* of Empedocles: adorned like a god, the famous practitioner enters the town, people swarm around him asking for private oracles in practical questions such as 'which is the way to profit', but also seeking 'a healing word for long-endured sufferings'.[22] About the same time we find the polemics of the Hippocratic treatise *On the Sacred Disease* against the magicians and charlatans of the day, *magoi, kathartai, agyrtai, alazones – hoioi kai nyn eisi*; to ridicule their 'craft', the author employs the word *banausia* instead of *technē*.[23] In fact this kind of 'craftsman' is not peculiar to the Greek world; the most ample evidence comes from ancient Mesopotamia where a whole literature of magical texts and incantations for various sorts of magical priests and healers has survived.[24] In view of the close oriental contacts of eighth- and seventh-century Crete, there may even be direct connection from there to Thaletas and Epimenides. At any rate there was continuous need for such people, and no doubt some of them were quite successful; considering the astounding role of comparable practitioners even in our days, we should acknowledge without prejudice the phenomenon of religious craftsmanship dealing with individual, practical problems.

Family organization

We do not know many details about the rites and formulae of these Greek 'craftsmen'; but we can get some idea of their social standard, organization and tradition: theirs is an esoteric knowledge handed down in personal succession, normally from father to son or to a spiritual heir, a disciple and adopted son. In surveying the evidence we may well take together the initiation priests (*telestai*) and the seers (*manteis*), since both functions often go together in the same person and activities. The art of the seer is hereditary in certain families: there are the *Iamidai* and the *Klytiadai* at Olympia, somehow related also to the mythical purification priest Melampus; Herodotus dwells on the case of Teisamenos imitating his great ancestor.[25] The most famous *teletai*, the mysteries of Eleusis, were in the hands of two families, *Eumolpidai* and *Kērykes*. The families were active in spreading their respective cults: Timotheus the Eumolpid helped to install the cult of Sarapis and probably that of Korē at Alexandria,[26] descendants of Theban Ino were called to Magnesia on the Maeander as *bacchae* of Dionysus.[27] One less famous case is known in some detail by a speech of Isocrates:[28] Polemainetos – a telling name – was a successful *mantis* about 450 BCE; being without son, he chose a disciple and left him his *technē*, his books, and his money; the heir 'made use of the craft', leading an itinerant life and seeing many cities, and thus enlarged his fortune considerably, until he married into a noble family at Siphnos; this was the end of his *technē*: he just left money, but no disciple. The mother of Aeschines the orator came, as an inscription has shown,[29] from a family of seers: her brother was a successful practitioner, aspiring to the tradition of Amphiaraos; thus it remained within the family that the woman, too, in difficult circumstances, should try to make a living as an initiation priestess. From a later period comes the document which gives the most direct evidence for the genealogical organization of *telestai*: in 214 BCE Ptolemy IV Philopator gave order that 'those who perform initiations for Dionysus', *hoi telountes tōi Dionysōi*, should report to Alexandria and hand in their 'sacred book' (*hieros logos*) in a sealed exemplar and give information 'from whom they have received the holy rites, up to three generations, heōs geneōn triōn.[30] Each of them is expected to know the spiritual forefathers from whom they got 'the books and the craft'.

An analogous system of 'family' tradition is known from singers – there are *Homēridai* and *Kreophyleioi*[31] – and from doctors; the Asclepiads of Cos remained famous through Hippocrates.[32] Still earlier, in fact, Homer, in an often quoted passage,[33] grouped together these kinds of wandering *dēmiourgoi*: the *mantis*, the healer, the carpenter and the singer. Outside Greece we find the Etruscan *haruspices* who 'propagated their craft in families'[34] and once more the Mesopotamian magicians: 'the wise man will teach his son, and he will let him take an oath';[35] the corresponding

7

formulae are still found in the Hippocratic collection, the famous 'oath' and the '*nomos*' which adopts the language of *teletai*: 'Things that are holy are revealed only to men who are holy. The profane may not learn them until they have been initiated into the mysteries of knowledge.'[36]

Books and myths

Notwithstanding the personal, esoteric, 'all in the family' form of tradition, books played a prominent role in all the cases surveyed, from the Mesopotamian tablets to the *libri haruspicini*, not to forget the books of Polemainetos; there are the books of the Homerids, the library of the Asclepiads – the Hippocratic corpus – and there are the 'books of Orpheus and Musaeus according to which they perform their sacrifices'.

It has been concluded from Plato's words that these Orphic books must have contained ritual prescriptions and liturgies, whereas the surviving fragments of Orphic literature are nearly exclusively mythological in character. It is, however, the Mesopotamian model which illustrates the use of mythology precisely in the sphere of the magical practitioner: he has to overcome disease and other forms of crisis, to reinstall normal order, and the most basic means of doing so is to repeat cosmogony. Thus cosmogony, including anthropogony, is not just for the much-discussed recital at the New Year Festival, it is equally suitable to facilitate childbirth or even to cure a toothache.[37] The relics of the poetry of 'Orpheus' concentrate on cosmogony and theogony including anthropogony; the most controversial item, the creation of man from the soot of the rebellious Titans who had killed and eaten the god Dionysus,[38] has its closest parallel in Mesopotamian anthropogony: the blood of a rebellious god is mixed with clay, 'that god and man may be thoroughly mixed in the clay . . . let there be a spirit from the god's flesh'.[39] Whatever the oriental connections of Orphism may have been, this much is clear from these parallels: even the cosmogonical and anthropogonical poetry of 'Orpheus' has its place and function in the practice of the itinerant craftsman.

It was the task of the seer and healer to discover the 'ancient guilt', *palaion mēnima*, underlying the present sufferings; thus Epimenides 'did not prophesy about the future, but about the past'.[40] This would mean to single out a specific offence in every single case of affliction. Orphic anthropogony, by contrast, has

8

The Problem of Orphics and Pythagoreans

the story of the most ancient and most general kind of *mēnima*
inherent in man as such, the 'ancient grief of Persephone' in the
words of Pindar.[41] There is, no doubt, penetrating reflection and
speculation in the myth, attested now since the seventeenth
century BCE, about the rise of mankind from rebellion and guilt;
but at the same time such a myth would indefinitely multiply the
prospective clients of the religious craftsman, as the average man
is far from perfect and happy and prone to depression again and
again. Thus the Orpheotelests apparently outdid the successors
of Epimenides. The myth, especially when combined with the
doctrine of transmigration and the ensuing ascetic life-style, could
have been the basis for a religion of salvation; but it seems that
these potentialities were not fully exploited before the advent of
gnosticism. In the parallel case of Empedocles, the account of the
primordial guilt was left remarkably vague (B 115), and he did
not found a sect, he chose a personal pupil. The system of
genealogically transmitted craftsmanship prevailed. It is in this
form that 'Orphism' is well attested, and it fits the archaic
Mediterranean world.

Neither guild nor sect

'Sect' and 'craft' are two different sociological models that cannot
be made isomorphic. If we apply the criteria for 'sect' to the
Orpheotelests, we find, it is true, (1) an alternative life-style,
which may be either above or below the normal standard: such a
man is without a home, barefoot, shunning baths, but he may
also wear wreaths and fillets and purple clothes, if he can afford
it; he has his special forms of diet.[42] There is also (4) some kind of
diachronic stability, thanks to the family tradition, and utmost
local mobility. What is lacking is communal organization and
spiritual unity. As Hesiod[43] put it: 'potter bears grudge against
potter, carpenter against carpenter, beggar against beggar and
singer against singer'. This is the way specialists behave; their
existence is dependent on the condition that they remain rare and
exceptional. In Greece even the 'normal' craftsmen were working
each at his own risk and profit,[44] without institutions such as the
late medieval guilds. All the more did religious practitioners
aspire for singularity, and they never came to form any kind of
'order' (though some might belong to the same 'family'). Of
course they would make use of traditional rites, formulae, and
books according to their training; they could call themselves

'servants' of a god, as Teiresias is the *doulos* of Apollo,[45] Abaris the servant of Apollo Hyperboreios. But the decisive criterion for being a *kathartēs* or *telestēs* must have been success, and this is unforeseeable and even independent of the belief of the practitioner himself: Lévi-Strauss has drawn attention to the case of a Kwakiutl shaman who became tremendously successful in spite of his own disbelief.[46] Thus we should not expect consistency of beliefs or even dogmas; each individual would select, adopt and discard according to the exigencies of his career. 'Orphism', in this sense, is a well defined phenomenon, 'modern' in the sense that it met individual rather than collective needs, and still anything but uniform.

Thus the main question of this symposium is answered even before it can be raised: at the level of religious craftsmanship the problem of normative self-definition is non-existent. There is tradition, there is trial and error, but there is no norm nor any form of control from the inside. It did not matter for an Orpheotelest whether he himself or his colleague was truly 'Orphic', but whether he was good at his profession.

There remains the polemical passage in the Derveni papyrus (n. 17) which we might tend to call a debate on 'what Orphism really is', sheer ritual practice or philosophical understanding. The author is an 'Orphic' in our sense, adamantly upholding the authority of Orpheus while reinterpreting his words in an allegorical fashion. Still the author is far from reflecting on his own status; he is concerned with reality, *ta eonta*; thus his position is analogous to that of the Hippocratic author hitting out against the charlatans, or of Plato condemning the magicians in the name of philosophical ethics. It is only within a community that the question of self-definition really makes sense; and Orphic communities remain elusive.

To be careful: there are germs from which a community may easily grow even in the practice of the 'craftsman'. Personal charisma will automatically find 'adherents' who come back bringing their friends, and possibly begin to imitate his life-style. The *telestēs* will bring together *thiasoi*, as Aeschines's mother did (n. 29), he will impose certain rules for a 'pure' life on his clients, such as those mentioned also in the treatise *On the Sacred Disease* 2 (LCL II, pp. 140ff.), avoidances of food and special forms of clothing. Euripides (Fr. 472) has *mystai* of Idaean Zeus wearing white garments and leading a vegetarian life. There is an *Orphikos bios*, the main characteristic of which is vegetarianism.[47] Such regulations may clash with socially accepted forms of behaviour, as even the modern vegetarian or anti-alcoholic may experience; but to turn this incipient 'alternative life-style' into a sect there would be need of organization according to criteria (2) and (3) above.

No doubt organizations of this kind would come into being time and again; but this was a dangerous enterprise. There is the example of Eunus, miracle worker and inspired prophet of the Syrian goddess who became the leader of the most dangerous slave revolt in Sicily, 136/2 BCE;[48] there was the relentless suppression by the Roman senate in 186 BCE of Bacchanalia, a movement started by one priest who migrated from Magna Graecia to Etruria.[49] We know very little about Theoris, who is variously called priestess, seer and sorceress and who was put to death together with her 'family' at the time of Demosthenes under the accusation of inciting slaves against their masters.[50] A 'sect', even *in statu nascendi*, might appear to be a *coniuratio* in the eyes of the authorities, and repression was severe. It was wise for the practitioner not to embark on such a career but to keep to himself his *technē*, his money, and his life.

'Hippolytus'

There is just one classical text which might make us surmise that Orphism went some steps further from craftsmanship towards sect: the much-discussed passage from Euripides' *Hippolytus* in which Theseus makes his son a hypocrite 'Orphic': 'Be proud of yourself, and with your vegetarian diet ply a retail trade in cereals, and with Orpheus for your lord celebrate Bacchic rites, honouring the vapourings of many books.'[51] This seems to presuppose a stereotype picture of an 'Orphic', an adherent of Orpheus who practises an alternative life-style, shunning meat and sex, who takes part in ecstatic festivals, who acknowledges a spiritual authority in connection with 'many books'. And Hippolytus definitely has an elitist self-esteem by which he sees himself in contrast to all the others. Still this very attitude does not leave room for a communal 'we' that is constitutive for a sect. Hippolytus is solitary, incomparable. Thus the reference is rather to the singular 'holy man', Tartuffe – *Orpheotelestēs*. Such a man is in fact a vegetarian and possibly sexually inhibited, he makes a trade with his *technē*, has his books, especially those of Orpheus, and he may experience 'madness' while performing his cures. There is nothing to prove that Orphism at the time of Euripides outgrew the typology of religious craftsmanship at Athens.

Olbia

All the more remarkable is the new evidence from Olbia;[52] it is at the same time enigmatic, and likely to remain so. These are bone plates, roughly rectangular, about 5 to 8 centimetres, polished on one or on both sides; they seem to have been found in sizeable numbers both in a sanctuary and in residential areas; very few of them bear any marks, graffiti, or drawings. Now one, from the sanctuary, has, in the upper margin, the words *bios thanatos bios*, 'life – death – life', beneath, *alētheia* 'truth' and an A, and in the lower margin *Dio(nysos) Orphikoi*; another has *Dion(ysos)* and an A again, *alētheia*, and *psychē*. Any attempt at interpretation is hazardous as long as the function of these plates has not been established. Were they some kind of token or amulet, possibly attached to votive garments in the sanctuary? What seems clear is not only the reference to the cult of Dionysus but also a claim to 'truth' in beliefs or teachings about a transition from 'life' through 'death' to 'life', somehow concerning the 'soul'. Most startling is the word '*Orphikoi*'. In its context it is difficult to imagine that it should refer to writers of Orphic books or to Orpheotelests. Thus we are left with the – hitherto missing – meaning (3), self-designation of a 'community'; note that the considerable number of such bone plates seems to point in the same direction. If we take account of the function of the *-ikos*-suffix[53] to characterize by differentiation, we arrive at the hypothesis that among the worshippers of Dionysus one group, possibly adherents of one *telestēs*, set themselves apart by their faith in the authority of Orpheus, and were thus called *Orphikoi*. But this is bound to remain speculative; it is, however, hardly a coincidence that this evidence comes from the utmost margin of the Greek world.

2. Pythagoreans

Source Problems

Any account of the activities of Pythagoras and Pythagoreans in Magna Graecia has to struggle first of all with the source problems.[54] There is no documentary evidence, such as contemporary inscriptions.[55] We are left with literary elaborations mainly by

Aristoxenus,[56] who wrote about the time of Alexander, and by Timaeus[57] about one generation later. Both of them had excellent information, coming from Magna Graecia themselves; both exhibit corresponding bias as they exalt its achievements for an Athens-orientated literary public; both are lost but for a few quotations and re-elaborations in the surviving histories of Diodorus and of Pompeius Trogus/Iustinus and in the biographies of Diogenes Laertius, Porphyry, and Iamblichus. There were also several books of Aristotle dealing with Pythagoras and Pythagoreans, probably *hypomnēmata* with limited circulation; they too are lost.

The most extensive text to survive was Iamblichus, 'On the Pythagorean Life', part of a large-scale enterprise to revive Pythagorean philosophy about 300 CE.[58] These are hasty compositions or, rather, compilations indiscriminately using earlier and later sources. There are verbatim excerpts for pages, preserving, no doubt, original texts of Aristotle and Aristoxenus. But one may never be sure which kinds of alterations were introduced by this author, who is both chaotic and dogmatic; in addition, there is the problem of intermediary sources.

The problem is not just one of philological minutiae. Iamblichus was writing precisely at the time when Neoplatonism turned anti-Christian, inaugurating the 'pagan reaction' while Christianity attained its wordly triumph with Constantine. The reaction, however, became more and more dependent on what it meant to fight. For Iamblichus, theurgy as well as Pythagoreanism seems to be an antidote to the progress of Christianity. When using the 'Pythagorean Life' as a historical source, we must be wary of detecting echoes of contemporary Christian concepts and institutions.

This is more than suspicion. There is philological proof at least in one case: the version of Nicomachus of the catastrophe of the Pythagoreans has been independently copied by Porphyry and Iamblichus; but only in Iamblichus we find the words: 'They (the Pythagorean refugees) led a lonely life in the deserts, wherever one happened to be, and in this way, shut in, each chose above all the company of himself more than anything else.'[59] Pythagorean monks in the desert, *monazontes en tais erēmiais*, this is rather a reflex of St Antony and his followers than a testimony for Pythagorean life-style 750 years before. Hardly less treacherous is the term *koinobious* for the Pythagorean coenobites, a word practically non-existent in pagan literature.[60] The problem is that

13

there may be many more and much more subtle anachronisms of this kind in the text of Iamblichus which are not easily unveiled and still are momentous for an inquiry into the sectarian character of Pythagoreanism.

The methodical basis left will be to start from the fragments of Aristoxenus and Timaeus. Even so there remains the fact that these authors are already looking back at nearly two hundred years of Pythagorean history. Both give the picture of a kind of golden age, when Pythagoreans ruled Croton, and a catastrophe which must have occurred about 450 BCE. The direct information they could attain belongs, however, to a later period, and still they were prone to speak of what had been before, obscuring the possibly decisive differences in status and organization before and after the great divide. We must finally be content to get an idealized picture with some realistic touches, some scraps of factual information – but a picture which has been quite influential in spiritual history again and again.

Pythagoreioi and Bios Pythagoreios

In marked contrast to the elusive 'Orphics', the basic fact about Pythagoreanism is the existence of *Pythagoreioi*, people generally designated as the followers of a certain individual. This kind of designation was current in party politics of *hetairia* style:[61] there were the *Kyloneioi* at Athens or the *Diagoreioi* at Rhodes, there were the *Dioneioi* at Syracuse with whom Plato was in contact; also adherents of what we call philosophers would get such a label as *Hērakleiteioi* or *Anaxagoreioi*. As to *Pythagoreioi*, we equally find them designated as 'friends', *philoi, hetairoi, gnōrimoi,*[62] *homilētai* of Pythagoras.

A *hetairia* would regularly meet for drinking parties, co-operate in political and legal proceedings and often wield political power. Pythagoreans, however, were evidently set apart by a very special life-style. The sources do not agree on all the details, least of all on the question of vegetarianism, but so much is clear: there was something very peculiar about a Pythagorean life, an *idiasmos*.[63] Pythagoreans had to know and to obey a set of very specific rules that would distinguish them from normal people and make them recognize each other; in this sense the rules were called *symbola*, tokens, but they were given symbolic explanations already by the time of Socrates.[64] These were prescriptions such as not to step over a yoke, not to stir a fire with a knife, or not to pick up food that falls from the table; especially there were complicated regulations concerning religious cult. Much of this would hardly be noticed by people outside, and still it would accompany a Pythagorean through the whole of his daily life, so that he should never forget he was not like the others. Dicaearchus, contemporary of Aristoxenus, has a story – which is hardly historical – on the Locrians refusing admission to Pythagoras when he comes as a refugee: we like our own ways, they say, and our constitution, and we do not want to change.[65] To turn Pythagorean means to change one's life.

Communal Life and Property

A special life-style, as we saw, might go together with many forms of purifications and *teletai*. What is definitely unique with Pythagoreans in the Greek world is a communal daily life and a sort of 'communism'. Here, though, the uncertainties become virulent whether this applies to the 'house' of Pythagoras himself or to a clique wielding political power at Croton or to various scattered groups after the catastrophe. Still the phenomenon in itself is of more than passing interest.

The reports of Pythagorean communism go back to Timaeus at least,[66] who brought the proverb *koina ta philōn*, 'common is what belongs to friends', into this context. Epicurus discussed, and discarded, the Pythagorean model.[67] Timaeus was apparently describing the advent of Pythagoras in Magna Graecia: 'As the younger men approached him and wanted to become his disciples, he did not allow this at once, but said that also their possessions must become common property'.[68] It was handed over to members specially assigned to the task.[69] If a fellow failed the five years' probation period, it was given back to him with interest; otherwise they 'became members of the house of Pythagoras'.[70] A more spectacular version of the foundation of the Pythagorean community is given by Nicomachus:[71] By his first 'lecture' in Italy Pythagoras converted more than two thousand people so that they 'did not go home again, but together with wives and children they built a gigantic auditory (*homakoeion*) and thus founded the so-called Magna Graecia . . . And they made their possessions common property and counted Pythagoras among the gods.' We are left with the question how on earth such a project could have worked. The notion of common property handled by Pythagoras recurs in the story about Abaris, who had collected gold for his god, Hyperborean Apollo, and was persuaded by Pythagoras to hand this fortune over 'to the fellows as common property'.[72]

Diodorus, probably following Timaeus, speaks of 'those who lived together all day', *hoi kath' hēmeran symbiountes*,[73] but also of others outside, a kind of corresponding fellows. Also various anecdotes about Pythagoreans helping each other in financial and other matters[74] presuppose that they were individuals living independently with their private household and fortune.

It is Iamblichus who has a coherent description of the common life of 'the' Pythagoreans.[75] In the morning, he says, they would take a lonely walk; then they met each other, preferably in sanctuaries, for edifying talks; after some bodily exercise there was breakfast at last, consisting of bread and honey. Then followed the working hours, spent on political duties. In the later afternoon they took another walk, in groups of two or three, and later, after a bath, they met for the common meal, usually in groups of ten, the perfect number. Dinner began with libations and the burning of incense; eating had to end before sunset. After concluding libations there was reading (*anagnōsis*), with the youngest member reading aloud what the eldest had chosen. Finally, with a last libation, the eldest imparted moral admonitions, and thus they went off to bed. The elements of this picture demonstrably come from Aristoxenus.[76] The similarity to a monastic rule is nevertheless overwhelming; 'reading' after dinner sounds especially strange even for the time of Plato and Aristotle. Iamblichus must have retouched the picture heavily. Still at closer inspection – and this must belong to the Aristoxenean outlines – these Pythagoreans are not really 'coenobites', they have their own houses and affairs to care for, they meet and dissolve; they form a kind of club or rather academy, and this may well have been the ideal of Aristoxenus.

More realistic is the situation of Pythagoreans implied in fourth-century anecdotes. There is first the story of Damon and Phintias which Aristoxenus claimed he had heard from Dionysus II himself.[77] Thus the incident is neatly dated 367/357 BCE. There are only two persons involved: they live together in a common household, without family, as it seems; Phintias handles all the economical affairs and therefore asks, after the tyrant's fake death-sentence, for one day to close his accounts, and gives his friend as a hostage. Both had drawn attention just by being *Pythagoreioi*; this made the tyrant single them out for his cruel

16

game. Evidently we are dealing with an experiment in alternative life-forms on a totally private basis: this is one form of Pythagoreanism of the time.

Another anecdote, told by the Hellenistic writer Neanthes,[78] evidently tried to outdo the Damon-Phintias-story: it is the 'great' Dionysius I (died 367 BCE) who becomes curious about Pythagoreans, and, as befits a 'real' tyrant, there is sheer cruelty, massacre, and torture. Still the background is once more remarkable: there is a group of about ten Pythagoreans who lead a common life; they used to spend the winter at Tarentum and the summer at Metapontum, attuning themselves to the ryhthmical changes of the year, and they are attacked while migrating all together between the two cities. There is one married couple among them, Myllias and Timycha, who is pregnant. Once more we have a very small group who wish to live their own life, a life different from others; they are not attached to one city; the taboo on beans is to play a crucial role in the story. Even if it is invented, it does indicate how we should see the realities of Pythagorean communities in the fourth century.

Sex and Women

Inherent in the Timycha anecdote is another feature that might strike us as no less 'modern' than communism: the equal status of women side by side with men. The fact that there were female as well as male Pythagoreans is often stressed in the sources. The 'Pythagorean woman', *Pythagorizousa*, even became a title figure in fourth-century comedy.[79] What goes beyond coeducation is that apparently in Pythagoreanism the same code of sexual morality is applied to men as it is to women: extramarital intercourse is forbidden to either sex; Pythagoras persuaded the Crotoniates to send away all their concubines, the story goes.[80] This, however, is not in the name of pure asceticism. Sex and procreation within marriage is encouraged beyond the average Greek standard.[81] Whereas in traditional ritual any kind of *aphrodisia* might be counted as 'polluting', it was to 'Theano the wife of Pythagoras' that a 'famous' saying was attributed: a woman, rising from her own husband, may approach the gods at once.[82] One must beget children, a Pythagorean rule said, in order to leave worshippers for the gods.[83] In the nether world, we are told, Pythagoras found out, among other things, that special punishment is reserved for those men who decline cohabitation with their own wives; no wonder the Italiote sisters of Lysistrata found Pythagoras a great man.[84] We recognize the sneer at Pythagorean morality, but there is more than a joke here. The 'new' sexual morality, well known to us from the Jewish-Christian tradition, meant abolishing those liberties which function as contraceptives, and thus enhancing the chance of the group for physical survival. In fact we are told by Iamblichus, probably echoing Aristoxenus,[85] that Pythagoreanism persisted 'from those who had known Pythagoras and through their offspring for many generations'.

Apostates

One trait remains to give the finishing touches to the picture: there was severe action on apostates. Once more the basic text seems to come from Timaeus, in continuation of the description of the probation period as mentioned above:[86] if a novice failed the protracted test, he was sent away with his money, and a grave monument was set up for him: he had died to the community, 'and whoever met him afterwards behaved as if this were a different person: the others, they said, were dead'. Iamblichus (74) refers to two specific cases, giving names. Timaeus, in addition, mentioned that Empedocles 'was found guilty of stealing the Pythagorean teachings, and was therefore prevented from participating'.[87] Thus, exclusion hits the traitor who has published secret lore. On this a Hellenistic forgery seems to elaborate, the 'Letter of Lysis to Hipparchus',[88] designed to introduce apocryphal Pythagorean *hypomnēmata* to the market; the addressee, who 'is said to teach philosophy publicly', is threatened: 'If you repent, I shall be glad; if not, you are dead for me.' The theme then becomes confused with another story of how a betrayer of mathematical secrets perished by drowning on account of divine wrath.[89] More realistic is the idea that those who overthrew Pythagorean rule at Croton were recruited among the reprobates who had prematurely been declared dead.[90] To establish facts with any confidence seems impossible. But the very idea is remarkable or even unique in the Greek world: ritual exclusion from the community in the most adamant form, by irrevocable death.

A full-fledged sect?

Now if we return to our sect criteria, the result will be quite different from the case of Orphism. In Pythagoreanism we find not only an alternative life-style fully developed to mark the differentiation from 'normal' people, but also a communal organization with regular meetings and some form of common property, a high level of spiritual integration based on the authority of the founder, and even action on apostates; there is, further, remarkable local mobility of groups and diachronic stability provided by sexual morals that encourage reproduction. What seems to be missing is the sacred scripture. The various editions of an *'Hieros Logos'* by Pythagoras were, as far as we can see, secondary falsifications without noticeable influence.[91] The belief in transmigration was important, but it does not seem to have taken a systematic, dogmatic form.[92] Still the whole complex of the Pythagorean life, with all its rules and avoidances, seems to have rested on the most authoritarian foundation, the Master's words; *autos epha*, 'he himself said it', and this is the end of the discussion.[93]

In other words: all the elements that constitute the phenomenon of a sect do appear in the Pythagorean evidence. The conclusion will be that there was indeed a Pythagorean sect, or possibly several sects using the name *Pythagoreioi*. At any rate, to use the most cautious phrasing, Pythagoreanism comes closest to the phenomenon of sect among all comparable 'movements' in pre-Hellenistic Greece.

This is not to overlook the fact that items of the other, the 'craftsmen' model of 'family' type, equally make their appearance in the Pythagorean conglomerate. The legend makes Pythagoras a miracle-worker in the style of Epimenides,[94] but he seems to have had no disciple in this kind of craft;[95] the Pythagorean life is not in need of a charismatic *telestēs*. As in the 'families' of craftsmen, a Pythagorean would call his teacher his 'father';[96] but this occurs as well in the context of early Christian baptism. What is decisive is the emergence of a communal 'we' instead of the exploits of the singular specialist; and this happened with the Pythagoreans.

What about the truly religious dimension of this 'sect'? Obviously there were not any new gods in the preaching of Pythagoras. Even if he was thought to be Apollon Hyperboreios himself, this was a traditional god's name. Still, dealings with the sacred were of primal importance in the Pythagorean life. 'The largest part' of prescriptions 'covers sacrifice . . . and death and burial.' 'Whatever they define about doing or not doing aims at the divine.'[97] In this sense Pythagoreanism was a quasi-puritan sect within the more general complex of Greek religion.

Akousmatikoi and Mathematikoi

It is confirmation and yet a surprise that a quarrel about self-definition was indeed started within the Pythagorean movement. There is just one document for this event, a text copied twice by Iamblichus, and wilfully altered in one of his versions.[98] Here is what must have been the original form, and there are arguments to suggest that it is based on no less an authority than Aristotle:

> There are two forms of Italiote, so-called Pythagorean philosophy; for there were two sorts of people pursuing it, the 'acousmatics' and the 'mathematicians'. Of these, the 'acousmatics' were recognized as Pythagoreans by the others, but they in turn did not recognize the 'mathematicians', saying that their activity did not even stem from Pythagoras but from Hippasus. . . But the Pythagoreans who deal with *mathēmata* admit that the 'acousmatics' are Pythagoreans, and say that they themselves are even more so, and that their own pronouncements are true. They say that the cause for the difference had come into being in the following way: Pythagoras came from Ionia and Samos at the time of tyranny of Polycrates, when Italy was at its prime, and the leading men in the cities became his friends. Now with the older men among them, who were busy in politics, Pythagoras spoke in simple terms, because it seemed difficult to teach them by way of mathematics and scientific proof; and he thought they would have no less profit if they knew what to do even without a reason, just as a doctor's patients regain their health even if they do not hear in advance why they have to comply with the prescriptions. But the younger people whom he met, those who were able to make some effort and to learn, were taught by way of scientific proof and mathematics. Thus they themselves, the 'mathematicians' say, stem from these, and the 'acousmatics' from the others.

We have, then, two rival groups within the common denomination of *Pythagoreioi* who disagree on what Pythagoreanism really is. For the 'acousmatics' this means strict adherence to the rules and sayings of Pythagoras as handed down in community tradition: 'They try to preserve whatever was said by Pythagoras as divine dogmas . . . and those among them they think outstanding in moral insight who have acquired possession of the largest number of *akousmata*.'[99] The others speak of truth, scientific proof, and mathematics: rationalists versus ritualists. The stance taken by each group against the other is complicated: the 'acousmatics' simply deny the Pythagorean status of their opponents and relish the story about divine punishment for Hippasus. The 'mathematicians', on the other hand, are not in a position to contest that the 'acousmatic' way of life is legitimately derived from the teaching of Pythagoras; but, they say, there is 'more' to it, as the 'younger' generation, with tactful forbearance, feels fit to surpass the older. Pythagoras, they say, found a way of rational thought, and if not everybody is able to follow suit, it is still the higher way; thus they are 'even more' Pythagorean. All of a sudden this designation can appear in the comparative: class inclusion turns into gradation of essence. In an additional defensive argument[100] they claim that Pythagoras had given rational explanations for all his apparently absurd commandments, but that these reasons had got lost in the course of transmission: modernism tries to define itself as re-discovery of origins, turning reaction into degeneration.

We cannot tell when exactly this interesting debate occurred; probability points toward the end of the fifth century BCE. In the fourth century, both strands of Pythagoreanism virtually disappeared, whereas in the field of literature, thanks to the writings of Platonists and of Aristoxenus, victory clearly fell to the 'mathematicians'. All the more valuable by its impartiality is the document preserved by Iamblichus. It is hardly necessary to comment further on the quite characteristic strategies adopted in this quarrel on Pythagorean self-definition. Suffice it to say that once again Pythagoreanism comes closest to features currently observed in the history of later sects and churches.

'de Grèce en Palestine?'

It is intriguing that the emergence of a religious sect in archaic Greece occurred just at the time when Judaism took the decisive steps to arrive at the form which has persisted to the present day. Correspondences between Pythagoreanism and Judaism have been noticed ever since Aristobulus,[101] and later writers were inclined to treat a Jewish sect such as the Essenes as a kind of Pythagoreanism.[102] Possibilities of mutual influences in the Hellenistic period have been ventilated by Isidore Lévy.[103] One might add that there was a common background in the stirring of oriental traditions at the onset of the Persian empire. Still this will not take us beyond generalities and possibilities. The pleasing story, in Neanthes,[104] of how Pythagoras was instructed at Tyre by Chaldaeans is not of much help.

The fact remains that in Greece Pythagoreanism was a unique experiment that failed and disappeared again, but for a vague ideal that lived on in literature.[105] It was evidently the overriding power of the *polis* with its thorough military and political organization that did not tolerate sects but upheld the claim to furnish the primary reference system for any 'we/they' dichotomy. And with rhetoric and philosophy taking over intellectual guidance, the tendency was towards universalism and not at all towards sectarianism. A Greek man, as witnessed by Aristotle, was much more *zōion politikon* than *homo religiosus*; his normal self-definition would be, in growing circles, I am (e.g.) an Athenian – I am Greek – I am human. It was a fundamental change when, later on, this self-definition as 'a man' came to appear as the mark of alienation rather than of identity and to necessitate transcendent salvation within the closing horizons of sect or church.

2

Are You a Stoic?
The Case of Marcus Aurelius

JOHN M. RIST

I have chosen in what follows to raise the question of self-definition among the Stoics by way of a particular example. An examination of the thought of Marcus Aurelius will show that it is legitimate to ask whether he is a Stoic or not. No one would doubt that Zeno or Chrysippus, or even Epictetus, were Stoics, and, of course, they claimed to be. But Ariston, Zeno's pupil, probably also made such a claim, yet was regarded as heterodox in so far as he understated the importance of physics, and indeed held that ethics alone is the essential part of philosophy. It is important to observe that though never denounced as such as heretical, his unorthodoxy was noticed in the ancient world itself. But, one might say, Zeno himself seems to have found Ariston unsatisfactory, and such disapproval might well do to label a man 'un-Stoic'. But, after the founder, whose disapproval could secure such an effect? Nor is the matter resolved by saying that Stoics functioned within Stoic schools: many Stoics had merely read their Stoicism or talked to Stoicizing individuals, and then claimed to be Stoics or desiderant Stoics. Marcus Aurelius is to be viewed as a test-case. If we can determine whether and why he is a Stoic, or how far he can be called a Stoic, perhaps we have made some progress towards understanding who was and who could claim to be a member of the school. Perhaps we can also see what happens when one's portion of Stoicism becomes minimal.

Marcus as Stoic

Though, in company with other scholars, I have claimed him for the school,[1] Marcus Aurelius himself never claimed to be a Stoic. Since in the *Meditations* and (marginally) in letters he is writing for himself (or in the case of letters for one other familiar), telling himself about forty times to 'always remember', there is no reason why he should act as a propagandist or teacher, speaking of technical details which he knows well. Of course, if, as has been suggested, he is indulging in a form of 'spiritual exercise',[2] the same argument would hold, but we should err if we accepted too formal a structure for the *Meditations*. [3] Marcus's mention of the Stoics, as a group, helps us to understand where he stood: 'Things are somehow in such a mystery (*egkalypsei*) that not a few philosophers, and those no ordinary ones, thought that they are quite beyond our grasp (*akatalēpta*). Even the Stoics find them hard to grasp' (5.10). The reason for this is that every assent is liable to be in error, for where is there a man who is not liable to error? These words are not so much those of the professed Stoic, but of a man for whom Stoicism is the superior philosophy, but who also concedes much to the Sceptical opponents of that school. We notice at once Marcus's feelings of uncertainty in matters epistemological.

Many but not all of Marcus's teachers were Stoics, or admirers of Stoicism. Such were Sextus of Chaeroneia, the nephew of Plutarch,[4] from whom Marcus learned his basic orientation to the 'concept of living according to nature', Apollonius of Chalcedon,[5] from whom he learned *inter alia* to look to nothing but Reason, pain and personal loss notwithstanding, and to be 'always the same' (*to aei homoion*), and, advancing beyond the professoriate, Junius Rusticus,[6] one time prefect of the City, twice decorated with the consulate. Rusticus advised him to keep off idle philosophical speculation – good Roman advice – and gave him a chance to look at a copy of Epictetus's *Discourses*. To these we should add Maximus, perhaps Claudius Maximus,[7] like Rusticus and Severus (1.14) a 'Roman statesman with a leaning to Stoicism', one time proconsul of Africa, who showed an indomitable soul during severe illness. There was also a certain Catulus.[8] It was a group much influenced by Stoicism, but there were others: Severus (probably, as Farquharson says,[9] Cn. Cl. Severus Arabianus [cos. 146]), a Peripatetic who, however, introduced Marcus to the 'Stoic' heroes, Thrasea Paetus, Helvidius Priscus, Cato, Dion (of Syracuse) and Marcus Brutus, and preached of a single state dispensing one law for all and freedom of speech; also the Platonist Alexander (of Cilician Seleucia?) who, however, only taught him not to use 'business engagements' as a device for evading personal obligations (1.12). There was also Fronto.

Marcus tells us he first acquired the concept of life according to
Nature from Sextus of Chaeroneia. It was an ideal preached, of
course, by the Stoics, and in varying forms advocated by others
too. Zeno first acquired the ideal from Polemon of the Old
Academy,[10] we are told, and Marcus (in 5.10.2) maintained it as
one of the two pillars of the good life. One should be comforted
with two thoughts, that nothing can befall a man that is not
'according to the nature of the cosmos' and that I can be compelled
to do nothing contrary to 'my god and daimon'.

What is the content of a life according to Nature? First some
caveats. Pain is not 'unnatural', and hence not evil. If a man
suffers, it is of no significance provided he does a 'man's work'
(*ta tou anthrōpou*, 6.33). Apparent evils, the lion's jaws, or pains,
are side-effects of what is good. Here indeed is the classic Stoic
theory;[11] they are consequences (*kat' epakolouthēsin*) of the common ruling principle of the cosmos. The marvel is not that there
are such things in the world, but that there are so few of them!
Evil in the world is like sawdust in a carpenter's shop (8.50). The
idea itself goes back at least to some remarks of Chrysippus, in his
book *On Providence*,[12] though Marcus's immediate source or
sources are unknown. It is interesting, however, to note that
Marcus does not quote Chrysippus's text exactly: Chrysippus
wrote *kata parakolouthēsin*; Marcus has *kat' epakolouthēsin*. But he
also mentions that he has no time to read these days; perhaps his
memory was inexact.

Life according to Nature, then, is doing a man's job, regardless
of any accompanying pain or discomfort. It is the shortest and
'soundest' path, which not only saves trouble in the long run, but
leads us immediately to the avoidance of 'mental reservations'
(*oikonomia*), affectation (4.51) and other such forms of speech –
which indeed are signposts of the perverse. As is appropriate for
an Emperor, Marcus is peculiarly conscious of freedom of speech
and the need to avoid dissimulation; together with this goes the
exhortation not to 'swing the dog', or, as he puts it 'play the
Caesar' (6.30; cf. 1.17.3). Such forms of dishonesty, says Marcus,
he had learned from Fronto to reject: the envy, deviousness
(*poikilia*) and dissimulation that are characteristic of the tyrant
(1.11). Freedom of speech (*parrēsia*, 1.6) a virtue both Roman and
Cynic, is both sign and itself part of the constant life, the being
always the same, the living according to nature. Listening to
flattery is therefore hateful – and dangerous (1.16.3; 6.26,30).
Flattery destroys one's natural modesty (1.2; 6.16; 8.5; 10.13;

11.1.2), a quality praised by Epictetus, as well as one's good faith (*pistis*; 3.11.2; 10.13); or indeed one's mental honesty.

It is not only the vanity of the tyrant that Marcus fears; other, perhaps more ordinary, vices threaten the 'lack of passion' (*apatheia*, 11.18.10) which is his ideal, and which, he is convinced, brings him the strength a man needs. Anger, in particular, is not only damaging to one's honesty, but to one's 'manliness,'[13] though Marcus claims to agree with Theophrastus that it is less heinous than lust (2.10), by which latter vice he is in fact much less troubled. But he is particularly concerned that the good man should not even be angry at the injustice, vice and toadying he sees, as Seneca saw, all around him.

Sexual excesses Marcus thinks he has overcome. He began his sexual career late (1.17.2), he tells us gratefully; he 'did not touch Benedicta and Theodotus', and even when involved in sexual relationships, was later cured of such passion (1.17.6). Early on too he had learned to avoid the fervour for Blues or Greens at the races (1.5); (he found the monotony of the amphitheatre like the monotony of life as a whole [6.46]) and to avoid superstition (1.6; 1.16.3). But if, on Marcus's conscious view, such moral victories were easy, subtler temptations remained, in particular – and importantly – the avoidance of 'showy' virtue, a vice at which some at least of the so-called Cynics and Stoics excelled, at least in the opinion of the historian Tacitus,[14] and of Epictetus.

The good man should not strike tragic poses in misfortune (3.7): neither tragic actor nor whore, Marcus comments laconically (5.28), presumably telling himself not to behave like such, though the phrase has understandably puzzled the commentators. Playing the tragic hero is unimpressive to other people (11.3), and in matters of life and death such play is associated in Marcus's mind with mere contrariness, opposition for opposition's sake to the divine and rational order of the world.[15] But Marcus's remarks on tragic acting – a possible vice of Philip of Macedon, Alexander and Demetrius of Phaleron (9.29) – are merely a prelude to an attack on what he feels to be the more serious problem. Posing in every form is objectionable, but it is worth noting how peculiarly undesirable is posing as a 'moral athlete', as again some of the Cynics had done (1.7). Similar remarks are made by Epictetus. Such posing is a more sophisticated form of the crude lust for fame, but 'the acclamation of the multitude is just a clamour of tongues. Then you've let poor little fame go too. What is left that is worth while? To act according to our own individual constitution' (6.16.2) – a phrase which reminds us that the goal of life according to some of the 'more recent' Stoics, as Clement of Alexandria tells us, was to live 'according to the constitution of man'.[16] Needless to say, if fame as statesman or moral athlete is unimportant (though Marcus recognizes the heroic status of Thrasea, Helvidius, Cato and Socrates, as we have seen), vain learning is equally to be rejected. Marcus gives thanks that he progressed only a little way in rhetoric or poetry (1.17.4) – he might have become preoccupied with them – and Rusticus in particular happily dissuaded him from speculative composition (1.7). But the temptation remained: cast away your thirst for books, he tells himself rather pathetically (2.3). They are temptations to be bracketed with those of the flesh (*tōn sarkiōn*, 2.2).

At the end of it all suicide is available. Epictetus is quoted appropriately: if the smoke is too great, then leave the house (5.29; cf. 8.47; 10.8). If a man cannot live as Reason dictates, he should die (10.32; 3.1; cf. 10.22). But suicide, being apparently a matter of indifference, should not be undertaken, of course, frivolously or for show. A man should die with a good grace (*eumenēs*, 8.47; cf. 11.3), without clinging to a degrading form of existence;[17] when considering his own death he should take the words of Epicurus seriously: it is not pain, but moral risk that should be feared, that provides 'too much smoke'. 'What is unbearable destroys us, what is chronic can be endured' (7.33).[18] Of course, pain should not be exacerbated by mere misgivings (7.64). Such material is traditional enough among practising Stoics.

Non-Stoic elements

Why then did we observe above that Marcus never calls himself a Stoic? So far we have seen little to which a Stoic would not subscribe. But the history of Greek philosophy should alert us, I think, to at least one reality, namely, that there is a difference between truth and appearance, between knowledge and true opinion. And if we look below the surface of what Marcus says to the reasons why he says what he says, we find much that is unexpected. Consider the basic topics of traditional Stoic philosophy – logic, physics and ethics – or even the weaker version of this triad preached by Epictetus. In each area, as well as in psychology, which somehow falls into the wasteland between physics and ethics, we shall find Marcus at least toying with, and at most accepting, un-Stoic theses. To him it seems that in practice such theories are often as good as or better than those of the Stoa for buttressing the ethical code we have briefly discussed, at least in some of its practical implications.

Logic obviously need not detain us; technical work in the subject had long ceased among Stoics, and Marcus does not even indicate the acquaintance with its technicalities shown by Epictetus, who had his own reasons for setting the value of logic low, but who is, after all, our chief source of knowledge for Diodorus Cronus's Master Argument, and whose reading in the subject, and perhaps also his thinking, was extensive. But for all we know, Marcus is ignorant of such things; and he only mentions syllogisms disparagingly.[19]

Turn now to Marcus's brief remarks about causation. See things as they are, he likes to say; distinguish them into Matter, Cause (apparently efficient cause),[20] and Objective (*anaphora* = final cause).[21] It looks like a traditional analysis of causation, but the language is not technically Stoic: *anaphora* does not occur in this sense in Von Arnim's collection of fragments of the Old Stoa and the detailed language of technical accounts of causation to be found there is absent in Marcus. Consider a further passage from Book 9: at 9.25 we find the almost unintelligible (and perhaps corrupt – should we read *poiētikon?*) phrase *poiotēta tou aitiou*,[22] which may refer to a final or efficient cause; and a material cause is also mentioned. Marcus then continues with an orthodox use of the phrase *to idiōs poion*, which here seems to mean 'individual object', as it does in at least one other text of the *Meditations*.[23] It is a curious mixture of technical Stoic terminology with vague analysis which could come from almost any source.

Marcus boasts not only of not taking much interest in meteorological phenomena (1.17.8), he tells himself to recall that the happy life depends on little or no knowledge of 'physics' as of logic (7.67), perhaps, as Farquharson says, thinking of Socrates. At any rate Chrysippus thought differently, if, as appears to be the case, Marcus meant that your physics has nothing to do with your morals. In his *Propositions of Physics*, as reported by Plutarch, Chrysippus argues that there is no more suitable way of approaching the theory of good and evil, the virtues or happiness, than from the study of the 'universal nature and the dispensation of the universe'.[24] But, it may be objected, perhaps Marcus is only following the usual Stoic line of saying that physics is of no importance for its own sake. The matter cannot be explained away so easily, for on certain rather important issues Marcus seems not to be concerned with the rightness of the Stoic view at all. Instead, he seems to take the rather Epicurean attitude that any explanation which enables him to say what he wants to say about ethics is adequate. But this really is un-Stoic, for orthodox Stoics hold that a proper ethics cannot in fact be based on Epicurean principles. In contrast to that, let us listen to Marcus on the basic structure of the universe: 'Either a well arranged cosmos or a confused medley (*kykeōn*), but still a cosmos' (4.27), i.e., the cosmos is either as described by (among others) the Stoics or as by the atomists; 'either all things proceed as in one body from one intelligent source . . . or there are atoms and nothing other than a medley and a dispersion. Why are you concerned?' (9.39).

Another text (4.3.2) is even more illuminating: Remember the choice, says Marcus, either Providence or atoms. This is a reply to a sense of discontent. The only alternative to allowing that this world is providentially arranged is to follow the atomists. The argument seems strange; its form would apparently run as follows: if your discontent leads you to deny that you are doing well *sub specie aeternitatis*, you are denying Providence. If you deny Providence, you are an atomist. For all Chrysippus's dislike of atomism, that is not how he would have proceeded. Yet this passage of Marcus does not stand alone. What matters is that Providence must be upheld – or perhaps the world is intolerable. Stoicism might seem to tell him not so much *how* Providence is upheld, but *that* Providence is upheld. In 6.10 the matter is put more apocalyptically. If the world is a chance medley and has no unity or Providence, why should I wish to remain alive? Elsewhere (10.6.1) Marcus backs off from the sharpness of the disjunction: whether there are atoms or nature (i.e. Providence), let it be agreed that I am part of the whole, controlled by nature. That is what matters. The same point is reached at 11.18 by another route: 'If not atoms, then whole-controlling Nature. If Nature, then the lower exist for the sake of the higher, and these for each other' (this axiom is said to be the genesis of justice, 11.10).

Finally there is the most reassuring line of all (12.14): either Providence or chaos. But *even if chaos*, you have a guiding reason (*noun hēgemonikon*); that is, even if the Epicureans are right and there is no Providence, you at least are safe. But normally Marcus is prepared to assume that since you have your guide, the Epicureans are wrong. In all this we must affirm that Stoic explanations of the ultimate nature of things are important *only* because they support the doctrine of Providence, and even

Providence itself may not matter provided the governing Reason can be maintained. And of that Marcus tells himself again and again he is certain, as we shall see. This is not an isolated passage, at least in the twelfth book; that all that is needful can be salvaged whether we posit chance *or* Providence occurs again in ch. 24.

From the evidence just cited it is apparent that what matters to Marcus is the nature and capabilities of the Reason within us. Normally he is happy enough to go along with the view, common enough in later Stoicism, that in some sense reason is a fragment (*apospasma*) of God. We shall return to this question, and to the nature of reason in general, when we talk specifically about Marcus's psychology. For the moment let us consider some ideas he displays both in physics and in psychology. We should attend to his talk of effluences (*aporroia*). Everything flows 'from there'; this phrase, to be found in 2.3, is perhaps the most striking of these ideas. The antithesis of 'this world' and 'there', as a way to express a generalized contrast between the life of the Divine Mind and the life of the 'flesh' or of the senses, seems to have only one strictly Stoic parallel: *ekeithen* (though without the notion of flowing) appears in Epictetus.[25] (Farquharson has noted two instances of *ekeithen* in non-technical senses in Dio Chrysostom.)[26] The idea of all things 'coming' from there is indeed also repeated by Marcus (6.36.2), though the 'flowing' is again absent.

So much for the derivation of the world as such: is 'All things flow from there' a development of the Heraclitean 'All things flow'? We shall discuss the relationship of Marcus to Heraclitus later. But if we restrict ourselves to the origin of the guiding reason in man (rather than the reason 'of all things'), the language of flowing – dare one say of emanation, or does that give the game away? – is much more frequent. It is true, as we have seen, that Marcus is quite ready, at times, to speak of mind's being a fragment (*apospasma*) or part; but in accounting for the origin, the process of derivation of that part or fragment, the 'flowing', emanative language appears. Farquharson finds it paralleled in earlier sources only in the Book of Wisdom (7.25) and in Clement of Alexandria (*Protr.* 6.6.8).[27] Marcus's language is not, however, a slip of the pen. He tells us that we are an effluence from the gods (2.4), that God is in touch with what has flowed 'from there', from another place (12.26). The word *aporroia*, of course, goes back to Empedocles, (at least in the version *aporroē*), but Stoics earlier than Marcus did not avail themselves of it. We must assume that Marcus's language is deliberate and novel, unless, of course, it derives (indirectly) from unattested themes of Posidonius and came to Marcus along with other débris about our *daimōn* from that and other sources. One of these other sources, as Farquharson perhaps indicated, not least for 12.2, may be Plato (*Republic* 485D).

The material we have just examined leads us on to the general psychology to be found in the *Meditations*. Note first that Marcus operates with a division of the human being into body (or flesh), *pneuma* and guiding reason,[28] for which, it seems, parallels can be found in the pneumatic tradition of medicine, admittedly a tradition influenced by Stoic, though not exclusively Stoic thought. An alternative triad is body, soul and reason (3.16). It is again possible that Posidonius, who certainly introduced Platonic doctrines of the tripartition of the soul into Stoicism, is ultimately responsible for these ideas; we are on surer ground, however, when we come to the nature of the reason itself, which Posidonius certainly viewed as the individual's true self, or *daimōn*, that is, as the most important part of his total being. On the evidence of Galen this is indisputable.[29] Seneca, undoubtedly influenced by Posidonius, follows the idea up, unaware of how dangerous it is to traditional Stoicism. Epictetus is more circumspect, but Marcus, whether or not he read Posidonius,[30] certainly followed the Posidonian line. Evidence for his belief that a guiding reason (*hēgemonikon*) is a distinct part of the total human being is unmistakable and abundant. But so, we should also notice, is evidence that he was also prepared to speak more directly in the fashion of Epictetus (and later of certain Platonists) of a moral personality (*proairesis*)[31] rather than as a physically separable part! As elsewhere theses jostle at the appropriate moments; perhaps the basic *philosophical* problem with Marcus is that he does not know whether he wants to talk of the *daimōn* in terms of 'mind' or of 'personality', or of both at the same time.

At any rate, in considering this question we should particularly notice how common the theme of the *daimōn* is; it is clearly fundamental in Marcus's mind. Here is the evidence:

2.13. It is sufficient for a man to be in company with the *daimōn* within him alone, and genuinely to serve it.

2.17. Philosophy consists in keeping one's *daimōn* within unviolated.

3.3.2. The ruling principle is mind and a *daimōn*; that which it serves (the body) is earth and corruption.

3.4.1. Don't be distracted from watching over your own ruling principle.

3.5.   Let the god in you be lord over a living creature, male, statesmanlike, and Roman. . .

3.6.2. Nothing appears better than the *daimōn* installed (*enidry-menou*) within you, which here acts like a conscience taming one's impulses and scrutinizing the images the senses provide.

3.7.   The man who puts his intelligence and his *daimon* first does not adopt the tragic pose.

3.16.   A fascinating section: Bodily senses are available for cattle; impulses, for beasts, homosexuals and tyrants (specifically Phalaris and Nero). Even those who disbelieve in the gods, desert their country and pull out all the stops behind closed doors (Christians?[32] Epicureans?) have intelligence as guide. The good man, however, can keep the *daimōn* seated within his heart pure and unmuddled by sense-impressions.

5.10.2. It is in my power to do nothing contrary to my god and *daimōn*. No one can compel me to disobey him.

5.27.   The man lives with the gods who does what his *daimōn* wishes, the *daimōn* which Zeus has given each of us as a commander and leader (*hēgemona*), a fragment of himself. This is each man's intelligence and reason (*logos*).

12.3.   Intelligence alone is strictly (*kyriōs*) your own. Live at peace with your own *daimōn*.

12.26. Each man's intelligence is god and has flowed 'from there'.

After all this we can have no doubt of Marcus's position. *Nous* is a *daimōn* within us; it is sometimes indeed a god (perhaps this merely means it is divine); certainly it is a fragment of the divine. Bonhoeffer even suggested[33] that Marcus proposed that it is not composed of the four basic elements, and certainly 4.4 seems to imply that. But this need not imply that it is immaterial.[34] It only means, as Marcus says, that being intelligent it comes from what is intelligent, presumably, that is, intelligent stuff. But however far this account of the physical composition of mind is from traditional Stoicism, or even from the view of Posidonius, it is chiefly of interest to us in so far as it shows Marcus prepared to offer a physical explanation of his separation of the Reason from the psychosomatic ego of Chrysippus.

It should be noticed that however non-Stoic, indeed 'Platonizing', this account of the *daimōn* may be, Marcus does not follow the Platonists in believing that the soul (or any part of it) is immortal, or even immaterial.[35] In one striking passage, he puzzles as to how the noble dead can be extinguished, but contents himself with the view that if they are, and it seems that they are, this must be for the best (12.5). Elsewhere, though he expresses himself able to face either extinction, or reassimilation to the *logos spermatikos* of the Universe (6.24), or removal to another place (4.21; 8.35, 58; 11.3; 12.31), he seems to incline towards extinction (8.5)[36] – the view of Panaetius. 'So you will be nowhere, like Hadrian and Augustus.' But a limited period of survival, as early Stoics taught, is certainly canvassed (4.21; 3.3); and in at least one passage, the choices are related to the ambivalence between Epicurean and Stoic cosmic theory we observed earlier; if atoms, dispersion; if a unity (*henōsis*, 7.32; cf. 7.50), either extinction or change of state. In all this, as we have seen, a definite view is not to be discerned. Marcus seems almost to be telling himself that the matter is unimportant. Whatever answer we give the question about survival, we need not be unhappy about it. Again, our *daimōn* need not be disturbed: it is safe and well looked after. It must be admitted that although this attitude sounds Socratic, or at least like some of the remarks of Socrates in the *Apology*, and even perhaps often Stoic in its conclusions and perhaps even its theories, the obvious anxiety which Marcus displays indicates that his mind needs constant reassurance, that the Stoic calm needs to be indicated, that he is a 'Learner' (*prokoptōn*) rather than a sage. But for all that, it is worth noting that his insecurity does not tempt him to toy with *Platonic* notions or the survival of the soul, a fact perhaps to be put down to lack of confidence rather than to Stoic design or dogma.

It has frequently been observed that Marcus's account of the *daimōn* is probably influenced by Roman ideas of the *genius*;[37] I have no wish to deny that. Indeed, it may help to explain his un-Platonic attitude towards the survival of the soul. For if Marcus's manner of thinking of the guiding reason is traditionally Roman rather than purely philosophical in its motivation, it is more intelligible that he did not proceed further down Plato's path – a fact, as we have seen, which is otherwise perhaps only to be explained in terms of an analysis of the quirks of Marcus's individual psyche, as was proposed by Dodds,[38] who speaks of his crisis of identity, and by Bowersock,[39] who speaks of his hypochondria, or more exotically (not to say comically) by Thomas W. Africa, who in an imprecisely worked out comparison of Marcus with Coleridge and Thomas de Quincey tells us with fine rhetoric and little evidence that 'A wall of narcotics insulated the Emperor from family disorders and all but public calamaties', though it is hard to see why it should have stopped so conveniently short.[40] Although we can, perhaps with a tinge of malevolent regret, leave Marcus the junkie on one side, we shall have to return to the remarks of Dodds at a later stage. As yet we are still not in the position to answer the question which seems to underlie Dodds's comments: Are Marcus's so frequent variations on or deviations from Stoicism due to a collapse of School Stoicism as a significantly identifiable intellectual institution, or are they merely functions of his individual preoccupations and neuroses?

Perhaps the path ahead from here may seem a little obscure; but let us look at what Marcus gives thanks for receiving from his father and the memory of him: modesty (*to aidēmon*) and maleness (*arrenikon*, 1.2). The first of these ideas is familiar, frequent in Marcus and more so in Epictetus; the second also occurs in Epictetus, but is perhaps more visible in Marcus, and is interestingly juxtaposed with the call to be a Roman. Every hour, he says, think steadfastly, like a Roman and a male (2.5). He continues by saying that we should perform each act of our life as though it were our last (2.5,11; 4.17). In these reflections should we think of the *genius* again? Consider a passage we have already mentioned where the two ideas are linked (3.5): 'Let the god in you be the leader of a male creature, an old man concerned with affairs of state, a Roman who has taken up his post as ruler. . .'

Certainly Marcus has the virtues of the old Romans in mind when he thanks the gods he did not advance too far in rhetoric and poetry (1.7; 1.17.4). But the emphasis on maleness: is that part of the old way? Certainly we see parallels in Epictetus and others; but the emphasis is more noticeable in Marcus. It does seem as though we have a personal note: Marcus notes with gratitude the amount of time spent with his mother in her last years (1.17.6), as well as the fact we noted that his time with his grandfather's concubine was cut short (1.17.2), apparently before he could enjoy her ('I preserved the flower of youth'); he then observes gratefully that his sexual life began late, that he did not touch Benedicta or Theodotus, and, as we again noted, that he was apparently cured of sexual desires without too much difficulty. Yet although cured of them, and despite his own repeated

34

self-exhortation against feeling anger, he concurred with the view
of Theophrastus that lust, *inter alia* because it is more female in its
mode of sinning, is more vicious than anger (thereby offending
against the Stoic canon of the equality of sins, 2.10); and he has a
particular (Roman?) contempt for passive homosexuals (*kinaidos*,
5.10.1) – in 6.34 they are compared with brigands, parricides and
tyrants. Is it that they are paradigmatically lacking in maleness?
We note too that he congratulates his 'father' Antoninus Pius for
restraining pederasty (1.16.1; cf. 3.2.2).

As Brunt has well observed,[41] Marcus's warnings to himself in
these matters are far less frequent than those concerned with the
restraint of anger or with truth-telling; but the small number of
references may be less important than the quality of what is said.
Marcus is very concerned to act like a male and a Roman; and he
associates such actions with the late Stoic *aidos* and, comparably
with Epictetus, with the Roman *fides*. *Fides*, of course, includes
truth-telling, which Brunt rightly remarks is a surprisingly frequent theme in the conscious part of Marcus's mind. In his youth
Marcus was called *Verissimus* by Hadrian;[42] his original name was
M. Annius Verus. The most valuable part of a man, he says, is the
seat of *pistis* and *aidos* (so far as in Epictetus), truth, law, and
finally a good *daimōn* (10.13; cf. 7.17). In this concept of the good
daimōn we see summed up the qualities Marcus so wishes for
himself: they are a blend of traditionally Stoic ideals with Marcus's
version of the ideals of *Romanitas*. This is a personal vision, and
Romanness and maleness go together in it. It springs perhaps
rather from a sense of inadequacy in these areas and a fear of
himself. To such fears we shall shortly return.

Marcus is uncertain about the fate of the soul after death,
perhaps also more uncertain about his success as a Roman and a
male. He is beginning to look *déraciné*; and Dodds's remarks
about a sense of identity begin to sound more plausible. Earlier
we saw an uncertainty too about the basic principles of Stoic
physics and a clinging at least to the un-Stoic account of the
daimōn and its providential situation. We have seen too traces of
a language of emanation which suggest a certain absence of Stoic
bearings. Let us now look at Marcus's account of the origins of
human knowledge to see whether and how far this sense of
uncertainty is explicable in terms of philosophical history.

Like Epictetus, Marcus is concerned with the proper evaluation
of the appearances (*phantasiai*) that come to us through the senses,
though there is lacking in his writings the Stoic text-book elabora-

tion of a doctrine of *chrēsis phantasiōn*. Despite this, his starting-point is clear: sense impressions are unreliable and we must struggle to avoid being led along by them holus bolus (5.36). Sometimes indeed they must be effaced (8.29); always we must take them literally: you hear that a man speaks ill of you. Very well, but you do not hear that this does you any harm (8.49). We must stick to 'first impressions'; what is to be avoided is the overvaluation of suppositions (*hypolēpsis*, 2.15). Everything is supposition, says Marcus un-Stoically, thus hyperbolically sub-stituting scepticism for Stoicism at a basic level. But perhaps he should not be taken literally. Presumably he is only talking of what might be emotionally disturbing. He means that the opinion supervening on the sense-impression should be recognized as such; it is not the original impression that is harmful. If the supposition is gone, the harm is gone (4.7; 12.22, 26). That sounds more Stoic; we are dealing, after all, with mistaken *judgments*. Troubles, as Marcus says, begin with suppositions (9.13), or, as he puts it more properly elsewhere (9.32), unnecessary troubles. So it seems all right; it really is Stoic. But a doubt remains, and Marcus's comments on the nature of physical objects in them-selves confirm that doubt. The talk of *all* (literally all) being supposition is not to be dismissed as hyperbole. To understand this we must consider the influence of the philosopher Heraclitus.

A. A. Long has recently complained that a number of modern scholars have neglected or denied the influence of Heraclitus on the Stoics from the earliest days of the school;[43] he wishes to return to a version of an earlier view,[44] which would see Heraclitus as a major source, alongside more nearly contemporary authori-ties, at least on Cleanthes. It is not my intention to examine his arguments here: suffice it to say that I believe them to exaggerate. Long does, however, draw attention to the established fact that Marcus Aurelius *is* indebted to Heraclitus, though he fails to note that what Marcus draws from Heraclitus is very different from what is at least arguably drawn by Cleanthes, indeed that Marcus derives ideas and more generally a 'feeling' of the cosmos which seem to lead him away from traditional Stoicism.

Let us look at some texts. As examples of great men (in contrast to the pseudo-greats like Alexander, Caesar and Pompey) Marcus cites (predictably) Diogenes and Socrates, but also Heraclitus (8.3), some of whose obscurities he quotes (4.46). Elsewhere Heraclitus accompanies Socrates and Pythagoras (6.47). But, as Long observed, the influence runs deeper: Marcus frequently uses the river-image to indicate the universal flux, and frequently alludes to the cycle of up and down. But the emphasis on flux is almost the ultra-Heracliteanism of Cratylus, the Heracliteanism which may lead to an ultimate scepticism:[45] all things of the body are a river, things of the soul are dream and mist (2.17); time (*aiōn*) is like a river (4.43); all substance is like a river in ceaseless flow. We come from the infinity of the past and all things pass into the 'chasm of the future' where they disappear (5.23).[46] And strikingly in 6.15, 'In this river of time which of these things that pass should one value? It is like loving a sparrow that flies away and is gone.' What these texts do is confirm a view we shall find very frequently in Marcus, that man is a dot, a pinpoint in everlasting time and space. It cannot be pointed out too strongly that this is an inappropriate attitude for a Stoic; it leads one to doubt the importance of human behaviour, any human behaviour, even moral behaviour. And Marcus draws from Heraclitus certain ideas with which he has to struggle: the insignificance and utter worthlessness of man, disgust at what happens in the world, disgust at himself. This sense of disgust, which we shall document, is fuelled by emphasis on a Heraclitean flux. Marcus does not draw comfort from the Heraclitean doctrine of the Logos, rather anxiety from the Heraclitean account of physical objects.

Texts in which Marcus emphasizes the passage of time, the fading of past glories, are frequent. One example will suffice:

> Think of the times of Vespasian and you will see it all; people marrying, rearing children, getting sick, dying, fighting, having festivals, trading, farming, flattering, boasting, suspecting, plotting, praying for others' deaths, complaining at their lot, loving, treasuring, lusting for a consulship and a kingdom. That life they led no longer exists. Go over to Trajan's times and it is the same story. That life too is dead (4.32).[47]

And as for posthumous fame, it is all empty (*kenon*, 4.33). The last point leads us on: it is not just that time quickly buries all; it also reduces it *sub specie* to triviality. It is like a stage-play (10.27). Sometimes even morally repulsive behaviour is bracketed together with a natural disaster and past excellence. 4.48 is striking; consider how many doctors are dead after pondering the fate of their patients, how many astrologers after predicting other people's deaths, how many philosophers after discussing death and immortality, how many leaders after killing many, how many tyrants after exercising their powers of life and death with dreadful insolence (*meta deinou phryagmatos*). Here the un-Stoic tendency to let time devour even the distinction between good and evil reaches the surface. Someties, it is true, a 'moral' from the passage of time is drawn: 'Soon you will be ashes and a skeleton, and a name, or not even a name . . . But what we value most in life is vain and rotten and small, and we are like puppies snapping at one another and querulous children, now laughing, now crying. But faith and modesty and justice and truth . . .'. The words 'have fled the earth' are omitted (5.33). Or again, 'You will soon be dead, and are you yet not simple, not undisturbed, not unsuspicious of being injured from outside, not gracious to all . . .?' (4.37). Or, finally (7.3), 'Empty love of pageants, stage-plays, flocks, herds, bones thrown to lap-dogs, a crumb thrown to fish, . . . scurrying of scared little mice, puppets on strings. Take your place graciously among them . . . but everyone is worth what they are keen on.' Marcus feels contempt for the world, but dredges out a moral by telling himself to take it calmly. But life is brief and therefore indifferent; the passage of time is morally deadening, it trivializes all.[48] It is important to recognize not just that Marcus's view of time is the product of pessimism, but that he locates reflections on the significance of the passage of time in a moral context: for Chrysippus time is a problem in physics, and the status of time as an incorporeal does not endow it with the sense of illusion. It neither makes the world unreal nor its passing events necessarily trivial. Now as Goldschmidt has beautifully shown, Marcus's theoretical account of time, in so far as it can be recovered, is Stoic, indeed Chrysippean, but his use of the material is his own. And we are left with the impression that it is the use of the theory, not its details, which matters. Goldschmidt, if I understand him aright, wants to argue that Marcus thinks like a Stoic, that he is in possession of a Stoic methodology, whatever differences he may show from Stoic 'dogma'. But my own analysis of Marcus's theory of time is that he may repeat certain Chrysippean ideas, but that if we talk of methodology, his way of thinking is not Stoic.

If Marcus's account of time suggests the unreality of things, even at times of all things, not merely the things of the senses which are, or are said to be, a dream and a delusion,[49] the same is also true of his view of space: Asia and Europe are corners of the universe, all the ocean is a drop in the universe . . . all the present (*to enestos*) – Chrysippus's technical term – a pinpoint in eternity.[50] As we confront endless time and boundless space, let us think again of the Caesars. Where are they now? Nowhere, or no one knows where (10.31). Look then on human things as smoke and nothing. It is indeed a Heraclitean vision, but often without any Stoic version of Heraclitean *logos*, the Heracliteanism, it seems probable, of one period of the Sceptic Aenesidemus. But even this is more Stoic than Marcus's frequent alternative: the world around, he says, is a tedious and disgusting place: 'Say at daybreak, I shall meet the busybody, the thankless, the thug, the treacherous, the envious, the antisocial. These people don't know the difference between good and evil.'[51] One's flesh is to be dispersed: gore and bones and nerves and veins and arteries. 'Everything around is decomposing or dispersing; look at it and see' (10.18). It is Heraclitus's world seen from the viewpoint of a highly sensitized individual who has learned hardly to endure himself. At the beginning of Book Eight Marcus observes that he has failed to live as a philosopher, that his life is in chaos, that neither logic nor wealth nor fame nor enjoyment nor anything else but a realization of the nature of good and evil can help him. It is this vestigial Stoicism, this sense of a moral reality somewhere, somehow that alone has survived the flux (8.1.1; cf. 10.8). But it is difficult; look again at the character of those around: it is difficult to tolerate the most sophisticated of them, indeed it is hard to endure oneself (5.10). The influence of Heraclitus as sceptic is visible, and the disgust and sense of illusion rule out any Platonic transfiguration. Marcus clings to the Providence of the world, the primacy of the Reason, the sense of the difference between good and evil; and that is almost all: driftwood in the river of time.

But in the immensity of time and space a new version of a traditionally Stoic theme sometimes gives comfort. Although the practising politician is wasting his time if he is hoping for Plato's Ideal State, and should be happy if he achieves even a very small success (9.29), the wise man is a member of the Dear City of Zeus (4.23; cf. 10.15; 2.16), the cosmos itself. It is precisely citizenship which is emphasized, with its rights and responsibilities, citizenship in the highest state of which existing societies are mere households (3.11.2). This is not, of course, the negative cosmopolitanism of the early Cynics, the belonging to no particular city; it is a positive belief in the universe itself as a city, with that peculiar feature of a Greek city which Marcus chooses to emphasize, its posssession of law.[52] Marcus insists that the terms 'rational' (*logikon*) and 'civic' (*politikon*) are identified (10.2). God himself, therefore, is the ideal statesman, and it follows that the Emperor in particular is following in God's steps, as Marcus so often exhorts himself to do.

Marcus seems almost to attempt a deduction of the cosmic city with its legal structure: if we are rational, then we share in a common rationality (*logos*). If a common rationality, then a common law to enjoin what ought to be done and what ought not. If we have a common law, then we are fellow citizens; if that is the case, the universe is a sort of state (*hōsanei polis*). Once we can see that this is so, we can understand where our intelligent, rational and legal characteristics come from: they come 'from there' (*ekeithen*), from the cosmos itself (4.4). And again, 'My nature is rational and social (*politikē*); my city and my country *qua* Antoninus is Rome, *qua* human being it is the cosmos' (6.44; cf. 7.9). At times, then, the cosmic city provides a place to which Marcus can emotionally belong. If man is citizen of the universe, and if he honours the rational principle within himself, he must not feel a stranger (*xenos*) in his own country (12.1.2; cf. 4.29); as we would put it, he need not feel alienated.

It is certainly with reference to the search for somewhere to belong, for a place in the whole world, that Marcus introduces two other related Stoic themes: the 'sympathy' of the parts of the cosmos for one another,[53] and the age-old *topos* of part and whole. If I am a part (or did Marcus actually write 'limb'[54]) of the cosmos, and remember the fact, I will be content with what I receive from the whole (10.6; cf. 2.9; 4.14). As for the bonds which culminate in what we call the doctrine of the bonds of 'sympathy', we can observe (as the old Stoics would have agreed) a more powerful unifying factor in bees and herds and birds and other eros-linked groups than in the 'soul-less' plants and sticks and stones.[55] But among rational beings (men) there are higher bonds still: households, political societies, etc. And in the more than human, in the cosmos itself, among the stars, for example, even though they are separate, a kind of unity (*henōsis*) exists. This bonding force, this 'sympathy' which rational creatures undoubtedly exhibit, helps us to feel at home. In all this we find Marcus using Stoic themes, types of souls, sympathy, the whole-and-part, the importance of our ruling principle, to find a rest from the Heraclitean flux and the corroding scepticism it often brings him. Finally, once again, it is the belief in Providence and in our mind's identity with God to which all the rest is subordinated. Men are inclined to forget many matters of importance, but two of the list Marcus gives should be singled out (12.26); we forget that the community of man with man is not based on our common origin as a mixture of menstrual blood and semen (2.1, as Marcus traditionally understands conception), but on our community of *nous*; and that this *nous* is divine and comes 'from there', from the lord of the cosmos. At death we shall be taken back into this *logos spermatikos*, this Seminal Reason of the world, by due process of change.[56]

When Marcus's spirits are raised, in such moments as this, his disgust at humanity lifts: we should not feel such disgust; on the contrary we should care for people and treat them gently (9.3). For we, as citizens of the cosmos, as fellow humans, are born for each other; and forbearance is a part of justice (4.3.2). One should not be angry at one's 'kinsmen'; they have not comprehended the nature and beauty of the good.[57] Goodwill towards one's fellows is a peculiar characteristic available to men (8.26), and the word 'fellowship' (*koinōnia*) is ever on Marcus's lips.[58] It was for fellowship that we were born (5.16; 8.59; 11.18.1; 9.1.1), God's *nous* is social (*koinōnikos*, 5.30). In the interest of such fellowship we should not only restrain our anger, but pity and forgive the wrongdoer (7.26). In the interest of fellowship we should even accept the (normally humiliating) idea of being helped: don't be ashamed of being helped, says Marcus, in a most unusual passage; you are a soldier on duty and you can't storm the ramparts unaided (7.7; cf. 10.12). Your duty is the duty of fellowship: 'save mankind' (*sōze anthrōpous*, 6.30), those who share your common divine citizenship. The duty to do so is bracketed with 'respect the gods'. Nor must you dissemble benevolence; you must be benevolent.[59] It is the peculiar mark of a man to love even those who stumble (7.22) – yet here we should notice the rationale – 'because they are our kin, because they sin through ignorance and involuntarily; because you and they will soon be dead anyhow; but above all because no man has done you harm or damaged your ruling principle'.

Coupled with helping our fellows, with the strictest regard for truth and justice (10.11; 3.16.2), goes following God (our source) (7.31; 12.31), which Marcus follows Seneca in advocating;[60] and, as Brunt and others have observed, his actions as Emperor bear witness to his carrying out the traditional practices of Roman religion devotedly,[61] even deifying several of his predecessors while noting in the *Meditations* that a number of the great *divi* of the past, Augustus, Vespasian, Hadrian, are mere dust and ashes. Yet his advice, 'Follow God' is sincere: for him it sums up the philosophical life, and it is to be accompanied by prayers to live in the right way:

Not 'Would that I might sleep with that woman!' but 'Would that I might not desire to sleep with her!' Not 'Would that I might be rid of that man!' but 'Would that I might not want to be rid of him!' Not 'Would that I might not lose my child!' but 'Would that I might not fear to lose my child!' (9.40).

All this is in the style of the religion of Epictetus. But a touch of Marcus's own: Reflect on the mysteries of conception and nutrition: they point to a directing force (10.26).

Lest we come to accept the idea of any full-blooded benevolence in Marcus, however, we should also recall a theme which does not spring from any sense of alienation or isolation, but is well rooted in the Stoic tradition. Benevolence has clearly defined limits in that it must not carry with it any kind of emotional disturbances to the giver. No one is responsible for the sins of his fellows; nor ultimately should he be concerned about them. Under no circumstances should he worry about them:

> However much we were born for each other, our ruling principles are independent. Otherwise my neighbour's vice might be harmful to me. It was not God's will that my unhappiness should depend on anyone else (8.56; cf. 9.20).

Marcus significantly quotes Epictetus to show that we are not only to be free of anxiety about our neighbours' well-being; the call for emotional detachment from human life comes nearer home: when kissing your child, you must say, Perhaps tomorrow you will die. Nothing ill-omened about it, just a reference to natural processes (11.34). And of course, if we revert to the matter of ordinary kindnesses, their bestowal depends on the value of the recipient, not, as certain passages might have led us falsely to deduce, on his mere existence as a human being.

In all these ethical attitudes, despite Marcus's peculiarities in psychology, there is much Stoic dogma, but little Stoic argument. Marcus even observes that in so far as we all sin, or are liable to sin, we are all *equally* corrupt (11.18.4) – an orthodox Stoic view which we saw earlier he was prepared to modify under certain circumstances – and to add that the only reason we do not sin with the worst of them is through cowardice, regard for our 'good name', or some other vicious pretext.

Marcus and late Stoicism

Is there any conclusion to be drawn about the connection between certain features of Marcus's mind that we have already noticed (his insistence that physics and dialectic are not necessary for the good life (7.67), his tendency to feel isolated in the Heraclitean flux of time and the vastness of space, his disgust at the human race, including himself, and his attempts to ward off such feelings by thoughts of cosmic providence and the laws of the cosmic city? The conclusion seems to be this: Marcus knows or perhaps 'feels' Stoicism as a set of ethical beliefs or dogmas, the philosophical origins of which he has lost to such a degree – perhaps, as he says, through lack of time for study – that he is tempted even to think that an atomistic physics might prop them up equally well. Anything, it seems, may be pressed into service against the overriding threat of scepticism in philosophy and isolation in personal life. For Marcus, in modern terms, if we are to call him a Stoic, then Stoicism is not a philosophy, as it was for Zeno and Chrysippus, nor a psychology, as at times it seems to be for Seneca, but a religion or 'philosophy of life'; and it is a religion devoid of any significant scholastic underpinnings. As we know, there is no Greek word which will adequately translate our word 'religion': *philosophia* has to do as well as it can in this regard, but we should not be misled.

But if Stoicism is a rather unphilosophical religion for Marcus, and if Marcus is in any way typical of his age in that regard, we can see why it lost its influence in the world of late antiquity. There was no reason why Stoicism should have survived as a religion alone; its growth to world influence depended on its philosophical rigour and unwillingness to compromise the truth, combined with a belief that the truth must be investigated in great detail. Marcus has lost all interest in the details, and is left with the almost unsupported dogmas of Providence, the divine ruling principle which he treats untraditionally, and the necessity to cling to what is right and do it. Throughout the *Meditations* we feel that spiritually Marcus is struggling to survive, at times almost gasping for breath. The Stoic doctrines which he uses to help himself along never remove the fear of the surrounding depths. All he can do in these circumstances is adopt a stiff upper lip and evoke the old atomist's call for courage (*euthymia*, 4.24), to which Seneca and perhaps other Stoics had also occasionally adverted.[62]

Part of the interest of Marcus's *Meditations* is that it was not written for public consumption, and that its author was not a professional philosopher, let alone a professional Stoic philosopher. There is no necessary reason why such a man should teach or reflect upon orthodox Stoicism. What the *Meditations* show us is how a particular powerful individual reacted to certain philosophical ideas available to him and used them for his own purposes. Nevertheless, despite the personal idiosyncrasies as well as the tendencies to Platonism that the *Meditations* reveal, it has to be admitted that if Marcus is to be classified somehow, it must be as a Stoic. Yet if Marcus's thinking is in any way typical, it is not surprising that Stoicism was dying as the dominant philosophy. As a decaying philosophy, it could only point to the resurgent Platonism. But, as we have already said, in modern terms Marcus's Stoicism is a religion rather than a philosophy. And as such it could easily be assimilated to another more self-assured and confident rival. The ethical positions of Marcus in fact disappear into the brand of Christianity purveyed by Clement of Alexandria (who resorts to the Stoicism of Musonius) as well as into the Platonism of the Middle Platonic and later Neoplatonic teachers who were prepared to give it more substantive philosophical or revelational backing than Marcus could obtain.

In 176 CE, among other chairs of philosophy, Marcus endowed a chair of Stoic philosophy at Athens;[63] and Stoics continued to teach there and elsewhere in the third century.[64] But if the example of Marcus is a sign of the times, they may have been mere moralists or academics in the worst sense of the word. Almost certainly they had nothing philosophically new to offer (though some of them wrote) and philosophers like Alexander of Aphrodisias who combatted Stoicism at this time fought the theses of Chrysippus rather than those of their own contemporaries; at most they refute their contemporaries only in so far as these merely repeat Chrysippus. It is sometimes said that the attacks of Alexander of Aphrodisias on the Stoic account of fate and other basic Chrysippean themes sounded the death-knell of the school. The evidence of the *Meditations* points in another direction. As a philosophical survival Stoicism could do little more than give away what it had left; in spirit it was already dead. Marcus's uncertainties are, among other more personal things, the uncertainties of a believer who has to fight hard to keep his faith, and beyond his faith, his will to live. He meditates on the death, the end, of a wise man – it might almost be a school of wise men – in a famous passage (10.36): 'No one is so fortunate that one or two of those standing by will not be welcoming his death. Even in the case of the sage, someone will say, "Now we can breathe again, freed from this schoolmaster." ' Note the image: the bystanders do not say, 'So much for this philosopher', let alone 'for this Stoic'. But they are malevolent as well as not wholly accurate; they do not even say, 'So much for this man who had an interest in philosophy.'

3

Self-Definition among Epicureans and Cynics

ABRAHAM J. MALHERBE

The problem of self-definition in ancient groups can be approached in various ways. One way is to start from the outside and to apply models constructed by the social sciences, as Walter Burkert does in his contribution to this volume. Another is to start from the inside, and to concentrate on statements made by members of the groups themselves. In the latter approach, the focus would vary from group to group, depending on where the issue of self-definition is perceived to emerge most clearly. Thus a group might be seen as defining itself over against its opponents, as John Dillon views the later Platonists in this volume. On the other hand, the concern with self-definition could also be found in confrontation within a group, when individuals in it debate who the true representatives of the group are or who exemplify its standards or ideals. This is the approach adopted in the treatment of the Cynics in this paper. A group might, however, be relatively free of debate, so that a concentration on confrontation could be expected to reap meagre results. This would seem to be the case with the Epicureans who, in the period under consideration, were more concerned with the explication and practical application of Epicurean doctrine and with its propagation than with debates.

An attempt will be made in this paper to examine the Cynics, and to a much lesser extent, the Epicureans, of the second and third centuries CE, from the symposium's interest without allowing the interest to impose categories foreign to the two schools. As in many other respects, they differed radically in the degrees to which they underwent change in their evolution, were characterized by diversity, and achieved normative self-definition.

The Epicureans

Lucian of Samosata mentions Christians and Epicureans together as opponents of Alexander the false prophet (*Alex*. 25. 38). It is not difficult to see why their critics could make the association. Both groups were charged with atheism, misanthropy, social irresponsibility, and sexual immorality,[1] and from their side Christians seem not to have been above demanding that they be accorded the same rights as the Epicureans.[2] In recent times attempts have been made to demonstrate a kinship between the two, and to argue that Epicureanism formed a bridge from Greek philosophy to Christianity.[3] Despite the similarities, however, that appear to have existed in their thought, and such external features as their allegiance to their founders and their teachings, the fact that both had highly organized communities, used oral propaganda and sought to hold their scattered communities together by an epistolary literature,[4] the early Christian attitude toward the Epicureans was polemical.[5]

Nevertheless, if one's interest were in the way in which a group maintained its identity after norms for its belief and practice had been established, the Epicureans would repay close examination as a possibly analogous phenomenon to early Christianity from the third century on, after Christianity had attained 'normative self-definition'. The interest of this paper, however, is in the possible movement from competing options open to a group to one which becomes normative, the direction of development Judaism and Christianity underwent during the first three centuries CE. Such a definition of interest permits the Epicureans to be treated very briefly, for they were singularly free from a variety of viewpoints within the school, and there is no evidence that the type of development considered here took place.

Epicureans are known for the conservatism with which they maintained the teaching of the master. Epicurus's immediate successors did not make major innovations in his teaching. Some refinements may have been attempted, but in general his writings remained canonical.[6] Even in their replies to anti-Epicurean attacks, his followers did not rethink the bases of his system,[7] although it is in such contexts rather than in the formulation of orthodox doctrine that innovations can be discerned.[8] This consistency of teaching in Epicurus and his followers, with differences primarily in nuance, can thus be appealed to in treating ancient Epicureanism as a unity.[9]

The uniformity of Epicurean doctrine was in no small part due to the veneration in which Epicurus was held and to the organization of and procedures within their communities.[10] Members of these highly structured communities swore an oath of obedience to Epicurus and acceptance of his teachings.[11] Epicurus himself had placed great stress on the importance of memorization of his teaching, and wrote epitomes of his doctrine with it in mind, and the practice of memorization found a firm place in the instruction of the communities.[12] Images of the founder were venerated, and this practice seems to have been integrated with Epicurean doctrine as part of a systematic plan to maintain cohesion and gain perpetuity for the communities and their teaching.[13]

The school seems to have been still vigorous in the second century CE,[14] and there are no indications of major changes in the conformity that had characterized it earlier. In the latter half of the century Numenius expressed the opinion that still prevailed:

> . . . The Epicureans . . . were never seen on any point to have opposed the doctrines of Epicurus in any way; but by acknowledging that they held the same opinions with a learned sage they naturally for this reason gained the title themselves: and with the later Epicureans it was for the most part a fixed rule never to express any opposition either to one another or to Epicurus on any point worth mentioning; but innovation is with them a transgression or rather an impiety, and is condemned. And for this reason no one even dares to differ, but from their constant agreement among themselves their doctrines are quietly held in perfect peace. Thus the School of Epicurus is like some true republic, perfectly free from sedition, with one mind in common and one consent; from which case they were, and are, and seemingly will be zealous disciples.[15]

The evidence provided by Diogenes of Oenoanda around 200 CE confirms this assessment. The interest of the fragments of his work consists in their orthodoxy rather than originality.[16] Diogenes differs from Epicurus more in the presentation of doctrine than in the doctrine itself.[17]

The Cynics

The Cynics and the Cynicism of the first century CE are known to us for the most part through Stoic interpreters, and the temptation is great, on the basis of Seneca's account of Demetrius, Musonius Rufus, Epictetus and Dio Chrysostom, to draw a picture of Cynicism that obscures the difference between Stoicism and Cynicism and among the Cynics themselves. In the second century, the diversity among the Cynics emerges more clearly as such personalities as Oenomaus of Gadara, Demonax and Peregrinus Proteus appear on the scene. Unfortunately, only fragments of Oenomaus's writings have been preserved, and only a few comments, mostly negative, are made about him by Julian, and we are largely but not wholly dependent on Lucian's interpretations of Demonax and Peregrinus for information about them. It is therefore fortunate that in the Cynic epistles we do have primary sources for the sect in the early Empire. These neglected writings are more than the school exercises they have been thought to be, and enable us to determine the points at issue among the Cynics themselves.[18]

The definition of Cynicism

Diogenes Laertius already experienced difficulty in describing common Cynic doctrine, and records that some considered it, not a philosophical school (*hairesis*), but a way of life (6.103).[19] He seems to incline to the view that it is a philosophical school, but notes that Cynics dispensed with logic and physics, and confined themselves to ethics. Cynics have generally been perceived as having an aversion to encyclopaedic learning and placing no premium on education in the pursuit of virtue. As a distinctively anti-social sect, they attached greatest importance to a way of life that gives chief emphasis to personal decision.[20] Yet this generalization holds only partly. While it is true that in the Hellenistic period Cynicism did not require adherence to an organized system of doctrine, the major figures known to us, in contrast to the charlatans Lucian describes, were by no means anti-intellectual. Oenomaus reflects a knowledge of philosophical arguments about free will and providence,[21] Demonax is said to have been eclectic although in dress he was a Cynic,[22] Peregrinus is thought to have been influenced by Neopythagoreanism,[23] and the Socratic epistles betray at least an openness to philosophy and its possible contribution to one's progress towards virtue.[24]

Cynics differed among themselves in their philosophical eclecticism as they did in other matters, but a personal preference for or use in debate of one system does not appear to have been a major issue in determining who was a Cynic. What made a Cynic was his dress and conduct, self-sufficiency, harsh behaviour towards what appeared as excesses, and a practical ethical idealism, but not a detailed arrangement of a system resting on

Socratic-Antisthenic principles. The result was that Cynicism was compatible with views that shared its ethical demands even if they were at cross purposes with its fundamentally different teaching in other matters.[25] The resulting diversity makes an attempt at a detailed definition of Cynicism difficult, especially if it is based on the idealized presentations of Epictetus, Lucian, Maximus of Tyre, and Julian.[26] Epictetus's description has often been taken to represent the true Cynic without due allowance being made for his Stoicizing or for the fact that he is presenting an ideal.[27] Although these accounts do contain genuine Cynic material and viewpoints, it is preferable to identify features that Cynics themselves considered central and to proceed from there. Among other sources, the Cynic epistles represent such information and must be introduced into the discussion. In view of the interest of the symposium, some major features of Cynic diversity in the second century CE will be touched on, and an attempt will be made to determine whether one form of Cynicism came to predominate in the third. Here, special attention will be given to the Cynic letters attributed to Socrates and his disciples.

The letters under consideration come from two authors, the former writing in the name of Socrates, probably in the first century CE (*Epp.* 1–7), the latter writing in the names of members of the Socratic circle in the third century (*Epp.* 8–27; 29–34). The letters may have originated in a school, but their value for the history of Cynicism is considerable. In addition to their propagandistic aim, they represent divergent Cynic views projected onto the Socratics to create an impression of Socrates and his disciples discussing issues important to Cynics.[28] The author of the Socratic letters, with the earlier collection before him, is embarrassed by the public fussing of Cynics among themselves,[29] and it is characteristic of his corpus that attempts are made to modify a radical Cynic individualism and attempt a *rapprochement* between the protagonists.

Lucian, in *Demonax* 21, records an illustrative encounter between Demonax and Peregrinus. Demonax is rebuked by Peregrinus for his levity and jesting with people, and is accused of not acting in the Cynic manner. Demonax replies that Peregrinus is not behaving with humanity.[30] Lucian's biased interpretation of the lives of the two does not obscure the fact that both were Cynics, and that the argument between them involves the manner of life that can justifiably be called Cynic. Reflected here is a divergence into two types of Cynicism, an austere, rigorous one, and a milder, the so-called hedonistic strain.[31] Despite Lucian's caricature of him, Peregrinus emerges as a Cynic of the austere type who modelled himself on Heracles. In his austerity he was not unlike Oenomaus.[32] Demonax, in contrast, was everybody's friend (*Demon.* 10; cf. 8 and 63) and, while he adopted Diogenes's dress and way of life, did not alter the details of his life for the effect it might have on the crowds.[33] He revered Socrates, except for his irony, and admired Diogenes, but loved Aristippus (6, 62). Lucian's stress on his culture and mildness does not hide the fact that he was not loved by the masses (11), and that his 'witty remarks' in 12–62 are reminiscent of Diogenes's apophthegms preserved in Diogenes Laertius 6.24–69. Demonax defended Cynic *parrēsia* (50), and even praised Thersites as a Cynic mob-orator (61). While retaining Cynicism's simplicity of life and dress and its indifference to presumed virtues and vices, he rejected its hostility to education and culture, excessive asceticism, and shamelessness.[34]

What can be detected in Lucian finds elaboration in the Cynic epistles, where attempts at self-definition utilize as models early Cynics and heroes from Greek myth, appropriately interpreted to reflect a particular writer's proclivities. Certain letters attributed to Crates and Diogenes represent austere Cynicism. In obvious polemic against hedonistic Cynicism, Crates affirms that Cynic philosophy is Diogenean, the Cynic someone who toils according to it and takes a short cut in doing philosophy by avoiding the circuitous route of doctrine, and wears the Cynic garb which is viewed as the weapons of the gods (*Ep.* 6).[35] The Cynic takes up this armament as a deliberate act to demonstrate that the simplicty of the soul finds expression in his deeds, in which he wars against appearances.[36] In contrast to Odysseus, who is made to represent the hedonistic Cynic, Diogenes is portrayed as consistent in his commitment to the Cynic life, austere, self-sufficient, self-confident, trusting in reason, and brave in his practice of virtue.[37] This brand of Cynicism does not simply consist in indifference to all things, but in the robust endurance of what others out of softness or opinion cannot.[38] The Cynic shamelessness is part of this rejection of opinions and conventions, and is the mark of the doggish philosopher.[39] The situation in which men find themselves requires, not philosophers like Plato and Aristippus, who in the tradition represent hedonistic Cynicism, but a harsh taskmaster who can bring the masses to reality.[40]

The issues between the two types are sharpened in six of the

Socratic letters in which Simon the shoemaker (and Antisthenes) and Aristippus speak for them (*Epp.* 9–13). The topic discussed is whether the Cynic could associate with a tyrant. Antisthenes asserts that the Cynic should strive for self-sufficiency, and that he cannot associate with tyrants or the masses, for they are ignorant of it (*Ep.* 8). With biting irony the hedonist Aristippus replies that he was a steward of the teaching of Socrates in Dionysius's court (*Ep.* 9), and that his position there had resulted in his saving certain Locrian youths (*Epp.* 10, 11). Simon denies that a life of luxury is Socratic; his cobbling is done to make possible his admonition of foolish men, and his austerity is of value in the pursuit of *sōphrosynē*. He takes umbrage at Aristippus's jesting about his way of life (*Ep.* 12). Aristippus responds in conciliatory fashion. He is not ridiculing the humble life, for there is wisdom in it. But Simon would also have opportunity to practise his craft, and on a larger scale, in Syracuse. Aristippus assures Simon that he is his friend, in contrast to the harsh, bestial Cynics (*Ep.* 13). The mild Cynic, therefore, defends his behaviour by arguing that it benefits others and is more human. What is to be found in Lucian's description of Demonax thus also appears here. It is the rigorous Cynics who explicitly discuss 'Cynicism' in their self-definition, and they do so in terms of their manner of life. The mild Cynic is more conciliatory, although this should not be overstated, and defends his behaviour by pointing to its usefulness in influencing a larger audience.[41]

The Human Condition

Something more, however, than a difference in method used to attain an end seems to have been at the basis of their self-conceptions. They shared the view that man has to be reformed by being taught to unlearn his vices (D.L. 6.7–8). Unlike vice, which enters the soul spontaneously, virtue is acquired by practice (Crates, *Ep.* 12), and happiness consists in living according to nature (D.L. 6.71: Julian, *Or.* 6, 193D). Virtue can be taught, and, once acquired, cannot be lost (D.L. 6.10,105). What they called for was a decision to improve oneself, to make a deliberate choice to change from one's previous condition (D.L. 6.56). Yet they differed in their assessments of the degree to which the human condition had been corrupted and, consequently, on the methods that were to be applied to effect the desired change. The rigoristic Cynics had an extremely pessimistic view of mankind, which earned them the charge of misanthropy.[42] This view is especially, but not exclusively, represented by most of the letters attributed to Crates, Diogenes, Heraclitus, and Hippocrates.[43] Most people, they held, are totally deluded, puffed up in their evil, and completely bereft of reason and self-control. Having sunk to the level of beasts in their ignorance and conduct, nature itself hates them, and takes vengeance on them by punishing them.[44] In contrast, the true Cynic, the epitome of virtue, knows nature and imitates it.[45] Whereas nature punishes them in deed, the Cynic does so in his speech (Diog., *Ep.* 28.5). It is by virtue alone that their souls can be purified of its diseases, and it is the Cynic who is the physician able to bring about their cure.[46] Their putrid condition requires no gentle treatment, but rather the cautery and surgery of scathing cynic *parrēsia*.[47] It is not that the Cynic wishes to be morbid; their wickedness made him sullen and excised his gentleness (Heraclitus, *Epp.* 5.3; 7.2f.). Nevertheless, the worse the human condition, the greater is the virtue of the Cynic perceived to be. Not everyone is capable of Cynic virtue, and most people, complaining about Cynic indifference, flee the Cynic regimen when they see how hard it is.[48] The Cynic alone has brought moral practice to perfection,[49] and, when people prove to be beyond cure, he withdraws from them.[50] He withdraws from the bestial crowd who know neither nature, reason or truth, and associates only with those who understand the word of a Cynic (Diog., *Ep.* 28.8). He may explain, in self-defence, that it is men's vice, and not themselves, that he hates (Heraclitus, *Ep.* 28.8), but his hatred for them and for association with them is nevertheless at times stated explicitly.[51]

This contempt for the masses raises the question of the harsh Cynic's motivation for speaking to them at all. It has been claimed that, despite the Cynic's consciousness of his superior virtue and his contempt for the masses, in reality he 'was influenced by altruistic motives in a far higher degree than his ethics required him to be'.[52] The Cynic, filled with philanthropy, acording to this view, recognized his goal to be the benefit of men.[53] His concern for others did not originate in a sense of duty, but stemmed from a real sympathy with human suffering and the unnatural bondage in which men find themselves. Having freed himself from evils, he was conscious of having a mission to free others.[54] This is not, however, the self-portrait of the harsh Cynic who hardly stresses his philanthropy, and whose altruism, such as it is, it not a major characteristic. As its proponents acknowledge, this view does not seem at odds with Cynic individualism. Julian, whose under-standing of Cynicism appears to be correct in this respect, provides us with some clarity on the matter. The Cynics' reproof of others, he says, was not their chief end and aim; rather,

> their main concern was how they might themselves attain to happiness and . . . they occupied themselves with other men only in so far as they comprehended that man is by nature a social and political animal; and so they aided their fellow-citizens, not only by practising but by preaching as well (*Or*. 6, 201C).

The Cynic must therefore begin with himself, expelling all desires and passions and undertaking to live by intelligence and reason alone.[55] Julian is aware that many Cynics failed in this, and allowed themselves to be influenced by the masses (*Or*. 6, 197B–D). The Cynic must free himself from popular opinion, but that does not mean

> that we ought to be shameless before all men and to do what we ought not; but all that we refrain from and all that we do let us not do or refrain from, merely because it seems to the multitude somehow honourable or base, but because it is forbidden by reason and the god within us, that is, the mind (*Or*. 6, 196D).

Julian wishes to retain the Cynic's individualism, and warns against his simply defining himself over against the multitude.

The superiority of the austere Cynic

The harsh, austere Cynics stress their radical individualism, but cannot withstand the temptation to do so by defining themselves in opposition to the multitudes whom they hold in such contempt. At the risk of overstating the matter, it is important to note that their comments on themselves are made when they lambaste the multitude who are beyond the hope of cure, or when they compare themselves with the Cynics of milder mien who hold out some hope for society, whom they accuse of pandering to the crowd. What we meet here is not philanthropy or altruism; rather, the concern with the multitudes serves to highlight the superiority of the Cynic who has committed himself without reservation to the life of Diogenes. That sense of superiority emerges from everything that this type of Cynic does or says.

To begin with, all men are evil, and hate the Cynic (Heraclitus, *Epp*. 2; 7.10). Although their folly causes him hardships, and they maltreat him, and he cannot avoid them, still his virtue remains untouched (Crates, *Ep.* 35). He is superior to them because he has chosen the difficult, Diogenean, way to happiness.[56] It is hard to find a real Cynic (Diog., *Ep.* 29.4). One must be born to that life, otherwise one fears it and despairs of it (Crates, *Ep.* 21; Diog., *Epp.* 12; 41). But he is superior in his moral exercise, is more simple in his life, and more patient in hardship (Diog., *Ep.* 27). It is, in the first instance, what he is, as exemplified in his deeds rather than his words, that is important. Thus, the Cynic dress, which he invests with great importance, sets him off from other people by freeing him from popular opinion (Diog., *Epp.* 7; 34) and effectively separating him from undesirable people (Crates, *Ep.* 23). Or again, he begs to sustain himself, but he does so for the right reasons and in the right manner, which set him further apart. Begging is not disgraceful, for it is to satisfy a need arising from voluntary poverty (Crates, *Ep.* 17). By surrendering his private property and thus being freed from evil (Crates, *Ep.* 7), he shows himself superior to the values of popular opinion (Diog., *Ep.* 9). Furthermore, he is not really begging, but only demanding what belongs to him, for, since all things belong to God, friends have all things in common, and he is a friend of God, all things belong to him (Crates, *Epp.* 26; 27; Diog., *Ep.* 10.2). Nor is he indiscriminate in his begging, for vice is not to support virtue. Thus, he begs only from people who are worthy of him and his teaching (Crates, *Epp.* 2; 19; 22; 36; Diog., *Ep.* 38.3f.) So, too, his offensive public acts are demonstrations of his deliberateness in choice and, rather than his being blamed for them, he should be recognized as the more worthy of trust because of them (Diog., *Epp.* 42; 44). His goal is to live quietly and not to participate fully in society (Crates, *Ep.* 7), for such pursuits compromise him. Nor does he accept political office, for philosophy, which teaches people not to do wrong, is superior to laws, which compel them not to (Crates, *Ep.* 5). He may be ridiculed, but he does not care what people think of him. The benefit that people will receive from him will not come to them because he had sought them out or tried to please them, but because they had observed the example he presented them in his life (Crates, *Ep.* 20).[57]

The mild Cynic

In comparison with the misanthropic Cynics, those of a milder disposition showed less pride. Their comparative tolerance did not exactly place them on the same level with people they exhorted, but they were decidedly more modest in the claims they made for themselves.[58] The Cynics of the Socratic epistles are not as preoccupied with nature or as pessimistic in their view of the human condition, yet they are certain that they know human nature, what people's shortcomings are, what is best for them, and that the greatest emphasis is to be placed on virtue (Socrates, *Epp.* 5; 6.3,5). They do not describe themselves, as Lucian does Demonax (*Demon.* 10), as everybody's friend, but their behaviour does reflect a more positive attitude. While their self-sufficiency and rejection of popular values makes them different from the majority (Socrates, *Ep.* 6.2–4), on the ground that the 'hedonistic' life does not affect their *phronēsis* (*Ep.* 9.3) they reject the misanthropists' claim that the only appropriate life for the sage is the austere one, and that he cannot associate with the ignorant masses (*Ep.* 8). Thus, in their various social roles they differ radically from the anti-social Cynics. Unlike Peregrinus, for example, they have no desire to upset the social order. This Cynic will accept no political office or military appointment, for it is beyond his powers to rule men. But he does remain in the city in the capacity that he does have, that of a counsellor who constantly points out what is profitable for it (*Ep.* 1.1, 10–12).[59] He seeks only that fame which comes from being prudent and just (*Ep.* 6.2), and remains constant in his endurance and contempt for riches (*Ep.* 5). He is fully aware of the injustice in the state (*Ep.* 7) and meets with opposition (*Ep.* 5), but Socrates is his exemplar, not only of the treatment that the sage may receive at the hands of unjust men (*Epp.* 14; 16), but also of the benefits that can accrue from his life and death (*Ep.* 17). This Cynic therefore does not despair of improving society, and consequently justifies his involvement by the potential benefit he might render. Like Demonax, he is mild in the exercise of his *parrēsia*, accommodating himself to his audience, and distancing himself from the anti-social Cynics.[60]

Living as a resident Cynic rather than an independent, wandering preacher required special justification, which 'Socrates' provides in *Epp.* 1 and 6.[61] It is clear that these letters are responding to charges of harsh Cynics that it is out of mercenary motives that the resident Cynic confines himself to esoteric teaching in lecture halls. In response, 'Socrates' denies that he is unapproachable or mercenary, and offers a number of reasons for his decision to remain in the city. First, he has done so because God had commanded him to remain (*Ep.* 1.2, 7). He knows that this argument may be unacceptable to many Cynics, and therefore uses the Socratic tradition to bolster it (*Ep.* 1.8f.).[62] Furthermore, he claims to meet the needs of his country in the capacity in which he can render some benefit (*Ep.* 1.5f.), unlike ignorant men who arrogate to themselves power that they do not have, who act disgracefully, are insulted, and then end in the wilderness (*Ep.* 1.10f.). He is self-sufficient, and does not beg from the masses (*Ep.* 1.2; 6.1), for he has ample resources in his friends.[63]

The Socratic epistles differ from other Cynic sources of the period in their emphasis on the circle of 'friends'.[64] Besides the financial assistance these friends render each other, they are pictured as in constant contact with each other, either in person,[65] or by means of letters, which are surrogates for their authors' physical presence (*Ep.* 18.1), and in which the philosophical discussion is continued.[66] The Socratics are made to represent differing Cynic positions, but their supposed contact with each other presents a picture of a school hammering out its differences in an attempt to come to some kind of harmony. As the major representative of the milder Cynicism advocated in the letters, Aristippus illustrates their irenic tendency. As already noted, he commends Simon. He is further on good terms with Xenophon and other Socratics (*Ep.* 18), and the enmity between him and Plato is played down as jesting and a reconciliation is hinted at (*Ep.* 23.3). By selective use of the anecdotal tradition, rivalries are played down and a harmonious picture is sketched. For example, although the tradition often records the austere Diogenes's criticisms of Plato, Diogenes does not appear in these letters, and even the less frequently attested opposition between Antisthenes and Plato is omitted, with Antisthenes left to rebuke only Aristippus.[67] The differences among members of the Academy after Plato's death are attributed to personal judgment and disposition (*Ep.* 4.2f.), and concern is expressed for the preservation and organization of the institution (*Epp.* 32; 33), yet the letters do not provide evidence for the institutionalization of Cynicism. The effort to bring Cynics into conversation with each other itself draws attention to their diversity, and there is no evidence that the authors are witnesses to organized Cynic schools. But there is at least an attempt made to mute their differences. The major confrontation that remains is between the harsh and the hedonistic Cynics, but attempts are made to ameliorate it.

No convincing generalization can be made about the Cynics' attitude towards religion. Opinions range from what is perhaps the classic one, that they were rationalists who had no patience with the supernatural or popular religion,[68] to one that describes them as conscious of a union with God which empowered them.[69] A mediating view is that two strains can be identified, a positive one accompanied by a moderate view of mankind, and a sceptical one associated with rigorism.[70] The latter view, while it may find support in Oenomaus, runs aground on the fact that Demonax, known for his mildness, was decidedly cool towards religion,[71] and that Peregrinus, the major example of Cynic 'mysticism', was known for his harshness.[72] Nevertheless, the Cynic epistles which reflect Cynicism of the austere type do tend towards a sceptical view,[73] and the Socratic epistles, while they do not make much of religion, do evidence a more positive attitude towards it. Thus, in the latter, Socrates offers a cock to Asclepius (*Ep.* 14.9), Xenophon builds a temple (*Ep.* 19), Socrates models himself upon God (*Ep.* 6.4)[74] and is divinely commissioned (*Ep.* 1.2, 7). Still, religion is not at the centre of the discussion and, as we have noted, where it does appear to justify Cynic behaviour, it does so in a polemical context and is appealed to with the recognition that it may carry no weight with other Cynics.[75]

Conclusion

The considerable diversity of second-century Cynicism is still evident in the third, although the author of the Socratic epistles does attempt to play it down. Diogenes Laertius, who may have been more interested in biography than doxography, nevertheless notes that some Cynics still preferred the austere regimen of Diogenes.[76] The evidence from Julian in the century that followed is more difficult to assess. His own austerity, susceptibility to religious mysticism, constant seeking for divine guidance, and the polemical nature of his addresses on the Cynics colour his views to an inordinate degree.[77] Some facts, however, do emerge. The Cynics he opposes scorned religion, and Julian uses the occasion to excoriate Oenomaus and present an interpretation of Diogenes as divinely guided, which may reflect his own predilections, but which is also part of the tradition.[78] Julian's own preference is evident when he complains that they ridiculed Diogenes for his austerity,[79] but demands that they exercise their *parrēsia* with charm and grace.[80] Julian could not tolerate their criticism of his administration, which he viewed as a subverting of the institutions of society.[81] Nonetheless, his tirade against Heracleius reveals that they did attempt to present themselves at his court, and that they therefore were not anti-social in the manner of 'Heraclitus' or 'Diogenes'.[82] Through Julian's invective glimpses are caught of rationalistic Cynics of the milder sort. The fifth century knew Sallustius the Cynic, a man with whom Julian might have been better pleased. He was austere in his way of life and, although not much is known of his religious outlook, he evidently shared Peregrinus's mysticism and practised divination.[83] In sum, Cynicism, which was essentially a way of life requiring no adherence to a canonical system of doctrine, continued to adapt itself to different viewpoints, and consequently retained the diversity which characterized it from early in its history.

4

Self-Definition in Later Platonism

JOHN M. DILLON

Self-definition by contrast to other groups

A terminological problem must be faced at the outset of this paper: self-definition in relation to what? An individual or an organization must define itself in relation to whatever stands over against it as 'other' at any given stage of its existence. During its long history, Platonism had to define itself in relation to various opponents, and I shall try to discuss all of them adequately, ending with Christianity, its last and most formidable adversary.

From the beginning of the Platonic School, as soon as a rival establishment was set up by Aristotle in the Lyceum, Platonists were under the necessity of defending themselves by defining themselves. Under the pressure of well-aimed attacks from Aristotle, himself a Platonist, Plato's successors Speusippus and Xenocrates had to hammer out a dogmatic system from the plethora of interesting suggestions and baffling puzzles which Plato had bequeathed to them. Responding to this challenge, Xenocrates in particular, through a large corpus of treatises on almost every area of philosophy (all of which are lost), became the true founder of Platonism as a system. Questions such as the nature of God, the Forms and their relation to the physical world, or the definition and role of Pleasure and Happiness, receive definitive treatment from Xenocrates, mainly in response to polemical assaults from Aristotle.

In the process of polemical self-definition, a notable phenomenon is the extent to which one finds oneself borrowing concepts and formulations from one's opponents. There is nothing very surprising about this process, which is just as much a feature of modern, as it was of ancient, ideological conflict. One's opponent, ruffian and charlatan though he may be, almost invariably scores a point or two in the controversy which one is forced to counter.

Aristotle scored a good many. The result for Platonism was that, although Aristotle himself remained beyond the pale, Aristotelian logic quickly superseded *diaeresis*, the Aristotelian doctrine of the mean became a basic feature of ethical theory, and God came to be accepted as a mind thinking itself, its contents being the Forms. A host of technical terms and concepts were taken on as well, 'matter', 'potential/actual', the four causes, the categories. It might be argued – and it was argued, vigorously, in later times – that most of these doctrines and formulations were not original to Aristotle, but arose in the Academy before he broke with it. There may be some truth in this. Later tradition (which we can see at work, for instance, in Albinus's *Didaskalikos*) managed to identify traces of these doctrines at one point or another in the dialogues (most varieties of syllogism in the *Parmenides*, all the Categories in *Timaeus* 37 AB – this from Plutarch, *An. proc.* 23, *Mor.* 1023E), but the adoption of these concepts into the Academy, in their fully-fledged form, is, I would maintain, the direct result of inter-school polemic.

In the course of the next century or so, from Arcesilaus's accession to the headship of the school in about 270 BCE to the death of Philo of Larissa in the 80s, Platonism ceased to be on the defensive, and, sheltering behind a cloud of scepticism, went onto the attack. Their chief enemy, or rather victim, in this period was the Stoic school, and their dogmatism in the area of epistemology. While not necessarily abandoning the conceptual baggage which it had inherited from the Old Academy and Peripatos, the Academy concentrated its efforts on undermining Stoic claims to certainty, and the ethical and physical superstructure based on this. For the majority of the Hellenistic age, 'Academic' meant sceptical, and this terminology persisted in later times, *Akadēmaikos* remaining distinct from *Platonikos*, as an epithet of members of the New Academy[1]. The advocacy of *epochē*, 'suspension of assent', and of *to pithanon*, 'the plausible', as a standard of conduct, became the hallmarks of a Platonist during this period, and left their mark later on Platonists such as Plutarch.

Identity crises and self-definition

At the turn of the first century BCE, however, there began a development away from scepticism, under the scholarchate of Philo of Larissa, which culminated in a return to dogmatism and the assimilation of much Stoic doctrine. This came to a head in the

61

80s, with Philo's dissident pupil, Antiochus of Ascalon, who broke away from the sceptical tradition to found what he defiantly termed 'the Old Academy', thus putting the intellectual world on notice that he was restoring the 'true' teachings of Plato and his immediate successors. This development brought on something of an identity crisis in the Platonic tradition, the reverberations of which continued for centuries, in the form of a running argument as to whether the New Academics were truly part of the Platonic tradition, and it is at this point that we may begin a closer examination of the process of self-definition.

What exactly the new position in epistemology taken up by Philo was is a matter of controversy, on which much light has been thrown recently by the exhaustive investigations of John Glucker.[2] Philo appears to have accepted the Stoic claim that things are knowable in themselves (*enargeia*), while rejecting the Stoic claim about certainty, that the mind can perceive impressions which are such as could only come from the object in question (*katalēpsis*).[3] Fortunately, the only aspect of his innovation which really concerns us here is the consequences it had for the self-image of the Academy. For it is with Philo, and his pupil Antiochus, that the controversy about the unity of the Academic tradition first arises, a controversy that was to remain active for the next few hundred years.

The New Academy, despite its sceptical stance, seems to have had no problem about claiming Platonic ancestry for itself. Arcesilaus, we learn from Diogenes Laertius, 'seems to have held Plato in admiration, and possessed his works' (4.32). However, it stressed, inevitably, the Socratic and aporetic element in Plato's works. Whether or not Arcesilaus or Carneades accepted the Theory of Ideas in any form is not clear, but as regards the possibility of certainty on the basis of sense-perception, which was what the Stoics were claiming, they could claim Plato as a sceptic, even in such a work as the *Theaetetus*.[4] When Philo veered back towards dogmatism, he was faced with a problem. If Plato was a dogmatist, as a reading of, say, the *Phaedo, Republic* or *Timaeus* would tend to suggest, did the sceptical Academy then constitute a deviation from true Platonism?

This was the second considerable crisis of self-definition in the Platonic school after the initial confrontation with Aristotle and Theophrastus. (Arcesilaus does not seem to have gone through a comparable crisis on taking over from Polemon and Crates, though his description of these distinguished predecessors as 'sort of gods, or left-overs from the Golden Race' may in fact conceal a measure of irony, such as would naturally escape Diogenes Laertius [4.22]). Philo tried to solve the crisis (perhaps in response to prodding by his Roman patrons, after his retreat to Rome in face of Mithridates in 89 BCE) by composing a treatise in which he argued that neither Plato nor the New Academics were thoroughgoing sceptics. He may simply have wished to claim that the principle of probability (or better, 'plausibility') involved no more than a relative scepticism (denying only the Stoic criterion) which was compatible with Platonic doctrine, but it is possible that he went further. Augustine, in his *Contra Academicos* (3.20.43), reports a statement of Cicero's in his *Academica* to the effect that the New Academy 'had a habit of concealing their opinions, and did not usually disclose them to anyone except those that had lived with them right up to old age'.[5] If Cicero got this notion from anyone, the only man one can imagine him getting it from is Philo – certainly not from Antiochus, who would have no interest in making such a claim – but if Philo said such a thing, what did he mean? Not necessarily, I think, that the New Academy preserved a whole system of dogmatic Platonism which they only revealed to trusted initiates; he need have meant no more than that in public Arcesilaus or Carneades would maintain total scepticism, simply posing difficulties for the Stoics, but in private they were prepared to express views on how to live to their permanent pupils. This would relate, perhaps, to the dispute that seems to have arisen in the school about Carneades's personal beliefs in the generation after his death, Clitomachus (his most authoritative exegete) maintaining that he had never been able to discern what the Master really believed about anything, whereas Metrodorus and Philo claimed that Carneades had held that the Wise Man would form opinions on the basis of *pithanotēs*.[6]

At any rate, Philo was concerned to maintain the unity of the Academic tradition. This aroused the indignation of Antiochus, who in these same years (the late 90s and early 80s) seems to have been provoked by Philo's rather vacillating stance in epistemology to a wholehearted acceptance of the Stoic theory of knowledge, and with it to a quite different view of the development of Platonic doctrine. Cicero makes Lucullus (*Luc.* 11) give a vivid description of a session in Alexandria in the winter of 87–6 BCE, in which Antiochus gives a heated refutation of Philo's position, which he is presented now as hearing for the first time. This circumstance is best explained, as Glucker has persuasively argued,[7] if we take it that Antiochus had not followed Philo to Rome in 89, but had stayed on somewhere in Greece, until picked up by Lucullus, who wanted him for diplomatic missions, in 87. This scene is probably taken by Cicero from a prefatory section of a treatise in dialogue form, the *Sosus*, which Antiochus is reported to have composed in refutation of Philo's position, dedicating it, significantly, to a Stoic philospher of that name from Antiochus's home town of Ascalon.

Antiochus in this work makes a clear break between the Old Academy down to Polemon, and the New, from Arcesilaus to Philo, condemning the latter as being untrue to the position of Plato. This is a significant development, but he does more. First, he declares that there is no essential difference between the Old Academy and the Peripatos; they are both equally parts of the great tradition. This is fully expounded by Varro, Antiochus's 'mouthpiece', in Cicero's *Acad. post.* 15ff., and more succintly at *Fin.* 5.7, where Piso, the spokesman of Antiochus, speaks of

> the Old Academy, which includes, as you hear Antiochus declare, not only those who bear the name of Academics, Speusippus, Xenocrates, Polemon, Crantor and the rest, but also the early Peripatetics, headed by their chief, Aristotle, who, if Plato be excepted, I almost think deserves to be called the prince of philosophers.[8]

This unity was that much easier to maintain before the rediscovery of Aristotle's esoteric works, which only saw the light (whether or not they had in fact been immured in a cellar in Scepsis) in Andronicus's edition somewhat later in the century,[9] but even so it must seem to us to gloss over a good deal. On the theory of ideas, after all, Aristotle had been pretty severe even in his exoteric works, such as the *Peri Ideōn*. Antiochus will presumably have taken such criticisms to refer only to early versions of the theory, or to perversions of it.

On the other hand, Antiochus sought to bring the Stoics into his new synthesis. For him, Stoicism was essentially an updated Platonism. Only in certain respects (such as making virtue alone sufficient for happiness, for example) did Zeno deviate from the Old Academy and these details can easily be isolated and corrected. At *Fin.* 4.3, Cicero says, speaking in his own person to the Stoic Cato:

> My view, then, Cato, is this, that those old disciples of Plato, Speusippus, Aristotle and Xenocrates, and afterwards their pupils Polemon and Theophrastus, had developed a body of doctrine that left nothing to be desired either in fullness or finish, so that Zeno, on becoming a

pupil of Polemon, had no reason for differing either from his master himself or from his master's predecessors.[10]

Antiochus thus staked out his base, pleasing nobody but himself (certainly not either Stoics or Sceptics), but defining a position for the Platonist school from which it did not deviate radically for the rest of antiquity. For the next few hundred years, Platonism moves between the opposing poles of Aristotelianism and Stoicism, different Platonists taking up different positions on the spectrum in accord with their personal predilections and the exigencies of inter-school warfare.

Almost immediately after Antiochus's synthesis, however, Platonism was forced to re-define itself to some extent. The rediscovery of Aristotle's esoteric works already alluded to, and Aristonicus's edition of them and commentaries upon some of them, led to defections from the school of Antiochus in the direction of Aristotelianism. Antiochus's pupil Cratippus appears in the 40s teaching in Athens as an Aristotelian, but he is a fairly harmless figure. More significant was Antiochus's pupil in Alexandria, Ariston, who wrote commentaries on the *Categories* and probably on the *Prior Analytics*, contributing a certain amount to the later development of Aristotelian logic.[11] It is probably in reaction to his activity that the Alexandrian Platonist Eudorus (who was probably not a pupil of Antiochus, but quite possibly of his pupil Dion),[12] in the 20s gave Platonism a distinct anti-Aristotelian turn, by initiating a series of polemical commentaries on the *Categories* which continued down to Plotinus (in *Enn.* 6.1–3). He also criticized Peripatetic ethical theory (and implicitly that of Antiochus) from a Stoic perspective.[13]

The other important contribution of Eudorus to the self-definition of Platonism was the revival of the Pythagoreanism which had been fostered by the Old Academy (or at least by Speusippus and Xenocrates). Making use of a host of Pythagorean pseudepigrapha which had sprung up, in mysterious circumstances, in the third and second centuries BCE,[14] Eudorus reintroduced a transcendental element into Platonism, rejecting Stoic materialism in physics, which Antiochus had admitted into the tradition. Eudorus's first principle is a One above a pair of Monad and Dyad, a thoroughly immaterial, not to say ineffable, entity.[15] With Eudorus, indeed, we begin to find that constellation of doctrines which are generally thought of as Middle Platonist – such characteristics as a belief in the transcendence and immateriality of

65

God, and the existence of immaterial substance in general, as well as a vivid interest in mathematics, and in particular in mystical numerology; and, in ethics, an ascetic, world-negating tendency, which takes 'likeness to God' as its slogan rather than the Stoic 'conformity with Nature', adopted by Antiochus. All these characteristics we see reflected in such a figure as the Jewish thinker Philo of Alexandria, who, while not himself to be reckoned as a member of the Platonist *hairesis*, certainly reflects to a large extent the state of contemporary Platonism.

Self-definition without institutional supports

Mention of a Platonist *hairesis*, or 'school', raises an important question in connection with Platonist self-definition in this period. It is relatively easy to define oneself if one has an institution to relate to, with all the physical plant, communal memory, and accreditation system that that might be taken to involve. Until recently, it was almost universally assumed, on the basis of the exhaustive researches of Carl Gottlob Zumpt (1792–1849), issuing in his study of 1844, entitled *Über den Bestand der philosophischen Schulen in Athen und die Succession der Scholarchen*,[16] that the Platonic Academy survived, albeit in great obscurity for much of the time, all through antiquity, until it was finally closed by Justinian in 529 CE. The excellent study of John Lynch, in the course of his book *Aristotle's School*,[17] and now the magisterial work of John Glucker,[18] have finally, I think, disposed of that comfortable illusion, and have revealed something much more interesting, a tradition maintaining itself unofficially, by word of mouth, without official certification, but yet preserving, in the process of transmission from master to pupil, a communal memory and consciousness. What one finds, in fact, is a series of individual schools, sometimes being handed on from a founder to his successor, as was the case with Antiochus, Gaius (to Albinus), or Plotinus (to Porphyry), but sometimes apparently going no further than their founder, as seems to be the case with the schools of Plutarch's mentor Ammonius, or Aulus Gellius's teacher Taurus. All these men, however, knew that they were Platonists. They knew where they came from, and had some sense, at least, of belonging to a 'golden chain' of philosophers (though this actual expression may only date from Neoplatonic times). Unlike the Epicureans (or the Christians), but like the Stoics, they imposed no rigid requirements for orthodoxy, though a belief in the transcendence of God, the theory of ideas, and the immortality of the soul is certainly a distinguishing mark of Platonists of this period. On the other hand, on such questions as the temporal creation of the world, the self-sufficiency of virtue, or the best system of logic, a wide measure of latitude was permissible, even though a man like Atticus, in a polemical mood, might castigate fellow-Platonists for being soft on Aristotelianism,[19] and Plutarch condemn his predecessors for their misunderstanding of Plato on the question of the creation of the world.[20]

Indeed, a running polemical battle was kept up throughout this period with the other schools, in which the Christians, as we shall see, were presently granted the compliment of being included. Eudorus, as I have noted, attacked Aristotle's *Categories*, and in this he was followed by the shadowy figures Lucius and Nicostratus (first to second centuries CE), by Atticus, and by Plotinus. Plutarch was friendly to Peripateticism, but aimed a number of polemical treatises at the Stoics (*SR, CN*) and at the Epicureans (*Non posse, Adv. Col., Lat. viv.*). Taurus wrote against the Stoics (Aulus Gellius, *NA* 12.5), and Atticus, as mentioned above, violently attacked the Peripatetics. All this activity, which is generally conducted on a disedifyingly low level, has the purpose rather of 'self-definition' (and the collection and preservation of pupils) than the disinterested search for the truth. It certainly did not prevent Platonists from borrowing terminology freely from both Peripatos and Stoa, presumably on the grounds that all this was common philosophical currency.

While on the subject of inter-school rivalry, it is necessary to raise again a topic which I discussed earlier, in connection with the quarrel between Antiochus and Philo, namely the unity of the Platonic tradition. This question was not finally settled by Antiochus's disowning of the New Academy. A nostalgia for the sceptical tradition of the Academy still lingered in certain Platonist breasts, notably in that of Plutarch, who wrote a work (now lost) *On the Unity of the Academy since Plato* (Lamprias Cat. no. 63), which perhaps recapitulated the arguments of Philo of Larissa, and the sophist Favorinus of Arles, who affected a New Academic stance when dealing with philosophical questions.[21] Plutarch found the arguments of Carneades and Clitomachus of great assistance in attacking the Stoics, but in his positive doctrine Plutarch was no sceptic. We do not even know the grounds on which he maintained the unity of the Academy. Very possibly he subscribed to the notion that from Arcesilaus to Carneades the positive doctrines of Plato were preserved as an esoteric teaching.

A diametrically opposed attitude to the New Academy was taken up somewhat later, in the mid-second century, by Numenius of Apamea, a Syrian Platonist of extreme Pythagoreanizing tendencies, who wrote an entertainingly satirical work, of which Eusebius has preserved large extracts,[22] entitled *On the Divergence of the Academics from Plato*, in which he traces what he sees as their defection from Arcesilaus down to Philo of Larissa, ending with some unkind words on Antiochus for his Stoicizing innovations. Numenius does not make it clear who pleases him, but since he affected, as I have said, a Pythagorean stance, he may have felt that the true faith was preserved by a Pythagoreanizing underground during the Hellenistic age, which emerged into the light with Eudorus. He also wrote a book entitled *On the Secret Doctrines of Plato*, which may have expressed such views, though the surviving fragment of it[23] is unhelpful.

Plainly the debate about the unity of the Academy, and the true line of succession to Plato, was still a lively one in the second century CE. Efforts to assert unity were also helped by the elaboration of a belief which I have noted above as going back in at least some form to Philo of Larissa, that even the Sceptical Academy had only used scepticism as a weapon against the Stoics, and had preserved the full array of Plato's doctrines as a secret 'mystery' to be imparted to the faithful behind closed doors. Numenius actually knows of, and rejects, this theory, which he attributes to one Diocles of Cnidus, of unknown date,[24] and Sextus Empiricus reports in more detail (perhaps using the same source) about Arcesilaus that:

> he appeared at first glance, they say, to be a Pyrrhonean, but in reality he was a dogmatist; and because he used to test his companions by means of dubitation to see if they were fitted by nature for the reception of the Platonic doctrines, he was thought to be an aporetic philosopher, but he actually passed on to such of his companions as were naturally gifted the dogmas of Plato.[25]

Whatever the accuracy of this belief, it grew in the next centuries to be an accepted truth, reaching Augustine as something generally agreed. The Neoplatonists actually show no interest in the sceptical Academy as such, and the question of unity may have been settled for them definitively by Porphyry in a lost portion of his comprehensive History of Philosophy. A distinction was always made in later times, however, between 'Academics' and

'Platonists', the former title referring to the members of the sceptical Academy, the latter to Platonic philosophers of the second century CE and later. Numenius utilizes this distinction (in the work above-mentioned); so do Plutarch (despite his beliefs about the unity of the movement),[26] Lucian,[27] and Aulus Gellius.[28] But the blurring of the self-image of Platonists consequent on the acceptance or rejection of Academic scepticism as part of the tradition ceased in the Neoplatonic era. The only contrast Proclus makes in his commentaries (particularly that on the *Timaeus*, where he is assiduous about quoting previous authorities) is between pre-Plotinian and post-Plotinian Platonists, the former being termed simply *hoi archaioi*, as opposed to *hoi neōteroi hoi apo Plotinou Platōnikoi* (*In Tim.* 2.88. 10–12).

Confrontation with Christianity

By the time we come to the confrontation with Christianity, then, the Platonist tradition knows, if not precisely where it stands, where it might retreat to. This self-consciousness it achieved, as has now been made plain, without the fixed repository of ortho-doxy which would be constituted by a physical Academy and a regular succession of scholarchs. What held Platonists together was simply a shared tradition, even a shared mythology. By the third century CE, in addition, they were in the position of being virtually the sole repositories of Hellenic philosophy and culture. The last notable Peripatetic was Alexander of Aphrodisias, at the end of the second century (unless Themistius be counted one, in the fourth century), and the Stoic and Epicurean schools became stagnant at about the same time (though presumably the profes-sorships of the four *haireseis* set up in Athens by Marcus Aurelius in 176 CE continued to function). The Platonists, therefore, from Plotinus and Porphyry on, through Iamblichus (and his devoted admirer, the Emperor Julian) to Proclus in the fifth century and Simplicius and Damascius in the sixth, become the bulwark of defence against the growing challenge of Christianity, 'this de-lusion that is rushing upon men', as Plotinus terms it in *Ennead* 2.9.6.

The first shots were fired before the end of the second century, by the Platonist Celsus. Unfortunately, even to Origen, who replied to his attack somewhat less than a century later, Celsus's identity was quite obscure. We are at least clear that he is not the Epicurean with whom Origen identified him, but whether he was a Platonist philosopher, or simply a Platonizing sophist, of the type of Maximus of Tyre, is not obvious. His Platonism has affinities with that of Albinus (if the *Didaskalikos* is indeed by him, and not by one Alcinous), but remains on a rather general level. At all events, he understands the conventions of inter-school polemic, and he uses them to good effect on the Christians. In the process, he sounds two notes of particular significance, one of which is echoed by his contemporary Galen, in various passing remarks, and both of which are taken up in the next century by Plotinus (with particular reference to Gnostics) and by Porphyry, in his great treatise *Against the Christians*. These are the charges of anti-intellectualism and irrationality, and of disrespect for tradition. By contrast, Platonism is represented as the supreme defender of Hellenic rationality and the antiquity of Hellenic (and other) wisdom.

To begin with anti-intellectualism, and the blind acceptance of authority: Platonists recognized that this was not peculiar to Christians. Pythagoreans, after all, had long been satirized for their submission to the *autos epha* of Pythagoras. But the characteristic of a philosopher, or even of a rational man (*logikos*), was felt to be the ability to give a *logos* of what he believed. Acceptance of authority as such was not the issue – no Platonist, after all, disputed the correctness of Plato's views; it is rather the disdain of any *logos* in one's beliefs that was offensive. To quote Origen (*Contra Celsum* 1.9):

> After this he [Celsus] urges us to 'follow reason and a rational guide in accepting doctrines', on the ground that 'anyone who believes people without so doing is certain to be deceived'. And he compares those who believe without rational thought to 'the begging priests of Cybele and soothsayers, and to worshippers of Mithras and Sabazius, and whatever else one might meet, apparitions of Hecate or of some other daemon or daemons. For just as among them scoundrels frequently take advantage of the lack of education of gullible people and lead them wherever they wish, so also', he says, 'this happens among the Christians.' He says that 'some do not even want to give or receive a reason for what they believe, and use such expressions as "Do not ask questions; just believe!", and "Thy faith will save thee!" ' And he affirms that they say: 'The wisdom in the world is an evil, and foolishness a good thing.'[29]

This is the voice of the establishment. Galen, who is not being polemical in his remarks, makes very much the same point:

> Those who practise medicine without scientific knowledge may be compared to Moses, who framed laws for . . . the Jews, since it is his

method in his books to write without offering proofs, saying 'God commanded, God spoke'.[30]

From the other references which Walzer has assembled, it is plain that the impression Galen has of the Jews and Christians is of those who accept dogmas without any attempt at scientific proof – though, as we see, he does not regard them as unique in this.

Celsus's second gibe is that of lack of ancestry. The Jews are peculiar, he says (ap. *CC* 5.25), but at least they have been around for some time. These people cannot even claim that (ibid. 33):

> Now let us take the second chorus. I will ask them where they have come from, or who is the author of their traditional laws. Nobody, they will say. In fact, they themselves originated from Judaism, and they cannot name any other source for their teacher and chorus-leader. Nevertheless they rebelled against the Jews.

A hundred years after Celsus, Plotinus, in *Ennead* 2.9, turns his scornful attention to the Gnostics (specifically Sethians and Valentinians) whose doctrines had affected some members of his own circle. He is not primarily concerned with Christians – indeed, his attack is partly directed against tendencies present in parts of the Platonic tradition itself, such as the school of Numenius – but his accusations are similar to those of Celsus. The Gnostics do not follow the dictates of reason, and they have no respect for truths sanctified by antiquity. In ch. 6, he complains against them that, though anything of any validity in their teachings is in fact borrowed from Plato, they try to disguise this by their abuse of ancient authorities:

> For these doctrines are there in Plato, and when they state them clearly in this way they do well. If they wish to disagree on these points, there is no unfair hostility involved in saying to them that they should not recommend their own opinions to their audience by ridiculing and insulting the Greeks but that they should show the correctness on their own merits of all the points of doctrine which are peculiar to them and differ from the views of the Greeks, stating their real opinions courteously, as befits philosophers, and fairly on the points where they are opposed, looking to the truth and not hunting fame by censuring men who have been judged good from ancient times by men of worth, and saying that they themselves are better than the Greeks.[31]

A good deal of the tractate is devoted to demonstrating the logical incoherences in the Gnostic doctrines of the fall of the soul and the creation of the world, by contrast with the Platonist account. In the same way, a hundred years further on, Julian, in his treatise *Against the Galileans*, sets side by side the cosmogonies of Moses and of Plato (in the *Timaeus*), to show the irrationality of Moses's account.[32]

But I do not wish to get sidetracked into a survey of the conflict between Platonism and Christianity. All that is relevant for my purpose is to show how the polemic against Christians, Jews and Gnostics serves the purpose of self-definition for Platonism, even as had previous struggles with Aristotelians, Stoics or Epicureans. One last feature of this polemic, however, should be adverted to, since it marks an important development in Platonism from Plotinus on, and seems to have been given particular focus as a consequence of Plotinus's ideological struggle with Gnostic tendencies. This is the essentially world-affirming attitude which one finds in *Ennead* 2.9, and in Plotinus's mature thought in general, as opposed to the radically world-negating attitude of the Gnostics, and of a good deal of Middle Platonism, particularly the Pythagoreanizing wing of it, represented by Numenius and Cronius. Plotinus is no friend of the flesh and its pleasures, but it is axiomatic to his system that the physical cosmos is a natural and necessary creation, and as good as it could in the nature of things be. He admits elsewhere, in *Enn.* 4.8.1, that Plato in some places (such as the *Phaedrus*) seems to reject the world as an aberration – he could have added the *Phaedo* – but he prefers to follow the doctrine of the *Timaeus*, which presents it as necessary and beautiful, though necessarily also inferior to its model. He therefore strongly condemns the Gnostic rejection and abuse of the world, as another example of their insolence and ignorance. In so doing, it seems to me, he adds something to the Platonist world view: Platonism affirms the world as it is. This was not always so clearly the case before Plotinus, but it remains a fixed characteristic after him. This is not to say that one should not fix one's eyes on a better level of existence, to which one hopes to withdraw at the appropriate time; it is just that one does not indulge in vulgar and indiscriminate abuse of what is, after all, a 'moving image of eternal things'. The distinction is made by Plotinus very well in one of his characteristic images, to which one might give the nickname of the Odd Couple.

> But perhaps they will assert that those arguments of theirs make men fly from the body since they hate it from a distance, but ours hold the soul down to it. This would be like two people living in the same fine house, one of whom reviles the structure and the builder, but stays there none the less, while the other does not revile, but says the builder has built it with the utmost skill, and waits for the time to come in

72

which he will go away, when he will not need a house any longer: the first might think he was wiser and readier to depart because he knows how to say that 'the walls are built of soulless stones and timber and are far inferior to the true dwelling place', not knowing that he is only distinguished by not bearing what he must – unless he affirms that he is discontented, while having a secret affection for the beauty of the stones.[33]

Platonism after Plotinus

In the generations after Plotinus, Platonism modified itself further by becoming much more hospitable to magical practice, in the form of theurgy, and by the admission of a wider range of 'inspired' texts, primarily the *Chaldaean Oracles*, a fabrication by one Julian, of the time of Marcus Aurelius, but also of the poems of Orpheus, and even of Homer and Hesiod, viewed allegorically. Plato himself was seen as inspired in a rather stronger sense than heretofore, and every part of those dialogues which were chosen for special comment, such as the *Timaeus* and the *Parmenides*, was taken to be filled with significance, the prefatory portions being interpreted allegorically to lend them suitable dignity and relevance. These developments in the direction of religion were no doubt stimulated by the challenge of Christianity, though this only becomes explicit in the efforts of the Emperor Julian to set up a theurgical Neoplatonism as a substitute for Christianity during his brief reign, in 361–3.

Admirer though I am of the Emperor Julian, I cannot regard his efforts, aided by the philospher-magician Maximus of Ephesus and the philosopher-statesman Sallustius, to set up a form of Platonism as a religion to rival Christianity, as other than an aberration, a bogus attempt at self-definition for Platonism. The experiment was rudely cut short by historical developments, but this combination of Platonic theology and the revival of old cults, together with a good deal of oriental theosophy, was surely too much of a hothouse plant to survive the chill winds of reality for very long.

More important for our purpose are certain significant remarks made by Proclus, with which we may fittingly close this survey. In the preface to his *Platonic Theology*, composed in the latter half of the fifth century CE,[34] Proclus gives an overview of the development of Platonism as he sees it, couched in the language of mystery-cult. Both what he says and how he says it are of interest. I noted earlier that the Neoplatonists do not seem to have concerned themselves with the Sceptical Academy, but they do in fact have a view of the development of this tradition which takes in that period. Since this view reappears in Augustine's treatise *Against the Academics* (3.17.37–19.42), it probably goes back to Porphyry.

Proclus sees theology as having been brought to a peak of perfection by Plato and his immediate successors, 'and then, as it were, after retreating into itself and rendering itself invisible to the great majority of those who professed philosophy, it once again emerged into the light'.[35] This period of darkness, where the truth was either underground (as Augustine presents it as being in the New Academy), or had retired to the heavens, takes in for Proclus not only the period of Scepticism, but also that of Antiochus and his Middle Platonic successors. Only with Plotinus, it seems, does theology emerge again into the light. Numenius's low opinion of Antiochus and his 'new departure' is maintained by the later school. However, in some mystical way the golden chain of true doctrine is not broken, and Plotinus is able to recover it and pass it on.

The other important aspect of Proclus's utterance here is the mystery imagery in which it is couched. Platonism, and philosophy in general, as a mystery into which one may be initiated is a conceit of long ancestry in Platonism. It is, indeed, something more than a conceit, since it embodies a claim by philosophers to uphold the truest form of religion. It thus constitutes an important slogan in the unending contest between religion and philosophy.

Plato himself provides a stimulus for this type of language in such passages as *Meno* 76E, *Symposium* 209E, *Gorgias* 479C, or *Theaetetus* 156A, all of which, however, are tinged, to a greater or lesser extent, with irony. Such irony as there may be vanishes, however, in later Platonic usage. It is actually not in a Platonist, but in the Platonist-influenced Philo of Alexandria that this imagery first reappears (in surviving authors), and then it reappears with a vengeance. So much use does Philo make of it that such a distinguished scholar as E. R. Goodenough was led to postulate Alexandrian-Jewish Mysteries into which Philo might have been initiated. No such hypothesis is necessary or likely. Mystery-imagery occurs in such Platonists as Plutarch,[36] Albinus,[37] and, most elaborately perhaps, in Theon of Smyrna.[38] Theon goes so far as to distinguish five stages in the 'initiation' – purification, communication of the ritual, vision (*epopteia*), 'adornment with garlands', and, finally, 'the joy that comes from unity and converse with the gods'. The concept of Platonism as a mystery is thus a commonplace in the Middle Platonic period.

Proclus, in this passage of the *Platonic Theology*, speaks of Plato's teaching as *mystagogia* and *epopteia*, and of Plato himself as 'the leader and hierophant of the truest rites (*teletai*), into which souls are initiated when they are separated from the earthly regions'. The situation is complicated by his time (and at any time after Iamblichus) by the fact that real Chaldaean and other magical rituals were now a part of philosophic practice, and Proclus's references are thus systematically ambiguous; but there is no doubt that he is drawing primarily on this age-old conceit.

Conclusion

Towards the end of antiquity, then, Platonism takes on some of the trappings of a religion, and a greater degree of organization (in the Athenian School after Plutarch of Athens, at least) then it had hitherto possessed, but the fact remains that the Platonic tradition attained self-definition without the aid of any regulating structure or hierarchy of accredited teachers, such as Christianity so quickly built up for itself. Its survival is all the more remarkable for that.

5

Hairesis and Heresy: The Case of the haireseis iatrikai

HEINRICH VON STADEN

It is the fate of new truths to begin as heresies and
to end as superstitions.   T. H. Huxley

The use of 'heresy' to refer to an opinion or a doctrine at variance
with orthodox beliefs seems to have its proximate roots in early
Christian uses of the Greek word *hairesis* (plural, *haireseis*). In most
phases of post-classical antiquity, however, *hairesis* had a considerably broader semantic spectrum than 'heresy' might suggest.
Its classical meanings – 'taking', 'choice', 'course of action',
'election', 'decision' – all continued to survive throughout the
Hellenistic and later ancient periods of Greek culture. But *hairesis*
also served to refer – positively, negatively, or neutrally – to any
group of people perceived to have a clear doctrinal identity.

The primary purpose of the present contribution is to trace the
development of this use of *hairesis* as a group referent in Greek
medical literature, and to explore what 'group definition' or
'group self-definition' might mean when the definiendum is
thought of as a *hairesis*. The fact that this analysis takes *hairesis* as
its starting point does not mean that other generic Greek terms
for 'school' or 'sect' are irrelevant to the question of definition and
self-definition in the ancient world. Much could be learned from
a careful scrutiny of *scholē, didaskaleion, agōgē, hoi ap' oikias tinos,
hoi peri, hoi amphi, mathētēs,* and similar expressions. But in view
of its prominence and its range, *hairesis* provides a useful starting
point.

From the late second century CE to at least the eighth century CE
the first book read in the medical curriculum of Alexandria – at
that time probably the most significant centre of medical learning
in the Mediterranean – was Galen's *On Haireseis for Beginners (De*

sectis). Galen himself had recommended *De sectis* as a suitable introduction to his works,[1] and hence, of course, to all of medicine, and his medieval Arabic translator, Hunain ibn Ishāq, confirms that *De sectis* continued to be the first of four Galenic works used to instruct novices.[2]

In *De sectis*, as in several late Alexandrian commentaries on this treatise,[3] three major *haireseis* or *sectae* are identified: the Empiricist (*empeirikē*) *hairesis*, Methodist (*methodikē*), and Rationalist (*logikē*) or Dogmatic (*dogmatikē*).[4] Several other Galenic treatises, notably *De optima secta*, and two pseudo-Galenic treatises which might predate Galen contributed to the popularization of this division of physicians into three major *haireseis*.[5] By the time Galen wrote his *De libris propriis* he could observe with both confidence and accuracy: 'Almost everybody already knows the names of the three *haireseis*.'[6] This ternary division became virtually canonical for centuries, and it has influenced medical historiography up to our own age.[7]

The firmness, apparent clarity, and longevity of this influential *hairesis* tradition has tended to obscure problems that are pertinent to the subject of this volume, e.g., (1) what does *hairesis* or, more specifically, *hairesis iatrikē* mean, and does it always refer to the same kind of group? (2) are there significant discrepancies between external perceptions and internal definition of these *haireseis*? (3) how stable or dynamic is a *hairesis* doctrinally and institutionally? (4) when and how does *hairesis* acquire the meaning 'heresy' or 'heretical faction'?

This paper attempts a fleeting, preliminary exploration of these and related questions under the following rubrics: I. '*hairesis* literature' in pre-Galenic medicine; II. three brief examples of the application of the *hairesis* label to a group: (a) 'Rationalists' vs. Empiricists, (b) Methodists, and (c) Herophileans; III. a few remarks on *hairesis* and institutionalization, with particular reference to the Herophileans; IV. a brief epilogue on the use of *hairesis* in early Christian literature, with specific reference to the question of *hairesis* as 'heresy'.

I *Pre-Galenic 'hairesis literature'*

While medical doxography owes much of its initial impetus to the Peripatos,[8] as has long been recognized, Alexandrian medicine of the pre-Christian era seems to offer the first examples of the systematic application of *hairesis* both to an opposing school of thought and to one's own. In doxographic treatises of polemical as well as apologetic character, early Alexandrian medical authors frequently employ *hairesis* for the purpose of partisan group characterizations.

The historical development of what I shall call – awkwardly, and for lack of inspiration – 'Alexandrian *hairesis* literature', might have derived, however obliquely, from the apostasy of Herophilus's famous pupil, Philinus of Cos, in the third century BCE. Herophilus, a revolutionary and highly scientific Alexandrian physician who is renowned especially for his anatomical discoveries and for his pioneering use of human dissection (but equally notorious for his use of human vivisection), attracted a circle of gifted followers to Alexandria, among them Philinus.[9] But Philinus turned renegade and founded a rival Alexandrian school with a radically different methodological and epistemological orientation: the Empiricist *hairesis*.[10] Philinus not only rejected several theoretical cornerstones of Herophilus's system; he also set an example for generations of Empiricists by devoting a treatise in six books to an attack on one of Herophilus's more substantial followers, Bacchius of Tanagra.[11] In the late third century BCE Philinus was succeeded as leader of the Empiricist 'School' by Serapion of Alexandria,[12] who wrote a treatise in two books *Against the haireseis (Ad sectas)*.[13]

Little is known about the content of Serapion's *Ad sectas*, but it seems likely that it offered not only criticism of rival – i.e., non-Empiricist – views but also his own therapeutic prescriptions.[14] More significantly, at least for present purposes, the plural, *haireseis*, probably refers to what later was lumped together as the 'rationalist' or 'dogmatic *hairesis*' (see II.1 below). Later Empiricists, perhaps taking their cue from the philosophical Sceptics, labelled all non-Empiricists 'Rationalists' or 'Dogmatists'; but here the plural perhaps still concedes considerable diversity within 'non-Empiricism' – a diversity which later becomes at least partially obscured by the popular but distorting and misleading notion of a single 'Rationalist' *hairesis*. While one cannot exclude the possibility that Serapion used *hairesis* to refer to something other than the distinctive collections of beliefs that characterize certain groups, subsequent uses of the term within the Empiricist 'school' – and, for that matter, in other medical *haireseis* – render this unlikely. There were enough such groups to provide Serapion with a plural target: Herophileans, Erasistrateans, Praxagoras and his pupils, and so on.

In subsequent generations both the Empiricists and the Herophileans contributed a number of doxographic works that made central use of the concept *hairesis*. A few examples might suffice: in the first century BCE the Empiricist Heraclides of Tarentum wrote an entire treatise *On the Empiricist hairesis*,[15] and the Herophileans Heraclides of Erythrae, Apollonius Mys, and Aristoxenus each followed with a treatise entitled *On the hairesis of Herophilus*.[16] These treatises were substantial: that of Apollonius consisted of at least twenty-nine books, that of Aristoxenus of at least thirteen, and that of the Herophilean Heraclides of at least seven books; Galen's synopsis of the Empiricist's treatise consisted of eight books.[17] And these treatises seem to have contained not only polemical but also apologetic material, as suggested by the fact that all three Herophileans' treatises dealt with their own 'school': *On the hairesis of Herophilus*.

By the end of the pre-Christian era the Alexandrian Empiricists and Herophileans therefore had identified themselves or their beliefs – and each other – as distinct *haireseis* and had produced a sizeable corpus of *'hairesis* literature', the main impetus for which continued to be derived from the sharp conflict between the two schools.

The dialectic of scientific growth often is marked by scientists' attempts to emancipate themselves from the theories of their precursors and contemporaries; scientific patricide and fratricide are part of the story of the development of science, and ancient medicine is no exception. But it is striking that the polemics of the Alexandrian *hairesis* treatises are no longer directed primarily at individuals, in contrast, for example, to early Peripatetic doxography (cf. e.g. Anonymus Londinensis or the famous passage in Aristotle's *Historia animalium* 3.2–3, 511B11–513A15: Syennesis, Diogenes, and Polybius – not their 'followers' or 'schools' – are taken to task for their erroneous views of the human vascular system). Rather, the *agōn* with outsiders now is often, though by no means always, depersonalized at least superficially to the extent that polemics are *ad sectam*, not *ad hominem*, and the apologetics likewise *pro secta sua*. Certain individuals, to be sure, remain villains or heroes, but they now are presented – or present themselves – as members of a larger group.

The paucity of testimonia concerning the content of the Alexandrian *hairesis* literature unfortunately leaves us only vaguely informed about what qualifies a group for the label *hairesis* or what qualifies an individual for membership in a *hairesis*. But the evidence suggests that a group with fairly coherent and distinctive theories, with an acknowledged founder (*hairesi-archēs*), and with publicly identifiable leaders who articulate (*a*) their rejection of rival theories through theoretically founded polemics, as well as (*b*) their own systematic alternatives, would qualify as a *hairesis*. Unanimity on *all* doctrinal questions is not a requirement (more on this below), and neither a single geographical centre nor any institutional organization is necessarily implied by this use of *hairesis*, although both the Herophileans and the Empiricists originally made Alexandria their only centre, and the members of each *hairesis* presumably had close and frequent association.

It might be noted in passing that the distinctiveness implied by *hairesis* does not seem to be compromised by the fact that several rival *haireseis* claim the sanction of the same patriarch. Almost every ancient medical *hairesis* claims Hippocrates as its *hairesi-archēs* (much as the various 'Socratics' claimed Socrates), some making him the founding father of medical 'rationalism', others of empiricism, still others of scepticism, etc.

A further complication arises from the expansion and redefinition of the *agōn* between Empiricists and Herophileans as a battle between Empiricists and 'Rationalists' or 'Dogmatists'. By the reign of Tiberius this putatively comprehensive, bipartite division of all physicians had become firmly established, possibly under Empiricist pressure, and it is reflected in Celsus's *De medicina*.[18]

This development represents a serious complication of the relatively straightforward though never satisfactorily explicated use of *hairesis* to refer to the Empiricist and Herophilean groups in Alexandria (who, along with the Erasistrateans, dominated Greek scientific medicine until the first century BCE). Despite all the internal debates, disagreements, and acts of revisionism within the great Alexandrian schools (see II.3 below), each school or *hairesis* constituted a relatively cohesive group with only one or two geographical centres. Not so the 'rationalist' or 'dogmatic' *hairesis*, as shown below in II.1.

It is worth noting that, no later than the second century BCE,[19] *hairesis* begins to occur in non-medical literature, too, as a designation for a group that is thought to be doctrinally distinctive, especially for a philosophical school.[20] The historian Polybius, for example, refers to Prytanis as a member of the Peripatetic *hairesis*.[21] Authors of the first century BCE who seem to have used *hairesis* in this sense include Diodorus of Sicily, Cicero, and Dionysius of

Halicarnassus. The latter refers to 'the leaders of the Stoic *hairesis'* and reports that Aristotle spent his time with Plato until he was thirty-seven years old, 'neither becoming the leader of [Plato's] school (*scholē*) nor having established his own *hairesis'*.[22] Diodorus complains that the Greeks, unlike the Orientals, try to make a profit from higher studies by always introducing doctrinal innovations in important matters and by 'founding new *haireseis'*.[23] In a letter of January 45 BCE, Cicero twits Cassius for having switched allegiance from one *hairesis* (Stoic? Platonic?) to another, viz. the Epicurean.[24]

In some of these non-medical texts 'doctrine', 'school', and 'sect' all might be defensible translations of *hairesis*, but in each case it refers to a group phenomenon, not to individual choice. Furthermore, here too, as in the Alexandrian medical *hairesis* literature, *hairesis* does not have any intrinsically pejorative overtones.

Unlike the medical *hairesis* tradition, however, the early philosophical usage is not associated with a substantial body of treatises called 'On *hairesis* x' or 'Against *hairesis* y.' This reinforces the impression that Greek medicine is the more significant early nurturing ground for *hairesis* as a doctrinal group designation. No later than the second century CE, however, *hairesis* also had become a standard term for philosophical 'school'[25] – and for religious 'sect',[26] as will be shown in IV below.

II *Examples of medical* 'haireseis'

1. *'Rationalists' vs Empiricists*

From Celsus to Galen a fundamental use of *hairesis* is to contrast the 'Rationalist' or 'Dogmatic' *hairesis* with the Empiricist. The Empiricists, as was suggested above, remained a relatively small, cohesive Alexandrian group with a clear, reasonably consistent core doctrine; even the Ptolemaic court seems to have recognized them as a significant, distinctive school.[27] Under the label 'rationalist', by contrast, one finds assembled a motley group of individuals and of fiercely independent *haireseis*, some of whom held sharply conflicting views on key issues: 'Hippocrates', Diocles of Carystus, Praxagoras, Herophilus and his *hairesis*, Erasistratus and his *hairesis*, Asclepiades of Bithynia, the *hairesis* of the Pneumatists, etc.

It seems clear that *hairesis*, as applied to 'Rationalists' or 'Dogmatists', cannot be used in the same sense as it had earlier been used of Herophileans and Empiricists. There never was a single 'rationalist' school which wrote treatises *pro secta sua*, which enrolled apprentices, and which attacked rival schools in the name of the 'rationalist' *hairesis* – let alone a cohesive group which called itself 'the rationalist (*logikē*) *hairesis*'. Herophileans, to be sure, did battle with Empiricists – but also with 'Hippocrates', with Praxagoras, with Erasistratus, and so on. The diverse group of so-called 'rationalists' admittedly are set apart from the Empiricists by their commitment to various forms of more speculative and theoretical medicine and, in particular, by their interest in aetiology and speculative systematization. But these interests were given such radically divergent, mutually incompatible expression by various 'Rationalists' and 'Rationalist' *haireseis*, that it is seriously misleading to imply that they represented a *hairesis* in the same sense as the Empiricists.

The Empiricists, by contrast, are united on central issues.[28] Thus they all believed that the search for hidden causes (as opposed to 'evident causes', such as heat, cold, and hunger) is useless, and hence that anatomy and physiology, along with dissection, should be banished from *ars medica*. Furthermore, they claimed that experience (*peira*) alone could form the foundation of the art of medicine, and that experience is assimilated in three basic forms: (*a*) transmitted experience (*historia*, understood as a passive reception of experiential traditions, of evident data seen and confirmed by previous observers); (*b*) 'transition by way of the similar', a relatively simple mental operation by analogy from one drug or disease or bodily part to another on the basis of as many observed similarities as possible; (*c*) *empeiria*, which in turn has three species: (i) involuntary, (ii) voluntary or improvising, and (iii) imitative or repetitive *peira*.[29] Hypothesis formation and verification by experimentation – of which Erasistratus and Herophilus made use – are ruled out firmly. Finally, the Empiricists chose their own label: *empeirikoi* or *empeirikē hairesis*.[30]

Among the so-called Rationalists there is no such agreement on either principle or detail. Divergent, even contradictory views prevail on the nature and knowability of causes, on the value and permissibility of dissection, on the place of experience in medical knowledge, on the value of experimentation, etc. – not to mention the irreconcilably divergent physiological and pathological theories (humoral, anti-humoral, atomistic, etc.) advocated by various 'Rationalists'.

Hairesis and Heresy: The Case of the haireseis iatrikai

For purposes of Empiricist propaganda it might have been useful to set up Empiricism as one of only two alternatives between which every physician had to choose, and for some doxographers it might have provided a welcome schematic simplification of complex traditions. But, by swallowing the Empiricist bait, some medical historians – ancient and modern – have helped to animate a doxographic fiction of convenience, viz. that there was a 'Rationalist' or 'Dogmatic' *hairesis* of medicine that was somehow comparable to the Empiricist *hairesis* in Alexandria.

This fiction does, however, establish an important point: while *hairesis* could be used of a socially cohesive, geographically centralized, and doctrinally relatively united group with its own, distinctive, publicly articulated system (e.g., Empiricist), it could also be given more expansive and even licentious application (e.g., the 'rationalist' or 'dogmatic' *hairesis*).

At the ouset I suggested that Galen's ternary division of *hairesis* into Empiricists, 'Rationalists', and Methodists – rather than the bipartite division with which we have been dealing – became canonical. I turn now to the entry of the Methodists (who, *pace* John Wesley, displayed little individual responsibility) into the *hairesis* doxography.

2. Methodists

By the beginning of the first century CE, the duel between the Empiricist *hairesis* and its collective 'rationalist' opponents had become bogged down in what Galen later aptly described as 'an undecided disagreement.'[31] Some educated members of Roman society nevertheless became fascinated with this struggle, perhaps not least because of the growing number of medical laymen (*philiatroi*) in Rome.[32] When a self-proclaimed 'new (*nea*) *hairesis*' with a promising name, 'Method-ists' (*methodikoi*), stepped onto the stage,[33] professionals and dilettantes alike applauded.

The 'new *hairesis*' proclaimed its independence from both Empiricists (*quod parum artis esse in observatione experimentorum credunt* [sc. *Methodici*])[34] and 'Rationalists' (*quod in coniectura rerum latentium nolunt* [sc. *Methodici*] *esse medicinam*).[35] Particularly welcome to laymen and, one might assume, to aspiring young physicians, was the Methodists' claim that medical science is simpler and more accessible than had commonly been assumed,[36] and that anatomy and physiology might – or rather, must – be dispensed with. The Methodist Thessalus, a contemporary of

83

Nero, is, for example, said to have claimed that anyone can master the art of medicine within six months.[37]

Although Celsus, probably writing toward the end of Tiberius's reign, still starts his *De medicina* with the comprehensive Empiricist-'Rationalist' dichotomy,[38] he subsequently sensed the need to add the Methodists as a third, distinct group (whom he does not show much respect),[39] and by the time of Galen the ternary division of *haireseis* was quite firmly in place.

It is perhaps not surprising that Thessalus and other Methodists became the most popular physicians of the first and early second centuries in Rome,[40] eclipsing Empiricists, Herophileans, Erasistrateans, and other *haireseis*. Thessalus unabashedly 'crowned himself victor on the world-stage',[41] and he attracted numerous apprentices who were as eager as they were unqualified. About Thessalus's pupils Galen caustically remarks: 'Cobblers and carpenters and dyers and smiths now are rushing to the tasks of the art of medicine, having abandoned their own ancient crafts.'[42]

The partisan flamboyance of some Methodists and their appeal to a broad lay audience seem to have stimulated further interest in accessible doxographic works that focus on the three major *haireseis*, and Galen's *De sectis* is one of many attempts to satisfy the needs of this general audience. (I hasten to emphasize that while Thessalus's theatricality might have gone over well in the Neronian period, Galen, as a good, archaizing representative of the Antonine period, had nothing but contempt for Thessalus.[43])

To return to some of the questions posed at the outset: despite their more popular appeal, the Methodists constitute a *hairesis* in roughly the same sense as the Empiricists and the Herophileans, rather than in the sense of the 'Rationalists'. In their epistemological statements the Methodists seem to show consistency: they are perhaps more sceptical than any other medical *hairesis*. Sextus Empiricus interprets the basic Methodist principle, 'indication (*endeixis*) derived from affections (*pathē*) which are apparent (*phainomena*)', as fully consistent with scepticism, and he remarks that a physician-sceptic could belong only to the Methodist school.[44] Yet all Methodists also seem to share the belief that medical practice must be based on the observation of three universal *communia* or *koinotētes*: costiveness, fluidity, and the mixture of these two.[45] Furthermore, like the Empiricists and the Herophileans, the Methodists chose their own *hairesis* label[46] and confidently proclaimed themselves as the only *hairesis* with access to the truth.[47] In these respects, then, the Methodists satisfy the criteria that emerged above for a narrower use of *hairesis*: a self-labelling, geographically centralized, doctrinally cohesive group, about whose core doctrine there seems to be general agreement.

Yet closer scrutiny raises serious doubts about the extent of a normative doctrinal consensus among the Methodists. Galen reports, for example, that the Methodists in fact agreed only on the names of the three *communia*, not on their referents: some Methodists determine 'costive', 'fluid', and 'mixed' according to natural secretions from the body, whereas others – 'not a small chorus' – look upon 'costive' and 'fluid' as pathogenic conditions that are found in the very dispositions (*diatheseis*) of the body.[48]

Furthermore, while the anti-Methodist polemics of other *haireseis* and of some non-aligned authors often are based on an assumption of dogmatic consensus and uniformity within the Methodist *hairesis*, Galen reports that the Methodists in fact all disagreed among themselves on almost all important doctrinal questions.[49] That Galen's references to Methodist discord or *diaphōnia* cannot be dismissed as a *topos* derived from sceptical polemics, is clear from the few instances of internal Methodist disagreement that are documented.

Precise details concerning internal dissension often are lacking in our extant sources, but external unity and internal disunity often co-exist in the Greek medical *haireseis*. A brief examination of dissent and revisionism within the Herophilean *hairesis* might shed further light on this aspect of the medical *haireseis* and on some of the other complex forces that militated against normative self-definition within ancient medical *haireseis*.

3. The hairesis of Herophilus[50]

The relation of Herophilus's followers to the founding father of their *hairesis* is complicated, first, by the dynamic nature of the Herophilean school – which, unlike Galenism and perhaps Epicureanism, always remained open to changes in emphasis and to doctrinal shifts – and, secondly, by the long history of the Herophilean *hairesis*, roughly from 300 BCE to 50 CE through periods in which varying demands and needs exercised frequently changing pressures upon scientists and physicians. Throughout these three and a half centuries the sanction provided by the common label 'follower of Herophilus' was sought and proudly shared by numerous distinguished physicians, but this nominal uniformity cannot conceal the diversity and the fierce, often contentious individualism accommodated within the *hairesis*.

Perhaps the single most striking development in this context is the general retreat from anatomy and from dissection, which had constituted Herophilus's most significant contribution to scientific medicine.[51] Few, if any, activities played a more powerful role in the rise of scientific medicine in Alexandria than the dissection – and possibly vivisection – of humans by Herophilus, and few were apparently as widely abandoned by Herophilus's successors. About the reasons for this surrender of a major tool of scientific medicine, one can only speculate. Among the possible causes are the reassertion of Greek and native Egyptian taboos, the fundamental insecurity of science within the social order under almost all but the first two Ptolemies, and the rising popularity of the Alexandrian Empiricists' theory of scientific method (which denied the scientific value and clinical relevance of dissection).[52] But whatever the reasons might be, with one or two notable exceptions (e.g. Hegetor), the followers of Herophilus, from the third century BCE to the first century CE, seem to have turned their backs on anatomy – at least if one may generalize on the basis of the roughly three hundred extant testimonia and fragments.

All was, however, not retreat, rebellion, and revision with the Herophilean *hairesis*. There are some clear strands of continuity between the founding master and his followers. Perhaps the most striking of these is the sustained interest Herophilus's followers showed in pulse theory, a branch of pathophysiology which assumed immense diagnostic significance in antiquity (and which owes its first thorough investigation to Herophilus).[53] From Bacchius (c. 275–200 BCE) to Demosthenes Philalethes (first century CE), the followers of Herophilus kept alive the sphygmological tradition initiated by the founding master of their school. Yet, even within this broad continuity, one is confronted with the independence and innovative ambitions of individual members of the *hairesis*.

Herophilus's analysis of the pulse was not simply transmitted with piety and reverence from one generation to the next, like an orthodoxy that had become obligatory. Instead, almost every Herophilean tried to improve not only on Herophilus's definition but also on those of his immediate predecessors and contemporaries within the school. The result is a striking example of the incessant shuffling and dissent that lurk not too far beneath the

homogenous surface suggested *prima facie* by the label 'Herophileans' or 'Herophilus's *hairesis*'.

> *Herophilus*: the pulse is a perceptible motion of the arteries received
> from the heart; it is born and dies with a living being; it exists naturally
> and attends us involuntarily at all times, occurring both when the
> arteries are filled and when they are emptied, i.e., when they dilate
> and contract.[54]
>
> *Bacchius*: (*a*) The pulse is a dilation (*diastolē*) and contraction (*systolē*)
> occurring simultaneously in all the arteries;[55] or (*b*) the pulse is a
> distention (*diastasis*) of the artery or of the arterial part of the heart.[56]
>
> *Zeno* (c. 200–150 BCE): The pulse is an activity of the arterial parts – an
> activity which is a mixture of contraction and distention.[57]
>
> *Chrysermus* (mid-first century BCE): The pulse is a distention and
> contraction of arteries, when the arterial coat, through the agency of a
> psychic and vital faculty, rises on all sides and then again shrinks
> together; it is a constant concomitant in both healthy and diseased
> conditions, and it can be apprehended by sense-perception.[58]
>
> *Alexander Philalethes* (c. 50 BCE–25 CE): Objectively, the pulse is an
> involuntary contraction of the heart and the arteries, such as can
> become apparent; subjectively, it is the beat of the continuous, invol-
> untary motion of the arteries against one's touch, and the interval
> occurring after the beat.[59]
>
> *Heraclides of Erythrae* (last half of the first century BCE): The pulse is a
> contraction and dilation of the arteries and the heart, accomplished
> through the agency of a vital and psychic faculty which is dominant.[60]
>
> *Aristoxenus* (first half of the first century CE): The pulse is an activity of
> the heart and the arteries – an activity peculiar to them.[61]
>
> *Demosthenes Philalethes* (c. 20 BCE – 50 CE): Objectively, the pulse is a
> dilation of the heart and the arteries, or their natural contraction,
> capable of becoming apparent; subjectively, it is a natural beat of the
> heart or of the arteries against one's touch and the interval which
> occurs after the beat.[62]

This selective enumeration of Herophilean pulse definitions
provides only one example of that diversity – within a common
thematic concern – which became characteristic of the Herophilean *hairesis*. Acutely aware of one another's views, in part through
doxographic treatises concerning their own school, each Herophilean strove for a fresh and more viable definition of the
essential nature of the pulse, attempting at the same time to meet
objections raised to his precursors' formulations. What might,
from a modern perspective, look like sophistic quibbling over
minor differences concerning a definition, to most of the participants in this revisionary process was anything but a mere exercise
in patricidal and fraticidal eristic. Rather, it was a search for a

correct understanding of the essential nature of a major diagnostic tool and, simultaneously, a reaffirmation of the value and relevance of theoretical investigations for the clinician.

What unites almost all followers of Herophilus is in fact precisely their interest not only in clinical but also in scientific or 'theoretical' medicine, and this is, of course, also what distinguishes them most sharply from their chief rivals in the early period, the Alexandrian Empiricists, who radically rejected anatomy and physiology as irrelevant for clinical purposes.[63] Even those Herophileans for whom no pulse-lore is attested (for example, Andreas) dealt with physiological questions that were taboo to the Empiricists – taboo, exactly because these questions required forming hypotheses concerning what nature has concealed.

With the exception of pulse-lore, the physiological questions which interested Herophilus do not, however, seem to have preoccupied subsequent members of his *hairesis* more than sporadically. The four faculties or humours,[64] the nervous system,[65] the problem of respiration,[66] dream theory[67] – none of these is tackled by any of his followers. Here and there we do get glimpses of continuity: Herophilus made a major contribution to the anatomy and physiology of the male and female reproductive organs;[68] Alexander Philalethes speculates on the origin and nature of sperm (and Andreas on conditions conducive to procreation);[69] Herophilus developed a theory of digestion and absorption; Alexander Philalethes returns to the same question.[70] But these strands of continuity tend to be the exception and they are relatively fragile. A similar pattern of spasmodically emerging affinities between the founding father of the *hairesis* and his followers is found in pathology.[71]

To find a part of medicine – other than sphygmology – both cherished by Herophilus and actively pursued by a majority of his followers, one has to turn to pharmacology. Herophilus had called drugs 'the hands of the gods'[72] and had made active therapeutic use of them. Not only is his expertise in simple drugs attested, but some of his compound drug prescriptions also are extant. From the earliest generation of Herophileans to the last, this pharmacological part of Herophilus's legacy was honoured and cultivated. Andreas, the court physician who probably was a direct pupil of Herophilus, made a monumental contribution especially to the study of simple drugs, compound drugs, and the toxic effects of certain plants and animals.[73]

Similarly, in the first generation of Herophileans, Callimachus and Bacchius displayed an active interest in pharmacology,[74] and in the second century BCE the Herophilean physicians Zeno, Demetrius, and Mantias again kept this tradition alive.[75] Mantias, in particular, more than once is recognized by Galen as the true father of the compound drug tradition.[76] Mantias apparently was the first to arrange his comprehensive compilations of drug prescriptions not only by kind or *per genera* (e.g., purgatives, clysters, emollients, etc.) but also by place or *secundum locos* (e.g., prescriptions for headaches, ear-aches, skin conditions, eye ailments, upset stomach, etc.) – a useful taxonomic principle which was also adopted by Galen in his massive and influential pharmacological treatises, and which hence became entrenched for centuries.[77]

In the first century BCE, too, Herophileans did not abandon their pharmacological legacy. Chrysermus, for example, became known both for his views on simple drugs, such as asphodel, and for his compound drug prescriptions,[78] and Chrysermus's pupil Apollonius Mys composed one of the more famous pharmacological treatises of antiquity, *Euporista* or *Readily Accessible Drugs* (also known as *On Common Drugs*), from which Galen quotes liberally, especially in his treatise *On the Composition of Drugs according to Place*.[79] Judging by Galen's accounts, Apollonius adopted one of Mantias's taxonomic principles, namely arranging his common remedies topically (i.e., by place of application), and the practicality of this arrangement, along with the fact that all the ingredients used by Apollonius were readily accessible, may account for its popularity in the first two centuries CE. About the state of pharmacology in the last visible generation of the Herophilean school we are less well informed, but it is possible that the drug prescriptions attributed to a 'Demosthenes' were authored by the great Herophilean ophthalmologist, Demosthenes Philalethes.[80]

This rapid survey of the pharmacological tradition within the Herophilean *hairesis* suggests, then, that pharmacology, like pulse-lore, represents a strong strand of continuity in the history of the 'school'. But whereas no spectacular advances over Herophilus's theory of the pulse were made by his successors, pharmacology is an area to which the Herophileans seem to have become more committed after Herophilus's death.

There is a further significant difference between these two instances of continuity. Whereas Herophilus's pulse theory was firmly rejected by the Herophileans' chief rivals – the Alexandrian

Empiricists – as a part of theoretical or speculative medicine and hence irrelevant to medical practice, the Empiricists warmly embraced pharmacology as an empirical discipline of unquestionable clinical import. From the time of Herophilus's 'heretical' pupil, the Empiricist Philinus of Cos (third century BCE), until the first century CE, the Empiricist *hairesis* repeatedly engaged in pharmacological activity: Philinus, Glaucias, Mantias's renegade pupil Heraclides of Tarentum, Diodorus, Lycus, and Zopyrus of Alexandria are examples of Empiricists who actively affirmed the significance of pharmacology.[81]

Having abandoned research in the area which brought Herophilus his greatest fame, i.e., anatomy, the Herophileans now therefore seem to have stressed a branch of learning found unobjectionable by their rivals. The same is true of two further areas in which Herophileans took a more active interest after Herophilus's death: surgery and Hippocratic exegesis.[82] This particular constellation – pharmacology, surgery, and Hippocratic exegesis – renders them virtually indistinguishable from their Empiricist rivals, and it is conceivable that the Empiricists' sustained polemics against theoretical medicine in general, and against the Herophilean school in particular, exercised pressure upon the Herophileans to concentrate on clinical medicine and the Hippocratic Corpus at the expense of anatomical exploration and physiological speculation.

The growing interest among Herophileans in Hippocratic philology is worth a brief comment. Whereas Herophilus's relation to 'Hippocrates' had been marked by ambivalence, polemics, and the need to establish himself as the emancipated founder of a new tradition, the later Herophileans, perhaps less burdened by the need to emancipate themselves from the Hippocratic shadow and to establish themselves as the vanguard of the new, scientific medicine, could approach Hippocratic texts in a relatively dispassionate, critical manner. Neither polemic nor an effort to legitimate their own views through an appeal to the sanction of the father of medicine marks their treatment of the Hippocratic texts.

Already in the first generation of Herophileans the new philological approach to Hippocratic texts becomes clear. The Herophilean physician Callimachus provided glosses on Hippocratic words,[83] and the *Lexeis* of his contemporary Bacchius became the most influential Hippocratic lexicon of the Hellenistic period. More than sixty testimonia and fragments from Bacchius's lexicon are still extant,[84] and the range of Hippocratic works it covered –

at least eighteen[85] – was unprecedented in the history of Alexandrian philology. But Bacchius was not only a lexicographer; he also edited the Hippocratic treatise *Epidemics* 3 (and possibly other Hippocratic works), and wrote commentaries on the Hippocratic *Aphorisms*, on *Epidemics* 6, and on *In the Surgery*.[86] Not much later the Herophilean Zeno provided further glosses on Hippocratic words[87] and apparently triggered the protracted Alexandrian debate about the authenticity and meaning of obscure letter-symbols found in an Alexandrian copy of *Epidemics* 3.[88] In the first century BCE two Herophileans continued this tradition: Dioscurides Phacas -- apparently a prominent counsellor and ambassador of Cleopatra, of her father, and of her brother – composed a Hippocratic lexicon in seven books,[89] and Heraclides of Erythrae not only wrote a commentary on *Epidemics* 2, 3, and 6 but also resumed, and perhaps terminated, the controversy concerning the provenance and significance of the letter-symbols in *Epidemics* 3.[90] Cydias, too, seems to have engaged in Hippocratic exegesis.[91]

This Herophilean trend can, therefore, be documented richly. Also significant is the fact that Hippocratic philology gained a prominent position in the school of the Alexandrian Empiricists, too. From the founder of the school, Philinus of Cos, who wrote a polemical work against Bacchius's Hippocratic lexicon, to Apollonius of Citium and Heraclides of Tarentum in the first century BCE, Empiricists engaged as actively as Herophileans in exegesis and lexicography.[92] This similar but not identical movement of two arch-rivals, Empiricists and Herophileans, from scientific research into philology, cannot be attributed to a diminution of royal patronage. On the contrary, there are indications that this development was encouraged, directly or indirectly, by at least some of the Ptolemies. Thus Apollonius of Citium, author of the only work of Hellenistic medicine to have survived intact, states in the introduction of his commentary on the Hippocratic work *On Joints* that he undertook the exegetical task on the king's orders and now offers the finished product to him for approval.[93] The Ptolemy in question is probably Cleopatra's father Auletes (c. 112–51 BCE),[94] and hence this is relatively late evidence, but it does reveal, as P. M. Fraser has argued, 'the direct' – but, I would add, not always scientifically fruitful – 'stimulus that writers received from a royal patron'.[95] It also vividly suggests the power of the patron to coax a physician into exegetical tasks.

Perhaps closely related to the burgeoning critical interest in precursor texts is another movement away from anatomical and physiological research, namely the growing importance of doxography within the Herophilean school, which brings us back full circle to explicit uses of the *hairesis* concept. As in the case of Hippocratic exegesis, the Herophileans could appeal to the example of Herophilus – who had also written a treatise with a doxographic thrust – to legitimate their own doxographic efforts. But here, too, there is a significant difference, namely the increasingly self-centred nature of Herophilean doxography. While Herophilus and Andreas were still primarily concerned with going on the offensive in their doxographic efforts – Herophilus wrote *Against Common Opinions*,[96] Andreas *On False Beliefs* and *On the Genealogy of Physicians*[97] – Bacchius set in motion a long Herophilean tradition of writing about, or in defence of, the opinions or *doxai* held by various members of one's own school. This trend reaches its culmination in the last years of the school's visible existence with treatises entitled *On the hairesis of Herophilus* authored by no less than three different Herophileans, as pointed out above: Apollonius Mys, Heraclides of Erythrae, and Aristoxenus.[98] This burst of works with an apologetic and protreptic purpose in the final stages of the history of the school might well reflect the growing insecurity of the followers of Herophilus in the midst of new challenges. Whereas they were reasonably successful in surviving the Empiricist challenge, in part, as suggested above, by distinguishing themselves in branches of medicine highly valued by the Empiricists themselves (pharmacology, surgery, semiotics or symptomotology,[99] Hippocratic philology), the last generations of Herophileans faced the challenge not only of the Empiricists but also of new, eclectic 'Dogmatists' or 'Rationalists' and Sceptics who were rapidly gaining in popularity: the 'Pneumatic' and 'Methodist' schools of medicine. Herophileans no longer had the appeal of novelty or the strength of anatomical and physiological excellence; with the exception of their sphygmological and gynecological persistence, the concerns of most Herophileans had become virtually indistinguishable from those of their Empiricist rivals. Furthermore, the rebellious and individualistic strain that marked the long, rich history of the Herophilean *hairesis*, from the time when Herophilus was abandoned by one pupil and ridiculed by another[100] down to Aristoxenus's sharp censure of almost all his Herophilean predecessors and contemporaries in the first century CE,[101] did not enhance its chances of surviving the fresh challenges. Herophilean polemics became increasingly fratricidal in nature – Herophilean pitted against Herophilean – and the self-centred doxography referred to earlier became its vehicle.

Yet even at the moment of its last visible gasps the *hairesis* of Herophilus displayed some of the ambiguity and tenacity that had characterized much of its history: while one of the last representatives of the school, Aristoxenus, was engaging in internecine, sophistic censure of his fellow-Herophileans, another, Demosthenes Philalethes, made enduring, if not always original, contributions to the pathology and therapy of eye ailments, contributions whose general impact upon ancient and medieval medicine was matched by those of no other Herophilean except Herophilus himself.[102]

Internal dogmatic scrutiny and heuristic triumph, looking over one's shoulder and looking ahead, preoccupation with the words of predecessors and aggressive discovery – these are some of the ambivalent dimensions of the history of Herophilus's *hairesis*, and they persist from its inception to its apparent death in the first century CE.

III   *Institutionalization and* hairesis

The institutional history of the school of Herophilus will serve as a single but fairly representative example of what *hairesis* does and does not imply about institutionalization, at least in the medical tradition. There is no clear evidence that Herophilus or his followers were organized institutionally in the first two hundred or two hundred and fifty years of the existence of this group of physicians. There is not even firm evidence that Herophilus, or any representative of scientific medicine, ever was associated with the Alexandrian Museum. Rather, the general Greek system of medical apprenticeship probably also prevailed in Alexandria, and Bacchius's use of the phrase 'those from the *house (oikia)* of Herophilus' to refer to early Herophileans[103] might well be an indication of the informal and non-institutional – but not necessarily unrigorous – nature of medical apprenticeships in Alexandria.

Despite this apparent absence of formalization and institutionalization of the *hairesis*, despite the individualism and dissent that marked relations between 'members' of the school, and despite the political and social vicissitudes which buffeted science and scholarship in Ptolemaic Alexandria (such as the expulsion of a large number of intellectuals, including physicians, from Alexandria in 145 BCE),[104] Herophilean medicine survived without noticeable interruption as a prominent force in Alexandrian life at least until the late first century BCE; there is no century in the history of Ptolemaic Alexandria in which Herophileans failed to assert their presence in the royal capital. Thus we find the Herophilean physicians Andreas, Callimachus, and Bacchius in Alexandria in the third century BCE; Zeno, Demetrius, Hegetor, and Mantias in the second century BCE; Dioscurides Phacas, Chrysermus, Apollonius Mys, and Heraclides of Erythrae in the first century BCE.

A novel phase in the institutional development of the school seems to have been reached, however, with the expansion of the school into Asia Minor in the mid- or late first-century BCE, after it had been associated exclusively with Alexandria for at least two hundred years. Founded by Zeuxis 'Philalethes' or 'Truth-Lover' (a reverential title traditionally reserved for Hippocrates) at the famous temple of the moon god Men Karou, in the vicinity of the Phrygian city of Laodicea on the great Eastern trade route, this branch of the school apparently had a more institutional character than the 'school' in Alexandria. Several factors seem to support this conclusion.

First, Strabo calls it a 'large place of instruction' or 'great school' (*didaskaleion mega*).[105] *Didaskaleion* is an expression rarely used of the Alexandrian 'school' of Herophileans – or, for that matter, of any other medical 'school'. The word usually is reserved for the kind of formal institution attended by school children and run by rhetoricians and grammarians; it is almost never applied to the apprenticeship arrangements that were characteristic of medical education in classical and Hellenistic Greece.[106]

Secondly, the association of the school with a cult centre also suggests an institutionalization of the kind well known from the Alexandrian Museum (but nowhere attested for the Herophilean *hairesis* in Alexandria): in the Museum a group of scientists and scholars were joined together not only as researchers sharing patronage and meals, but also as members of a cult association presided over by a priest.[107] A similar arrangement probably prevailed at the Museion in Ephesus, which was famous for its *synedrion* of physicians and its annual 'medical Olympics'.[108] While the Herophilean school at the temple of Men Karou might not have shared all these characteristics with the Alexandrian

Museum and similar institutions, its association with a cult is suggestive.

Furthermore, by the Imperial period the *Lex Julia de collegiis* seems to have stipulated, as the first of several conditions for establishing medical schools or formal medical associations, that cult worship must be fostered by such an association or institution.[109] It is conceivable that the Herophilean school at Men Karou was constituted as just such a *collegium*.

The history of the Herophilean school in Asia Minor extends roughly one century or three generations, from about 40 BCE to 50 CE. The successive leaders of the school were Zeuxis Philalethes, Alexander Philalethes, and Demosthenes Philalethes. Another influential member of the school was a student of Alexander Philalethes, Aristoxenus, whose sharp criticism of a number of Alexandrian Herophileans might be indicative of rivalry, or at any rate of disharmonious relations, between the Alexandrian mother school and her Asian offspring. But among the Asian Herophileans, too, disagreements soon arose; institutionalization was no guarantee of unity or doctrinal homogeneity.

It has been suggested that a notorious earthquake which struck the area around Laodicea during the reign of Nero, in 60 CE, coincided with the end of the Herophilean school.[110] Other factors mentioned above should, however, not be ignored in favour of a cataclysmic hypothesis. The Herophileans' disputes with the Empiricists and with each other became internecine; the partial usurpation of Herophilus's emphasis on anatomy and physiology by Hippocratic philology and doxography left many Herophileans vulnerable at a theoretical level (as did the restriction of physiology to pulse-lore, at least by a majority of Herophileans); and the rising popularity and influence of new schools of medicine with vociferous claims to sweeping theoretical innovation exercised strong pressures upon Herophileans.

This brief survey of doctrinal (II.3) and institutional (III) change and continuity in the Herophilean *hairesis* has yielded results which are fairly representative of the medical *haireseis*. The sectarian cohesion suggested by the common label 'Herophilus's *hairesis*' masks complex forces that generated constant internal debate, doctrinal disagreements, and shifts in emphasis. These shifts and disagreements often render even the minimal 'distinctive' core doctrine of the *hairesis* no more than a shell. The proclamation of *haireseis*, and the extensive *hairesis* literature, do not seem to have advanced the cause of normative self-definition significantly.

IV   Hairesis *and Heresy*

In the Acts of the Apostles the orator Tertullus charges Paul with being a ringleader of the *hairesis* of the Nazarenes.[111] Paul's reply to his accusers acknowledges that 'I serve the God of my fathers according to the way which *they* [sc. my accusers] call *hairesis* . . .'.[112] These two passages belong to the earliest text in which *hairesis* seems consistently used to designate a 'sect', 'faith' or 'school' that opposes one's own. Its author also refers to the Sadducees and Pharisees as *haireseis*, and he reports that the leading Roman Jews remarked to Paul, 'We consider it worthwhile hearing from you what you think; you see, as far as this *hairesis* [sc. of the Christians] is concerned, it is known to us that it is spoken against everywhere.'[113] In each of these cases an opponent is identified by a Christian or a Jew as belonging to a group called a *hairesis*. In and of itself such a reference to a doctrinally adversary group as a *hairesis* is not novel; as shown above, it represents one – but only one – strand in standard Hellenistic usage.

Hairesis, however, not only refers to an opposing sect or school of thought in early Christian and Jewish contexts. The neutral and positive Hellenistic uses of *hairesis* as a group referent also occur both in Christian and Jewish texts. In his *Life* Josephus, for example, reports:

> When I became about sixteen, I wished to get experience of the *haireseis* among us. There are three of these; first, the *hairesis* of the Pharisees, second that of the Sadducees, and third [the *hairesis*] of the Essenes . . . In my nineteenth year I began to follow the *hairesis* of the Pharisees, which resembles the *hairesis* called 'Stoic' among the Greeks.[114]

In his *Jewish Wars*, Josephus reaffirms this as the standard division of Jewish 'schools of thought', this time using a derivative of *hairesis* to refer to the members of each 'school':

> There are three forms of practising philosophy among the Jews: the *hairetistai* of one of these are the Pharisees, of another the Sadducees, and the third is called the Essenes.[115]

In none of these uses are *hairesis* and its derivatives defined by reference to orthodoxy. As in the Hellenistic texts discussed above in I and II, *hairesis* here does not necessarily imply heresy, sectarian defection, heterodoxy, or apostasy; rather, it refers without pejorative overtones to 'sects' or 'schools of thought', including one's own. This usage survives into later antiquity, i.e., even after *hairesis* also has come to mean 'heresy' or 'heretical faction'. Thus Eusebius quotes Constantine as saying, '. . . some people wickedly and perversely began to separate themselves from the universal [*katholikē*, i.e., orthodox and true Christian] *hairesis* . . .'.[116]

The authoritative claim that 'within Christianity *hairesis* always denotes hostile societies . . .' and that when *hairesis* is used in the early church, 'what the church usually has in view is Gnosticism'[117] therefore does not hold, at least not without serious modification.

Clement of Alexandria provides a representative illustration of the wide range of uses to which patristic authors tend to put *hairesis:*

> One must investigate and learn conclusively how some *haireseis* have become fallible, while the most accurate *gnosis* and the truly best *hairesis* is in the only true, ancient church.[118]
> . . . Both among the Jews and among those philosophers most esteemed by the Greeks there have been very many *haireseis;* I presume you're not saying that one should hesitate to practise philosophy or Judaism just because of the disagreements that these *haireseis* have with one another?[119]

Like most patristic authors Clement, however, does not restrict *hairesis* to the Christian church, to Jewish 'sects', and to Greek philosophical 'schools'; he also gives it a meaning not characteristic of the texts and contexts discussed in I–III above, viz. 'heresy' or 'false, apostate doctrine':

> A person who has fallen away into *hairesis* goes through a waterless desert, having left behind the truly real God; deserted by God, he seeks waterless water, traversing uninhabitable, parched land, collecting unfruitfulness with his hands.[120]

Falling away, breaking away, separation, estrangement, alienation – these are new elements in the definition of *hairesis*: it now becomes defined primarily by reference to that from which it is separated or different.[121] Thus Ignatius tells his readers that 'the love of Jesus Christ enjoins you to use only Christian nutriment, and to abstain from alien [*allotria*] plants, which are *hairesis*'.[122] Origen, Justin Martyr, Hegesippus, Irenaeus, and Basil are among the numerous other patristic authors who use *hairesis* to refer to 'heresy' or to 'heretical faction'.[123]

It is important to recognize that there is a significant difference between (*a*) the use of *hairesis* by Jews and Christians in the Acts of the Apostles to refer to an adversary 'school' and (*b*) this patristic use of *hairesis* to refer to 'heresy'. It lies in the fact that the Pharisaic and Sadducean or 'Nazarene' *haireseis* did not stand accused by their Christian and Jewish opponents, respectively, of breaking away from the true doctrine they once had possessed – as little as did the Herophilean *hairesis*[124] – whereas the *haireseis* in the new patristic sense – 'heretical factions' – are accused precisely of separating themselves from the true church, and hence are defined by reference to Christian orthodoxy.[125] A Hellenistic medical or religious or philosophical *hairesis* could exist alone and without necessarily being regarded as errant, whereas a Christian *hairesis* now becomes a *hairesis* (qua 'heresy', 'heretical sect') only when condemned as such by the authors or bearers of ecclesiastic orthodoxy.

This new, early Christian use of *hairesis* to refer to a body of false beliefs or believers did not entirely usurp the standard Hellenistic uses, as the passages from Clement quoted above confirm. But it soon gave rise to elaborate new taxonomies of doctrinal and institutional error (in which *hairesis* played a central role), and to a substantial body of canon law. An examination of *hairesis* in these new contexts, and of its relation to *heterodoxia* and *schisma*, lies beyond the scope of this contribution, but a brief allusion to two texts that signal the increasingly technical uses of the word might be of use.

First, in a discussion of Montanist baptismal practices, Basil remarks:

> . . . To some, they [sc. the ancients] gave the name *haireseis*, to others *schismata*, and to others again *para-synagōgai*: *haireseis* [they call] the ones who have completely broken away and who have become estranged with regard to their faith itself; *schismata* those who are in disagreement with each other for reasons having to do with the church and with remediable issues; and *para-synagōgai* [they call] those assemblies which arise through the agency of insubordinate elders or bishops or lay people . . . *Haireseis* are, for example, the *hairesis* of the Manichaeans, of the Valentinians, of the followers of Marcion, and of these very Pepuzans . . .[126]

Somewhat different, but again a harbinger of technicalities to come, is an earlier effort by Clement of Alexandria to classify *haireseis* according to the derivation of their names from personal names (Valentinians, Marcionists), from places (the Gnostic 'Peratikoi'), from ethnic origin (the 'Phrygian *hairesis*', a name for the

Montanists), from their practices (the Encratites or 'continent ones', a sect that abstained from marriage, meat and wine), from distinctive doctrines (the Docetists, who maintained the illusory character of the incarnation), from their hypotheses and from whom they honoured (the Gnostic 'Kainistai', who honoured Cain, and the 'Ophianoi' or serpent-worshippers), and from their acts of nefarious audacity (the 'Entychitae', an offshoot of the Simonian sect, probably so-called because of the belief that they practised promiscuous sexual intercourse at their meetings).[127]

I have traced various aspects of the development of *hairesis* from 'taking' and 'individual moral or intellectual choice' to 'doctrinal group choice' and 'school', and finally to the Christian sense of 'heretical sect' or 'heresy'. It has become clear that some of the pre-Christian uses of *hairesis* continue to survive in Christian literature, alongside 'heretical sect', and that patristic authors even use *hairesis* to refer to their own orthodoxy. What remains unresolved, however, is how the use of *hairesis* to refer to one's own 'school' or to an external 'school', whether adversary or not, gave rise to the use of *hairesis* to refer to internal breaking away, to doctrinal dissent or deviation *within* Christianity.

A key text in this murky transition seems to be the New Testament. The consistent application of *hairesis* to a doctrinally adversary group in Acts was pointed out above. More explicitly *in malam partem* are statements by other New Testament authors deploring the existence of *haireseis*, 'factions' or 'factious beliefs', *among the Christians themselves*. Thus Paul expresses his disapproval of contentiousness and divisions (*schismata*) among the Corinthian Christians, while conceding that 'there must be *haireseis* among you in order that the approved persons may become clearly distinct among you'.[128] Similarly, he warns the Galatians against 'factious intrigues, seditious dissensions, and *haireseis*', all of which are among 'the works of the flesh', not 'the fruit of the spirit'.[129] In the letter to Titus, 'Paul' says: 'After a first and second warning, reject the person who is *hairetikos*, knowing that such a person has turned astray and sins, being self-condemned.'[130] In Peter's second letter, too, a warning is sounded against false teachers, *pseudo-didaskaloi*, 'who will surreptitiously introduce *haireseis* that cause destruction'.[131] The church could not accept any schools or new societies within or alongside itself, since the *ekklēsia* is the assembly of the whole people of God and accommodates this people both exclusively and comprehensively; 'the concept of party necessarily excludes that of the people or state'.[132]

From the 'factiousness' and 'factions' deplored in the New Testament it is neither an impossibly long nor a very tortuous road to the 'heretical sects' and 'heresies' so elaborately defined, classified, and condemned in Christian orthodoxy. But old habits die hard, and for several centuries the tenacity of the secular Hellenistic uses traced in I and II above continued to muddy the semantic waters in which *hairesis* drifted. As Cicero wrote to Cassius, 'in ista ipsa *hairesei* metuo, ne plus nervorum sit, quam ego putarim . . .'.[133]

6

Sarapis and Isis

TRAN TAM TINH

Sarapis: Hellenistic hybrid god, whose main cult centre was in Alexandria; later worshipped by the Greeks as Helios or Zeus. The name is a combination of Osiris and Apis; accordingly he has Isis as his consort and is regarded as god of the nether world and fertility, but also becomes physician and general helper in distress. He never became fully accepted by the Egyptian element of the population in the Ptolemaic kingdom.[1]

This definition, of which every term seems to have been carefully weighed and every element sets interpretative problems, shows how difficult it is to describe this god who, to all appearances, is so familiar but yet has remained an 'unknown god'. Sarapis is one of the rare 'historic' gods the era of whose first appearance is known. But he is also among the gods whom the ancients (historians, philosophers, theologians) discussed with a certain vagueness, for the makers of this new cult apparently wished to bathe it in the mysterious clouds worthy of a mythical god. Four centuries after the introduction of his cult, Tacitus, Plutarch and Clement of Alexandria[2] found it difficult to trace his origin, or to understand his nature: all three were satisfied with detailing various versions of the god's 'arrival' at Alexandria, by emphasizing that their own contemporaries did not hold the same view on his nature.

A hybrid god, Sarapis bears a composite name derived from the Egyptian: Sarapis = Osirapis = Osorapis = Osar-Hapi or Osiris-Apis.[3]

Although he is a hybrid god with a Hellenized Egyptian name, he is nevertheless Greek in appearance, bearing features common to the 'father gods' (*Vatergottheiten*) of that time, which may well have facilitated the beginning of syncretism with other Greek gods: Zeus, Asclepius, Pluto, Hades, Dionysus.

Sarapis and Isis in the Mediterranean

Despite and perhaps because of the rather fluid contours of his personality, Sarapis had seven centuries of glorious history, from the third century BCE to the end of the fourth century CE, not only at Alexandria but also in all the countries around the Mediterranean including Egypt from the Roman period onwards. In this achievement he was not alone. His cult was intimately bound up with that of Isis, an Egyptian goddess who became Hellenized as well towards the beginning of the third century BCE. We know almost nothing of the vicissitudes of the establishment of this joint cult outside Egypt. There are evidences, however, allowing us to say that sometimes it is Sarapis who precedes his partner, sometimes it is Isis who has made it possible for her companion to become known.

A look at the map of the Mediterranean shows that before the birth of Christianity the cult of Sarapis and Isis already existed in most of the lands of the Eastern Mediterranean, in Greece and in Italy. The history of how the cult took root differs from one area to another, but in most cases it was a slow, patient advance effected by the conversions of individuals or families. At Delos, for example, towards 280 BCE, a certain Apollonius, probably an already Hellenized Egyptian of Memphis, took up residence accompanied by a statue of the god. At first it was a private cult practised by the family. Two generations later the cult assembled a group of devotees and a college of therapeutae; Sarapis made it known to Apollonius II, grandson of the Apollonius mentioned above, that he should dedicate a temple to him. The first Sarapeum on the island thus arose 'with the help of the god'. Soon afterwards two other sanctuaries would be built, and towards the middle of the second century, Delos was, after Alexandria, the largest Sarapis centre in the world.

The list of other centres dedicated to Isis and Sarapis is rather long:

Attica: Athens, Megara;

Peloponnesus: Corinth, Sicyon, Epidaurus, Methone, Argos, Mantinea, Phigalia, Pellene;

Boeotia: Tanagra, Thebes, Thespiae, Aegosthena, Coronea, Orchomenus, Chaeronea; in the last two cities, as at Tithorea in Phocis, slaves were freed by a form of fictitious sale to Sarapis and Isis or to Sarapis alone in the temple of these deities;

Phocis: Daulis, Hyampolis;

Locris: Naupactus;
Euboea: Chalcis, Eretria;
Thessaly: Hypata, Crannon, Larissa, Demetrias;
Macedonia: Salonika, Philippi, Maronea;
Thrace: Byazantium, Perinthus, Mesembria, Dionysopolis.

Insular Greece also showed up as well, offering a long list of cultic centres of which many were quite important, though not as important, of course, as Delos.

Among the Cyclades: Astypalea, Anaphe, Thera, Melos, Ios, Amorgos, Tenos, Chios;

Among the Sporades: Potidea, Cos, Samos, Chios, Methymna, and Rhodes where, outside the city of Rhodes, the sanctuaries at Lindos and Camiros were especially renowned;
Crete: Gortyna, Chersonesus;

Among the islands off the Thracian coast: Lemnos, Imbros, Thasos, where there was a lively collegium of *sarapiastai*.

On the coast of Asia, in almost all the important cities, we find devotees of the cult of Sarapis and Isis. Among these cities, Halicarnassus has often been cited as underscoring the importance of political influence in the expansion of the Sarapis cult. Here Arsinoë II is invoked together with Sarapis and Isis. On the contrary, other cities, situated outside the Ptolemaic orbit – Bargylia, very early in the third century, Priene, Magnesia-on-the-Meander – were by no means opposed to the presence of the cult of these deities. Then, after the decline of the empire of the Ptolemies, the cult spread to Caunus, Cnidus, Mylasa, Olympus, Heraclea of Latmus, Didyma, Cyme, Ephesus, Smyrna, Pergamum, Cyzicus. The cult took on concrete form with mystes, priests and collegia of *therapeutai* (Cyzicus, Cnidus), *synanoubiastai* (Smyrna), *katochoi* (Smyrna). These faithful, mystes and priests, were mainly Greeks or Hellenized autochthons.

Even in the kingdom of the Seleucids, hostile to the Ptolemies, Sarapis extended his power to Laodicea-ad-mare and to the shore of the Caspian Sea, where the freeing of slaves took place in the temple of Sarapis just as at Coronea and Tithorea.[4]

Reason for their success

Sarapis and Isis plainly attracted these populations throughout the two or three centuries that constituted the turning point of mankind's history.

Off-hand one might attribute this success to the charm of Egypt, which from the time of Herodotus onwards was considered as pre-eminently the land of gods, the land of mankind's most religious people. Even in the mid-fourth century of the Christian era Egypt could be spoken of as the country that

> produces the most eminent worshippers of the gods: in fact, the mysteries are celebrated nowhere else as they are there. From the most ancient times down to our own day Egypt has been almost alone in teaching the world the cult of the gods.[5]

Yet this myth of religious Egypt failed, prior to the Hellenistic era, to elicit more than a merely theoretical admiration. In no country, not even in regions subject to the political domination of the Pharaohs, do we find the adoption of Egyptian gods by the native peoples. Even the temples of the Egyptian gods built in Nubia and in Syria, were mainly for Egyptian civil servants or soldiers quartered in those countries or were there to mark Egypt's political ascendancy. That is not surprising. Like all the religions of antiquity, Egyptian religion had an ethnic and national character. There are even texts stating precisely that access to the temples, participation in the religious ceremonies, were forbidden to non-Egyptians.[6] Moreover, the notion of a universal god without national ties did not yet exist.[7]

The reason for the success of Sarapis and Isis, then, is not to be found in the reputation of Egypt nor in the political or military support for the dynasty of the Ptolemies. The 'imperialist' thesis, according to which Sarapis conquered the Mediterranean, thanks to the Ptolemies, has failed the test of critical scrutiny and is no longer accepted.[8] Apart from Thera, where the temple was managed by mercenaries of the Ptolemaic army, and Halicarnassus, where the divinized queen Arsinoë II was honoured together with Sarapis and Isis, we have no evidence, direct or indirect, of royal directives bearing on the establishment of the cult of Sarapis. This holds for regions subject to or allied with Alexandria and, *a fortiori*, for independent or hostile cities.

Private initiative, like that of Apollonius of Delos, succeeded in spreading the new religion. I say 'new', for we are dealing here with deities who were adopted and adored by non-Egyptians but not, it would seem, as Egyptian deities. To be sure, it was known that they came from the land of Egypt and that they carried with them elements of Egyptian religion. But they were also known to have something special. The great gods and goddesses of Egypt, anthropomorphic or zoomorphic, remained forever in their sumptuous temples in the Nile valley, served by a hierarchical clergy in accord with thrice-millenary rites. They did not leave their country. They were not ready to be expatriated. They remained always the gods of Upper and Lower Egypt, immobile in their eternal power. It is very likely that most of the Roman votaries of Isis never heard of Atum, of Rē, of Ptah, of Neith, of Hathor, etc.

Did, then, Sarapis and Isis come to non-Egyptian peoples as deities of the Nile valley, bringing them the traditional doctrine of Egypt, or rather as deities announcing a new message, which transcended national frontiers and cultural barriers?

We find ourselves faced with a contradiction, at least a seeming contradiction. Sarapis, little known by native Egyptians, becomes the Egyptian god universally venerated outside Egypt.

After a difficult start he would soon be promoted by some Roman Emperors to the rank of protector of the Empire. And Isis, his partner, would go before him everywhere. To say nothing of the sanctuaries that already existed in the Hellenistic era, other temples would rise in Palestine, in Syria, in Asia Minor and Greece. In the West more than a hundred Isis centres are known, especially in Italy, in Dacia and Pannonia, in Gaul, in Spain, and in North Africa.[9]

Isis's identity

During the imperial period, thanks to the *pax augusta*, thanks to the unification of the whole Mediterranean under the same power and the same laws, a new religiousness began to blossom. Little by little the peoples, like the nations, were losing their identity. Traditional, ethnic, civic deities thus saw their brilliance dim. Peoples, and individuals as well, were looking for a religious response to the new order of things. At that very moment, Isis presented herself to them: 'I am Isis, sovereign over all countries.'[10] The idea is new. Although she was 'born' in Egypt, she is no longer the goddess only of Egyptians. 'My single godhead is adored by the whole world in varied forms, in different rites and with many diverse names.'[11] In this expression and in similar formulae, there is something unusual, something that breaks with the traditions of the peoples of antiquity. The universalist and syncretistic objective is evident. Isis is not an unknown. But she is invoked under different names in accord with different peoples: Cybele, Astarte, Artemis, Demeter, Aphrodite, Hecate, Bellona, Kore, etc. Only the Egyptians, mighty in knowledge, know her real name: Queen Isis, or *Thiouis*: being One goddess, who at the same time is 'all other goddesses venerated by the races of men' (*una quae es omnia Isis*).[12]

This doctrine exhibits an accommodating suppleness that is remarkable. Isis is 'one', but she is not exclusivist or 'jealous', like Yahweh of the Jews. She accepts the existence of the other gods. But she recognizes at the same time that the honours paid to other goddesses are only diverse forms of cult in her own favour. And yet there is power in the name of the deity, and this accounts for the invitation to search out and find the goddess's true name, in which the eminent might of the deity is acknowledged.

In the light of these characteristics, two important religious facts are ascertainable. First, in the sanctuaries of Isis and Sarapis, homage was paid to a multitiude of deities considered as *sunnaoi theoi*. At Delos, for example, over and above Anubis and Harpocrates, who belonged to the family, several dozen gods were invoked and received dedications, notably, Osiris (distinct from Sarapis), Aphrodite, Astarte, Asclepius, Artemis, Demeter, Dionysus, Mater deum, Hygieia, Hermes, Pluto, Heracles, Nike, Agathodaimon, Agathe Tyche, Zeus Soter, etc. On this sacred island of Apollo the throng of Greek and Oriental gods venerated within the enclosure of the Sarapea proves the efficacy of the prayers offered here, in these temples, on the basis of the similarity of divine functions which, in the last analysis, corroborated one another for the good of the faithful. In the temple of Isis at Pompeii, Bacchus and Venus were likewise venerated as *sunnaoi theoi*.

Second, owing to the workings of syncretism, Isis multiplies her attributes. These lasting or passing unions allow her to realize in her own person the acquisition of divine qualities which she did not have. From the powerful goddesses venerated by other peoples she borrows attributes and assumes functions; she puts herself in their place to succour the faithful. Finally, she succeeds in eliciting a belief, unusual in antiquity prior to advanced Hellenism: *henotheism*. Henceforward she brings together in herself all the attributes, all the powers, that belong to the gods. 'You, you alone, are all the goddesses invoked by the races of men (each in his own language, in his own land)!' declares one of her votaries, Isidorus of Medinet Madi.[13] This belief is shared by most of her faithful, particularly in the Roman era, if we are to believe the *litany of Oxyrhynchus*, Apuleius, numerous inscriptions and, as well, the mass of Isiac iconographical documents found in the

Roman world. She is *one*, just as her fellow is acclaimed '*Heis theos Sarapis*' or '*Heis Zeus Sarapis*'.[14]

Polyonymous or even myrionymous (goddess of a thousand names), she is all-powerful both because the force of divinity abides in her name and because 'the gods of heaven pay her homage, the gods of the netherworld worship her' (Apuleius).

We have no text summing up the Isis *credo* but we do possess aretalogies and *prayers*[15] that clearly illustrate the belief of her faithful.

Isis is sovereign over the universe; she separates earth from heaven, fixes the course of the stars, particularly that of the sun and of the moon; moreover, she is in the quadriga of the sun (as his partner) or she even dwells in the sun's rays.

Mistress of the elements, she rules over winds, lightning, rain, snow; she raises up islands and continents, she determines river-beds and springs.

Inventor of human civilization, she founded laws and customs: the abolition of cannibalism, the right of legitimate defence, regard for the suppliant, the observance of oaths, the institution of marriage, the fidelity of spouses, filial regard for parents. In this domain, her blessings are immense: with Hermes she invented writing; she taught all peoples the cultivation of wheat and of the vine; she showed men how to venerate the gods.

In the 'litany of Oxyrynchus' there are other remarkable affirmations, which still astonish us by their novelty: 'you ruin whom you wish and you exalt the ruined; you purify all things; you have appointed each of the days made for joy. . . You have given to women a power equal to that of men.'[16]

Omnipotent, Isis is particularly attractive by the fact of her willingness to be of help. A saviour goddess (*sōteira*) as Sarapis is saviour god (*sōtēr*), she is ready to help all human beings in all the difficulties of life: sickness, war, prison, exile, the dangers of the sea, travel, shipwreck, and finally death. These powers, especially that over death, raise her above all the traditional deities of Greece and Rome. She is above Fate, which neither Zeus nor any other god can resist. 'I have vanquished Fate; Fate obeys me', declares Isis.[17] And elsewhere: 'I alone have the power to prolong your life beyond the span determined by your destiny.'[18] Thus, the Isis cult, by the belief in a clairvoyant, previsionary Fortune who illumines even the gods with the radiance of her light, introduces a new image of the Saviour Goddess, victorious over blind Fortune: Isis – Fortuna. Goddess of help (*Epēkoos*), she lends her miraculous assistance to all who address prayers to her.

The above résumé allows us to ascertain that Isiacism was not only a cult but a religion demanding an act of faith (a theme to which I shall return after examining Sarapis).

Sarapis's identity

It is an astonishing fact that the omnipotence of Isis does not detract from the omnipotence of Sarapis. Like his partner, Sarapis too unites in his person all the powers of the gods. Emergent from the combination Osiris-Apis, he is essentially the sovereign of life beyond death, the Greek equivalent of Hades-Pluto. But very early he encompasses the powers of 'the father of the gods and of men' to become Zeus Sarapis. Saviour and *Epēkoos*, he lends a helping hand to sea-voyagers in distress, to the shipwrecked, to the ill. This power over the elements permits him to become a cosmic god, the *kosmocratōr*. Since Isis directs the course of the sun and is even found in the quadriga of the sun, and since the Sun god gains in power and domination especially in the imperial era, Sarapis soon has himself invoked as the 'great Zeus Helios Sarapis' (*Zeus Helios Megas Sarapis* or *Jupiter optimus maximus Sol Sarapis*).

To express this creed, the faithful use the wondrous formula 'HEIS ZEUS SARAPIS' inscribed on gems, in stones, and above all proclaimed in meetings and ceremonies. This unambiguous henotheistic proclamation will remain after the triumph of Christianity as the last challenge of a religion that nearly gathered together all the peoples in one and the same belief: '*Heis Zeus, heis Aides, Helios esti Sarapis*' proclaimed Julian the Apostate.[19] The inscription found in the Mithraeum of the baths of Caracalla in honour of 'the unique Zeus Sarapis Helios, invincible, master of the world',[20] demonstrates the assimilative power of this composite god who thenceforward accepts the other attributes deriving from Oriental deities (Mithra, Helios-Baal). According to the orthodox doctrine Isis is the spouse of Osiris. This notion figures in cosmogony, beliefs and mysteries. Despite the syncretism of Osiris-Sarapis, the personality of Osiris was not blurred. He continued to be worshipped in the temples of Egypt even in the Hellenistic and Roman periods. The mysteries of Osiris continued to be celebrated according to ancestral rites. Aelius Aristides assures us that in his time 42 Egyptian nomes each possessed temples dedicated to Sarapis. We do not know whether the Greek author meant to speak specifically of Sarapea in the proper sense, but we do know that Sarapis gained more ground in Egypt in the imperial age than he did in the period of the Ptolemies.

At the same time, outside Egypt, Osiris was mentioned only rarely in funerary invocations: 'May Osiris give you refreshing water!'[21] In the sanctuaries of Isis and Sarapis, however, great ceremonies were celebrated annually, recalling the passion of Osiris, the quest of Isis, the *inventio* (i.e., discovery) of the limbs of the mutilated and scattered corpse of Osiris.

The votaries of Isis thus lived in a religious atmosphere that itself included mysterious and paradoxical elements. They did not worship Osiris, a purely Egyptian god, but each year they commemorated his myth, which was at the basis of Isiac eschatology, the source of beliefs in life after death and of mythical inspirations. They honoured Sarapis, a god without myth, but thanks to the union Osiris-Sarapis, they could find in his cult the bases of a new spirituality.

By a *tour de force* Sarapis was made the spouse of Isis and the father of Harpocrates. The aretalogy of Delos was the first effort in this direction:

> They are innumerable and prodigious, O glorious Serapis, the works of your power: some are sung in the cities of Egypt, land dear to the gods; others fill Greece. Isis, your spouse (*homeunos*), is celebrated as well.[22]

The aretalogy of Maronea is clearer:

> You (Isis) have taken Sarapis as companion (*sunoikos*) and after you had instituted marriage, the world has shone beneath your faces, set under the gazes of Helios and Selene.[23]

The hymn of Chalcis begins with a proclamation: 'I am Karpocrates, son of Sarapis and Isis.'[24]

In the Roman era Sarapis seems to have given way to Isis. She is always named first in the invocations. Despite modern research we still do not know the relationships between these two most closely related cults. From Apuleius we learn that there was 'an essential unity of the two deities and of the two cults' but a very great distinction between the rites of initiation proper to each. We also know that in certain cities there existed separate temples of Sarapis and Isis.

Missionaries

This theology, however attractive, could not touch the people without the activity of missionaries who themselves were firm believers. One may speak now of 'faith' (though perhaps less than in the case of Christian faith), for the religion of Isis requires a personal adhesion to a god, even if this adhesion does not always imply a total conversion of the type 'burn what you worshipped and worship what you burned'.

Who were these missionaries? How did they transmit their message?

We know a certain number of cases, for example, that of Zoilos, according to the archives of Zeno dated from 257 BCE, and that of Apollonios of Delos, also in the third century. In a letter addressed to Apollonios, one of the collaborators of Ptolemy II Philadelphus, Zoilos narrates that Sarapis ordered him in a dream to build a temple for him in a city of Asia Minor, to install a priest and have sacrifices offered there. Zoilos tried to pay no attention to this, and he fell ill. The god later cured him, after he had promised to do what had been asked of him. In the meantime, someone coming from Cnidus began to erect a private sanctuary dedicated to Sarapis but this did not please the god, who forced him to leave the city. Zoilos, for his part, arrived in Alexandria but, absorbed by his personal business, failed to ask the assistance of Apollonios for the god's project. Again he fell ill, this time more gravely, for four months. For this reason he decided at last to write to Apollonios, asking the latter to carry out the orders of the god.[25]

The story includes several points of importance; (*a*) Zoilos receives the orders of the god in a dream; (*b*) he is punished for not having done what the god asked of him; (*c*) someone comes from Cnidus and spontaneously propagandizes for the new cult by building a private Sarapeum; (*d*) finally, Zoilos writes to a partisan belonging to the court of Ptolemy. While implicitly reminding Apollonios that devotion to Sarapis was a sign of loyalty to the dynasty of the Lagids, Zoilos did not mention that the propagation of the cult of Sarapis was encouraged by royal policy.

The case of Apollonios of Memphis, who settled in Delos in the first half of the third century, is more striking. For two generations the family of Apollonios venerated the god in his own home and probably spread the cult in his surroundings. The number of the faithful must have become considerable, for Sarapis ordered

Apollonios II, grandson of Apollonios I, in a dream, to dedicate a temple to him. The god himself showed where the future temple should be located.

> Since the god wanted it, the purchase of terrain was effected and the sanctuary built rapidly, in six months. It happened then that some individuals joined forces against us and against the god and they brought a public action against the sanctuary and against me. I had to pay a fine or undergo a painful punishment. But the god announced to me in a dream that we would be victorious.[26]

The story told by Apollonios II shows once again that the spread of the new religion on Delos took place owing altogether to private initiative and that the god took pleasure in communicating with human beings in dreams.

How non-Egyptians adopted Isiacism

Other testimonies show us how non-Egyptians adopted the new belief.

1. Dreams and miracles

First, over and above warnings given in dreams – a phenomenon frequent enough to justify the presence, for example, in the Sarapea of Delos, of *Oneirokritai* whose role was to interpret prophetic dreams – Sarapis and Isis often healed the ill who practised incubation in the temples. Ex-voto offerings with the formula *kata prostagma* or *ex visu* abound.[27] Tibullus implored Isis to save his failing Delia, for, judging from numerous painted ex-voto offerings in her temples, he knows that the goddess can heal.[28] And for the health of Corinna Ovid offered incense on the altars of Isis, brought the goddess offerings, said prayers, made promises like a true devotee.[29] Again, let us recall some other celebrated cases. Demetrius of Phalerum, having regained his sight thanks to Sarapis, composed paeans which were long sung in the sanctuaries.[30] The author of the aretalogy of Maronea wrote his praise to thank Isis for having cured him of ophthalmia.

> With these eyes. . . I saw the sun and I see the world, which is yours: I am convinced that you will help me in every way. Indeed, you came when I invoked you for my health. . .[31]

The title of healers, of *sōtēres*, applied to Sarapis and Isis,

111

confirmed the power and the benevolence of these deities towards human beings.

By these cures and by other miracles, e.g., protection from and survival of storms, and shipwreck, Sarapis and Isis attracted an increasingly various clientele. Aelius Aristides, saved by Sarapis when shipwrecked, composed a hymn to glorify him,[32] while a certain Isidorus of Medinet Madi in his first poem emphatically affirmed the power of Isis in storms.[33]

With a view to public notice it is significant that miracles were not only recounted *viva voce* but recorded in hymns, registers and prayers that often end with acclamations such as *Heis Zeus Sarapis* or *Isī Nikēi* or *Mega to onoma tou Sarapidis*.

2. Asceticism

Second, the cult was also propagated by a somewhat paradoxical phenomenon: its rigorism and its ascetic aspects. The ancients, used to pre-eminently ritualist cults, were amazed at the religion of Isis. One thinks, for instance, of those Roman women who observed days of chastity, avoiding sexual relations: the Delia of Tibullus, the Cynthia of Propertius, etc. One may imagine these devotees plunging three times into the icy Tiber and, trembling with cold, going on their bleeding knees round the temple of Isis.[34] Apuleius's Lucius, who after having shaved his head, showed his shaved head to all, proud of being an Isis follower, could well draw people by his devotion, his joy in life, and his happiness in the service of the gods.

The mysteries, moreover, rather than frightening people, were attractive to some and objects of respect to others. By initiation into the mysteries the faithful are assured of spiritual salvation in the beyond. Many testimonies attest the existence of Isiac mysteries, the character of which nevertheless still escapes us. The law of the secret was so well kept that it is only by cross-checking the sources that we can come to know or, rather, surmise their essentials. Plutarch[35] tells us that Isis instituted the initiations on the model of sufferings that she had herself undergone. It is perhaps this awesome *hieros logos* that she taught the mystes, according to the statement in the hymn of Andros.[36] According to Apuleius, the very initiation itself represents a voluntary death and a resurrection, salvation by grace. The last-mentioned author gives us some extremely precious details especially if one would compare these rites with similar acts in other religions. To be initiated the candidate must spend ten days in fasting and abstinence. Then, on the evening chosen by the priest following an order of the goddess, he receives an instruction given by the mystagogue after a liturgical and penitential purification. The ceremony itself is extremely secret. We have only an echo of it in a deliberately obscure description:

> I approached the boundary of death and, treading on Proserpine's threshold, I was carried through all the elements; after which I returned. At dead of night I saw the sun flashing with bright effulgence; 'I approached close to the gods above and the gods below and I worshipped them face to face.'[37]

The next day, clothed in a richly ornamented tunic, his right hand holding a lighted torch, his head encircled with a palm-crown whose leaves stand up like sun rays, the initiate presents himself to the public to be adored like the Sun god.

By 'sacramental' power, the initiate is identified with the deity. Like Osiris he is dead. And like Osiris he is born again. The initiate is henceforward placed under the special protection of the goddess, assured of his material well-being, health, prosperity, riches, and, above all, freed from the chains of Fate ('When you have begun to serve the goddess, then will you better realize the result of your freedom', says the priest to Lucius).[38]

3. Mysticism

Third, the story of Apuleius's Lucius leads us to consider another aspect of the cult of Isis which also must have played an important role especially for those who were in search of the spiritual. Because of his sins Lucius is punished, transformed into an ass and dogged by blind and brutal Fortune. The miracle that Isis worked in his favour, giving him back human form, is primarily the symbol of his purification from the sins of the past and of the call to spiritual salvation. After the miracle the Isiac high priest says to Lucius:

> . . . on the slippery path of your hot-headed youth you fell into low pleasures and you have gained a grim reward for your ill-starred curiosity. . . Now you have been received into the protection of a Fortune who is not blind, but sees, and illumines the other gods too with the radiance of her light . . . Let the unbelievers take note, let them take note and acknowledge their mistake.[39]

These words contain an idea of conversion which was new to the mentality of this age.[40]

Converted, Lucius henceforward acknowledges the beliefs, the rites and the commandments of the religion he has just embraced. He will be initiated. But there is something more. His conversion is not only that of the mind but also of the heart. Repeatedly he gives himself up to the contemplation of the goddess, enjoys her sweet presence either alone or in the daily ceremonies. The image of Isis haunts him day and night. And after obeying her divine orders, he petitions his initiation. After this happy event his mystical transports of joy multiply: 'Having tarried there for a few days longer, I enjoyed the ineffable pleasure of the image of the goddess to whom I was now pledged by a favour that could not be repaid.' Finally, before returning home at the goddess's command, he feels the pain of having to say good-bye. He prostrates himself before the image of the goddess; with his face he wipes the divine feet he had wet with his tears; he prays, sobbing.[41]

Psychologically, the impassioned devotion of Lucius, his emotional and mystical transports, can be accountable for only in terms of a communion of heart between Lucius and the goddess. He loves her. He believes in the love of Isis. In the blessings he has received, in the spiritual consolations, he feels the goddess's love within himself. And in return he loves her. His tears of joy, his long contemplation before the image of his beloved goddess, are but the expressions of an overflowing piety.[42]

4. *The religious ceremonies*

Fourth, for the great mass of the people, the cult further offers spectacles unknown to the traditional Graeco-Roman religions: the ceremonies. Like most of the Oriental religions, the cult of Isis and of Sarapis draws people's curiosity, and thence their admiration, by grandiose festivities. The *navigium Isidis* of 5 March included a grandiose procession and the dedication of a votive ship to open maritime navigation. The *Isia* and/or the *Heuresis* in the month of November commemorated the *quest of Isis* or the *finding of Osiris*. Like the goddess, the faithful mourned, beat their breasts, aped the gestures of a mother in distress; on the third day, they shouted acclamations whose echo resounded in the streets; they proclaimed that Osiris had been found, brought back to life.

But what differentiates this cult from the others are the daily rites. In the morning, it is the morning service. The priest draws the white curtain veiling the cella to allow the faithful to worship the image of the goddess. Then come the libations, the priestly prayers echoed with the voice of the faithful. In the evening, prayers resound again, the sounds of the sistrums and the intonation of hymns.[43]

A universalist doctrine abolishing ethnic and social barriers, the promise of a happy life here below and of felicity in the Elysian Fields in the hereafter, precepts of continence and abstinence, a daily liturgy giving life to piety: these are the factors creating the aura of the Isis cult.

5. *The divine iconography*

Fifth, to this should be added that religious imagery also made its contribution. One hardly finds great artistic masterpieces of Isis and Sarapis, but their iconography reflects the popularity of these deities and the subtle skill of visual theological expression. It should be noted incidentally that this imagery penetrated all spheres of ancient religious life: cultic images in the temples, or in domestic sanctuaries, pendants in gold, silver, or precious stone for devotees, amulets, magic intaglio engravings for personal protection, statuettes in metal or clay for ex-voto offerings, and even figures on coins for official propaganda. It is in iconography that one discovers the true face of the cult of Isis and Sarapis, a face at once moving and enigmatic.

First of all, Sarapis has the appearance of a Greek bearded god. In the beginning probably he was only given the attributes of a Lord of the netherworld (Osiris-Hades); theological evolution attached other attributes to him, thus permitting people to express their beliefs about the true nature of the god such as he was or appeared to be to the believer. Soon he was seen with sun-rays round his head like Helios, with ram's horns in his hair like Ammon, with a horn of plenty in his left hand like Pluto or Agathodaimon, with a serpent encircling his sceptre like Asclepius, with a club like Heracles, with a helm like the sovereign of the sea. Like Zeus he holds a sceptre in his left hand and raises his right hand as a sign of well-being and majesty. Once he has become the god of the cosmos, his image takes on the most supple forms to answer to the expectations of the faithful who believe in him, the saviour god, helpful and all-powerful.[44]

For her part Isis, too, despite her purely Egyptian name, presents herself in Greek form, though keeping some Egyptian symbols like the *basileion* (Isiac emblem), the sistrum, the situla.

As distributor of riches, she holds the horn of plenty. Syncretistic goddess of a thousand forms, her attributes are very numerous: she will have the sheaves of wheat and torches like Demeter, poppy seeds like Persephone, wings like Nike, a crescent moon like Artemis-Selene, a helm like Fortune; she sometimes appears like Astarte or Aphrodite, or with a body in the form of a serpent like Thermouthis, clothed in a star-spangled tunic like Aphrodite Ourania; mother of Harpocrates, she suckles him; nymph-goddess, she is to be found in nymphaea.[45]

This iconographic richness, completely unknown to any other cult, is the counterpart of the theological richness referred to above.

Isiacism and Christianity

Christianity was born in a spiritual milieu permeated with a new religiousness to which the cult of Isis and of Sarapis made an important – perhaps fundamental – contribution. Everywhere the devotees of Isis preceded the missionaries of Jesus. By their henotheistic and universalist theology, by their personal piety, their rites and their mysteries, they readied the peoples of the Mediterranean for the quest of the new. Historical circumstances naturally played a part. (a) Historical events overturned the old order of countries and cities. National or civic deities as powerful as Zeus or Athena saw people under their protection humiliated, scattered. At the same time, however, frontiers were opened. The *oikoumenē* took shape without the good will of statesmen. (b) The break-up of traditional religions created a void. People tried to fill it first by a futile return to tradition, to the religion of their ancestors, then by a turn to the wondrous East (Persia, Egypt). Anxiety incited men to the quest and the quest set numerous metaphysical questions especially about the immortality of the soul, about assurance of the hereafter. In this field the religion of Egypt was ahead of the Graeco-Roman religions. (c) Though polytheism was not repudiated, little by little there took shape in the old system a hierarchy of values which granted to some one deity supremacy over the others and approximating to some extent Semitic monotheism. *Isis panthea, Sarapis pantheus,* or *Sol invictus* were born in this spiritual atmosphere where the deities and their prophets were bent on expressing truth regarded as revealed by the deity himself.

On the other hand, it is also in this cultural atmosphere

permeated with Graeco-Roman tradition and thought that Isiacism and Christianity developed, spread, defined themselves. It
was to men of this time and this culture that these religions were
preached. Isiacs and Christians lived in the same world; used the
same language as means of communication, first Greek, then
Greek and Latin; recruited co-religionists almost in the same way,
by personal contacts, for example, in comparable belief in a divine
call; and probably they could not but have met one another.

The self-definition of Isis offers an analogy to Judaism and
Christianity, where the *'ego eimi'* formulation is very frequently
used. It does not, however, permit us to suppose any kinship
between them.[46] The religion of Isis and Sarapis was involved, as
was Christianity, in a historical process of personal religion, but
it was not structured by church organization. If the devotees were
related to each other by common devotion to Isis and by a common
credal commitment to her divine power and her mysteries, if they
attended similar ceremonies everywhere in the Roman world,
they did not have any structural link permitting them to be
incorporated to an 'Isiac assembly' distinct from the community
in which they had been initiated. Each Isiac community was very
likely autonomous and independent. So at Rome, Apuleius's
Lucius 'was a stranger to the temple of Isis Campensis although
he was at home in the faith'.[47]

Believers, devotees and initiates had the same objectives: to
love the goddess and to spread abroad the creed claimed to belong
to every human being. We do not have any evidence of prosely-
tism similar to the Christian mission or of any missionary mandate
from a priestly hierarchy of Alexandria or Memphis. But, as we
have seen above, we have evidence of a divinely mandated
mission: Sarapis or Isis themselves gave instructions through
dreams. In other cases, the devotees, without formal order from
the gods, proclaimed the supremacy of Isis by aretalogies, literature and personal persuasion. Since Isiacism became cosmopolitan and universalist, the missionaries were not necessarily
Egyptian. Like Apuleius's Lucius, they were converts who, out of
conviction or gratitude, tried to convert others to the same faith.

7

Self-Definition in the Asclepius Cult

HOWARD C. KEE

In the history of the cult of Asclepius, self-definition comes into sharp focus at two points: (I) in the late third/early second century of the Hellenistic era when the familiar tablets of testimony to the virtues of Asclepius were prepared for his shrine at Epidaurus; (2) in the mid-second century of our era, when Aelius Aristides prepared his *Sacred Tales* to recount his ailments and the divine manifestations and ministrations of the god in his behalf. The fidelity of the picture that emerges from the literary sources is remarkably confirmed by the inscriptional evidence from Pergamon, as we shall see. Earlier studies have drawn attention to some of the differences between the stages of the cult as represented by these two *corpora* of texts. It seems that it might be fruitful, however, not only to examine the contrasts in content among the various testimonies to Asclepius, but also to explore some of the major shifts that occurred in personal and social outlook between the two eras from which our documentation has been preserved. Rather than a bland blend or a simplistic synthesis of diverse evidence, we must inquire whether self-definition among devotees of the cult changed, concurrently with and in direct relationship to the changes in the outward cultic phenomena.

Methods

What is involved in this proposed undertaking is more than an attempt at a fresh examination of familiar texts and archaeological evidence concerning Asclepius. Our inquiries are undertaken in a period of competing methodologies, some of them adopted as self-evidently valid, while others are self-consciously in process of development. The approach adopted here offers an alternative to the traditional history-of-religions approach, which assumes that external similarity of religious phenomena attested in different ages or cultures is to be perceived as evidence of identity or of direct causal links. Some recent work in historical analysis of ancient religions considers its goal to be the discernment of timeless patterns which are assumed to underlie religious phenomena, whether of the Jungian symbolic type represented by the learned studies of Kerényi, or the tracing of mythological motifs best exemplified in the encyclopedic work of Mircea Eliade, or the currently popular identification of the so-called deep structures in the anti-historical, anti-contextual hypotheses of Lévi-Strauss and his school. What seems called for among responsible historians is rather to explore how, in a religious tradition, human self-understandings – personal, social and cosmic – undergo significant shifts even though the external features of a religion's myth and ritual seemingly perdure. Under the impact of basic changes in the social, cultural and economic setting of a religious tradition, the world-view or (to use the term offered by sociology-of-knowledge) 'life-world'[1] may change. Concurrent with that alteration in self-understanding, and in a dialectical relationship with it, the story and circumstances of human consort with the divinity are almost certain to function otherwise in the experience of the community of devotees than they did in an earlier and therefore different cultural era.

To speak of '*self*-definition', therefore, is a modern intellectual abstraction. The self adopts an identity through acceptance – either by passive conformity or by conscious choice – of a framework of meaning through which one's origins, purpose and destiny are defined. Self-definition is achieved through group identification, whether that be a tribe, a nation, or a voluntary association. In the case of the Asclepius cult, we see that the god functions in one epoch almost exclusively as an instrument for resolving personal difficulties – usually physical ailments. In another cultural context, the god has become the central focus of existence and meaning for a stratum of society that consciously and of its own volition identifies itself with him. Common to both sets of historical phenomena are the healing benefactions of Asclepius and the advent of seeking pilgrims to his shrine. But how the seeking self is defined is in each case shaped by, and in turn helps to shape, the 'life-world' of the seeker.

Literary evidence

The evidence available for our study of the Asclepius cult, including its life-world dimension, is sufficiently diverse and derives from historical circumstances that can be known with precision sufficient to enable us to test such an historical method and perhaps to demonstrate its usefulness. Our point of entry to the investigation will be the older literary material which antedates the Hellenistic evidence from Epidaurus. In the Iliad Asclepius appears in a passing reference to his sons, Podaleiros and Machaon, who led the contingent from Trikka and Oichalia that joined the Greek coalition against Troy. The clear implication is that their father is a healer, since they are 'good healers both themselves'.[2] There is here no hint of a hero-cult of Asclepius at Trikka,[3] nor from this evidence alone could one infer anything more than that Asclepius was a man whose gift of healing was transmitted to his sons – whether by heredity or instruction cannot be determined from the Homeric text.

With Pindar, however, the details become clearer, and include links between Asclepius and the realm of the divine which are essential to his origin, his destiny, and his role in human existence. In his Third Pythian Ode, Pindar longs for the return to life of Cheiron, who had reared Asclepius, 'that gentle craftsman (*tektona*) who drove pain from limbs that he healed – that hero who gave aid in all manner of maladies'.[4] Struck by jealous Artemis for having consorted with Apollo and conceived his child, Asclepius's dying mother (Coronis, daughter of Phlegyas) was delivered of her child by his divine father, who took him away and gave him to the Magnesian centaur to rear. The centaur was ordered specifically 'to teach the child how to heal mortal men of painful maladies'.[5] What follows in Pindar describes in detail the benefactions human kind received from Asclepius, as he was perceived in the fifth century before our era:

> And those whosoever came suffering from the sores of nature, or with their limbs wounded either by gray bronze or by far-hurled stone, or with bodies wasting away with summer's heat or winter's cold, he loosed and delivered divers of them from diverse pains, tending some of them with kindly incantations, giving to others a soothing potion, or, haply, swathing their limbs with samples or restoring others by the knife.[6]

Pindar associates with Asclepius a factor which will stand in tension with the god's role as benefactor throughout the epochs scrutinized in our inquiry: that is, how medical technique relates to the healing action of Asclepius.

Somewhat later than the time of Pindar, Aristophanes's parody of the Asclepius cult and its devotees includes, as does Pindar, the dimension of medical methods. In his *Plutus*, Aristophanes includes a detailed account by one Cario to his wife of a visit to an Asclepion in Piraeus in the company of the god, Plutus, and an Athenian politician named Neoclides.[7] After Platus had been taken to bathe in the sea, they all entered the sacred precincts, offered the requisite loaves and sacrifices, and bedded down for the night. The sacristan ordered all to remain quiet no matter what noise they heard, and then extinguished the lights in the incubation chamber. Cario's account is livened by humorous details, satirical and earthy, of the priest filching the edibles from the altar after the lights are out; of his own successful theft of a bowl of porridge (he scared the old woman to whom it belonged by hissing and pretending to be one of the sacred snakes); of his embarrassing the god's daughters by breaking wind as the deity approached. But of substantive importance for our purposes are the details concerning the epiphany of Asclepius and his healing technique in the course of the incubation. The god is portrayed as an apothecary, with mortar, pestle and box. He prepares a plaster with hot spices and vinegar, which when applied to Neoclides's eyes, causes him to run around in understandable pain. Then the patient is calmed. As for Plutus, however, a scarlet cloth is placed on his eyes, and then the divine dimension of the healing is disclosed: two serpents appear from the sacred depths of the temple, creep under the scarlet cloth and lick his eyes, whereupon his sight is restored. The god disappears and the serpents return to the innermost recesses of the temple.[8]

Precisely because Aristophanes's scorn for and scepticism towards the Asclepius cult are so patent, the information he offers about the healing processes is the more revealing. For reasons which are not at all clear, Neoclides is treated by a simple medicinal device: a hot plaster. Plutus, on the other hand, is given no orders and receives no thaumaturgic treatment, except for the scarlet cloth placed on his eyes. The healing is performed directly and solely by the serpents, the chthonic symbols and agents of the god's healing powers. Thus in Aristophanes's comedy the two elements – medical technique and divine healing – are merely juxtaposed; no logical link or causal connection between them is even implied. One overarching feature of the Asclepius cult is clear, however: the god is regarded as the benefactor of those in need of healing. He is accessible in his shrines, directly and immediately efficacious in therapy, whether by simple medical treatment or by direct action of the god in epiphanic or emblematic mode.

Epidaurus

The oldest and fullest documentation for the cult of Asclepius at Epidaurus is of two kinds: literary and archaeological. Both date from the Hellenistic period, with some confirmatory evidence from the early imperial period.[9] Although he was writing in his *Description of Greece* in the second half of the second century of our era, Pausanias reports sympathetically the mythological tradition that Asclepius was born near Epidaurus, the son of Apollo. His divine qualities were evident from his birth, when lightning flashed from his new-born body.[10] as his divine generation was attested by the Delphic oracle;

> O Asclepius, born to bestow great joy upon mortals,
> Pledge of the mutual love I enjoyed with Phlegyas's daughter,
> Lovely Coronis, who bore thee in rugged land, Epidaurus.[11]

The central feature of the main sanctuary within the sacred enclosure at Epidaurus, Pausanias tells us, was the famous chryselephantine statue of the god, accompanied by the serpent and the dog. Also visible in his time, presumably in the *tholos* – which he remarks blandly is 'worth seeing' – were still standing six slabs (of an originally larger collection) on which were inscribed the names of men and women healed by Asclepius, as well as the means of their cure. The nineteenth-century excavators of the sanctuary of Asclepius at Epidaurus found four of these tablets, three of them preserved almost completely.[12] R. Herzog is almost certainly correct in stating that these represent an official collection of testimonies, as the quality of writing and the stylized nature of the accounts attest.[13] There are no traces of rhetorical art in them; the accounts are artless and popular;[14] their aim is not so much propaganda as pre-conditioning of pilgrims to convey courage and hope as they await the epiphany and the healing of the god.[15]

The central feature of the Asclepius experience was the incubation, or sacred sleep in the *abaton*, a kind of dormitory located only a few metres from the *tholos* and the Asclepius shrine proper. More than three-quarters of the tablet testimonies at Epidaurus make specific reference to the sacred sleep and dreams as the mode of Asclepius's self-disclosure to the needy. The *tholos* was the most beautiful building in the entire precinct. Built between 370 and 360,[16] the circular structure surrounded by a colonnade had a kind of labyrinth below with four circular walls. The fact that these were pierced by doors and arches, however, suggests that access was encouraged rather than hindered. The function of the building was probably to make water from the sacred springs available to large numbers of people simultaneously.[17] Ceremonial cleansing prior to incubation was an essential feature of the cult, according to the testimonies on the tablets, and as is also implied by the nearly universal links between Asclepius shrines and springs and wells in the long list offered by Pausanias.[18] At the same time, the *tholos* may well have served as the official headquarters of the sacred snakes.[19] Defrasse and Lechat in their early report on the excavations at Epidaurus noted that the serpent in Greece was regarded as a being of mystery; it glides noiselessly but observantly along the ground. Like springs and exhalations, it comes out of the earth, and thus is associated with chthonic divinities. The annual shedding of skin is seen as a sign of eternal renewal and hence of divine cure.[20] Attested on the tablets are cures accomplished through the pilgrim's being licked by the tongues of snakes and dogs, a phenomenon which occurs with about the same frequency as the visible manifestation of the god himself. Indeed, the serpent and the god are alternate forms of one kind of epiphany. It takes little imagination to identify with the pilgrim lying in the pitch-dark dormitory, hearing the slithering of the snakes, the padding or panting of the dogs – or in a climax of divine favour, the footstep of the god himself.

In one of the Hippocratic Epistles (15), 'Hippocrates' is describing a vision he had received of Asclepius. He was not gentle and calm, as the statues suggest, but lively and frightening.

> Serpents followed him, enormous sorts of reptiles, they too hurrying on, with their tremendous train of coils, making a whistling noise. . . . His associates followed him carrying boxes of drugs tightly bound. Then the god stretched forth his hand to me.[21]

Thus personal encounter with the god conveys both compassion and awe.

What sort of people came seeking the benefactions of the god? Childless women, mute children, blind men, a father seeking a missing son, those with long pregnancies and those with crippled hands. Ailments of the pilgrims included infestation with lice, leeches, and worms; growths, pus, abscesses, sores, ulcers; paralysis, headaches, baldness, embedded spear points, epilepsy, dropsy. All were healed by the compassionate Asclepius. This does not mean, of course, that all who came to Epidaurus in search of a cure found it. There are no tablets of testimony left by the disappointed, who must have outnumbered the healed by a vast margin. It was essential, in any case, that those who came seeking the god's assistance brought with them appropriate offerings. In two of the Epidaurus testimonies, punishment fell on those who failed to make the proper sacrifice, though in each case the failure was remedied and the ending was happy as the pilgrim experienced a cure.[22]

What was at stake in the pilgrimage to Asclepius at Epidaurus in the Hellenistic period, as far as we can trace it, was the god's gracious action in meeting the need of a faithful individual. Although the testimonies include expressions of gratitude for benefits received, the focus is solely on the solution provided by the god. There is no hint of a broader religious experience of conversion, with attendant effects on the pilgrim's later life or even on his or her general outlook on life. The process is *ad hoc* and pragmatic: need *x* evokes request *y* made to the god, who responds with remedy *z*. Thanks be to Asclepius. There is, for example, no social or political dimension of the Asclepian piety. The Paean of Isyllos (early third century BCE), which appeals to an epiphany of Asclepius to the Spartans in the fourth-century struggle with Philip as a way of persuading the Epidaurians to ally themselves with Sparta, is idiosyncratic and propagandistic.[23] Although Asclepius was the panhellenic god of healing, his ministrations were personal. Other than the priestly group which managed and operated the shrine, there is no evidence of a movement or an organized religious group gathered in his name.

Asclepiads

To deny the emergence of an Asclepius sect or conventicle, however, is not to ignore the existence of a group known as Asclepiads or to overlook the extent to which the cult of Asclepius spread over the Greek lands and islands, as well as to Rome. The links between Hippocrates of Cos and Asclepius go back at least to Plato,[24] and evidence a very different stance towards healing from that of the Epidaurian tablets. The Hippocratic treatise *On*

Ancient Medicine proceeds entirely on the basis of observation, experimentation and generalization, although its theoretical base in a notion of humours and structures has a determinative effect on diagnosis and prescription. The only major tie to Asclepius is in the designation of Hippocrates and his followers and students as Asclepiads. W. H. S. Jones rejects the suggestions that the term means 'priests of Asclepius', or that it was adopted by a medical guild; rather, he thinks, it was the clan of hereditary physicians, who claimed descent from the god, or who were regarded as adopted members of the medical family.[25] We shall return briefly to the question of the relation of ancient medical science – or art – to the Asclepius cult when we consider the relations and differences between Galen and the devotees of the god in the Antonine period. But we should note at this point that, although the medical tradition at Cos is centuries older, the Coan temple of Asclepius dates from only the third century BCE; it seems to have had no predecessor there, and represents the importation from Epidaurus of a type of Asclepian piety at variance with the medical-training tradition found at Cos at least back to the time of Plato.[26] But, by the middle of the third century, the poet Herondas depicts women offering sacrifices in the temple of Asclepius.[27] Of the details of the Coan cult, we learn nothing, although one would assume a general similarity to that prevailing at the same time in Epidaurus.

Two accounts from antiquity describe the happy journey of Asclepius from Epidaurus to Rome. According to Livy's sober report, a pestilence which swept the city and its environs was so severe that the Sacred Books were consulted. The instruction derived from them was that Asclepius was to be summoned from Epidaurus to Rome.[28] The envoys dispatched to carry out the command brought back a serpent which crawled into their ship and which was generally believed to be the bodily presence of the god. On reaching Rome, the serpent went ashore on the island in the Tiber, whereupon a temple of Asclepius was erected there.[29] The year was 291 BCE; traces of the cult are still evident in rock-carvings, and the site remains a centre of healing down to the present.

In Ovid's splendidly dramatic description of the same incident, the messengers were sent to the Delphic oracle, which gave orders to go to Epidaurus, where Apollo's son would come to their aid. Although the council in Epidaurus was understandably reluctant to release their resident god – and their chief source of renown and revenues – the god appeared in serpentine form, left the temple, boarded the ship and sailed for Rome, with a pious stop en route to honour his father at an Italian shrine of Apollo. As the ship sailed up the Tiber, the banks were lined with devotees and altars laden with bloody sacrifices; the air was filled with the sound of crackling incense and the fragrance of perfume. As the city was reached, the serpent-god mounted the masthead, spying out a place fitting for his abode and chose the island in the Tiber, where he disembarked and resumed his heavenly form. By his coming as 'health-bringer' to their city, he put an end to the people's woes.[30] As is the case with our knowledge of the Asclepion at Cos, we have no clues as to the forms or modes that the piety in honour of the god took at Rome, but both the earlier account and the later romanticized variant of it concentrate on healing benefits as such, as Ovid's description of him as *salutifer* attests.

The Antonine Era

When we turn to the evidence about Asclepius in the Antonine period, however, the changes are fundamental and dramatic from those features which we have traced in Hellenistic and republican times. At Epidaurus, the older prohibitions against childbirth or death occurring in the precincts sacred to Asclepius were modified. A Roman senator, Antoninus, is reported by Pausanias to have built, 'in our own day' a bath of Asclepius in addition to other shrines for the god, for Apollo and Hygieia. But further,

> As the Epidaurians about the sanctuary were in great distress, because their women had no shelter in which to be delivered and the sick breathed their last in the open, he [Antoninus] provided a dwelling so that these grievances were also addressed. Here at last was a place in which without sin a human being could die and a woman be delivered.[31]

More than additional buildings and a relaxation of earlier strictures against birth and death had occurred; Defrasse and Lechat state that 'by the Antonine age, the hostel had become a spa; baths had replaced the *tholos*, and the cures included detailed dietary and medicinal advice.'[32]

That generalization is confirmed by the inscriptions and other testimony from Epidaurus dating from the Antonine era. Sick with indigestion, one Julius Apellas arrived at Epidaurus about 160 CE and underwent a regimen of diet and exercise that included bathing, swinging, walking, rubbing himself with oil, smearing himself with mud, gargling with cold water, as well as imbibing milk with honey and lemon-rind, and eating lettuce and celery. The treatment went on for days on end, sometimes within, sometimes outside the sanctuary. The subjective factors are patent: his congestion came from too much study; the journey from Aegina 'did not upset him greatly'; he tipped the bath-master an Attic drachma; the god prescribed for a headache even though Apellas had none at the moment. The reader gets the impression that he is glimpsing a few of an extended series of episodes of illness or at least of indisposition.[33] Apellas is not so bold as to say with Aelius Aristides that he actually enjoys bad health, but the implication is there.

Before looking at the testimony of Aristides to the powers of Asclepius, it may be useful to inquire as to whether historians of the Antonine period regard this prolific rhetorician-diarist as unique or as representative of his period. Historians dealing with this era do, in fact, see in Aristides an eloquent spokesman for what Rostovtzeff has called the 'mentality' of the Antonine age. With specific reference to Aristides's encomium to Rome, Rostovtzeff considers this rhetor to have given vivid expression to the widespread admiration with which Rome's achievement of unifying the civilized world was regarded by so many of its thoughtful inhabitants. The intellectuals had led the attack on Vespasian, and had shaped the paradigm of responsible leadership under the model of the king who, unlike the tyrant, is chosen of the gods for his role, whose power is transmitted on the basis of ability rather than heredity, and whose actions are in consonance with the will of the gods. That role was assumed by Trajan, in whose reign 'peace was concluded between the mass of the population of the Empire, especially the educated classes of the city *bourgeoisie*, and the imperial power'.[34] It is precisely that segment of the population for which Aelius Aristides is an eloquent spokesman. As G. W. Bowersock expressed it, 'Lucian (of Samosata) and Aelius Aristides brilliantly mirror the world in which sophists flourished.'[35] Although the sophists came from wealthy families, and therefore were drawn from a narrow segment of the population, the respect they enjoyed is attested by the constant pressure on them to accept major public office. The generous acts of the sophists in providing public facilities and monuments for their fellow citizens were obviously a factor in their popular appeal, but as Bowersock has observed, 'the benefactions of sophists are a palpable expression of the union of literary, political and economic influence'[36] that characterizes this period. In an era when the masses had almost no access to literature, except through public rhetorical displays, the rhetors were shapers of public opinion, objects of popular admiration, and the articulators of widespread values and aspirations.

Religiously, this epoch had only a waning interest in the Olympian gods; far more significant for most persons were the gods and goddesses who were immediately available, who were directly interested in and sympathetic towards the needs of individuals. As André Boulanger asserted, 'After a long period of religious indifference, this epoch displayed a great attraction for oracle and miracle, especially in Asia.'[37] Heightened interest in miracle is likewise evident in Philostratus's *Life of Apollonius of Tyana*, designed as it was for a readership within the imperial household.[38] Speculations about demons, prophets, and fascination with ancient deities – especially those from Egypt – permeated the upper classes.[39] It was precisely in such a coterie of poets, politicians, philosophers and sophists that Aristides lived and for whom he was an eloquent spokesman.

What was the piety that Aristides exemplified, and how did he come to espouse it? Born into a well-to-do-family with large land-holdings in provincial Mysia, Aristides enjoyed social and economic stability, as well as the political advantage of citizenship. At about the age of fifteen he was sent to Athens to study under Alexander, one of the most renowned teachers of that day. Probably his earliest education was in the lower school at Smyrna, which city he was later to adopt as his home town. The extensive quotations from classical historians, playwrights, poets and bio- graphers – often from memory apparently – attest the range of his study and the quality of his mind. Then he studied rhetoric in Smyrna and finally in Athens, under Herodes Atticus, the leading rhetorician of his day.[40] After an extended journey in Egypt, he determined to go to Rome, presumably to establish himself as a rhetorician. En route he was taken ill, and continued to suffer much at the hands of the doctors in Rome. Unable to give public declamations in Rome, and harassed by sickness, he returned to Smyrna. His petitions to Sarapis were in vain. But in 144 he turned to Asclepius at the Warm Springs near Smyrna, and the dream- vision that came to him changed his entire life.[41]

The following summer he took up residence in Pergamum, where he was an incubant at the Asclepion. Significantly for our purposes, the shrine to the god had been elaborately rebuilt in the

Antonine period, replacing a structure that dated back to the mid-fourth century BCE. Adjacent to the impressive temple of Zeus-Asclepius was a huge rotunda, about 60 metres in diameter, with pipes, channels and a connection with the sacred well, all for the purpose of medicinal bathing.[42] As at Epidaurus, there is no evidence of medical equipment in the ruins at Pergamum.[43] Nor was there a dormitory: the incubants slept in the temple itself, but lived in accommodation nearby in the city.[44] Let us turn to the details of the healings and of the life world linked with them in the experience of Aelius Aristides, as evidenced in his writings.

Healings and life-world

C. A. Behr differentiates three types of healings in the Asclepius tradition: (1) the surgical type, where miraculous cures are effected overnight or over a brief period; (2) the dream prescriptions, which Behr characterizes as totally irrational, but in conformity with the praxis of the time; (3) regimens, which are rational and also in keeping with medical practice of the period. Behr eliminates Type 1 from the discussion 'as not germane to Aristides', and states further that the testimony to this type in the tablets at Epidaurus is the result of the 'fraudulent desire of that temple's priesthood to magnify the power of their god'. What Behr has ignored here is the significant shift in life-world from Hellenistic times in Epidaurus to the sophisticated ambience of Smyrna and Pergamum in the Antonine period. Modes of cure of the dream prescription type include the following: baths in rivers, wells and the ocean, as well as abstinence from warm baths and from strenuous and unreasonable exercise in summer or winter. Cures of the so-called rational types involve enemas, vomiting, internal and external drugs, foods and fasts, change of climate, blood-letting.[45] Within the upper strata of Pergamene society Aristides participated in what Behr has characterized as a 'small, cultivated circle comparable to that of the European sanatoria in modern times. They lived in harmony, devoted to the exercise of their literary and intellectual interests, the discussion of their ailments, and the interpretation of their dreams.'[46]

But from the *Sacred Tales* in which Aristides recorded his dreams and thoughts as well as his ailments and their alleviation, much more of his world-view becomes apparent to the inquiring reader. Most important is the heavily documented claim that Aristides found the meaning of his life and the ability to fulfil his destiny through the god. Because of his illness he had abandoned the study and the practice of rhetoric, but the god commanded him not to do so. He was told that he was qualified to 'converse with Socrates, Demosthenes and Thucydides'. Indeed, in a dream he was informed by a philosopher that he surpassed Demosthenes in dignity, so that not even the philosophers, though they were traditional enemies of the sophists, scorned him (4.16–20). Following these dream communications, Aristides resumed practising rhetoric and was commended by his hearers for his skill. In spite of his ailments, he was given the strength to prepare for a rhetorical contest, and was shown in dreams 'many things which excelled in purity of style and were gloriously beyond' the models according to which he had been trained by the finest rhetoricians. He is 'too modest' to repeat what other great orators had to say about his excellence (4.22–27). After describing his struggles to master techniques which did not come naturally to him, such as *ex tempore* speaking and learning his speeches word-for-word, he declares that Asclepius had greater plans for him than salvation alone: 'Therefore he saved me by means worth more than the act of being saved' (4.29f.). Under inspiration of the god, he wrote a lyric poem – an art-form he had not attempted before. Later he wrote songs and lyric verse, many of which he recalled by memory from his dreams (4.38–41). Thus the achievements of his career under the aegis of the god include his being linked with Sophocles and Aeschylus (4.59–61), and with Plato (5.57–67). It would be wrong for him to recount only his bodily cures and to keep silence about the strengthening of his soul and the 'glory' of his rhetorical career (5.36f.). He thinks that he is free from pride of achievement, 'but the continual activity of the god is marvellous, as for example the matter of that great rhetorical display' in Smyrna when the crowd sat through dull preliminaries, listened with rapt attention to his long speech, and then demanded a second discourse (5.38–41). His admirers were the more astounded when he told them that Asclepius had specifically prepared him for this rhetorical display, including the advice to strengthen himself beforehand by eating.

It is apparent that no less impressive than the superior quality of rhetorical skills granted him by the god was the dimension of his self-esteem. The emperors, Marcus Aurelius and Verus, who heaped unequalled honours on Aristides – 'in all their marvellous and unsurpassable activities – counted themselves fortunate to have known such a man (1.46). Even the gods acclaimed him, as he saw in the vision which portrayed him as honoured in the temple of Olympian Zeus, crowned with gold, and hailed as 'invincible in rhetoric'. A monument he found in the temple of Asclepius portrayed him and Alexander the Great as receiving equal honours, since both achieved the pinnacle of their respective careers (4.48f.).

In addition to his mastery of rhetoric as a gift of the god, Aristides was also aware of his influence on the forces of nature. Of the reports about his divinely-bestowed insights preserving him from disaster at sea, the most detailed is the incident in which he refused to sail from Delos because he foresaw an impending storm. When it struck with such severity that the crew and passengers knew they would have been lost, they hailed Aristides as *Euergetēs* and *Sōtēr* (4.32–37). Supernatural phenomena appear at points in Aristides's career in order to confirm the divine purpose at work in his career. Thus, for example, when he was sacrificing an ox to Zeus following a severe earthquake, a shining star darted through the agora to sanction the offering. He was advised to sacrifice at the temple of Olympian Zeus, whereupon he learned that his ancestral estate had escaped destruction (3.38–40).

Although Asclepius had become the central focus of his life, the god did not have exclusive claim on his devotion, nor did the other gods ignore Aristides. In despair at the death of Zosimus, one of the servants who had reared him with loving care, Aristides had an epiphany of Sarapis and one of Isis, who not only comforted him but also became the divine replacements for the mentor-companions who had died (3.45–49).[47] This same pair of divinities appeared to him again when he was engaged in a series of successful legal efforts ('there was more the air of a rhetorical display than of a lawsuit') to be granted immunity from public office in order to pursue his career as a rhetorican (4.94ff.). His journeys included calls at temples of Zeus and Apollo, as well as the shrines of Asclepius and his favourite Egyptian pair of divinities. Even elements of imitative magic appear in the *Sacred Tales*, as when Aristides was ordered by the god to smear himself with mud at the time of the vernal equinox. A magical feature is also reported in the Stele of Apellas: as dedicatory incense was being offered, a flame shot out and singed his hand so that it had blisters, which healed shortly.[48] In the overwhelming majority of cases, however, action is by the direct will of the god.

The concept of vicarious sacrifice is apparent in two different forms in the Asclepius cult. Aristides was informed in a vision a year after his return from Rome to Pergamum that he had only two days to live. His instructions included sacrifices to be offered in a trench outside the city, coins to be thrown away on the bank of a river, and a full complement of sacrifices to be presented in the Asclepion and shared with his fellow pilgrims. Finally, he was to cut off some part of his body, though the god relented, permitting him to dedicate a ring instead. If this were done, he would be saved (2.26–28). The acts of burial, of discarding the old, of shedding one's identity are clearly a ritual of transfer and renewal.

The other dimension of vicarious sacrifice is explicit in the touching incident in which Aristides, after hearing of the serious illness of a daughter of one of his servant-mentors, dreams that he had immolated a sacrificial animal, and on inspecting it, saw that it was called 'Deliverer'. Neither he nor the seers whom he consulted understood the import of this, but he learned from the girl's father following her death that inscriptions on her entrails had signified that Aristides was to be divinely preserved. From this he concluded that her soul and body had been given for him (2.19–24), just as he came to understand his brother's death as vicarious in his behalf (2.25).

In the first of his *Sacred Tales* Aristides tells how the god revealed himself to him by direct presence as well as by dreams, and how he submitted to Asclepius as to a doctor, ready to do in silence all that was commanded (1.2–4). These moments of divine communion were experienced by Aristides as mystic transport, as 'inexplicable high spirits', when the power and providence of the god were disclosed (2.23f., 55). He compares his ecstasy with initiation into a mystery, 'since the rituals were so strange and divine', but there was 'something marvellous and unaccustomed', which filled him at once with cheerfulness and joy but also with anguish and fear, lest his former woes return (4.6f.). Perhaps the high point of the mystic transport came after Aristides had received visions of his public crowning before the temple of Olympian Zeus and his identification with Alexander the Great (mentioned above) when he entered the temple of Asclepius, apparently the one adjacent to his boyhood home (4.48f.). With the other assembled worshippers he hymned the praise of the god, who at the conclusion of the liturgy signalled for the devotees to disperse – except for a private indication to Aristides that he was to remain. In gratitude for the special honour, Aristides acclaimed the oneness of god, only to have the compliment turned back on him: he is 'the one'. For Aristides, that honour was the greatest thing to occur in his life, '. . . greater than human life, every disease was less than this, every grace was less than this. This made me willing and able to live' (4.51). As a consequence of this experience his mind was transformed to make it 'associate with the god' and therefore be 'superior to man's estate', just as he received a new name, Theodorus. The final stage of the mystic vision came when he was permitted to see what Plato called the Soul of the Universe: gazing into heaven he saw established there Asclepius of Pergamum (4.56).

Far more was at stake for Aristides in the Asclepius cult than the healing of his ailments, numerous and chronic as they were. The rhetor's career and his capacity to fulfil it were the gift of the god. His personal identity, his sense of destiny, his hope for a link with transcendent reality, his ability to cope with elation and depression, with personal success and deeply-felt bereavement – all flowed from his relationship with the god in whose purpose and being he shared. That link with the divine provided Aristides with direct knowledge of the gods themselves which came to him in spite of his illnesses. Divine communication rested on divine initiative rather than on human art or achievement, since it is the gods' concern for human beings that leads them to disclose themselves and their purposes to humankind through dreams and visions. What is important for the aims of our investigation is that he did not regard his experience in any way unique:

> Through their [*sc.* the gods'] aid, contrary to the likelihood of the circumstances, I am alive, having escaped at different times through various kinds of consolation and advice on the part of the god from things which no doctor knew what to call, to say nothing of cure, nor had seen befall the nature of man. There are many others like me who can bear witness to these tales, not only Greeks but barbarians, both the flocks of those who dwell at times in the temple of Asclepius and all who attend upon the god of Egypt. Yet no one of us, I think, has any share of art (*technē*) in regard to these matters, but the scorn of art is, one might almost say, the beginning of taking refuge with the gods. Still, to speak by their grace, neither do the gods dishonour our judgment (*logismon*) such as it is, nor have many of those who have preferred fortune (*tychē*) from the god to art repented. But we employ dreams, not knowing in advance of the evening, surely, what we are going to see, and we know what we must do to be saved (*sōthēnai*), although we are in ignorance up to that minute in which the benefit has come from the gods.[49]

The extended quotation is necessary to show that the healings are only the most obvious facets of the more complex benefits received from the saviour-god. What is at stake is not merely health, but life-orientation, communion with the god, destiny (*tychē*) itself.

The inscriptions from the Pergamene Asclepion confirm to an astonishing degree the picture of the shrine and the life that surrounded it that is to be derived from Aristides. They show, for example, that the heyday of Asclepius in this city began at the end of the first century of our era and reached its zenith in the age of the Antonines. This period of ascendancy was characterized by a surge of syncretism, according to which Asclepius both eclipsed the Olympian deities and was closely associated with them, especially Zeus, Athena and Dionysus.[50] It was then that the god and his shrine were honoured by the emperors, particularly Trajan, Hadrian and Antoninus Pius, and by their associates and admirers in the imperial establishment, as the inscriptions placed by order of senators and members of the equestrian order attest.[51]

Concurrently there was a movement among intellectuals and wealthy sophisticates whose personal devotion to the god led them to erect tablets or to adorn the shrine in his honour.[52] Although the importance of dreams[53] and incubation[54] is evident, completely missing are narratives of miraculous healings, such as were typical of the Epidaurus tablets. Only once is there a detail of healing technique,[55] and only occasionally are there indications of the ailments of those who sought Asclepius's benefactions.[56] The donors of the dedicatory inscriptions included sophists and philosophers,[57] just we should expect from Aristides's sketch of a second-century Baden-Baden, a health resort for the rich and influential.

The medical profession

Since Asclepius was linked with both miraculous healing and with the practice of medicine, how are we to understand Aristides's attitude towards the medical profession? Modern exploration of this issue has led scholars to attribute to devotees of Asclepius psychological or medical insights which anticipate modern developments along those lines. Kerényi portrays Asclepius as symbolically midway between Apollo and Chiron, between the uranic and the chthonic, suffering an eternal wound and yet precursor of 'the luminous divine physician'. He concludes

> To be at home in the darkness of suffering and there to find germs of light and recovery with which, as though by enchantment, to bring forth Asclepius, the sunlike healer – this is as contradictory as Chiron, and yet it is no less a part of the gift of medicine than the tapping of Paieon's salutary sources of light.[58]

There is no disputing, of course, the interconnections between psychological and physiological factors, however one perceives the causal connections. But it is scarcely likely that, either in the Hellenistic or the Antonine periods, those who experienced healing would have viewed themselves in the symbolic categories of depth psychology, however serviceable that approach to human experience may be for modern scholars seeking to embrace these ancient stories of Asclepius and his benefactions.

Historians of religion have sought to provide rational explanations for the healings. Typical is the proposal of H. Idris Bell 'that priests, qualified doubtless by a medical training and disguised as the god, tended the sick and even performed successful operations while the patient, under the influence of strong religious belief and probably of narcotics administered by the priests, was in a state of trance.'[59] The most elaborate and sensitive attempt to account rationally for the healings, especially of Asclepius, is that of R. Herzog. Although he recognizes that in the Asclepius cult, therapy does not take place through the skill of a mortal physician, but through the divine healer,[60] he goes on to attempt 'by philological and historical methods with insights from modern medicine to approach the real state of affairs of the *hiamata*'. This he undertakes in spite of the acknowledged limitation that the original witnesses 'can neither be determined nor interrogated'.[61] Expressing the hope that no one will accuse him of either apologetics or Enlightenment-type rationalism, he proceeds to trace the mixture of medical technique and power of suggestion by which we are to understand 'what actually occurred' in the healings attributed to the gods. Herzog is probably correct that, although Aristides's medical contemporary, Galen, shares the Hippocratic view ('Give nature a chance and most diseases will cure themselves'),[62] he also recognized that healing could be effected through dreams and visions and shared Aristides's view that divine prescription supersedes that of the physician.[63] Galen did not find this incompatible with clinical observation and prognosis based on recognition of the typical ways in which the human organism functions.

Aristides's own position, however, is crystal clear. On several occasions when the doctors heard Asclepius's prescription to treat an ailment, they immediately abandoned their own plans and bowed to the wishes of the god (e.g. 1.57, 62). At other times, the physicians acknowledged their inability to prescribe for Aristides's illness (2.5, 69). When our rhetor decided to follow the doctor's advice, the god cured him forthwith in his own way (3.8–13). On at least one occasion, the counsel of the doctor was patently useless (3.16–20), while on another the divine instructions and those of the physicians exactly coincided (5.49–55). There is not a single reference to a physician in the preserved inscriptions from Pergamum. We may conclude, therefore, that while Asclepius was firmly established as the divine patron of the medical school at Cos – from which we hear nothing of miraculous healings – at Pergamum there was an uneasy alliance between the god and the medical practitioners. Yet, in a test, the god always won. In a contest between epiphanic thaumaturgy and rational medicine (as it was then understood), revelation always triumphed over reason.

Conclusion

The Asclepius cult, therefore, underwent far more than a mere geographical shift when it journeyed from Epidaurus to Asia Minor. And the change from Hellenistic culture to the Antonine life-world is readily apparent in the transformation of the cult that occurred in these three to four centuries. At Epidaurus men and women went to the Hellenistic equivalent of an out-patient clinic, seeking speedy relief from ailments, or remedies for problems. At Pergamum, on the other hand, the shrine of Asclepius in the period of the Antonines had become an all-purpose sanatorium. Their wounded psyches were comforted and caressed. Bodily ailments were alleviated, and occasionally cured. Intellectuals stimulated and encouraged one another. Above all, the vulnerable found in the company of Asclepius a safe retreat from the slings and arrows of a fortune, which if not outrageous, was at least profoundly disconcerting.

8

Changing Dionysiac Identities

ALBERT HENRICHS

Like other deities of exuberant life Dionysus could have a special relation with the underworld. As is clear from the *Bacchae* of Euripides, however, this relationship was not always prominent and might not provide the principal reason for adherence to his cult. In their later, more hierarchical form, Dionysiac initiations had the advantage of giving not only possibly a new status to the individual, as did initiation at Eleusis or Samothrace, but also admission to a society of like-minded persons who used common symbols and met for common purposes. These societies, furthermore, with their grades and titles, were not bound to a single place or season, but could function anywhere. Dionysiac associations spread to every part of the Hellenistic world and continued with unabated popularity afterwards in the Imperial period. Dionysus was a god capable of many interpretations and forms of worship, with a mythology that included salvational epiphanies in this world as well as a hope for the afterlife. For these reasons he excited more widespread ceremonial devotion than any other Greek divinity.[1]

The preceding quotation from a recent survey of Hellenistic soteriological religions illustrates the high suitability of the cult of Dionysus for a comparative study of Judaeo-Christian versus pagan self-definition and religious identity. The following three qualities in particular make Dionysus and his worship ideal pagan candidates for such comparison. First, Dionysus appealed to fundamental human interests which were shared by men and women alike; secondly, his cult had a very long history which produced an abundant documentation in Greek and Roman literature, art, and cult inscriptions from the late Bronze Age well into late antiquity; lastly, at all periods of its recorded history, the cult of Dionysus attracted large numbers of followers who were extremely well organized locally or regionally and who shared universal symbols which gave verbal and visual expression to their faith.

Students of Dionysus and his cult cannot complain about any lack of evidence. The sheer quantity of the extant documentation, and its distribution over almost two millennia, over widely different geographical areas and over a variety of media, are equally overwhelming. If one wants to illustrate consistent trends or new departures in the ancient conception and worship of Dionysus, it is necessary to avoid vague generalizations as well as mere accumulation of data, and to aim for a reasonable balance, which is difficult to achieve. The question of how worshippers of Dionysus identified with the god, with their religion and with one another has been raised implicitly in the extensive literature on Dionysus. In particular, the different roles of the sexes in the cult of Dionysus have often received the attention which they deserve, most recently from the feminist point of view.[2] But no full and systematic answer to this question has been attempted, and to give one now would require a whole book. For our present purposes, I suggest that we focus our attention on four principal factors which contributed to the emergence and articulation of different identities in Dionysiac religion: natural differences, such as sex and age, among his worshippers; regional varieties of Dionysiac cult and attested connections between them; the role of language and art in fostering Dionysiac identities; and finally, the various ways in which men and women who worshipped Dionysus emulated and achieved ultimate identification with the god and his multiple divine identities.

I   Sex roles and age groups

Greek society was male-oriented and patriarchal. Men were active in politics, agriculture and warfare, while women of citizen status were confined to the house and their domestic chores.[3] The different roles of the sexes were a key factor in the early establishment and historical evolution of Greek cult.[4] The Greek emphasis on sexual differentiation in cultic matters was a corollary of the predominantly anthropomorphic conception which the Greeks of the archaic period had formed of their gods and which distinguished Greek religion from Egyptian animal-cult or from the aniconic worship of the Jewish god.[5] In sharp contrast to the universal saviour-gods of the Hellenistic period, especially Asclepius and the Hellenized pair of Isis and Sarapis, who did not discriminate between the two sexes, religious allegiance to male or female members of the traditional Olympian pantheon was

138

often predetermined by the sex of their worshippers. Gods who embodied masculine traits or occupations, such as Apollo or Hephaestus, attracted male followers. With few exceptions (e.g. the Eleusinian mysteries), only females (girls, married women, or both) were admitted to the inner circle of participants in local rites for such feminine deities as 'the two goddesses' (Demeter and Kore), Athena, Artemis or Hera.

Whereas the other Olympians were portrayed as exclusively male or female, Dionysus embodied characteristics of both sexes and attracted men and women alike, but for different reasons which reflect different aspects of the god's identity and of the human condition. In the Greek view, the realm of Dionysus comprised three separate provinces, wine, maenadism, and after-life, each of which had its own distinct population. Ritual wine-drinking in the name of Dionysus was the privilege of Greek males, whereas ritual maenadism was practised exclusively by women. Although sexual differentiation was rigidly observed in these two areas of Dionysiac cult, it was ignored or abandoned whenever more universal qualities of Dionysus himself, or more general concerns of his human followers, were emphasized. Specifically, public festivals in honour of the god's annual epiphanies required active participation of the whole citizen body regardless of sex. For similar reasons, identical hopes for a happy afterlife under the protection of Dionysus were entertained by both sexes.

This close correlation between different cultic manifestations of Dionysus on the one hand and different sexual identities of his worshippers on the other hand constitutes one of the most conspicuous and consistent features of Dionysiac religion. Occasional departures from this norm are attested, characteristically in literary rather than epigraphical sources. Male maenads, for instance, occur on the Euripidean stage as a striking illustration of the perversion of genuine maenadism.[6] Bibulous old women – an abomination in Greek eyes – who drank themselves to death are commemorated in Hellenistic funerary epigrams in connection with Dionysus as Bakchos, whose name stands metonymically for wine.[7] In both cases, the exceptions are artificial and provocative, and confirm the validity of the traditional distinctions, which require closer study.

1. Wine

Throughout antiquity, Dionysus was first and foremost the god of wine.[8] The grapevine was his sacred plant.[9] The vine (*ampelos*), its fruit (*botrys*), the fermented drink made from it (*oinos*) and the various vessels from which the wine was poured or drunk (especially the *kantharos*) were the most ubiquitous visual symbols of his cult. In his Hellenistic role as culture hero, Dionysus ranked as 'inventor of wine' and bringer of civilization through viticulture.[10] Bread and wine, the two staple foods of the Mediterranean diet, were considered the respective 'gifts' of Demeter and Dionysus.[11] In principle, the gift of Dionysus was destined for 'mortals' in general.[12] In actual practice, however, men alone were the true beneficiaries of the wine: Greek and Roman women were discouraged from drinking wine, and penalized if they did.[13] In Greek poetry of the archaic and classical period, wine-drinking and intoxication are invariably introduced to establish male identities. Dionysus as wine god inspired Archilochus to write dithyrambs,[14] encouraged sexual activity in men,[15] and induced drunken illusions of sudden wealth at stag parties (*symposia*);[16] in times of war, wine epitomized the blessings of peace in the minds of weary warriors;[17] in general, Dionysus as wine helped Greek males, both freemen and slaves, to escape the harsh realities of their lives,[18] while the symposium served as a social catalyst for men of the upper class and for their political ambitions.

Apart from the drinking of wine, its cultivation too was primarily associated with the male sex. In vintage scenes on Attic vases (c. 540 to 430 BCE), satyrs who gather and process the grapes conspicuously outnumber the occasional maenads who are assigned either auxiliary or amorous roles.[19] In later Graeco-Roman art, the vintagers are represented by male figures from the real or mythical world – peasants, satyrs, Erotes or small boys (*putti*).[20] Vintage scenes in ancient art are a mirror of real life. The laborious task of collecting and treading the grapes required strength and stamina, and was naturally left to men.[21] Greek and Roman manuals on viticulture are addressed to a male readership, and Propertius vows to plant vines and tread grapes if Dionysus frees him from his lovesickness through wine.[22] In his bucolic description of the vintage on Lesbos, Longus assigns the active roles of grape-harvesting, wine-making and wine-drinking to men, while the maiden Chloe pours wine and women generally assist the men.[23] Unmarried girls (*parthenoi*), apparently not married women, would occasionally carry baskets of grapes from the vines to the wine-vat.[24] It is safe to conclude that the cultivation of the grapevine required and received male attention, while the consumption of wine reinforced the male ego.

The wine shared the ambiguities of its god.[25] Potentially a dangerous drug (*pharmakon*),[26] wine was normally diluted with water, both for everyday use and on ritual occasions.[27] Getting drunk (*eis methēn pinein*) was not considered proper behaviour, 'except at festivals of the god who gave the wine'.[28] The difference between regular and ritual wine-drinking did not lie solely in the quality (mixed versus unmixed) or quantity of the wine but even more in the mental attitude of the wine-drinker who came to Dionysiac wine festivals with raised expectations. As a reflection of such heightened awareness at Athens and elsewhere, the 'newness' of the wine, as opposed to its regular use and general availability, was emphasized in annual festivals, either through commemoration of the mythical origins of wine-making and wine-drinking,[29] or in connection with various wine-producing miracles which illustrated the supernatural appearance of wine.[30]

Ritual wine-drinking in the cult of Dionysus was a 'social' rather than a 'sacramental' experience.[31] The 'Day of Pitchers' (*Choes*) of the Athenian Anthesteria, a Dionysiac spring festival, featured a wine-drinking contest.[32] Participation was restricted to male Athenians who were three years and older, and to social outsiders such as slaves and female entertainers (*hetairai*);[33] Athenian girls and women are nowhere mentioned in our sources and must have been excluded.[34] Adult Athenians celebrated the *Choes* even abroad and in exile,[35] and participation in them was recorded in the curriculum vitae of Athenian boys as an important event in their lives.[36] These facts suggest that the ritual wine-drinking at the *Choes* reinforced the civic identity of the Athenian male.

In the Hellenistic and Roman period, worshippers of Greek and foreign gods were commonly organized in local cult-associations of private character.[37] The ubiquitous Dionysiac clubs are particularly well documented.[38] Although the consumption of wine at club-meetings, which continued the older Ionian practice of the male symposium, was apparently as common in non-Dionysiac as in Dionysiac cult-associations, organized worshippers of Dionysus elevated social wine-drinking to a ritualized form of religious group experience, thus making it a hallmark of their Dionysiac identity.[39] The Athenian Iobakchoi of the late second century CE were unusually conspicuous for their total devotion to wine-drinking ceremonies and for their fastidious statutes, which regulated every conceivable aspect of the activities of the club's all-male membership.[40] Donations of wine for communal use (called solemnly 'libations', *spondai*) were required of all Iobakchoi as an entrance fee, as regular monthly contributions and as compulsory largesse on joyous occasions in the member's life; in addition, high-ranking club members such as the priest (*hiereus*), chief bakchos (*archibakchos*) and treasurer (*tamias*) had to provide special *spondai* for certain festivals.[41]

Apart from their preoccupation with wine-drinking, the Iobakchoi advertised their relaxed lifestyle through Dionysiac catchwords and visual symbols which were immediately intelligible both to insiders and the outside world.[42] Like other Dionysiac clubs with whom they competed, the Iobakchoi were known as a Bakcheion, named after Bakchos, the most frequent epithet of Dionysus as wine-god.[43] Although their club house was located in the heart of Athens to the west of the Acropolis, the hall for their drinking parties was called *stibas* (lit. a makeshift bed or couch of branches and leaves), an idyllic name which evoked merry associations of country life, outdoor picnics and escape from urban confinement.[44] The statutes of the Iobakchoi are inscribed on a stele decorated with a pediment in bas-relief which displays a drinking cup (*kantharos*) flanked by a pair of panthers and crowned with grapevine and a bull's skull (*bukranion*).[45] The wine-drinking of the Iobakchoi was a civilized affair; 'good order' (*eukosmia*) was rigorously enforced, and members who were noisy or violent were expelled from the *stibas*.[46]

But merrymaking and wine-drinking were not the only ways in which the Iobakchoi honoured Dionysus. One of their priests composed a hymnbook (*theologia*).[47] Occasionally they would even slip out of their everyday identities and escape into the realm of Dionysiac myth by assuming assigned parts in a sacred play whose cast included divinities (Dionysus, Kore and Aphrodite) as well as obscure figures of Dionysiac cult (Palaimon and Proteurythmos).[48] Their spirits elevated by the wine, the Iobakchoi temporarily surrendered their secular personalities and indulged in the oldest form of Dionysiac transformation, that of disguise and impersonation in the service of the god of the mask, from which Attic tragedy and comedy had originated at the same location some seven hundred years earlier.[49] The Dionysiac stage remained on the whole as inaccessible to women as the wine. Theatrical performances and dramatic re-enactment of mythical episodes, whether by amateurs or by professional actors (who were organized in guilds under the patronage of Dionysus[50]), were the privilege of men. Women were offered a Dionysiac experience which was radically different.

2. Ritual Maenadism

While men escaped into the dreamland of Dionysiac intoxication, women sought Dionysus and 'the blessings of madness'[51] outside the secure confines of the Greek polis. Maenads (*mainades*, 'mad women') were female followers of Dionysus who were differentiated from ordinary worshippers by their ceremonial garb, their ritual activities and, if their name is any indication, their exalted state of mind. In short, they were practitioners of ritual maenadism, the most fascinating branch of Dionysiac cult.[52] In the case of maenadism, myth and ritual are even more than usually inseparable: maenadic myth mirrors maenadic ritual, while ritual practice mollifies the mythical model. Unfortunately maenadic myth is infinitely better known than actual maenadic ritual. This discrepancy has been the source of much controversy among modern students of maenadism.[53] Even now the prevailing stereotype of the Greek maenad is almost exclusively determined by maenadic myth. The result is a romantic vision of wild ecstasy and bloodthirsty violence. Seized by Dionysus and oblivious of husbands, looms and all standards of decency, these creatures of poetic imagination don maenadic gear, take to the woods in untold numbers and turn into a destructive mob who at the height of their frenzy climb mountains (*oreibasia*), tear apart animals or even human beings (*sparagmos*), and devour the raw flesh of their victims (*ōmophagia*).[54] Their pent-up frustrations released and their senses recovered, they quietly return to their normal lives, outwardly bloodstained but inwardly blissful.

This exaggerated picture of spontaneous, unmitigated wantonness is incompatible with three principle features of ritual maenadism: its fixed biennial periodicity;[55] its regional character which confined its practice to Boeotia and Delphi, to the Ionian cities of Asia Minor and to some areas of the Peloponnesus;[56] and finally, the organization of maenads in local congregations (*thiasoi*) of limited membership.[57] Unlike the mythical maenads of Euripides's *Bacchae* who are impervious to spears, fire and pain, the maenads of actual cult were creatures of ordinary flesh and blood who suffered from exhaustion,[58] got stuck in snowstorms[59] and were respectable enough to be honoured by their cities after their death.[60] No substantial eyewitness report of ritual maenadism has come down from antiquity, but scattered references add up to a composite picture.[61] Diodorus mentions the biennial periodicity of maenadic rites, the participation of girls and married women, the carrying of the *thyrsos* (*thyrsophorein*), Dionysiac sacrifices (*thysiazein*), and the performance of ecstatic Bacchic rites in general (*bakcheuein*).[62] Plutarch and Pausanias add important details about a local group of maenads, the Delphic Thyiads.[63] The epigraphical evidence confirms that ritual maenadism existed in the Hellenistic period; that the maenads conducted initiations (*teletai*), went 'to the mountain' (*eis oros*), handled sacred implements and were organized in *thiasoi* under the leadership of a chief maenad; and that the decline of ritual maenadism began in the second century CE.[64] On the delicate subject of maenadic diet, an inscription from Miletus (276/5 BCE) suggests that pieces of raw meat (*ōmophagion*), presumably cut from regular sacrificial victims, were handled rather than eaten by Hellenistic maenads.[65] If so, their 'omophagy' was hardly more than a token tribute to the ritualistic savagery of maenadic myth. In Attica too the close ritual alliance between Dionysus and his women worshippers was reflected in public sacrifice. The sacrificial calendar of the deme of Erchia from the fourth century BCE records separate goat sacrifices to Semele and Dionysus on the 16th of Elaphebolion (the time of the City Dionysia). Once ritually killed by the priestess (of Semele and/or Dionysus), the goats were to be 'handed over to the women' (*aix gynaixi paradosimos*), the meat had to be consumed there and then (*ou phora*), and the priestess was to receive the skin.[66] It is unlikely, though, that this is a case of ritual maenadism. Although a women's cult of Dionysus existed in late fifth-century Athens (Aristoph. *Lys.* 1), ritual maenadism proper was apparently not practised in Attica: Athenian women went to Delphi to celebrate maenadic rites on Mount Parnassus.

But the epigraphical evidence offers no information on such important matters as maenadic dress,[67] *sparagmos*,[68] or the maenadic state of mind. How 'mad' were the maenads? No immediate answer to this urgent question is available. No ancient maenad tells us how she felt religiously when engaged in her ritual. This is hardly surprising. Greek ritual in general was traditionally action-oriented (*drōmena*), repetitive and stereotyped, externalized and unreflecting, or in other words, a studious re-enactment of an inherited response rather than a personal expression of inner feelings or religious sentiment.[69] These characteristics of Greek ritual explain why the physiological and psychological condition of maenads in ritual action remains unknown. The true nature of their 'telestic madness'[70] is therefore a matter of speculation. Ancient and modern authorities agree that intoxication with wine was not the source of maenadic madness (*mania*),[71] even though mythical maenads often hold drinking vessels or miraculously produce streams of milk, honey and wine. But even the maenads of myth, while distributing the undiluted gift of Dionysus, do not drink from it themselves. Their close association with the wine in its raw state is a trait which they share with Dionysus himself, the divine embodiment of life-sustaining saps and liquids. In structural terms, raw meat and undiluted wine reflect the abnormality, otherness or 'liminality' of the extreme Dionysiac experience,[72] which was given conceptual rather than ritual expression.

The enigmatic state of mind of the maenads has been explained in various ways by modern scholars, and with interdisciplinary recourse to comparative anthropology, cross-cultural and clinical psychology, Freudian psychoanalysis, and social anthropology.[73] Depending on one's theoretical model or point of comparison, Greek maenadism has been variously diagnosed as religious group possession or hysteria which involved control by a spirit and 'dissociation' from one's normal self;[74] as a 'ritual outlet' for 'infectious irrational impulses', especially 'the impulse to reject responsibility';[75] and more specifically, as a form of social protest by an oppressed group,[76] a Greek case of 'Frauenaufstand'[77] or temporary reversal of 'sociobiological roles'.[78] In concrete terms, maenadic mountain-dancing has been compared to epidemic outbreaks of 'dancing madness' in the late Middle Ages in Western Europe;[79] confirmation for typical body movements of mythical maenads, for instance their tossed-back head, as authentic symptoms of possession has been found in anthropological descriptions of ecstatic dancers and in clinical accounts of hysteria;[80] the snake-handling of the maenads, which was a genuine feature of Macedonian maenadism, has invited comparison with the rattlesnake ritual of Christian sects in southern states of the USA;[81] and in the most amazing demonstration of blind comparatist faith, a whole generation of scholars has interpreted maenadic omophagy in light of a bloody ritual practised by Muslim sectarians in Morocco and Tangier.[82]

Against exaggerated trends to ascribe to the maenads attitudes which are alien to Greek religion, it must be emphasized that Greek maenadism with its ritual limitations of time, place and membership was not the result of psychic illness or a cure for mental problems; that it was not an infectious mass seizure which 'spread like wildfire';[83] and that the role of Dionysus in connection with maenadism is not comparable to the relationship of a modern gynaecologist to his patients.[84] Even the possibility that maenadism was a periodic and socially sanctioned rebellion against 'a male-dominated society'[85] is rather remote, if only because the percentage of women involved in maenadic rites was apparently never high enough to have an impact on representative segments of the female population. The conflict between modern psychological explanations and the known characteristics of Greek religion and mentality forced E. R. Dodds, the pioneer of the modern theory of maenadism, to posit a development from originally 'spontaneous attacks of mass hysteria' to the 'harmless outlet' of the organized maenadic rites in alternate years.[86] But 'historical' interpretations of Dionysiac myth are highly problematic, and have been largely abandoned in the case of the so-called resistance myths which illustrate public opposition to Dionysiac religion.[87] Theories of religious origins, however fascinating, are poor substitutes for documented religious history.[88] Whether we like it or not, we must accept the basic dichotomy of maenadism into a mythical and a ritual realization as an irreducible datum of Greek religion as we now know it. In the case of maenadism, myth proved to be stronger than ritual, and the mythical maenad who is violently 'mad' made a more lasting impression on the ancient and modern mind than her cultic replica.

It cannot be demonstrated that 'madness' understood as an abnormal psychological state was an authentic quality of the historical maenad, despite her name. 'Maenad' (*mainas*) was essentially a poetic word[89] which has decidedly reprehensive connotations even in the *Bacchae* of Euripides.[90] The maenads of actual cult are usually called *Bakchai*.[91] The few cases in which they are called 'maenads' are due to imitation of poetic diction[92] or to an archaizing tendency.[93] Pausanias makes it clear that the Delphic Thyiads ('women who are in a ritual hurry') 'are mad' (*mainontai*) in the service of Dionysus because they practise mountain-dancing on Mount Parnassus;[94] in other words, his explanation of maenadic 'madness' is ritualistic, not psychological. By all indications, the peculiar religious identity of the maenads had more to do with sweat and physical exhaustion than with an abnormal state of mind. To exhaust oneself for Dionysus became a 'sweet toil',[95] a source of exhilaration and relief. Once that elation had been achieved by ritual means, the maenads came down from their mountain, resumed their normal lives, and waited for the return of the ritual two years later.

3. Sexual Union

'Le ménadisme est chose féminine'.[96] Male maenads in the ritual sense did not exist, although they were played by men on the Attic stage.[97] Even the alleged male leaders of maenadic *thiasoi* are a modern fiction.[98] But beginning in the fifth century BCE at the latest, men too 'went mad' (*mainesthai* used in combination with *bakcheuein*) for Dionysus and enrolled in private congregations which admitted both sexes, met in secret, and required initiation ceremonies (*teletai*).[99] These sexually unrestricted Dionysiac groups with esoteric pretensions mushroomed during the Hellenistic period and provided the model for the ubiquitous Dionysiac mystery cults of the imperial era.[100] In Euripides' *Bacchae*, the non-maenadic, esoteric and private cult of Dionysus coexists with maenadism.[101] In actual Hellenistic cult, too, the ritual distinction between maenadism proper and less restricted forms of Dionysiac worship became occasionally blurred. In Miletus, for instance, initiations and fees were obligatory for all-female *thiasoi*;[102] in nearby Magnesia, professional maenads led non-maenadic *thiasoi* which included men.[103] In the late Hellenistic and the imperial period, members of Dionysiac associations were usually recruited from both sexes. The Delphic Thyiads and Athenian Iobakchoi, the most notable exceptions, are anachronistic survivals from the old times.

As the two sexes came into closer contact on Dionysiac occasions, sexual activity under a religious pretext became a controversial issue rather than a regular cultic institution. The issue of illegitimate sex in Dionysiac circles is raised by Euripides, and was reportedly a major factor in the Roman Bacchanalia scandal of 186 BCE.[104] In both cases, the allegations reflect understandable suspicions of public officials opposed to the cult of Dionysus, and belong to a well-known type of propaganda against cults that were new, foreign or otherwise socially unacceptable. In reality, however, there is no evidence for large-scale sexual promiscuity in Dionysiac cults. Sexual acts in the cult of Dionysus were apparently more symbolic and mythical than real, perhaps nothing more than an ongoing attempt to incorporate the natural conditions of human reproduction ritually and visually in the religious realm of Dionysus, the divine archetype of 'indestructible life'.[105] In Athens, the wife of the king-archon was sexually united with Dionysus each spring at the Anthesteria;[106] phallic obscenity, though rampant in connection with Dionysiac festivals, is naturally confined to the male sex;[107] in late classical art, Dionysus and Ariadne begin to appear as the divine prototype of the human couple;[108] in late Hellenistic art, scenes of Dionysiac initiations show young women in awed contemplation of a phallus exposed in a winnowing basket (*liknon*).[109] Maenads undress in Hellenistic art as early as the fourth century BCE, and become half-nude and sensuous; but unlike some of their older counterparts on archaic and classical vases, they are not shown mating with satyrs or men.[110] On the whole, Dionysiac religion emphasized human sexuality through allusive concealment or crude exposure of the male organ and the female body (but not the female genitalia), thus reversing the normal conventions of decency. Sex as such was the special province of Aphrodite; but like Demeter, Aphrodite too is occasionally found in cultic association with Dionysus.[111] Dionysus (wine) and Aphrodite (sex) are often paired in Greek and Latin literature,[112] and their combined pleasures found visual expression on numerous Roman sarcophagi which projected hopes for an afterlife in eternal Dionysiac bliss.[113]

The major public festivals of Dionysus such as the Anthesteria and rural Dionysia, which were still observed in the imperial period,[114] brought together men, women and children ('the whole city', *pasa polis*[115]) in joint celebration of Dionysus as the god of the spring growth and the grape harvest. On such occasions, religious sentiment was concentrated on the annual epiphany of the god and on his gifts,[116] while Dionysiac ostentation took shape in processions and parades which were led by local priests and priestesses of Dionysus[117] and which displayed his colours and symbols.[118] As a figure of public cult, Dionysus thus became a source of new strength, and his festivals a ritual mechanism of periodic revitalization, for Greek cities and their inhabitants, especially in Attica, Boeotia and Ionia.[119]

4. Age Groups

Dionysus has been described as 'a democratic god' who imposed no limit of age or status and who invited worship by young and old, freemen and slaves alike.[120] Dionysiac inscriptions confirm for the imperial period that Roman citizens, freedmen and slaves were often members of the same Dionysiac mystery cults which were invariably of local and private character.[121] The inscriptions tell us next to nothing about the age of the worshippers of Dionysus.[122] But literary evidence, though scant, suggests that each age group served Dionysus in its own way. Attainment of puberty in particular was a decisive line of demarcation for religious purposes, because Greek religion was inseparable from the larger social fabric.[123] Euripides in the *Bacchae* differentiates between maenads who are married and those who are young and unmarried (*parthenoi*).[124] Diodorus confirms that the two age-groups had distinct ritual identities and that the married women could actually celebrate full Bacchic rites (*bakcheuein*) whereas the unmarried girls played subordinate roles as thyrsos-bearers (*thyr-sophorein*) rather than full-fledged *bakchai*.[125] Again, Dionysiac religion, at least for the Hellenistic period, reflects and reinforces social structures based on biological differentiation.

'Truly, I say to you, unless you undergo a change and become like children (*paidia*), you will not enter the kingdom of heaven' (Matt. 18.3). For a variety of religious and cultural reasons, children, or more precisely, small boys (*paides*), were admitted into mystery cults of Dionysus, and add a striking perspective to the complex picture of post-classical Dionysiac religion.[126] The Greeks of the late classical and the Hellenistic period were particularly fond of children, who are conspicuous in their art and literature.[127] Scenes from the world of Attic children grace the miniature cups (*choes*) used by young boys at the drinking contest of the Anthesteria.[128] The romantic story of Dionysus's own childhood, which was set in an exotic ambience, became a favourite subject of Dionysiac mythology and art.[129] Dionysus *Pais*, the infant god who exudes charm, innocence and divine power at the same time, is shown while being nursed by nymphs or riding a feline on numerous mosaics.[130] Swarms of winged boys and girls, Erotes and Psychai, populate Bacchic sarcophagi.[131] In this highly imaginative world, myth and reality merge constantly, and Dionysus and his worshippers seem to change identities at will. Children were treated like adult citizens of the Dionysiac paradise, and adults nursed childhood dreams of a careless and innocent existence as eternal members of Dionysus's entourage. While trying to escape from the real world and their own lives, both children and adults wishfully identified themselves with Dionysus in his changing mythical roles.

5. *Individual and Group*

'Group solidarity reinforced by ritual' is instrumental in establishing and preserving civic, cultural and religious identities.[132] Public and private worshippers of Dionysus would have agreed that there was strength and solidarity in numbers. Dionysiac inscriptions sponsored by groups far outnumber dedications to Dionysus by individuals.[133] Dionysus encouraged the 'merging of the individual consciousness in a group consciousness'.[134] The individual personality of the worshippers of Dionysus was either transformed (as in all impersonations and masquerades of the Dionysiac type[135]) or functionally reinterpreted in Dionysiac terms to suit the identity of the group (as in the elaborate hierarchies of Dionysiac associations[136]). But even Dionysus could not fully erase human vanity and personal ambition. Full religious equality was never achieved in his cults. There were always individuals who rose above the Dionysiac rank and file by dint of their spiritual or secular superiority and status: 'many carry the *thyrsos*, but few are *bakchoi*';[137] maenadic *thiasoi* were led by chief maenads;[138] seniority, family ties and social rank determined one's place in the Dionysiac hierarchy;[139] and at the very apex of the Dionysiac ascent stood, unrivalled, the recipient of ruler-cult as a 'New Dionysus' (*Neos Dionysos*).[140]

The sheer size of Dionysiac groups is often impressive. Throngs of satyrs and maenads surround Dionysus on Attic vases. The mythical circle of the god became visual reality in the satyr-choruses of the Attic stage and, on a larger scale, in more ambitious Dionysiac histrionics. In the seventies of the third century BCE, Ptolemy II Philadelphus displayed his Dionysiac aspirations and the Ptolemaic version of a dynastic, mythically inspired ruler-cult by parading a Dionysiac pageant through the stadium at Alexandria.[141] The parade included, apart from countless other groups, 'forty satyrs crowned with gold crowns in ivy pattern'; three different varieties of Macedonian maenads; a gigantic wine-press full of grapes which were trod by sixty satyrs; 'one hundred and twenty crowned satyrs and sileni, some carrying

wine-pitchers, others shallow cups, still others large deep cups –
everything of gold'; Dionysus returning triumphant from India
and seated on an elephant was followed by 'five hundred young
girls dressed in purple tunics with gold girdles' – and so the show
goes on and adds up to a portrayal of the Hellenistic Dionysus,
and of the human ambitions associated with him, that is almost
too superlative even for the god of luxury and plenteousness.

Ptolemy's demonstration of royal splendour and wealth had its
more modest parallels in actual cult. Two membership lists of
Dionysiac associations from the second and third centuries CE
contain, respectively, nearly five hundred and more than fifty
names. Various cult-titles of their members suggest that they
participated in Dionysiac processions carrying thyrsi (*nartheko-
phoros*), phalli (*phallophoros*), 'sacred chests' (*cistae mysticae*) made
of wickerwork (*kistaphoros*), winnowing baskets (*liknaphoros*),
standards (*semeiophoros*), and images of the emperor (*sebastophan-
tes*).[142] Organized worshippers of Dionysus in the imperial period
always acted as groups identified by generic names of religious
(*thiasoi*), political (*systema*) or military (*speira*) origin.[143] In addition
to their generic names, many Dionysiac groups acquired more
specific identities by including the name of their founder or
benefactor, or a particular epithet of Dionysus, in their title.[144]
With few exceptions, 'initiates' (*mystai*) of Dionysus in the second
or third century CE satisfied their Dionysiac ambitions simply by
becoming one of many *boukoloi, bakchoi* or *bassarai* in the *speira* or
thiasos of so-and-so. Membership in a Dionysiac group enhanced
a person's status in the community, gave access to the amenities
of a social club, and encouraged flights of fancy, or occasionally a
true 'mystical' experience, which opened the door to the mythical
world of Dionysus. His cult remained always as congregational
and gregarious as his mythical entourage. Dionysus was the lord
of maenads and satyrs, of *bakchoi* and *bakchai*, and of symposiasts
and actors. But he did not attract loners, individualists or single
souls in search of ultimate truths.

II *Regional differentiation and cult mobility*

The so-called 'religion of Dionysus' is a convenient modern
abstraction, the sum total of the god's numerous facets, symbols
and cults. Dionysus had no central priesthood, no canonical
books, and not even a panhellenic shrine of his own. His cults
were regional and emphasized different aspects of the god. In

ritual terms, a Delphic maenad, an Athenian celebrating the Anthesteria, and a Greek from southern Italy who was an initiate of an Orphico-Dionysiac sect had very little in common, and their separate Dionysiac identities were not interchangeable. The Italian initiate, esoteric and in possession of a sacred text, would not climb a Dionysiac mountain, either in this world or in the nether world; a Theban maenad would not be buried with an Orphic gold plate in her tomb; and unlike the Athenian at the Anthesteria, neither the maenad nor, presumably, the esoteric believer in an exclusive afterlife would drink wine as part of their ritual role. Although Dionysus was ubiquitous in Greek lands and far beyond, different cultic manifestations of his religion tended to be concentrated in different areas. Information about religious contacts between worshippers of Dionysus in different regions is scarce. In most cases, such connections will have existed only between groups and individuals of comparable ritual identity. While cults of Dionysus as wine-god apparently did not travel at all within Greece proper (which may be an indication of their deep-rooted antiquity), even the mobility of maenads was extremely limited. In sharp contrast to the immobility of maenadism and of the wine-oriented cults, the so-called private mysteries of Dionysus, bent on expanding their ranks, moved so rapidly and widely that they became the predominant form of Dionysiac worship in the course of the Hellenistic period.

In Euripides's *Bacchae*, Dionysus is portrayed as an active and itinerant missionary of his own religion. Myths of the god's arrival and global travels as a culture hero were so popular that his mobility and ubiquitous presence must be added to his religious activism as major aspects of the Hellenistic image of Dionysus.[145] Surprisingly then, Dionysus is not a prominent name in the pages of the two standard studies of mobility and conversion in Hellenistic cults.[146] Various explanations for this curious discrepancy come to mind. In the first place, the various myths and aretalogies which characterize Dionysus as a god who makes his powerful appearances here and now are best explained as spontaneous articulations of the religious concept of Dionysus as *deus praesentissimus*,[147] and should not be taken as direct evidence for actual regional propagation of his cult. In addition, we may safely assume that Dionysiac inscriptions do not give an adequate picture of the actual propagation of Dionysiac cults through public and private initiative. And lastly, it must be kept in mind that two major types of Dionysiac religion as practised, maenadism and wine festivals, were locally fixed and difficult to transplant because of their traditional connection with local wine-growing regions and with particular mountains. Despite the relative paucity of authentic records for the mobility of Dionysiac cults, two or three spectacular cases are known and deserve mention.

If the joint maenadism of Attic and Delphic women on Mount Parnassus goes back to the fifth century BCE, as seems more than likely,[148] it would be the earliest known contact between homogeneous Dionysiac groups, and the one with the longest history. A different case of maenads on the move is that of the three professional maenads from Thebes, the metropolis of maenadism, who were dispatched to Magnesia ad Maeandrum between c. 279 and 250 BCE at the suggestion of the Delphic oracle.[149] The differences are instructive: in one case, biennial ritual maenadism practised jointly by women of two cities; in the other, a one-time transfer of thoroughbred maenads overseas who establish Dionysiac *thiasoi* which are non-maenadic and include men among their members.[150] In both cases, mythical centres of maenadism are recognized as strongholds of maenadism as practised.

The maenadic shuttle between Athens and Delphi and the trip of the Theban maenads to Magnesia were quiet exchanges which did not make headlines in antiquity. By contrast, a private cult collided with the political system and the Roman senate was scandalized when in 186 BCE initiations into a Dionysiac mystery cult allegedly turned into orgies involving sex and crime.[151] The Greek roots of the cult are said to have been in Etruria and Campania. Although the senate decree which restricted the rites in all Roman territories was found in Bruttium, several hundred miles south of Rome and Campania, it would be rash to conclude that an orgiastic Bacchic movement swept through southern Italy until it was stopped when it reached Rome. Given the local and private character of Bacchic mysteries in general, it is more likely that the Bacchic cults which Roman authorities tried to eradicate in southern Italy had no direct connection with the Bacchic groups in Etruria or Campania from which the Roman Bacchanalia originated.

Finally, Dionysiac cults of the esoteric and mystery type, propagated through private initiative, occasionally travelled over long distances. Although the evidence for such far-reaching cult transfers is less explicit in the case of Dionysus than it is for the Egyptian gods, the so-called Orphic gold plates and the private *thiasos* of Agrippinilla in particular open fascinating geographical perspectives.

Of the ten 'Orphic' gold plates from the late classical and the Hellenistic period which contain similar directions for the dead upon their arrival in the nether world, two come from Petelia and from Hipponion in Bruttium (now Calabria), southern Italy (where an additional five plates of different content were also found, at the site of Thurioi), two from Thessaly, and six from Eleuthernai on the island of Crete.[152] This is an impressive geographical spread. It shows that esoteric beliefs in a blissful afterlife based on sacred texts which were buried with their owners travelled from southern Italy (whence the oldest specimen originates, from c. 400 BCE) to Thessaly (where copies existed in the second half of the fourth century BCE) and ultimately to Crete (which produced the youngest copies, from perhaps the second century BCE).[153] But these plates and their wide geographical distribution illustrate more than merely the shipment of sacred texts from one end of the Greek world to the other. The gold plates are the only epigraphical documents of Greek religion with a text history that can still be followed and verified.[154] Presumably remembered by heart and transmitted orally by individual specialists in Bacchic and Orphic initiation,[155] these texts circulated within distinct but loosely structured groups commonly identified as 'Orphic'. The Hipponion plate, however, with its reference to 'Bacchic initiates' (*mystai kai bakchoi*) who walk the same 'sacred way' (*hieran hodon*) to their destination in the nether world, has added a new Dionysiac perspective to the enigmatic background and 'Sitz im Leben' of the 'Orphic' tablets by connecting them with private Bacchic (i.e. Dionysiac) mysteries from the end of the classical period which promised temporary liberation on earth and eternal life after death through Dionysiac rites.[156]

The case of Pompeia Agrippinilla, a member of the Roman imperial aristocracy and of Greek extraction, who early in the reign of Marcus Aurelius founded a Greek Dionysiac *thiasos* near Rome, whose members were recorded on stone, is more straightforward.[157] Where exactly did the Greek roots of Agrippinilla's *thiasos* lie? Whereas most scholars traced them back to the island of Lesbos – the home of Agrippinilla's family, a traditional centre of Dionysiac cult since the archaic period, and the location of Longus's Dionysiac novel about Daphnis and Chloe – Nilsson suggested more plausibly that Agrippinilla received her Dionysiac inspirations in the Greek cities of Asia Minor where her husband served as pro-consul c. CE 165.[158] In either case, her *thiasos* remains the most spectacular example of a private Dionysiac cult transplanted from the Greek east to the very heart of the Roman empire.

III Dionysiac self-portrayal through verbal and visual symbols

Whereas sex, age and provenance are natural differences over which worshippers of Dionysus had no control, outward symbols, in particular uniforms and slogans,[159] were largely a matter of personal choice which distinguished Dionysiac groups and their members from the rest of the world. Cutting across sex roles, age groups and geographical areas, some Dionysiac slogans – especially *eu(h)oi (evoe)* and *eis oros* – and numerous symbols – including the vine, grape-cluster and ivy, the *thyrsos*, *tympanon* and *pedum*, the *kratēr* and the *rhyton*, the panther, goat and ass, as well as the phallus and the *liknon* – attained universal currency and remained in use from the archaic or, in some cases, Hellenistic period down to the end of antiquity. Although their interpretation can pose occasional problems in specific contexts, their general importance as reliable indicators of the Dionysiac mood is undisputed.

1. Cult Language

The cult of Dionysus has been called 'a religion without a language'.[160] It is true that visual symbols exceeded cultic slogans both in number and in importance. But whereas Dionysiac art addressed an unlimited public, much of the verbal articulation of Dionysiac beliefs was intended for the insider rather than the world at large, which explains why so little of it survived. Apart from Euripides's *Bacchae*, which is a gold mine of information on Dionysiac cult language but treacherous for anyone unfamiliar with this kind of terrain, and from a few scattered hints in other authors, Greek inscriptions from the Hellenistic and imperial period are our most valuable sources. A full study of Dionysiac *Sakralsprache* in the widest sense, still a desideratum,[161] would have to include, for instance, the titles of the god and of his worshippers, names of cult objects and cultic activities, ritual exclamations, hymns, prayers and other invocations, and 'beatitudes' (*makarismoi*) as well as esoteric texts (*hieroi logoi*[162]), all of which are attested in some form or other. As appropriate illustrations of verbal self-identification, I select two radically different types of Dionysiac slogans, the public rallying-cry and the secret password, for brief comment.

One does not have to be a psychologist, or a Nietzsche or a Rohde, to feel both the physical exertion and the liberating effect usually associated with the repeated utterance of ritual cries in Dionysiac group rites.[163] Of the various Dionysiac cries, the cry of joy, *eu(h)oi* or its variant *eu(h)ai*, is heard more often than any other.[164] Until recently, the earliest attestations of it were all literary, and confined to Attic tragedy and comedy of the second half of the fifth century BCE. In 1968, a bronze mirror of the late sixth century BCE from Olbia revealed an inscription in which *eu(h)ai* occurs twice in juxtaposition with the Dionysiac proper name Lenaios – valuable proof of the antiquity and tenacity of such key words in the Dionysiac vocabulary.[165] The most memorable articulation of maenadic ritual is the exhortation *eis oros* ('to the mountain'), which can be found both in Euripides's *Bacchae* and in two cult inscriptions of much later date.[166] The nature and chronology of these attestations raise a methodological problem. Are all three instances directly derived from the actual practice of maenadism, or (a disturbing possibility) did the maenads of Miletus in the late third century BCE and the members of a Dionysiac club at Physkos in the second century CE describe their pilgrimage to the mountain in terms borrowed from the classical literary treatment of maenadism? I wish I knew the answer.

The 'Orphic' gold plates contain solemn passwords, to be recited before the guardians of the nether world, which identified the deceased as belonging to a special race.[167] Bacchic associations of the esoteric type, which used such gold plates, were secret societies which shut their doors in the face of outsiders, as the Pentheus of the *Bacchae* quickly found out.[168] Their members employed prearranged verbal 'signs' of recognition (called *signa* or *symbola*[169]), apparently a widespread practice which is attested by Plautus[170] around 200 BCE for Rome if not Athens, and by Plutarch for central Greece.[171] But as often, antiquity kept its secret well: no ancient author quotes the *ipsissima verba* of a single Dionysiac *signum*.[172]

2. Visual Symbols

Homonymous with the secret passwords, and equally hidden from profane curiosity, were the sacred 'tokens' (*signa* or *sym-*

bola[173]) which initiates of the Dionysiac mysteries kept at home as visible proof of their religious identity.[174] Again, what exactly these symbols were remains unknown. Perhaps the 'playthings' of Dionysus Zagreus, as one scholar suggested,[175] or the mysterious content – cakes, a snake, perhaps a heart, a thyrsus, a phallus, and ivy, in short, *mysteria* or *orgia* in the sense of 'sacred objects' – of the *cista mystica* described by Clement of Alexandria?[176] But it is unlikely that the Bacchic *signa* treasured by Apuleius were very different from the Bacchic symbols found on dozens of mosaics from his native North Africa.[177]

These mosaics are teeming with the animal and plant life traditionally associated with Dionysus, especially with wild cats and ivy, two of the most ubiquitous 'symbols' of Dionysus in the Hellenistic and Roman period.[178] It is often difficult to distinguish between a strictly religious application of Bacchic iconography and its purely decorative use.[179] The ivy illustrates this problem well. Ivy was widely used as a decorative emblem, not only on Bacchic mosaics but even in countless Greek and Latin inscriptions which lack any Dionysiac reference.[180] Yet it is evident that the ivy-leaf served indeed in certain cases 'as a sign of recognition among Bacchic initiates'.[181] The evidence is sporadic but unambiguous. Ptolemy IV Philopator was tattooed with an ivy-leaf as a visible mark of his well-known Dionysiac aspirations.[182] Tattooing was practised by Thracian maenads,[183] and Dionysiac initiates in the imperial period apparently presented their tattoo marks after death as an admission ticket into Elysium.[184] And finally, two Hellenistic funerary inscriptions from Erythrai are prominently decorated with a single standing ivy-leaf,[185] which has been convincingly interpreted as a Dionysiac *signum*.[186] It is conceivable, though we lack explicit evidence, that other Dionysiac symbols were similarly employed to establish personal religious identities among followers of Dionysus.

IV   *Ultimate identification with Dionysus*

The choice of Dionysiac roles available to worshippers of Dionysus either in actual group ritual or in solitary flights of fancy became more varied and exotic as the centuries went by. Dionysiac religion in the Hellenistic and imperial period is characterized by the omnipresence of myth which pervades all aspects of ritual and iconography. Bacchic initiation scenes in Dionysiac art, especially from Italy, are filled with mythical members of Dionysus's circle (maenads, satyrs, Sileni) and with Dionysiac animals (the goat and the panther) who assume cultic roles and puzzle the modern observer.[187] Conversely, Bacchic initiates cast themselves in Dionysiac roles, reflected in their dress and nomenclature, through assimilation to the god's mythical environment, including his male and female entourage,[188] his animals,[189] and his plants. The essence of the Dionysiac experience apparently culminated in visible *imitatio Dionysi*, accomplished through external and mechanical means. Even the long series of Hellenistic and Roman rulers who emulated Dionysus as triumphant conqueror or beneficent culture hero did so by appropriating the god's mythical symbols and entourage.[190] At their most Dionysiac, they were regarded by their subjects not as a full incarnation of Dionysus but as a 'New Dionysus', or a latter-day replica of the god and of his manifestations in the distant past.[191] Yet modern students of Dionysus are at one in their claim that his ancient worshippers, who shared the title *bakchos* with their god, experienced a more substantial and deeper identification with Dionysus.[192] It remains to ask how much we know about this ultimate experience, and what it was like.

1. Role Reversal

More than any other Greek god, Dionysus lacks a consistent identity. Duality, contrast and reversal are his hallmark. The wide range of experiences embodied by him was described in pairs of opposites such as male/female,[193] young/old,[194] war/peace,[195] and life/death.[196] Such opposite predications reflect similar role reversals experienced by his worshippers. Inspired by Dionysus, old men feel young again,[197] slaves enjoy freedom,[198] and women act like men, men like women.[199] Established identities are thus overturned, and replaced with others of an opposite nature. In most cases, such role reversals must have been an invisible psychological phenomenon which was temporary and which ended with a harsh awakening to the true realities of life. But in one exceptional case, that of reversed sex roles, the change was visibly acted out in actual ritual. Male transvestites are found in various situations which share a common connection with Dionysus although they are ritually unrelated:[200] as komasts at Ionian drinking parties,[201] a sympotic practice later revived at the court of 'Ptolemy surnamed Dionysus';[202] as male impersonators of female characters on the Attic stage;[203] as chosen ministrants of

Dionysus at the Attic Oschophoria when two young men dressed as girls carried vine-branches heavy with grapes;[204] and finally, Dionysus himself raised in girls' clothes according to Hellenistic myth.[205] Of all the Dionysiac transvestites known to us, only the Pentheus of the *Bacchae*, in Euripides's psychological portrayal, undergoes a true 'change of personality'.[206] Whether or not his experience was shared by other Dionysiac transvestites in the real world is a question which no scholar can answer in good conscience. In any case, ritual tranvestism was never prominent in Dionysiac cult, and apart from the concept of the effeminate Dionysus, it has left no trace in the Dionysiac iconography of the Hellenistic or imperial period.

2. *Dionysiac Sacramentalism*

'The blood is the life.'[207]

The practice (of omophagy) seems to rest in fact on a very simple piece of savage logic.[208] The homoeopathic effects of a flesh diet are known all over the world. If you want to be lion-hearted, you must eat a lion; if you want to be subtle, you must eat snake; those who eat chickens and hares will be cowards, those who eat pork will get little piggy eyes. By parity of reasoning, if you want to be like god you must eat god. . . . And you must eat him quick and raw, before the blood has oozed from him: only so can you add his life to yours, for 'the blood is the life'.[209]

'Whoever eats my flesh and drinks my blood will live in me and I in him.'[210]

The juxtaposition of Semitic, heathen and Christian beliefs illustrates the intellectual roots which sustain the widespread habit among modern interpreters of Dionysus of attributing a sacramental character to maenadic omophagy and, less frequently, to ritual wine drinking. Under the spell of Robertson Smith's totemistic theory of Semitic sacrifice[211] and of J. G. Frazer's pages on 'Killing the God',[212] Jane Harrison concluded that maenadic 'sacrifice is a sacrament, that the bull or goat torn and eaten is the god himself, of whose life the worshippers partake in sacramental communion'.[213] While some prominent continental classicists protested,[214] others adopted the sacramental theory of maenadic omophagy,[215] which received fresh support from E. R. Dodds.[216] The idea of eating and drinking Dionysus is intrinsically attractive to modern minds steeped in Christian sacramentalism and Frazerian anthropology, and it is difficult to resist.[217] But as long as we cannot even be sure that the Greeks identified Dionysus with his sacrificial animals, or that historical maenads practised omophagy in the literal sense,[218] the whole theory remains a splendid house of cards.

Wine lends itself more easily to sacramental interpretation than raw meat. In the eyes of most Greeks and Romans, Dionysus was the inventor of wine, and nothing more.[219] But others, presumably not very many, thought that 'he who drinks wine has drunk deity'.[220] They considered wine the blood of Dionysus, even drew a parallel between wine-making and the god's dismemberment, and apparently believed that wine-drinking was a sacramental act, the literal consumption of Dionysus.[221] Only fermented wine, however, encouraged such beliefs, while grapes did not have the same effect: the alleged 'Traubeneucharistie' in Dionysiac mysteries is a modern invention.[222]

3. Dionysiac Life After Death

Permanent Dionysiac identities, however, were not established in this life but only after death. Like the Eleusinian mysteries, although on a much larger scale, Dionysus promised his followers a happy afterlife. Such high hopes were rarely put into words.[223] Instead, they found abundant symbolic expression on countless funerary monuments which speak to us in the visual language of a complex Dionysiac eschatology.[224] This symbolism reflects the total range of the Dionysiac experience, and includes, for instance, the *kantharos* on Attic tombstones of the fourth century BCE;[225] Bacchic eroticism on Apulian funerary vases;[226] the maenad with the features of the deceased woman on an Etruscan sarcophagus lid of the mid-third century BCE;[227] the Dionysiac reliefs on the monumental tomb of the Roman veteran L. Poblicius at Cologne, of c. 50 CE;[228] and finally, the massive Bacchic scenes on neo-Attic and Roman sarcophagi of imperial date, which visualize the Dionysiac afterlife in military, rural, erotic or sympotic coloration.[229] Invariably, the eschatological message is the same. It tells us that the follower of Dionysus has finally acquired a lasting Dionysiac identity, either as a permanent member of the god's eternal entourage, or more ambitiously, as another Dionysus who has accomplished his own apotheosis through identification with one of Dionysus's mythical roles.

9

The Formation of Authoritative Tradition in the Greek Magical Papyri*

HANS DIETER BETZ

The body of material collected under the heading *Papyri Graecae Magicae* (hereafter *PGM*) seems at first sight to be unrelated to the overarching theme of this symposium, normative self-definition. The discussions have shown, however, that normative self-definition should be regarded as a heuristic concept and not as a fixed pattern to be imposed on the phenomena. One should, therefore, expect that the philosophical schools and the different religious cults and sects in antiquity engaged in quite different forms of self-definition. The professional magician whose spells are contained in the *PGM* belongs to the phenomenological type of the 'craftsman' so well described in Walter Burkert's essay in this volume.[1] This magician may have an apprentice, but his professional practice is basically a one-man show. He has no school, no organization, no building, and no institution upon which he can rely.[2] One should, therefore, not expect the magicians to have developed forms of self-definition that are typical of religious or philosophical groups, nor should one declare that self-definition was altogether unknown to these magicians.

Fundamentally, there seem to be two forms of definition related to the magician. One form of definition is the role expectation provided by the society at large,[3] the other is the peculiar way by which the magician defines himself through the formation of an authoritative tradition. The following paper will investigate the

* I am indebted to Morton Smith not only for his valuable comments upon an earlier draft of this paper, but for many years of learned advice about the intricacies of the world of magic.

latter, the formation of authoritative tradition as a way of self-definition in the *PGM*. This form of self-definition seems partly typical of magicians at all times, partly peculiar to the religious situation in Egypt in the later Roman Empire.[4]

The Greek Magical Papyri[5] appear at first sight to be a chaotic mass of charms and spells, diverse in nature, origin and length, and ever increasing through new discoveries and publications. But as Origen has already observed, the first impression is deceptive. He says in *Contra Celsum* I. 24:

> . . . so-called magic is not, as the followers of Epicurus and Aristotle think, utterly incoherent (*pragma asystaton*), but, as the experts in these things prove, is a consistent system (*synestos*), which has principles (*logoi*) known to very few . . .[6]

At one level, of course, all magical literature is or pretends to be tradition. No magician who is worth his reputation would ever claim to have invented or made up his own spells. On the contrary, he always operates on the assumption that his spells are ancient and venerable tradition. To this extent the magical literature and tradition are coterminous.

The question to be investigated in this paper, however, is this: To what extent does the magical literature in *PGM* reflect a conscious approach by the magicians to forming an authoritative tradition, and which are the indicators in the material itself of such formation?

Surprisingly, perhaps, the *PGM* do reflect in many ways such self-consciousness and redactional work by those persons who wrote the spells down and thus preserved them. Without their efforts we would not possess the magical material today. In the *PGM* material, it is obvious that the conscious formation of an authoritative tradition is a secondary activity.

In its original state, the material is indeed a disorganized mass of spells of all sorts, a mass which appears to have been handed down from one magician to the next, allegedly since times immemorial. Writing down individual spells, names, formulas, hymns, and so forth, represents a shift from the oral to the written stage, while at a third stage the written material is sorted out and collected in hand-books. Preisendanz's edition of the *PGM* contains both individual spells and collections of such spells made by ancient magicians. In fact, it represents nothing but one more phase in this long process of collection of magical material in Greek on papyrus. At the stage of the collection, it also became necessary to develop names and technical terminology by which the various spells could be classified and arranged. Such arrangements also made use of available literary genres, like the book or the letter, and thereby lifted some of the material from the level of the merely practical hand-book to the more ambitious level of magical *literature* in the stricter sense of the term.

It is at this latest stage of the formation of the tradition that we also find theoretical reflections about the nature and purpose of magic, definitions of magic and magician, and regulations for the transmission of the tradition. These theoretical reflections occasionally show the influence of Greek philosophy. They are, therefore, evidence of the rise of magic from the lower strata of society reflected in many of the spells to the higher levels of the cultural *élite* in the Roman empire, a development which is confirmed by the discussions about magic and theurgy among Neopythagorean and Neoplatonist philosophers.

The names designating magic in the *PGM* are few and are found only in the later strata of the tradition. The term *mageia* ('magic') is always used in a positive sense, but it occurs only infrequently and mostly in connection with definitions.

The Epistle of Pnouthis (I. 42–194) purports to be written by a temple-scribe (*hierogrammateus*) named Pnouthis to a certain Keryx who is called a 'devotee of the god' (*sebazomenos ton theon*). The author presents himself as one who knows how to instruct Keryx in the proper way. From all the innumerable prescriptions contained in endless numbers of books he claims to have selected the one that really works and yet creates no harm for him who uses it. A formal definition at the beginning sets things straight (I. 53):[7]

> The spell of Pnouthis has the power to persuade the gods and all the goddesses.

This definition is noteworthy because it takes up the old literary definition of magic as 'persuading gods' (*peithein theous*)[8] and expands it to include all the goddesses as well. After performing the rituals prescribed, Keryx is told, 'you will be worshipped like a god because you have the god as your friend' (I. 191f.). Lavish praise is heaped upon the addressee even prior to the performance. He is called: 'O blessed initiate of the holy magic' (*ō [ma]karie mysta tēs hieras mageias*, I. 127), and 'O friend of the wandering aerial spirits' (*ō phile aeriōn pneumatōn chōroum[enōn]*, I. 49f., cf. 171) because he is now working with such awesome *logoi theologoumenoi* ('words of divinity') (I. 50).

Similarly complimentary is the Epistle of Nephotes to King Psammetichos (IV. 154–260). While 'the great god' has installed Psammetichos as 'eternally living King', 'nature has made him the greatest sage' (*aristos sophistēs*, IV. 155–7). He is the 'professor of magic' (*magōn kathēgemōn*, IV. 243) because he has the 'magic soul' (*magikē psychē*, IV. 120).[9] In the Epistle of Pitys to King Ostanes (IV. 2006–2124) the procedure for calling up a *nekydaimōn* ('demon of the dead') as *paredros daimōn* ('assistant demon') is so powerful that most magicians, after they have learned to use it, put away their tools (IV. 2081f.). It is at this higher cultural level in the *PGM* that we find the terms *mageia* ('magic'), *magikos* ('magical'), and *magos* ('magician') as designations of magic as a whole. But in other sections other terms are used. There is a clear tendency in some texts to interpret magic in terms of the mystery cults.

The whole of magic as well as its parts can be called *mystērion* or *mystēria*[10], *mega mystērion*[11], *mystērion megiston*[12], *mystērion tou theou*[13], *theion mystērion*[14], *megalomystērion*[15], *ta hiera mystēria*[16]. Therefore the magician is the 'mystagogue' (*mystagōgos*).[17] Furthermore, handing over the magical tradition to a student becomes the purpose of a mystery-cult initiation.[18]

Yet other sections of *PGM* show evidence of Hermetic-gnostic thought and therefore interpret magic as *gnōsis*. The Prayer to the Sun (III. 494–611) contains a long list of traditional wishes for life, health, wealth, etc., but in the midst of these worldly goods occurs *gnōsis*, apparently a secondary interpolation.[19] The second part of this prayer is devoted entirely to *gnōsis*. Especially the thanksgiving, which has parallels in the Hermetic treatise *Asclepius* 41 and the *Nag Hammadi Codex* VI.7: 63.33–65.7 states how this part of the tradition wishes to be understood:

> Thanks to you we know (how to give), with the whole soul, as the heart is lifted up to you, the Unutterable Name, honoured by the divine title and blessed with divine holiness, by which you have shown fatherly good-will, affection, friendship and sweetest power to all people and with regard to all things, granting us *nous*, *logos*, and *gnōsis*; *nous*, that we may apprehend you; *logos*, that we may call upon you; *gnōsis*, that we may know you. We rejoice that you have revealed yourself to us; we rejoice that while we are (yet) in bodies you have deified us with the knowledge of yourself. . . .[20]

In this way all magic can be subsumed under *gnōsis*. This *gnōsis* pertains first, of course, to the secret divine names[21] as facilitating the powers of magic.[22] Moreover this *gnōsis* includes almost everything of interest to the magician, from foreknowledge of the divine plans for the future[23] to the range of things we would regard as scientific.[24] Impressive in this respect is the section called 'Hermes's Ring' (V. 213–303), in which the magician prays to Helios, identifying himself with Thoth:

> I am Thouth, discoverer and founder of drugs and letters. Come to me, you under the earth, exalt me, great daimon. . . . Unless I know what is in the minds of everyone, Egyptians, Greeks, Syrians, Ethiopians, of every race and people, unless I know what has been and what shall be, unless I know their skills and their practices and their works and their lives and the names of them and their fathers and their mothers and brothers and friends and deceased (relatives). . . . I will not let (any) god or goddess give oracles until I, NN know through and through what is in the minds of all men, Egyptians, Syrians, Greeks, Ethiopians, of every race and people, those who question me and who come into my sight, whether they speak or are silent, so that I can tell them what happened to them (in the past) and their present (circumstances) and what will happen to them hereafter, and I know their skills and their lives and their practices and their works and their names and (the names) of their dead (relatives) and of everybody, and I can read a sealed letter and tell them everything <in it> truly.[25]

As to the sources of magic, the tradition is agreed in tracing its origins back to the gods themselves.[26] Among the many gods named in this connection, some are prominent. Hermes-Thoth is regarded as the founder and originator of the magic arts (*pantōn hōs magōn archēgetēs, Hermēs ho presbys, Isidos patēr*, IV. 2289–91). He is the author of the secret 'names which Hermes Trismegistos wrote in Heliopolis with hieroglyphic letters' (IV. 885). A new magical papyrus from the first century CE opens with this statement of origin: 'An excerpt of charms from the holy book called Hermes, found in Heliopolis in the adyton of the temple, written in Egyptian letters and translated into Greek.'[27] Hermes first fashioned the little wax-figurine called *epaitētarion* for Isis (IV. 2376–8). His enthusiasm for magic, however, made him even plagiarize: the *Eighth Book of Moses* suggests in an editorial comment that Hermes stole from that book the seven incense substances akin to the deity and copied them into his book *Pteryx* (XIII. 14–16). Osiris is said to be the author of the holy book, from which III. 424–43 claims to be an excerpt: the spell was spoken directly by Osiris who gave it as a gift to Manetho (III. 439f.). The book called *Klaudianou Selēniakon* is said to belong to the Twelve Gods but to have been found in Aphroditopolis near the temple of Aphrodite Ourania (VII. 862–5).[28] Often the deity is simply named as the authority that has issued the order to perform the rituals.[29] Of course, the syncretistic nature of the magical tradition is all too obvious. One example may suffice here: in V. 108–17 Moses presents himself to the deity with these words:

> I am Moses, your prophet, to whom you have transmitted your mysteries performed by Istraēl [sic]. . . . I am the messenger of Phaprō Osoronnōphris. This is your true name which has been transmitted by the prophets of Istraēl [sic].[30]

This example is one among many that shows that the deity has first revealed the magical tradition to one of the great diviners of the past. In the Greek tradition the most prominent figure is Orpheus, from whom a formula is cited in XIII. 933–44, introduced by the words: 'as the diviner Orpheus handed it down through his book *Parastichis*' (*hōs ho theol<o>gos Orpheus paredōken dia tēs parastichidos tēs idias*).[31] Dardanos, the legendary founder of the mysteries at Samothrace, is said to have contributed the piece called 'The Sword of Dardanos' (IV. 1716ff.). Verses from Homer cited in the *PGM* serve as magical formulae or as oracles in the 'Homeromanteia' (VII. 1–52). From the philosophers, Pythagoras and Democritus are mentioned as co-authors of an astrological dream-divination (VII. 795–845); from Democritus there are others, admittedly puzzling pieces: the *Dēmokritou paignia* (VII. 167–85) and the *Dēmokritou sphaira* (XII. 351–4). Unique is a text ascribed to Apollonius of Tyana, called 'The Old Woman Servant of Apollonius of Tyana' (*Graus Apollōn[io]u Tyaneōs hypēretis*, XI.a). On the other hand, there are conspicuous gaps. The great Zoroaster is mentioned only once (XIII. 967), and for many other famous ancient magicians we may look in vain in the *PGM*. There is no doubt that Egyptian magicians are represented best: Astrampsychos (VIII. 1), Manetho (III. 440; XIII. 23); Nephotes (IV. 154): Ostanes (IV. 2006; XII. 122), Pachrates (IV. 2447), Pibechis (IV. 3007), Pitys (IV. 2006),[32] Pnouthis (I. 43, 52), Psammetichos (IV. 154). From the Roman side, only the Emperor Hadrian made it into the *PGM* (IV. 2448), while from Judaism came the most prominent figures of Moses, whose name is mentioned frequently,[33] Jacob (XXII.b) and Solomon (IV. 850–929, 3039f.).

These great magicians of the past set the standards which present practitioners aspire to follow. In order to be elevated to their lofty height, however, the present magician must become a god himself, for only a god or 'divine man' can be the friend and companion of the deity.[34] To bring about deification is the purpose of the initiation ceremony. In spite of the importance of the initiation, the *PGM* do not contain many rituals of this kind. Whether or not there existed some form of ordination for professional magicians we do not know. The initiations found in the *PGM* indicate that the ceremonies are repeatable and that no one who is 'uninitiated' (*amystēriastos*) in the practice of magic is acceptable to the deity.[35] The so-called 'Mithras Liturgy' has an interesting instruction for initiating a fellow-initiate before his participation in the ritual. This initiation shows signs of being typical rather than exceptional.

> If you also wish to use a fellow-initiate (*synmystēs*), so that he alone may hear with you the things spoken, let him remain pure together with you <seven> days, and abstain from meat and the bath. And if you are alone, and you undertake the things communicated by the god, you speak as though prophesying in ecstasy. And if you also wish to show him, then judge whether he is completely worthy as a man: treat him just as if in his place you were being judged in the matter of immortalization, and whisper to him the first prayer. . . . And say the successive things as an initiate, over his head, in a soft voice, so that he may not hear, as you are anointing his face with the mystery. This immortalization takes place three times a year. And if anyone, O child, after the teaching, wishes to disobey, then for him it will no longer be in effect.[36]

There are a few other instances which show that the tradition may be handed over only to a 'son', that is, an apprentice.[37] Frequently, this apprentice is told that he must keep the holy tradition secret: e.g., 'keep secret, son' (*krybe, hyie*, IV. 2512), or 'what you possess in secret as a great mystery, keep secret, keep secret . . .' (*ho eche en apokryphōi hōs megalomystērion, krybe, krybe* . . ., XII. 322).[38] Secrecy is necessary especially for the 'secret and unspeakable names' (*krypta kai arrhēta onomata*)[39] because they cannot be spoken with just a human mouth (XIII. 763).

There can hardly be any doubt that the collections of the magical material extant in the *PGM* were made by magicians for their own use. In regard to literary genres, a variety were employed to mould the holy 'tradition' (*paradosis* I. 54). The material could be collected as a 'book' (*biblion*[40] or *biblos*).[41] As mentioned before, special literary skills are claimed by the epistles[42] of Pnouthis (IV. 42ff.), Nephotes (IV. 154ff.), Pitys (IV. 2006ff.), and Ieu (V. 96ff.). Some of these works are said to be due to active research. The activity of copying is attested: *antigraphē* (III. 483) or *antigraphon* (III. 424).[43] Other pieces are said to be copies from steles (e.g. IV. 1115).[44] The study of hieroglyphic letters is sometimes mentioned but the results are rather limited.[45] Extraordinary in this regard is the section XII. 401–45, a secret book of plant names whose origin is described in this way:

> Interpretations which the temple-scribes employed, from the holy (writings) in translation. Because of the curiosity of the masses they (i.e., the scribes) inscribed the name of the herbs, and other things which they employed, on the statues of the gods, so that they (i.e., the masses) since they do not take precautions, may not practise magic, (being prevented) by the consequence of their misunderstanding. But we have collected explanations (of these names) from the many copies – all of them secret – (of the sacred writings).[46]

(The Egyptian letters are then interpreted as cryptic lists of plants.)

Once the material has been collected it must be put into some kind of order. In the *PGM* we indeed find the beginnings of systems of classification, but none of the competing classification systems was carried through systematically.

We find these attempts at classification in two places. There are in the formulae themselves lists of operations which the particular spells are said to be able to carry out. These aretalogical sections strive to be both comprehensive and competent in using the technical terms needed to designate operations.[47] The same technical terms are then used by the collectors/redactors as section titles indicating and separating spells in the collections, such as 'love spell' (*philtrokatadesmos*), 'spell to gain favour' (*charitēsion*), 'spell to gain victory' (*nikētikon*), 'request for dream revelation' (*oneiraitēton*), 'spell for protection' (*phylaktērion*), and so forth. Other titles arrange spells by imitating the physician's prescription book, e.g., 'against scorpion sting' (*pros skorpiou plēgēn*), 'against running eyes' (*pros rheuma ophthalmōn*), 'against headache' (*pros hēmikranion*), and so forth. Duplicates are simply introduced by *allo*. Still another approach is to cite and remember famous spells by distinctive names, such as 'The Sword of Dardanos' (IV. 1716), 'The Prayer of Jacob' (XXII.b), 'The Key of Moses' (XIII. 21, 229, 382, etc.), 'The Diadem of Moses' VII. 619), 'The Seal of Solomon' (IV. 3039f.) or 'The Ring of Hermes' (V. 213). None of these systems, however, is used with any degree of consistency; we find them mixed up and combined in every conceivable way. Any classification is frustrated by the exaggerated boast for some spells that they are good for everything, as in the epistle of Pnouthis, where the 'assistant daimon' (*paredros daimōn*) is recommended thus:

> . . . He will serve you suitably for whatever you have in mind, O

blessed initiate of the sacred magic, and will accomplish it for you, this most powerful assistant, who is also the only lord of the air; and the gods will agree to everything, for without him nothing happens.[48]

Why was the sacred tradition collected? As far as the *PGM* are concerned, some cautious observations can be made. On the surface, one notices the constant recommendations attached to spells, the 'commercials' asserting 'tested and approved', 'this really works', and the like. These commercials may be taken as evidence of a concern to sift through the whole mass of magical materials available at the time and select the best and most effective of the spells. Was this done to beat the competition? Was there an urge to assemble the tradition because of the competing Christian and Jewish canons of the Bible? Did the debates in contemporary Neoplatonism about magic and theurgy stimulate the formation of the tradition? There is no evidence in the *PGM* that lends itself to answering any of these important questions. All we are able to see is that the professionals of magic were concerned with the preservation of their traditions. Apart from the need for the individual magicians to have their own handbooks ready for the day-to-day business, there is a faint notion throughout the material that it may soon be lost unless a real effort is made to preserve its best. Although many magicians probably were bilingual, the language barrier is quite apparent which prevented the Greek-speaking magicians from really understanding and properly pronouncing the old sacred languages of Egyptian, Hebrew, and whatever other languages may be contained in the *voces magicae*. This problem cannot have escaped the magicians' notice. In fact, the general impression one gets is that of a literature not very well preserved. In a literature where the precise pronunciation of foreign language spells appears absolutely crucial, the badly corrupted textual tradition characteristic of much of the *PGM* material signals a deadly threat to the very existence of the tradition itself. Perhaps some of the larger collections owe their existence to authors who were making a serious attempt to prevent the final corruption of the Greek magical material. Indeed if, as Karl Preisendanz[49] has suggested, it appears that all of the great papyri acquired by d'Anastasy belonged to one man's library at Thebes, this man may have been more than an average magician. He may have been one of the learned priests at Thebes who worked at the preservation of the Greco-Egyptian magical literature.[50] As a result, his efforts, more than any other factor, shaped this tradition, and apart from the lucky circumstances of the discovery and rescue of the material by d'Anastasy, it is due to his work that we today have access to this important sector of Hellenistic literature.

10

The Imperial Cult: Perceptions and Persistence

G. W. BOWERSOCK

In the cities of the classical and Hellenistic Greek world there had gradually developed a system of honouring benefactors.[1] The honour was as much a means of securing favour in the future as it was an acknowledgement of favour already received. The form of the honour varied in accordance with the importance of the individual and the magnitude of the benefaction, real or potential. The honorand might look forward to a municipal decree (authorizing some local privileges and priorities), a statue with a eulogistic inscription, festival games bearing his name, or a cult complete with priests and sacrifices. The benefactor might be hailed as such (*euergetēs*), or recognized as a saviour (*sōtēr*) or even a founder (*ktistēs*). The outlines of this fertile institution are now reasonably clear, although much still remains to be done in detail. From the cults of benefactors emerged the dynastic cults of Hellenistic monarchs. By a separate evolution from the same origin came the cult of the Roman emperors.

Governors sent by the republican government of Rome to the eastern provinces found themselves increasingly subjected to the Hellenic homage of benefactor cults. Tacitus later called it *Graeca adulatio*,[2] and few had Cicero's courage in rejecting it.[3] The cults of governors were above all an expression of political adhesion in anticipation of favourable treatment. The honours accorded to Augustus at the beginning of the Principate came as readily and naturally as they had to Q. Mucius Scaevola, Pompey, P. Servilius Isauricus, Julius Caesar, and many others.[4] Provincial cults of such Romans were generally the responsibility of the provincial councils (*koina*), which, as we now know, were functioning in the Greek-speaking regions already in the time of the late Republic and at the initiative of the provincials themselves. The new dispensation which Augustus brought to the Mediterranean world under the guise of a revival of the old ways soon led to the formal suppression of benefactor cults for Roman governors.[5] The field was to be left clear for the *princeps* and his house; if at the outset he insisted that his cult be joined with that of *Roma*, this was no impediment to the diffusion of the cult not only in the East but in the West as well. And there was no one to stop private cults of the emperor on his own.

Obviously the growth of the imperial cult served the aims of the Roman government. It provided an unparalleled guarantee of loyalty throughout a vast and varied empire, and it served to engage the more affluent and better educated provincials in the ceremonies of devotion to the ruling power. Priesthoods of the cult, especially at the provincial level but also in individual cities, were prestigious posts and rapidly became an identifiable stage in a pattern of social mobility that could take an energetic family to senatorial status in a mere three generations.[6] Scholars have emphasized the political and social role of the imperial cult over and over again. There is very little evidence that the cult ever became comparable to the traditional religions of pagan antiquity. As Arthur Darby Nock pointed out many times,[7] there are no *ex voto* proofs of fulfilled prayer involving any emperors on their own, alive or dead. (There are only a few instances in which emperors are mentioned together with traditional gods.[8]) Nock compared the cult of the emperors to the cult of the Roman standards in the army. The standards were symbols rather than divine entities, and in the same way the emperors were *divi* – deified – rather than *dei*. The miracle stories concerning Vespasian evoke wizardry rather than deity.[9] The emperors were honoured and celebrated, but they were not the same as Zeus, Heracles, or Asclepius. Even though Greek is less able to accommodate the distinction between *divus* and *deus*, Greek writers show unmistakably that they felt the difference.[10]

It is for this reason that accounts of religious life in the Roman Empire tend to be rather thin on the imperial cult. This is simply a reflection of the ancient evidence. The religious obsessions of the age were with deities of personal salvation and of healing. Hence Mithras and Asclepius come to play important parts in the spiritual life of the second and third centuries. Mystery religions and orgiastic cults commanded attention. The imperial cult was not much talked about. In documenting the silence of our literary sources on this matter it is unfortunately easy to ignore the indications that the imperial cult nonetheless flourished.

Although it is absurd to state, as A. H. M. Jones once did,[11] that every time someone was deified, a new temple was built for him, it is still true that the construction of new temples for the imperial cult is probably the most conspicuous form of building activity for religious purposes in the Roman Empire of the second and third centuries.[12] Civic pride accounts for this in large measure. A city that could boast several imperial temples could hope for the formal honour of as many neocorates. This honour, which could be bestowed only by the emperor after the bureaucratic procedures of petitioning, enhanced the status of a city and usually of its more influential citizens.[13] But the cult offered more than prestige and the possibility of advancement. It furnished festivals and rituals, and these have properly been given greater emphasis in recent years as a legitimate reaction to earlier work on political and social issues.[14]

The imperial cult, like the original benefactor cults, included the celebration of competitive games in honour of the imperial house, together with sacrifices and (in some instances) the revelation of mysteries to initiates.[15] The games were most commonly athletic and provided opportunities for both famous and aspiring athletes to demonstrate their prowess before admiring crowds. There were also competitions in music and poetry, for which the emperor's greatness would be the theme.[16] All of this took place in a holiday atmosphere, with the high priest of the imperial cult presiding. Of the sacrifices and mysteries we know less, but it seems evident from the names of various celebrants (*sebastophant*, *sebastologos*) that imperial images were displayed and sacred tales recounted about the Augusti. In view of the popularity of mystery religions in the Roman Empire, it is reasonable to suppose that this feature of the imperial cult may have enjoyed some vogue among citizens who participated in the better known imperial festivities.

Most persons in the empire of Rome could only have known their emperor from his bust or statue, and it was this which dominated the celebration of his cult.[17] At games and sacrifices as well as in sacred processions, the images of the emperor and his predecessors could be seen. The impact of this spectacle must have been considerable, even if the emotions it inspired could not be described, in the modern sense, as particularly religious. No one, it seems, was moved to stretch out his hands in prayer; but he cannot have escaped a consciousness of temporal power at least, and of divine power potentially. By looking upon the emperor's image, by joining in sacrifice, and by enjoying the imperial games, a citizen of the Roman Empire was reminded of who ruled the world.

It should not have been a surprise, therefore, to find that the imperial cult was, at the same time, both a flourishing institution and a rare topic of discourse. It was taken for granted not because it was insignificant but precisely because it was so integral to life in the empire. Its importance can best be seen at the times when it was resisted or transformed. Neither the Jews nor the Christians were able to accept the worship of the emperors. Hence resistance. And yet the imperial cult was continued by Constantine and his successors. Hence transformation.

It is well known that the Jews had a privileged status in the Roman Empire, and neither Augustus nor Tiberius thought to involve them in the imperial cult.[18] The emperor Gaius (Caligula), both deranged and tyrannical, tried to force the Jews to acknowledge his divinity, inasmuch as he had no doubts about it himself. Their desperate resistance is a familiar story, and despite the brutality to which they were subjected by Roman forces in the ensuing reigns they continued to enjoy special consideration in respect to religious observance. In the early third century Severus and Caracalla explicitly affirmed their right to civic honours without the imposition of obligations that would offend their *superstitio*.[19] Naturally this meant exemption from the observances of the imperial cult, in which prominent local citizens would normally be expected to take part.

As for the Christians, the imperial cult forms the background for many a martyr story, since persecuting Roman officials found it best to test a believer's faith by demanding worship of the emperor. The origins of this practice can be seen in Pliny's well known letter to Trajan about the Christians in Bithynia:

> An anonymous pamphlet has been circulated which contains the names of a number of accused persons. Among these I considered that I should dismiss any who denied that they were or ever had been Christians when they had repeated after me a formula of invocation to the gods and had made offerings of wine and incense to your statue (which I had ordered to be brought into court for this purpose along with the images of the gods) – *cum praeeunte me deos appellarent et imagini tuae, quam propter hoc iusseram cum simulacris numinum adferri, ture ac vino supplicarent.*[20]

Distinguishing carefully between the *imago* of the emperor and the *simulacra* of the gods (a distinction comparable to that between *divus*, of an emperor, and *deus*, of a true god), Pliny thus makes use of the imperial cult as a test; and suddenly this often unnoticed institution blazes into prominence. As a result of his efforts Pliny can report to his emperor that sacred rites which had been allowed to lapse are being performed again, 'and flesh of sacrificial victims is on sale everywhere, though up till recently scarcely anyone could be found to buy it'. One suspects that games had interested the Bithynian populace more than sacrifice. At any rate it would be hard to conclude from Pliny's words that most of Bithynia had turned Christian and then promptly lapsed as soon as he began his inquisition.

In view of the importance of the imperial cult in martyrologies it has seemed puzzling to some that the Christian apologists have almost nothing to say about it.[21] Their silence is not unlike that of the pagan intellectuals of the same period. Apart from a passing reference in Justin (or Melito),[22] the principal exception to this neglect of the theme is Tertullian in the *Apologeticum*. But even he is surprisingly moderate in his opinions. He objects to oaths sworn by the *genius* of an emperor but has no objection to an oath *per salutem*; and he notes that the emperor is but a man, for if he were not he could not be an emperor. *Non enim deum imperatorem dicam, vel quia mentiri nescio vel quia illum deridere non audeo vel quia nec ipse se deum volet dici.*[23] This is tame and respectful language, with which all but the most megalomaniac emperors would have concurred.

Swearing by the emperor's *genius* and venerating his statue with wine and incense (as well as sacrifice) clearly did pose problems for Christians when they were instructed to make these observances. Service in the army was therefore ruled out for them until well into the third century.[24] But apart from the army and deliberate persecutions the imperial cult appears paradoxically to have been an institution which Christians could tolerate around them.

The statue as a potential point of trouble turns up in rabbinic literature for reasons that are presumably little different from those of the Christians. Mishnah Abodah Zarah 3.1 reports:

All statues are forbidden because they are worshipped (at least) once a year: the words of Rabbi Meir. And the sages say, only those with a staff or bird or sphere are forbidden. Rabbi Shimon ben Gamliel says, all statues with anything in their hands are forbidden.

175

The Tosefta adds to the list of sages commenting on the Mishnah text, and both the Palestinian and the Babylonian Talmud provide further commentary.[25] It is evident from the various discussions that the forbidden statues were judged to be those of emperors, and it therefore becomes immaterial in the present context whether or not the original formulation of the prohibition was aimed at statues of gods in general or of emperors in particular. The Palestinian Talmud even appears to separate the statues of emperors from those of governors:

> With what are we dealing (in the Mishnah controversy between Rabbi Meir and the sages)? – If it is clear that the statues are of kings, all agree that benefit from them is forbidden. – If it is clear that the statues are of governors, all agree that benefit is allowed.[26]

Since no cults of governors were permitted in the Roman Empire after Augustus, it is obvious why there was no difficulty in regard to the presence of their statues. But the political implications of the cult of emperors were not inconsiderable. Indeed one exceptionally holy Jew took so seriously his obligations not to look upon the image of the emperor that he refused to look even at any coin, since the face of the emperor would invariably appear there.[27]

The persistence of the imperial cult in the Christian empire which Constantine founded provides a unique opportunity to determine what the cult means in the Roman world. One might well wonder what sort of cult it was that the earliest Christian emperors not only tolerated but encouraged. The deceased Constantine was proclaimed *divus*, and his reception into heaven was commemorated by the celebrated coinage first issued from Lyons and subsequently from many parts of the realm with a depiction of the emperor on his way to heaven in a chariot and with a hand reaching down to receive him from above.[28] The significance of this issue is underlined by a chapter which Eusebius devoted to it in his *Life of Constantine*.[29] The scene is, of course, different in certain respects from the traditional pagan consecration imagery with its pyre and eagle to indicate the immolation by which the divine part of the emperor rose heavenward. But, for all that, it is apparent that the epithet *divus* was not a simple equivalent of the expression 'the late'.

Eckhel, Hirschfeld, and Beurlier have been among the most notable scholars to explain the imperial cult of Christian emperors in terms of a secularization of the cult.[30] Certainly it was altered, as the iconography of the Constantinian coins shows; but it does not necessarily follow that it was secularized. The coins imply some kind of divinization or identification with the divine.

Constantine himself and his three sons, in a famous letter preserved on an inscription from Hispellum in Umbria,[31] formally authorized the cult of themselves and their house, the *gens Flavia*. The letter gives the emperors' resolution of a difficulty between the towns of Vulsinii and Hispellum arising from the contribution of priests from Hispellum to the imperial observances (theatrical and gladitorial shows) at Vulsinii. Complaining that their obligations to Vulsinii were burdensome and noting furthermore that they were building their own temple to the emperors at Hispellum, the representatives of that town sought permission for their own priests to perform their duties there. The emperors agree to the completion of the new temple and the performance of spectacles to go with it, while at the same time they insist that the observances at Vulsinii not be curtailed. They also require that their temple, which is to be built in magnificent style (*magnifico opere*), not be polluted 'by the deceptions of any contagious superstition' (*ne aedis nostro nomini dedicata cuiusquam contagiose superstitionis fraudibus polluatur*).

All this seems to amount to active support of the cult by the emperors along with an oblique prohibition designed to satisfy a Christian conscience. To what this prohibition referred is not altogether clear, but the obvious reference is to sacrifice. To judge from a ruling of Constantius in 341, Constantine had forbidden sacrifices:

> Superstition shall cease; the madness of sacrifices shall be abolished. For if any man in violation of the law of the divine emperor, our parent, (*contra legem divi principis parentis nostri*) and in violation of this command of our clemency should dare to perform sacrifices, he shall suffer the infliction of a suitable punishment and the effect of an immediate sentence.[32]

In his *Life of Constantine* Eusebius also ascribes to him a ban on sacrifice.[33] It is therefore likely that the cult observances at Hispellum and elsewhere did not include sacrifices. But it is certain from the inscription that there were officials with the title of priest and that theatrical and gladiatorial competitions (*ludi scenici et gladiatorum munus*) were held. It is equally certain that the centre of the cult was a temple.

Overall the transformation of the cult under Constantine meant the elimination of sacrifice. But, as we have seen, the strength of the cult in the previous centuries had lain in the festive games and in the celebration of the emperor's divine image. In neither of these aspects did Constantine and his successors effect any change. The divinization implied by the coinage at Constantine's death gave authority to his sons and heirs. It seems quite wrong to follow the current tendency to interpret the ascent of Constantine to heaven as an ambivalent scene cunningly chosen because it was acceptable, for different reasons, to both pagans and Christians. Calderone eloquently argued some years ago against the inherent implausibility of the *Zweideutigkeit* which Otto Seeck and others had tried to discern in Constantinian symbols.[34] In the latter part of his reign Constantine was not trying to deceive anyone about his Christianity or his interest in making the empire Christian. The situation is less clear for the period between 312 and 324, but even for that time it is unlikely that anyone intended one symbol to convey two distinct messages. If one were unsure of what was happening or what would please the emperor, then deliberate vagueness was the answer. Hence the unspecified *divinitas* which is so important in the inscription on the arch of Constantine and in the panegyrics of 313 and 321.[35]

It is unlikely that in real life the chariot of Constantine on the coins suggested Elijah to Christians and the old pagan consecration rite to pagans. Such subtlety is an invention of resourceful scholars. The chariot suggested no more and no less than appeared on the coins: the reception of the Roman emperor into heaven without the appurtenances of pyre and eagle. Everyone could and would take it in this way. And there was, moreover, an important antecedent which would probably not have been ignored by the more knowledgeable of Constantine's contemporaries. (Modern scholars have tended to miss this evidence.) Constantine's father, Constantius, had become a *divus* himself and had been appreciatively regarded throughout Constantine's career by pagans and Christians alike for his character and his administrative tact.[36] Christians were prepared to see in him either Christian sympathies or an outright espousal of their faith. From the pagan panegyric of 307, the year after Constantius's death, we discover that he had ascended to heaven in a chariot led by the sun (*sol*): . . . *dive Constanti, quem curru paene conspicuo . . . Sol ipse invecturus caelo excepit*.[37] What is more, the panegyrist of 310 informs us that in making the transit to heaven (*transitus in caelum*)[38] Constantius was received by the gods while Juppiter himself stretched out his right hand: *receptusque est consessu caelitum Iove ipso dexteram porrigente*.[39] The consecration coins of

Constantius, obviously issued after his death, include an issue in gold that depicts a chariot led by the Sun rising heavenward above a four-tiered funeral pyre.[40] The imagery of Constantius's deification could scarcely be clearer.

The importance of the Sun in the house of Constantine needs no emphasis, but the role of the Sun in escorting Constantius I to heaven does. The iconography of Constantine's deification simply repeats a motif already familiar from the apotheosis of his father. That motif, in turn, had been no less acceptable to Christians than to pagans. A famous mosaic discovered after World War II in a Christian mausoleum under the Constantinian basilica of St Peter's and dated on stylistic grounds to the middle or late third century shows a radiate figure standing on a chariot drawn by four white horses.[41] Since there can be no doubt that this is a Christian tomb, it has been fashionable to describe the figure as Christ-Helios, whatever that is supposed to mean. (No ancient, it may be argued, ever thought of a character called Christ-Helios.) What we have here is another clear and unambiguous representation of apotheosis in a *quadriga* driven by the Sun. This scene in a Christian funerary context, perhaps evoking the ascent of the deceased to heaven, depicts the same kind of scene as the pagan panegyrists of 307 and 310 offer for the ascent of Constantine's father to heaven. The parallel provides an easy explanation of the iconography of the imperial cult under Constantine and immediately after.

By the end of Constantine's reign, Sol seems to have been replaced by the emperor himself as driver of the chariot, but the divine hand that received the deceased is now actually visible in the iconography. Constantine's divinization is essentially like that of his father. The hand, formerly assigned to Juppiter, has become as vague as the *divinitas* of the eulogies. It is divine, but not explicitly Juppiter's nor God's. Nor does Eusebius in describing the coin identify the owner of the hand. It is simply a right hand stretched out from above: *hypo dexias anōthen ekteinomenēs autōi cheiros analambanomenon.*[42]

The imperial cult, as revised by Constantine and his successors, was not a pale remnant of an old rite but rather an institution that drew new vigour in its traditionally strong elements from the divinity of both Constantius I and Constantine. The importance of the games is evident in the Hispellum inscription. The importance of the emperor's image can be seen nowhere better than in a *constitutio* of Theodosius II as late as 425:

> If at any time, whether on festal days, as is usual, or on ordinary days, statues or images of us are erected, the judge shall be present without employing the vainglorious heights of adoration (*sine adorationis ambitioso fastigio*) . . . Likewise if our images are shown at plays or games, they shall demonstrate that our divinity and glory live only in the hearts and the secret places of the minds of those who attend. A worship in excess of human dignity shall be reserved for the supernal divinity (*excedens cultura hominum dignitatem superno numini reservetur*).[43]

The language of this text shows not only the extent to which the emperor's image was adored a century after Constantine but also the remarkable endurance of that ancient formula by which emperors from the time of Augustus had forsworn an excess of worship that would obliterate the distinction between a true deity and the divine emperor.[44] Theodosius here does not sound very much different from Tiberius in his reply, as given by Tacitus, to a request for a cult in Spain: *Ego me, patres conscripti, mortalem esse et hominum officia fungi satisque habere, si locum principem impleam, et vos testor et meminisse posteros volo . . . Haec mihi in animis vestris templa, hae pulcherrimae effigies et mansurae.*[45] Dio Cassius had made Maecenas advise Augustus that if he wished to be truly immortal he had only to be enshrined and glorified within the thoughts of all men.[46]

The fundamental separation of the emperor's divinity from any kind of equality or identification with a god was inherent in the imperial cult from the start, and therefore a Christian emperor who ultimately became *divus* when he died was in no sense a rival to God but only a recipient of his goodness and power. Like the adoration of the emperor's image, the actual use of the word *divus* persisted well into the fifth century, as late as Valentinian III[47] in the West, and later still in the East. With the increasing strength of the clergy it is not surprising that by the fifth century measures were finally taken to stop these practices. But the cult itself was ingrained, and it is interesting to read in an early sixth-century inscription from Ammaedara in North Africa, beneath the christogram and an alpha and omega, the proud boast of a certain Astius Mustelus that he was *flamen perpetuus Christianus.*[48]

The curious but explicable symbiosis of the imperial cult and Christianity had an influence on the pagan perception of the cult. It was only after the Christians had appropriated it for their own emperors that the pagans introduced what the worship of the emperors had conspicuously lacked for so long – prayer and fulfilment. Libanius reports that images of the deceased Julian were honoured in many cities and that worshippers had prayed to him with success. 'To such an extent has he literally ascended to the gods and received a share of their power from them themselves'.[49] Several decades ago Nock suggested that this development in the pagan imperial cult was a direct response to the efficacy of Christian martyrs and saints.[50] Julian had become a kind of pagan saint, capable of at least as much influence with celestial powers as St Babylas. In this matter one should note the importance of statues or busts of Julian, keeping his memory alive.

Nock's point is reasonable, but we may be nearer the mark in thinking that the pagan behaviour was not so much an imitation of Christian attitudes towards martyrs and saints in general as a reflection of the imperial cult itself as managed by the Christians. In other words, it may be argued that the Christians had already set an example for the pagans by introducing prayer and its fulfilment into the cult. Constantine, viewed as a saint, certainly became the object of cults very soon after his death:[51] if prayers could so promptly be addressed to him as a saint, it is unlikely that they were not as an emperor or indeed that many people were conscious of the difference. It is clear that the veneration of Constantine continued in this way into the early fifth century. Photius records that the Eunomian church historian Philostorgius criticized those Christians who offered sacrifice, candles, and incense at the statue of Constantine on the top of a porphyry pillar in Constantinople. Furthermore, according to Philostorgius, these Christians prayed to Constantine as a god, *hōs theōi*.[52] In view of the elaborate funeral and subsequent interment of Constantine among the Cenotaphs of the twelve apostles[53] it is easy to understand why cults of so potent a *divus*, so visibly ranked with the apostles, grew up almost immediately both inside and outside the structure of the imperial cult.

The use and even the rationale of the imperial cult for Christian emperors is nowhere so explicitly and eloquently stated as in the panegyric addressed by Pacatus to Theodosius in 389. The emperor draws special power from sharing a secret with God, and on this account he is worshipped and prayed to:

Tibi istud soli pateat, imperator, cum deo consorte secretum; illud dicam quod intellexisse hominem et dixisse fas est: talem esse debere qui gentibus adoratur, cui tot orbe terrarum privata vel publica vota redduntur, a quo petit navigaturus serenum peregrinaturus reditum pugnaturus auspicium. (Let that secret lie open to you alone, O Emperor, with God as your partner. I shall say what it is right for a man to have understood and said: Such should he be who is adored by the nations, to whom throughout the world so many vows, private and public, are made; from whom one about to sail petitions a calm sea; one about to travel, a safe return; one about to do battle, a good omen.)[54]

In short, the pagan prayers to Julian were not a reaction to the saints and martyrs but proof of the swift transformation in the cult of emperors. If one prayed to saints and the *divus* was a saint, then there was no reason not to pray to the *divus*. Prayers to Constantine would have led naturally to prayers to Julian. By then the pagans who offered those prayers would not have known that what they were doing was almost unheard of in the imperial cult before Constantine.

The Christians thus imported into the cult of the emperors the possibility of sainthood. That suddenly gave a religious force to the cult that it had lacked earlier, and this together with the games and spectacles that had traditionally given strength to the institution, made it gradually suspect to the leaders of the church. Ambrose perceived sharply the dangers of religious authority vested in the emperor. That is why he opposed the title of *pontifex maximus*. The disappearance of this title and the cessation of the divinization coinage of Constantine both occurred under Gratian; and Christian Habicht had good reason to propose that there was a connection between these two changes and that Ambrose was involved in both.[55]

The testimony of Philostorgius shows, however, that adoration of the imperial image continued. His words deserve to stand alongside those of Theodosius II in 425 as evidence of the pertinacity of the imperial cult even as it was finally yielding to the spiritual leadership of the church. The Jews had well understood the implications of imperial statues. The statues themselves (or the busts) and the festive events with which they were associated gave an astonishing longevity to an institution that had taken its origin in political adhesion. Any religious institution that lasted over four hundred years and could accommodate both pagans and Christians was not without vitality. It endured so long because it succeeded in making multitudes of citizens in far-flung regions feel close to the power that controlled them. It did not, for most of its duration, respond to those desperate human anxieties over salvation in the next world and disease in this one; but at least it kept a Roman citizen from feeling helpless and alone in a faceless crowd.

Notes

1. Craft Versus Sect: The Problem of Orphics and Pythagoreans

1. The Derveni papyrus was found in 1962; partial edition by S. G. Kapsomenos, 'Ho Orphikos papyros tēs Thessalonikēs', ArchDelt 19, 1964, pp. 17–25; it is a scandal that a complete edition is still missing; transcripts of unpublished parts are circulating privately. See also R. Merkelbach, 'Der orphische Papyrus von Derveni', ZPE 1, 1967, pp. 21–32; W. Burkert, 'Orpheus und die Vorsokratiker. Bemerkungen zum Derveni-Papyrus und zur pythagoreischen Zahlenlehre', Antike und Abendland 14, 1968, pp. 93–114; P. Boyancé, 'Remarques sur le papyrus de Dervéni', REG 87, 1974, pp. 91–110; M. S. Funghi, 'Una cosmogonia orfica nel papiro di Derveni', PP 34, 1979, pp. 17–30.

2. A. S. Rusajeva, 'Orfizm i kult Dionisa b Olbii', Vestnik Drevnej Istorii 143, 1978, pp. 87–104. This is not the place to enter the debate about the 'Orphic' gold plates; on the important recent discovery at Hipponion see G. Pugliese-Carratelli and G. Foti, 'Un sepolcro di Hipponion e un nuovo testo orfico', PP 29, 1974, pp. 108–26; M. L. West, 'Zum neuen Goldplättchen aus Hipponion', ZPE 18, 1975, pp. 229–36; G. Zuntz, 'Die Goldlamelle von Hipponion', WS 89, 1976, pp. 129–51; the new Malibu plate in ZPE 25, 1977, p. 276; W. Burkert, 'Orphism and Bacchic Mysteries: New Evidence and Old Problems of Interpretation', Protocol of the 28th Colloquy of the Center for Hermeneutical Studies in Hellenistic and Modern Culture (ed. W. Wuellner), 1977, pp. 10, 19. The diffusion of the gold plates is easily accounted for on the 'craftsmen' model of telestai.

3. In Burkert, 'Orphism and Bacchic Mysteries', p. 21.

4. For a survey, see Burkert, 'Orphism and Bacchic Mysteries' and Griechische Religion der archaischen und klassischen Epoche, 1977, pp. 432–51. The basic collection of fragments remains O. Kern, Orphicorum Fragmenta, 1922. Notable for their critical position are U. von Wilamowitz-Moellendorff, Der Glaube der Hellenen II (henceforth: GdH), 1932, pp. 182–207; I. M. Linforth, The Arts of Orpheus, 1941; G. Zuntz, Persephone, 1971. Much more sympathetic are W. K. C. Guthrie, Orpheus and Greek Religion, 1952[2]; K. Ziegler, 'Orpheus', PW XVIII, 1939–42, cols. 1200–1316, 1341–1417. The terms 'Sekte' and 'Gemeinde' with reference to Orphics have been used ever since E. Rohde, Psyche II, 1898[2], pp. 103f.; O. Kern, Orpheus, 1920, added 'Dogma' and 'Bibel' (pp. 39, 43); the term 'church' in A. J. Toynbee, A Study of History I, 1935[2], p. 99; V, 1939, p. 84

(referring to Nilsson) and (polemically) W. Jaeger, *The Theology of the Early Greek Philosophers*, 1947, p. 61.

5. M. Detienne, 'Les chemins de la déviance: Orphisme, Dionysisme et Pythagorisme', in *Orfismo in Magna Grecia*; Atti del Quattordicesimo Convegno di Studi sulla Magna Grecia, 1975, pp. 49–78 (henceforth Detienne, *Taranto*) and *Dionysos mis à mort*, 1977, pp. 163–207, ET, *Dionysos Slain*, 1979, pp. 68–94; cf. 'Pratiques culinaires et esprit de sacrifice', *La cuisine du sacrifice en pays grec*, 1979, pp. 14–6.

6. Cf. Burkert, 'Orphism and Bacchic Mysteries', pp. 6f.

7. Cf. n. 4; Detienne, *Taranto*, p. 53 etc.; methodical circumspection in L. Gernet, *Le génie grec dans la religion*, 1932 (repr. 1970), pp. 121f.

8. B. R. Wilson, *Sects and Society*, 1961, esp. 325–27; *Religious Sects*, 1970, 22–35; cf. D. E. Miller, 'Sectarianism and Secularization: The Work of Bryan Wilson', *RSR* 5, 1979, p. 163; A. Momigliano, 'The Social Structure of the Ancient City', in *Anthropology and the Greeks* (ed. S. C. Humphreys), 1978, pp. 190f.; a survey of modern research in K. Rudolph, 'Wesen und Struktur der Sekte', *Kairos* 21, 1979, pp. 241–54; he holds that sects in the strict sense presuppose 'Bekenntnisreligionen' from which they diverge. I shall not discuss here the ancient concept of *hairesis*, on which see H. von Staden in this volume.

9. See C. Andresen, *Die Kirchen der alten Christenheit*, 1971, pp. 7–10.

10. Wilamowitz, *GdH*, pp. 192f., 199.

11. Apollodorus, *FGrH* 244 F 139 = Sch. E. *Alc.* 1; A. Henrichs, 'Philodemos "De Pietate" als mythographische Quelle', *Cronache Ercolanesi* 5, 1975, pp. 35f. (new text of Philodemus, *Piet.*, p. 16 = *Orph. Fr.* 36); further Iamblichus, *VP* 151 and Stobaeus 1.49.38; Porphyry, *Gaur.* 34.26 = *Orph. Fr.* 124; frequently in Proclus, *Orph. Fr.* 90; 110; 122; 168; 210, etc.

12. Achilles Tatius, *Intr. Arat.*, p. 33.17; 37.8 = *Orph. Fr.* 70.

13. Theophrastus, *Char.* 16.11 = *Orph. Fr.* T 207; Philodemus, *Poem.* Fr. 41 Hausrath = *Orph. Fr.* T 208; Plutarch, *Lac. apophth.*, *Mor.* 224E (an anecdote referring to the early fifth century; D.L. 6.4, in a parallel version, has *hiereus*).

14. Cf. Proclus, *In Ti.* III 297 = *Orph. Fr.* 229: *hoi par' Orphei tōi Dionysōi kai tēi Korēi teloumenoi.* – *Orphikoisi* in Herodotus 2.81 refers to *Orphika*, E. R. Dodds, *The Greeks and the Irrational*, 1951, p. 169 n. 80; W. Burkert, *Lore and Science in Ancient Pythagoreanism*, ET 1972, pp. 127f.

15. Plato, *Phdr.* 244DE (accepting Hermann's *ēn* D7, and leaving *heautēs* E3).

16. Euripides, *Alc.* 967; Wilamowitz, *GdH*, p. 193.

17. Col. 16 of the preliminary transcript; cf. n. 1.

18. Strabo 10.3.23; on his theological excursus, see K. Reinhardt, *Poseidonios über Ursprung und Entartung*, 1928, pp. 34–54, and 'Poseidonios', *PW* XXII, 1953, col. 814.

19. 'Thaletas', *PW* VA, 1934, col. 1213; esp. Plutarch, *Mus.* 42, *Mor.* 1146BC = Pratinas, *TGFI*, 4 F 9 Snell, and Philodemus, *Mus.* 4, p. 85 = *SVF* III, p. 232 (Diogenes of Babylon); Plutarch, *Mus.* 9f., *Mor.* 1134B–E,

following Glaucus of Rhegion. On *Wundermänner* in general see Rohde, *Psyche* II, pp. 89–102; Burkert, *Lore and Science*, pp. 147–54.

20. Epimenides, *FGrH* 457 esp. T 4b; Burkert, *Lore and Science*, pp. 151f.

21. Burkert, *Lore and Science*, pp. 149f.; the foundation of a Kore temple at Sparta is attributed either to Abaris or to Orpheus, Pausanias 3.13.2.

22. Empedocles, *Katharmoi* B 112; cf. Zuntz, *Persephone*, pp. 186–92. C. Gallavotti, *Empedocle, Poema fisico e lustrale*, 1975, p. 268, wishes to spiritualize the 'profit' besought of Empedocles; but cf. the authentic questions from Dodona, H. W. Parke, *The Oracles of Zeus*, 1967, pp. 268–71.

23. For the magicians and charlatans: Hippocrates, VI 354 Littré, *On the Sacred Disease* 2 (LCL II, p. 140); see now G. E. R. Lloyd, *Magic, Reason and Experience*, 1979, pp. 15–29, 37–49. For *banausia*: VI 396 L., *On the Sacred Disease* 21 (LCL II, p. 182 n. 4).

24. Listed in R. Borger, *Handbuch der Keilschriftliteratur* III, 1975, pp. 85–93; a good survey still in B. Meissner, *Babylonien und Assyrien* II, 1925, pp. 198–282; a selection of translations in G. R. Castellino, *Testi Sumerici e Accadici*, 1977, pp. 519–732.

25. Herodotus 9.33–36; see Hepding, 'Iamos', *PW* IX, 1916, cols. 685–9; a seer from the 'blood of Melampus' in Pausanias 6.17.6; in general, I. Löffler, *Die Melampodie*, 1963; P. Kett, *Prosopographie der historischen griechischen Manteis bis auf die Zeit Alexanders des Grossen*, 1966.

26. Plutarch, *Is. et Os.* 28, *Mor.* 362A; Tacitus, *Hist.* 4.83f.; see now A. Alföldi, 'Redeunt Saturnia regna VII: Frugifer-Triptolemos im ptolemäischen Herrscherkult', *Chiron* 9, 1979, pp. 554f. with lit.; in general, K. Clinton, *The Sacred Officials of the Eleusinian Mysteries*, 1974.

27. *IMagn.* no. 215, see A. Henrichs, 'Greek maenadism from Olympias to Messalina', *HSCP* 82, 1978, pp. 123–37.

28. Isocrates, *Or.* 19.5f.; 45; on the legal situation, H. J. Wolff, *Das Problem der Konkurrenz von Rechtsordnungen in der Antike*, SHAW 1979.5, pp. 15–34. This passage was brought to my attention by F. Heinimann.

29. *SEG* XVI 103, alluding to the judgment about Amphiaraos, *Thebais*, ed. Allen, Fr. 5; Pindar, *Olymp.* 6.17; Kett, *Prosopographie*, pp. 52f.; on Aeschines's mother, Demosthenes 19.249, 281; 18.129, 259f.

30. W. Schubart, 'Ptolemäus Philopator und Dionysos', *Amtliche Berichte der Preussischen Kunstsammlungen* 38, 1916–17, pp. 189f.; *Sammelb.*, p. 7266; G. Zuntz, 'Once more the so-called Edict of Philopator on the Dionysiac mysteries', *Hermes* 91, 1963, pp. 228–39, 384.

31. Porphyry, *VP* 1 = Neanthes, *FGrH* 84 F 29; W. Burkert, 'Die Leistung eines Kreophylos. Kreophyleer, Homeriden und die archäische Heraklesepik', *MH* 29, 1972, pp. 77f.

32. Plato, *Prt.* 311B, *Phdr.* 270C, Soranus, *Vit. Hippocr.* 1f. ('taught by his father'); extremely sceptical are E. J. and L. Edelstein, *Asclepius* II, 1945, pp. 53–62.

33. Homer, *Od.* 17.384ff.

34. Tacitus, *Ann.* 11.15; cf. Cicero, *Div.* 1.92; C. O. Thulin, *Die etruskische Disziplin* II. *Die Haruspizin*, 1906; A. Pfiffig, *Religio Etrusca*, 1975, pp. 36–41; 115–27.

35. H. Zimmern, *Beiträge zur Kenntnis der Babylonischen Religion* II, 1901, nr. 24, 19–22; cf. E. Ebeling, *Tod und Leben nach den Vorstellungen der Babylonier* I, 1931, pp. 37, 47: 'Der Wissende soll es dem Wissenden zeigen'.

36. Hippocrates, IV 642 L; *Law* 5 (LCL II, p. 264); on the 'oath', see L. Edelstein, *Ancient Medicine*, 1967, pp. 3–63 (making too direct connections with Pythagoreanism).

37. *ANET*, pp. 100f.; 99f. was taken to be an 'incantation', but proved to be part of the Atraḥasīs epic: W. G. Lambert and A. R. Millard, *Atraḥasīs, The Babylonian Story of the Flood*, 1969; but the epic clearly retells magic, and sections of it were in turn used by magicians, Lambert and Millard, *Atraḥasīs*, p. 28.

38. Olympiodorus, *In Phd.*, p. 2.21 Norvin = pp. 41f. Westerink = *Orph. Fr.* 220. It is important that the 'four divine monarchies' mentioned here disagree with the Orphic 'Rhapsodies', but agree with the Derveni theogony; see also Burkert, *Griechische Religion*, pp. 442f.

39. Atraḥasīs I 212–7, Lambert and Millard, *Atraḥasīs*, p. 59; the different interpretation of W. von Soden, 'Die erste Tafel des altbabylonischen Atramhasis-Mythus', *Zeitschrift für Assyriologie* 68, 1978, pp. 50–94, of what is translated 'spirit' here seems to be very far-fetched. A similar anthropogony occurs in *Enuma eliš* VI 1–34, *ANET*, p. 68.

40. Aristotle, *Rh.* 3.1418A24 = Epimenides, *FGrH* 457 F 1.

41. Pindar, Fr. 133, cf. P. Tannery, 'Orphica fr. 208 Abel', *RPh* 23, 1899, p. 129; H. J. Rose, 'The grief of Persephone', *HTR* 36, 1943, p. 247; Burkert, *Griechische Religion*, p. 443.

42. The first description of such a person seems to occur in Semonides (ed. West), Fr. 10a, cf. M. L. West, 'Notes on newly-discovered fragments of Greek authors', *Maia* 20, 1968, pp. 195–7. Seers do not eat beans, Cicero, *Div.* 1.62; *Gp.* 2.358.

43. Hesiod, *Op.* 25f.

44. On wandering craftsmen, see Laws of Solon, Plutarch, *Sol.* 24.4 and Ben Sira 38.30; in general, A. Burford, *Craftsmen in Greek and Roman Society*, 1972.

45. Sophocles, *OT* 410.

46. C. Lévi-Strauss, *Structural Anthropology*, 1963, pp. 175–8, following F. Boas, *The Religion of the Kwakiutl*, II, 1930, pp. 1–41.

47. Plato, *Lg.* 782D; J. Haussleiter, *Der Vegetarismus in der Antike*, 1935, pp. 79–96; on the importance and function of this 'protest' see esp. Detienne (n. 5); on Aristophanes, *Ra.* 1032, see F. Graf, *Eleusis und die orphische Dichtung Athens in vorhellenistischer Zeit*, 1974, pp. 34f.; contra, Detienne, *Taranto*, pp. 60f., *Dionysos*, pp. 169f., ET, 71f.

48. Diodorus Siculus 34.2 following Poseidonius.

49. Livy 39.8.3f. *sacrificulus et vates*. See A. Bruhl, *Liber Pater*, 1953, pp. 47–116; A. J. Festugière, *Études de religion grecque et hellénistique*, 1972, pp. 89–109. The authorities made provision that henceforth *Bacchanalia* should have neither priests nor 'common money', *Senatus consultum* 11f., Livy 39.18.9.

50. (Demosthenes) 25.79 *pharmakis*; Philochorus, *FGrH* 328 F 60 *mantis*;

Plutarch, *Dem.* 14.6 *hiereia*; cf. *Dem.* 19.281; 'Theoris', *PW* VA, 1934, cols. 2237f.

51. Euripides, *Hipp.* 952–4; cf. W. S. Barrett, *Euripides, Hippolytos*, 1964, pp. 342–5 with lit.

52. See n. 2. I have to thank J. Vinogradov for additional information.

53. A. N. Ammann, *-ikos bei Platon*, 1953, pp. 259–66.

54. See K. von Fritz, 'Pythagoras', *PW* XXIV, 1963, cols. 172–9; Burkert, *Lore and Science*, pp. 97–109. W. K. C. Guthrie, *A History of Greek Philosophy* I, 1962, pp. 148–81.

55. Scholars tried to use the evidence of the coins; on those of Croton, see C. J. de Vogel, *Pythagoras and early Pythagoreanism*, 1966, pp. 52–7; on the Pythagoras-coins of Abdera, W. Schwabacher, 'Pythagoras auf griechischen Münzbildern', *Opuscula K. Kerényi dedicata*, 1968, pp. 59–63; D. Mannsperger finds a representation of Pythagoras on a fifth-century coin of Metapontum, Iamblichus, *De Vita Pythagorica* (ed. L. Deubner), 1975², p. xx.

56. Aristoxenus in *Die Schule des Aristoteles* II (ed. F. Wehrli), 1967²; *PW* XXIV, cols. 172–5.

57. Timaeus, *FGrHist* 566 F 13; 14; 16; 17; 131; 132; K. von Fritz, *Pythagorean Politics in Southern Italy*, 1940, pp. 33–67; *PW* XXIV, cols. 176f.; Burkert, *Lore and Science*, pp. 103–5.

58. Iamblichus, *VP*, ed. L. Deubner, 1937, repr. 1975; the basic analysis of the sources was given by E. Rohde, 'Die Quellen des Jamblichus in seiner Biographie des Pythagores', *RhM*, 1871–2 = *Kleine Schriften* II (ed. F. Schöll), 1901, pp. 102–72, whose thesis that Iamblichus used only two books, Nicomachus and Apollonius, has, however, been refuted: Burkert, *Lore and Science*, p. 100. On his life and his 'Pythagorean sequence', see now B. D. Larsen, *Jamblique de Chalcis*, 1972, pp. 34–42, 66–100, and J. M. Dillon, *Iamblichi Chalcidensis in Platonis dialogos commentariorum fragmenta*, 1973, pp. 3–25. Iamblichus's lifetime is about 245/50 to 325 CE; Dillon, *Iamblichi*, pp. 18–25, very tentatively dates the 'Pythagorean sequence' to about 280; it may well be later.

59. Iamblichus, *VP* 253, p. 136. 1–3; cf. Porphyry, *VP* 58, p. 50.2. Iamblichus did not use Porphyry directly, Burkert, *Lore and Science*, pp. 98f. Similarities between Iamblichus, *VP* and Athanasius, *Vita S. Antonii*, have been noted since K. Holl and R. Reitzenstein, see esp. A. J. Festugière, *Études de philosophie grecque*, 1971, pp. 443–61.

60. Iamblichus, *VP* 29; *LSJ* s.v. adds Ptolemaeus, *Tetr.* 3.6.4, p. 119, where the word is introduced for *koinonous biou* by some later manuscripts.

61. Burkert, *Lore and Science*, pp. 30, 8; cf. F. Sartori, *Le eterie nella vita politica ateniese del VI e V sec. A.C.*, 1957; W. Rösler, *Dichter und Gruppe*, 1980, pp. 33–5; for *kreophyleioi* see n. 31.

62. *Gnōrimoi* appears to be a catchword of Aristoxenus, Fr. 11–25 Wehrli; Suidas s.v. *gnōrimoi*; Porphyry, *VP* 22; Iamblichus, *VP* 34; cf. n. 85 below; *hetairoi* Porphyry, *VP* 54, Iamblichus, *VP* 246, cf. *prosetairizeto* Aristoxenus Fr. 43. The term *hairesis* (Aristoxenus Fr. 18) cannot go back to Aristoxenus himself.

63. Iamblichus, *VP* 255, cf. *idiotropos agogē* 247; *idiazein* 257; *ta ex archēs ethē* Aristoxenus Fr. 18. On vegetarianism, Haussleiter, *Vegetarismus*, pp. 97–157; Burkert, *Lore and Science*, pp. 180–3; on beans, Burkert, *Lore and Science*, pp. 183–5.

64. Anaximander the younger, *FGrH* 9 T 1; see F. Boehm, *De symbolis Pythagoreis*, 1905; Burkert, *Lore and Science*, pp. 166–92.

65. Dicaearchus Fr. 34 Wehrli = Porphyry, *VP* 56.

66. Timaeus, *FGrH* 566 F 13; R. von Poehlmann, *Geschichte der sozialen Frage und des Sozialismus in der antiken Welt* I, 1925³, pp. 41–4 high-handedly dismisses the Pythagorean evidence.

67. D.L. 10.11 = *Epicurea* 543.

68. Timaeus, *FGrH* 566 F 13 = Scholion on Plato, *Phdr.* 279C; closely parallel, but more extensive in Iamblichus, *VP* 71–4, in fact two parallel texts, pp. 40.15–42.4‖42.4–22; see von Fritz, *Pythagorean Politics*, p. 39 – Hippolytus, *Haer.* 1.2.16 *pipraskein ta hyparchonta* seems to echo NT Matt. 19.21; Acts 4.36f.

69. Iamblichus, *VP* 72.

70. Timaeus, *FGrH* 566 F 13B = D.L. 8.10.

71. Iamblichus, *VP* 30 = Porphyry, *VP* 20; on *homakoeion*, see Burkert, *Lore and Science*, p. 176.

72. Iamblichus, *VP* 92.

73. Diodorus Siculus 10.3.5; cf. *biou koinonia* 10.8.2; Diogenes Antonius in Porphyry, *VP* 33; two categories also in Hippolytus, *Haer.* 1.2.17; Iamblichus, *VP* 80f. Iustinus 20.4.14 assigns to the *hetairia* of 300 Pythagoreans at Croton *separatam a ceteris vitam*.

74. Diodorus Siculus 10.4; cf. 10.3.5; Iamblichus, *VP* 127f.; 237; 239.

75. Iamblichus, *VP* 96–100; parallel is Diogenes Antonius in Porphyry, *VP* 32; cf. P. Boyancé, 'Sur la vie pythagoricienne', *REG* 52, 1939, pp. 36–50. Similar is the account of the daily life of the Essenes in Josephus, *BJ* 2.128–33.

76. Aristoxenus, Fr. 27, cf. D.L. 8.19.

77. Aristoxenus, Fr. 31 = Iamblichus, *VP* 233–7, Porphyry, *VP* 59–61.

78. Neanthes, *FGrH* 84 F 31 = Iamblichus, *VP* 189–94. Similar 'seasonal migrations' are ascribed to Diogenes the Cynic, Dio Chrysostom 6.1–6; Sch. Luc., p. 125.8–14.

79. Alexis Fr. 196f. = Athenaeus 4.161CD; Cratinus Iun. Fr. 6 = D.L. 8.37; on female students of Pythagoras, Dicaearchus Fr. 33 = Porphyry, *VP* 18f.; Philochorus, *FGrH* 328 T 1; Iustinus 20.4.8; D.L. 8.42; Iamblichus, *VP* 30; 54; 132; 267; in general, J. Vogt, *Von der Gleichwertigkeit der Geschlechter in der bürgerlichen Gesellschaft der Griechen*, 1960, pp. 2, 248.

80. Iamblichus, *VP* 50, cf. 48; 55; 132; 195 (quoting Plato, *Lg.* 841D).

81. According to the often-quoted principle, (Demosthenes) 59.122, Greeks had *hetairai* for pleasure and wives for the sake of legitimate offspring, i.e., preferably *one* son (Hesiod, *Op.* 376).

82. D.L. 8.43 with the parallels noted by A. Delatte, *La vie de Pythagore de Diogene Laerce*, 1922, Iamblichus, *VP* 55; 132; see E. Fehrle, *Die kultische Keuschheit im Altertum*, 1910, pp. 155f., 232f.

83. Iamblichus, *VP* 83.

84. Hieronymus Fr. 42 Wehrli = D.L. 8.21.

85. Iamblichus, *VP* 34, with the catchword *gnōrimoi* (n. 62).

86. Iamblichus, *VP* 73; 74; cf. n. 68.

87. Timaeus, *FGrH* 566 F 14 = D.L. 8.54.

88. *Epistolographi Graeci*, ed. R. Hercher, 1873, pp. 601–3; Iamblichus, *VP* 75f.; Burkert, 'Hellenistische Pseudopythagorica', *Philologus* 104, 1961, pp. 17–28.

89. Burkert, *Lore and Science*, pp. 454–62; Iamblichus, *VP* 246.

90. Nicomachus in Iamblichus, *VP* 252.

91. H. Thesleff, *The Pythagorean Texts of the Hellenistic Period*, 1965, pp. 163–8.

92. Burkert, *Lore and Science*, pp. 120–36.

93. See D.L. 8.46 and Cicero, *ND* 1.10, with the parallels noted by Delatte and A. S. Pease (*M. Tulli Ciceronis de Natura Deorum Libri III*, 1955) respectively.

94. Burkert, *Lore and Science*, pp. 136–47.

95. The tradition about Pythagoras's son Telauges seems to be totally apocryphal, though pre-Hellenistic; see K. von Fritz, 'Telauges', *PW* VA, 1934, cols. 194–6; he never appears as a miracle-worker.

96. Epameinondas towards Lysis, Aristoxenus Fr. 18 = Iamblichus, *VP* 250; Pythagoras towards Pherecydes, Diodorus 10.3.4; cf. Paul, I Cor. 4.15; Burkert, *Lore and Science*, pp. 179f.

97. Iamblichus, *VP* 85; 86.

98. Iamblichus, *Comm. math.* 25, pp. 76.16–78.8; *VP* 81; 87–9; K. von Fritz, *Mathematiker und Akusmatiker bei den alten Pythagoreern*, SBAW 1960.11; Burkert, *Lore and Science*, pp. 192–208, esp. 195f. on Aristotle; pp. 232f. on a later distinction between 'genuine' and less genuine Pythagoreans.

99. Iamblichus, *VP* 82.

100. Iamblichus, *VP* 87.

101. Clement of Alexandria, *Strom.* 1.22.150.3; cf. M. Hengel, *Judaism and Hellenism*, ET 1974, I, pp. 163–9.

102. Josephus, *AJ* 15.371, still followed by Eduard Zeller, *Die Philosophie der Griechen* III 2, 1902⁴, pp. 365–77. A striking verbal coincidence is *BJ* 2.137 and Timaeus, *FGrH* 566 F 13, Festugière, *Études de philosophie grecque*, p. 446.

103. I. Lévy, *La légende de Pythagore de Grèce en Palestine*, 1927; *Recherches esséniennes et pythagoriciennes*, 1965.

104. Neanthes, *FGrH* 84 F 29 = Porphyry, *VP* 1.

105. The 'Neopythagorean' revival is heterogeneous (cf. Burkert, 'Hellenistische Pseudopythagorica', pp. 226–46): At the time of Cicero, there is Nigidius Figulus, specialist in occult literature and centre of a conventicle; then there is Anaxilaus of Larissa, a solitary *Pythagoreus et magus*. The imperial period saw philosophical writers such as Moderatus of Gades and Nicomachus, but also those charismatics of persisting fame, Apollonius of Tyana and Alexander of Abonuteichos. In his case, the local cult, i.e. probably the local clientele, outlived the founder, yet apparently did not develop sectarian organization.

2. Are you a Stoic? The Case of Marcus Aurelius

1. J. M. Rist, *Stoic Philosophy*, 1969, p. 283.

2. So P. Hadot, 'La physique comme exercise spirituel ou pessimisme et optimisme chez Marc-Aurèle', *RTP* 22, 1972, pp. 225–39, and 'Une clé des Pensées de Marc-Aurèle', *Les Études Philosophiques*, 1978, pp. 65–84.

3. The *Meditations* are hereinafter cited only by book and paragraph.

4. 1.9; cf. *SHA* 4.3.2.

5. 1.8; 1.17.4; *SHA* 4.2.7; Fronto, *Epp.* V.36 (51), (ed. S. A. Naber, p. 86).

6. 1.7; cf. 1.17.4.

7. 1.15.1; cf. 1.17.4; 11.16.9.

8. 1.13; cf. *SHA* 4.3.2.

9. A. S. L. Farquharson, *The Meditations of the Emperor Marcus Aurelius* II, 1944, p. 458; *Med.* 1.14; cf. *SHA* 4.3.3 and n. 52 below.

10. For Aristo and life according to nature see J. M. Rist, 'Zeno and Stoic Consistency', *Phronesis* 22, 1977, pp. 161–74.

11. See A. A. Long, 'The Stoic Concept of Evil', *PhilosQ* 18, 1968, pp. 329–43.

12. Cf. A. Gellius, *NA* 7.1.7 (*SVF* II, p. 1170).

13. Cf. P. A. Brunt, 'Marcus Aurelius in his *Meditations*', *JRS* 64, 1974, pp. 11f., 19.

14. '*Ambitiosa mors*', Tacitus, *Agr.* 42.

15. 11.3. *hōs hoi christianoi* seems to be interpolated. So now P. A. Brunt, 'Marcus Aurelius and the Christians', *Studies in Latin Literature and Roman History*, ed. C. Deroux, I, 1980, pp. 483–520, esp. p. 493. Most of Marcus's 'references' to Christians must be abandoned after Brunt's discussion, but I am still inclined to think he refers to them among others at 3.16.

16. Clement of Alexandria, *Strom.* 2.21.129.5.

17. 10.8.11; cf. 'It is more graceful (*chariesterou*) to die untainted with falsehood' (9.2).

18. As Farquharson suggests (*Meditations* II, p. 737), this may not be what Epicurus (who perhaps thought of *intermittent* pain) had in mind; but other Epicureans (including Diogenes of Oenoanda) were less precise and took the text in the same way as Marcus.

19. 8.1; 1.17.8; cf. 7.67, where being a *physikos* is also discredited.

20. Cf. 12.18; 12.29.

21. 12.10. For *anaphora* as 'objective', 'object of desire', see 12.8; 12.20; cf. 7.4.

22. Farquharson's translation 'individuality of the cause' must be mistaken.

23. 10.7.3; for an apparently orthodox use of *poiotēs* (quality) see 6.3. For general discussion, M. E. Reesor, 'The Stoic Categories', *AJP* 78, 1957, p. 81.

24. Plutarch, *SR* 9, *Mor.* 1035C (*SVF* II 68).

25. Epictetus, *Disc.* 1.9.13.

26. Farquharson, *Meditations* II, p. 503.

27. Farquharson, *Meditations* II, p. 506. See further Clement in GCS 3,

p. 202.21. H. Dörrie, 'Emanation – ein unphilosophisches Wort im spätantiken Denken', *Parusia. Studien zur Philosophie Platons und zur Problemgeschichte des Platonismus. Festgabe für J. Hirschberger* (ed. K. von Flasch), 1965, pp. 119–41, argues that the pre-Plotinian uses are 'theological' rather than philosophical.

28. 2.2; 11.20; 12.3. For 'pneumatic' doctors see G. Verbeke, *L'évolution de la doctrine du Pneuma du Stoicisme à S. Augustin*, 1945, pp. 191–206.

29. Galen, *Hipp. et Plat.* 5.6 (V.469 Kuhn; p. 448. 15 Müller); cf. Rist, *Stoic Philosophy*, p. 266. Clement of Alexandria (*Strom.* 2.21.129.5 = Fr. 186 Edelstein-Kidd) observes that Posidonius included 'not being led by the irrational part of the soul' in his definition of the 'end' of life.

30. Cf. H. Erbse, 'Die Vorstellung von der Seele bei Marc Aurel', *Festschrift F. Zucker*, 1954, pp. 136f.; R. Neuenschwander, *Marc Aurels Beziehungen zu Seneca und Poseidonios*, 1951. But Neuenschwander habitually makes the assumption that similarity entails direct derivation. The oddity of Marcus's theory (in Stoic terms) was already clear to A. Bonhoeffer, *Epictet und die Stoa*, 1890, pp. 30f.

31. J. M. Rist, *Stoic Philosophy*, p. 232. For *proairesis*, 8.56; 11.36; 12.33.

32. For association of the two see Lucian, *Alex.* 38, though the charge of desertion (technically true of Epicureans) is more factually true of Christians.

33. Bonhoeffer, *Epictet*, p. 31.

34. J. M. Rist, *Stoic Philosophy*, p. 269.

35. Erbse, ('Die Vorstellung', p. 129) gets this wrong.

36. So R. Hoven, *Stoicisme et Stoiciens face au problème de l'au-delà*, 1971, p. 148.

37. E.g. Farquharson, *Meditations* II, p. 529.

38. E. R. Dodds, *Pagan and Christian in an Age of Anxiety*, 1965, p. 29 n. 1.

39. G. W. Bowersock, *Greek Sophists in the Roman Empire*, 1969, pp. 71–5. For a reply, J. E. G. Whitehorne, 'Was Marcus Aurelius a hypochondriac?', *Latomus* 36, 1977, pp. 413–21. Whitehorne shows that by comparison with Fronto, Marcus was healthy in this regard!

40. T. W. Africa, 'The Opium Addiction of Marcus Aurelius', *JHI* 22, 1961, pp. 97–102. A more moderate, though still unconvincing proposal along the same lines is offered by C. Witke, 'Marcus Aurelius and Mandragora', *CP* 60, 1965, pp. 23f.

41. Brunt, 'Marcus Aurelius in his *Meditations*', p. 8.

42. Dio Cassius, 69.21.2.

43. A. A. Long, 'Heraclitus and Stoicism', *Philosophia* 5–6, 1975–6, pp. 133–56; for Marcus, p. 153.

44. Basically that of R. Hirzel, *Untersuchungen zu Cicero's philosophischen Schriften* II.1, 1882, pp. 115–82.

45. As in the case of Aenesidemus; cf. J. M. Rist, 'The Heracliteanism of Aenesidemus', *Phoenix* 24, 1970, pp. 309–19.

46. For other rivers and cycles, 6.17; 9.2.8; 4.46. For other references, 6.11 (perhaps); 6.42; 9.19, etc.

47. Cf. 4.19; 6.24; 6.47; 6.59; 8.31.

48. For further discussion see J. M. Rist, *Stoic Philosophy*, pp. 283–88; V. Goldschmidt, *Le système stoïcien et l'idée de temps*, 1977³, pp. 197, 207, 248f.

49. 7.3; 2.17. The latter text is misleadingly said to refer to the 'life' of man's mind by Dodds (*Pagan and Christian*, p. 21).

50. 6.36; for *aiōn* cf. 4.3; 5.24.

51. 2.1; cf. 8.37, quoting Epictetus.

52. 12.36; 2.16. For law see G. R. Stanton, 'The cosmopolitan ideas of Epictetus and Marcus Aurelius', *Phronesis* 13, 1968, pp. 183–95, esp. p. 191. In contrast to Marcus, Epictetus concentrates on the individual as citizen, Marcus on the universe as state. Was his source Severus? See Stanton (p. 193) on 1.14.1 and its sources.

53. The theme of *sympatheia* has been connected with Posidonius; perhaps Epictetus is a better proximate source (see n. 55 below). Note however Posidonius's account of the goal of life: *to zēn theōrounta tēn tōn holōn alētheian kai taxin kai sygkataskeuazonta autēn kata to dynaton, k.t.l.* (Fr. 186 Edelstein-Kidd), and compare it with 8.26: *epitheōrēsis tēs tōn holōn physeōs kai tōn kat' autēn ginomenōn.*

54. As in 7.13 (*melos-meros*).

55. 9.9.2; cf. Epictetus, *Disc.* 1.14.

56. 4.14; 4.21. Notice that the passages occur nearby. Marcus seems to dwell on bits of Stoic theory from time to time, then pass to others.

57. 2.1; cf. 7.26. Brunt ('Marcus Aurelius in his *Meditations*', pp. 11f.) comments on the serenity of the sage as traditionally Stoic.

58. 6.23; cf. Stanton, 'The cosmopolitan ideas', p. 188.

59. 6.39. For Marcus's hatred and awareness of dissimulation see 1.16.5; 9.29.

60. Seneca, *De vita beata* 15.

61. Brunt, 'Marcus Aurelius in his *Meditations*', pp. 14–17.

62. 4.24; cf. Seneca, *Tranq.* 12.

63. R. B. Todd, *Alexander of Aphrodisias on Stoic Physics*, 1976, p. 1.

64. Porphyry, *VP* 20.

3. *Self-Definition Among Epicureans and Cynics*

1. See A. D. Simpson, 'Epicureans, Christians, Atheists in the Second Century', *TAPA* 72, 1941, pp. 372–81; Abraham J. Malherbe, 'Hellenistic Moralists and the New Testament', *ANRW* II.26 (ed. W. Haase), nn. 235–38 (in press).

2. Tertullian, *Apol.* 38. Cf. R. L. Wilken, 'Collegia, Philosophical Schools, and Theology', *The Catacombs and the Colosseum* (ed. S. Benko and J. J. O'Rourke), 1971, pp. 268–91, esp. 282–4.

3. N. W. DeWitt, *Epicurus and His Philosophy*, 1954, pp. 336ff., and esp. *St Paul and Epicurus*, 1954, both of which vastly overstate the case.

4. B. Farrington, *The Faith of Epicurus*, 1967, pp. 144ff., who is far more restrained than DeWitt.

5. On Christian polemic against the Epicureans, see W. Schmid,

'Epikur', *RAC* V, 1962, cols. 780–803; H. Steckel, 'Epikuros', *PW*, Suppl. XI, 1968, cols. 647f., and further on the subject, R. Jungkuntz, *Epicureanism and the Church Fathers*, PhD Diss, University of Wisconsin, Ann Arbor, Mich. 1961, and 'Fathers, Heretics and Epicureans', *JEH* 17, 1966, 3–10.

6. Schmid, 'Epikur', cols. 708f., 755f. Cf. A. A. Long, *Hellenistic Philosophy*, 1974, p. 19, who suggests that Zeno of Sidon (150–70 BCE) may have gone beyond Epicurus in his work on logic.

7. Steckel, 'Epikuros', col. 647.

8. P. H. De Lacy, 'Lucretius and the History of Epicureanism,' *TAPA* 79, 1948, p. 13.

9. Cf. R. Müller, *Die epikureische Gesellschaftstheorie*, 1972, pp. 9f.

10. See A. J. Festugière, *Epicurus and His Gods*, 1956, pp. 40f., for the veneration of Epicurus.

11. Philodemus, *Peri parrēsias* 45.8–11. See N. W. DeWitt, 'Organization and Procedure in Epicurean Groups,' *CP* 31, 1936, pp. 205–11.

12. Diogenes Laertius (henceforth D.L.) 10.35–37; cf. Cicero, *De finibus* 2.20. On the procedure, see P. Rabbow, *Seelenleitung*, 1954, pp. 127–30; N. W. DeWitt, *Epicurus and His Philosophy*, pp. 25, 112; I. Hadot, *Seneca und die griechisch-römische Tradition der Seelenleitung*, 1969, pp. 47ff.; H. G. Ingenkamp, *Plutarchs Schriften über die Heilung der Seele*, 1971.

13. DeWitt, *Epicurus*, pp. 100f.

14. DeWitt, *Epicurus*, pp. 349–53; C. W. Chilton, *Diogenes of Oenoanda: The Fragments*, 1971, pp. xxivff., although the matter is possibly overstated.

15. Numenius ap. Eusebius, *PE* 114.5, 727D–728A, according to Gifford's translation.

16. M. F. Smith, 'More New Fragments of Diogenes of Oenoanda,' *Études sur l'Epicurisme antique* (ed. J. Bollack and A. Laks), 1976, p. 282.

17. J. M. Rist, *Epicurus: An Introduction*, 1972, pp. 72f., 113f.; Schmid, 'Epikur', col. 755.

18. The texts are readily available in R. Hercher, *Epistolographi Graeci*. For introduction, text, and translation of the most important letters, see *The Cynic Epistles: Study Edition*, (ed. Abraham J. Malherbe), 1977.

19. Cf. D.L. 1.19–20, for Hippobotus's refusal to list the Cynics as a philosophical school. For *hairesis* as a school of thought, see John Glucker, *Antiochus and the Late Academy*, 1978, pp. 166–92. On Diogenes's passion for classification, see J. Mejer, *Diogenes Laertius and His Hellenistic Background*, 1978, 52. Julian, who also describes it as a way of life (*Or.* 6, 181D, 201A), nevertheless insists that it is a form of philosophy, a gift of the gods, but that it should be studied from the Cynics' deeds rather than their writings (ibid., 182C–189B).

20. See, for example, R. Hoistad, *Cynic Hero and Cynic King*, 1948, 34 and *passim*.

21. See D. R. Dudley, *A History of Cynicism*, 1937, p. 169; D. Amand, *Fatalisme et liberté dans l'antiquité grecque*, 1945, pp. 127–34.

22. Lucian, *Demon.* 5, 62, but see 14.

23. Cf. K. Praechter, *Die Philosophie des Altertums*, 1926, p. 512; Dudley, *A History of Cynicism*, p. 180. H. M. Hornsby, 'The Cynicism of Peregrinus

Proteus', *Hermathena* 48, 1933, pp. 65–84, discusses the evidence and is sceptical of Neopythagorean influence on Peregrinus.

24. Socrates, *Ep.* 25. In *Ep.* 18.2 and *Ep.* 20 there is a positive evaluation of Socrates's *logoi*, in contrast to Lucian, *Vit. auct.* 11, where education and doctrine are regarded as superfluous. Cf. Julian, *Or.* 6, 189AB: 'For Diogenes deeds sufficed.'

25. Praechter, *Die Philosophie des Altertums*, p. 659.

26. Epictetus 3.22; cf. M. Billerbeck, *Epiktet: Vom Kynismus*, 1978; Lucian, *Demonax*; cf. K. Funk, 'Untersuchungen über die Lucianische Vita Demonactis', *Philologus*, Suppl. 10, 1907, pp. 561–674; Maximus of Tyre 36; Julian, *Or.* 6, esp. 200C–202C.

27. This has been the case particularly with New Testament scholars who, impressed by Epictetus's view of the ideal Cynic as a messenger of God, have used his interpretation of Cynicism to illustrate the Christian apostolate and other Christian and pagan emissaries. See e.g. K. Rengstorf, '*Apostolos*', *TDNT* I, pp. 409–13, who qualifies the usefulness of Epictetus's description by saying, 'in so far as Epictetus describes for us the reality and not merely the ideal of the true Cynic' (p. 409). W. Schmithals, *The Office of Apostle in the Early Church*, ET 1969, p. 111, impatiently dismisses any other possible descriptions of religious emissaries in Hellenism and confines himself to Epictetus's description of the 'Cynic-Stoic' sage as the pre-eminent source for a figure close to the Christian apostle. D. Georgi, *Die Gegner des Paulus im 2. Korintherbrief*, 1964, pp. 32ff., 110f., 187ff., is similarly dependent on Epictetus and combines his picture of Cynicism with that of other types of religious propagandists to construct a *theios anēr* figure on which Paul's Corinthian opponents are claimed to have modelled themselves. These scholars have not done justice to the Stoic elements in Epictetus's description, nor have they sufficiently recognized that he is describing an ideal Cynic. As to Epictetus's Stoicism in 3.22, the debate among classicists has not been whether it dominates the diatribe, but whether it reveals Epictetus as a follower of early Stoicism, as A. Bonhoeffer, *Die Ethik des Stoikers Epictet*, 1894, had argued, or whether the influence of Musonius and the evidence of Seneca for contemporary Stoicism should not also be taken into consideration, as Billerbeck, *Epiktet*, does. Billerbeck, however, is more successful in distinguishing between Stoicism and Cynicism in Epictetus than between the varieties of Cynicism in the early Empire. Furthermore, Epictetus describes an ideal Cynic – from a Stoic point of view. Stoics were not at all sanguine about attaining the ideal. Epictetus himself claimed not to have done so, and his description is given to correct the popular misconception of Cynics for young men who may be considering entering that way of life. On the attainment of the ideal, see Abraham J. Malherbe, 'Pseudo Heraclitus, Epistle 4: The Divinization of the Wise Man', *JbAC* 21, 1978, pp. 54–56.

28. On the composition and dating of the corpus I follow J. Sykutris, 'Sokratikerbriefe', *PW* Suppl. V, 1931, cols. 981–87 and *Die Briefe des Sokrates und die Sokratiker*, 1933. See also L. Köhler, 'Die Briefe des Sokrates und die Sokratiker', *Philologus* Suppl. 20.2, 1928. On the appeal

to Socrates by the Stoics and Cynics in the early empire, see K. Döring, *Exemplum Socratis*, 1979, esp. pp. 114–26 on the Socratic epistles. For the school setting of the letters, see Köhler, 'Die Briefe', pp. 4–5, and W. Obens, *Qua aetate Socratis et Socraticorum epistulae quae dicuntur scriptae sunt*, 1912, p. 6. For their propagandist aim, see E. Norden, 'Beiträge zur Geschichte der griechischen Philosophie', *JCPh* Suppl. 19, 1893, p. 393, and O. Schering, *Symbola ad Socratis et Socraticorum Epistulas Explicandas*, 1917, p. 32. I am indebted to my student, Benjamin Fiore, SJ, for much of what follows.

29. Socrates, *Ep.* 23.3. Cf. Lucian, *Pisc.* 44, and for his awareness of the diversity among the Cynics, see R. Helm, 'Lucian und die Philosophen-schulen', *NJA* 9, 1902, p. 364 n. 2; M. Caster, *Lucien et la pensée religieuse de son temps*, 1937, p. 71.

30. For the Cynic as bestial and inhumane, see Lucian, *Vit. auct.* 10f.; Julian, *Or.* 7, 209A.

31. For the types, see G. A. Gerhard, *Phoinix von Kolophon*, 1909, pp. 67ff., 165ff.; and 'Zur Legende vom Kyniker Diogenes', *ARW* 15, 1912, pp. 388–408, and for a different interpretation, R. Hoistad, 'Cynicism', *Dictionary of The History of Ideas* I, 1968, pp. 631f. and J. F. Kindstrand, *Bion of Borysthenes*, 1976, pp. 64–67.

32. Despite their eclectic tendencies, Peregrinus's disciples also considered themselves Cynics (cf. *Peregrinus* 2–4, 24, 26, 29, 36, 37, 43), and he was remembered by others as an austere Cynic (A. Gellius, *NA* 8.3; 12.11; Philostratus, *VS* 563). For Oenomaus's severity, see Eusebius, *PE* 5.21, 213C; 5.23, 215D; 5.29, 224C–225A; 5.33, 228D; 6.6, 254D; 6.7, 261B, and Julian's criticism of his inhumane, bestial life (*Or.* 7,209B).

33. *Demon.* 5f. Lucian's *ou paracharattōn ta eis tēn diaitan* may be an allusion to the Cynic *paracharattein to nomisma*, cf. D.L. 6.20, 71.

34. Praechter, *Die Philosophie des Altertums*, p. 511.

35. See V. Emeljanow, 'A Note on the Cynic Short Cut to Happiness', *Mnem.* n.s. 18/2, 1965, pp. 182–84.

36. Cf. Diogenes the Cynic (henceforth Diog.) *Epp.* 7; 15; 27; 34; 46.

37. Crates, *Ep.* 19. For Cynic interpretations of Odysseus, see Abraham J. Malherbe, 'Pseudo Heraclitus, Epistle 4', pp. 50f.

38. Crates, *Ep.* 29; Diog., *Ep.* 27; Lucian, *Peregrinus* 27.

39. Diog., *Epp.* 42; 44. On Cynic *anaideia*, see Gerhard, *Phoinix*, pp. 144f. H. Schulz-Falkenthal, 'Kyniker – Zur inhaltlichen Deutung des Namens', *WZHalle* 26.2, 1977, pp. 41–9, and I. Nachov, 'Der Mensch in der Philosophie der Kyniker', *Der Mensch als Mass der Dinge* (ed. R. Müller), 1976, pp. 361–98, overstress the social and political motivations for Cynic conduct.

40. Diog., *Epp.* 29; 32. For Plato in the Cynic tradition, see A. Swift Riginos, *Platonica*, 1976, pp. 111–18, who does not, however, discuss the way the Plato anecdotes function in the debate under review. For Aristippus as representing the hedonistic Cynic, see R.·F. Hock, 'Simon the Shoemaker as an Ideal Cynic', *GRBS* 17, 1976, pp. 48–52.

41. Cf. Diog., *Ep.* 46, for the rigorist's insistence that his way of life, too, is beneficial as a demonstration of self-sufficiency.

42. See Gerhard, *Phoinix*, pp. 67ff., 156ff., 170ff.

43. The charlatans Lucian criticizes frequently affected the style of these Cynics, but for different reasons. They made up for the lack of content in their speeches by railing at the crowds (*Vit. auct.* 10f.) who, being simple people, admired them for their abusiveness (*Peregrinus* 18), delighted in their 'therapy', and thought them to be superior persons by virtue of their belligerence (*Fug.* 12; *Conv.* 12–19).

44. Diog. *Epp.* 28; 29. Cf. Heraclitus, *Epp.* 2; 4; 5; 7; 9; Hippocrates, *Ep.* 17.

45. Heraclitus, *Epp.* 5.1; 9.3, 6.

46. Diog., *Epp.* 27; 49; Hippocrates, *Ep.* 11.7.

47. E.g. Diog., *Epp.* 27; 28; 29. On the medical imagery, see Abraham J. Malherbe, 'Medical Imagery in the Pastoral Epistles', in *Texts and Testaments: Critical Essays on the Bible and Early Church Fathers* (ed. W. E. March), 1980, pp. 19–35.

48. Crates, *Ep.* 21; Diog., *Epp.* 21; 41.

49. Cf. Diog., *Ep.* 27; Heraclitus, *Ep.* 4.3; cf. D.L. 6.71.

50. Heraclitus, *Epp.* 2; 4; 7; 9; Socrates, *Ep.* 24. He would prefer, however, to live with men in order to provide an example for them to follow. Cf. Crates, *Epp.* 20; 35.2.

51. Diog., *Ep.* 28.2. Socrates, *Ep.* 24 is more ambiguous: 'Plato' is convinced that Timon was not a misanthrope. On Timon remembered as a Cynic, see F. Bertram, *Die Timonlegende*, 1906, pp. 33 n. 1, 38, 44ff.

52. T. Gomperz, *Greek Thinkers* II, 1908, p. 163.

53. Gerhard, *Phoinix*, pp. 32f.; Gomperz, *Greek Thinkers* II, p. 166. For a more nuanced treatment, see Hoistad, *Cynic Hero and Cynic King*.

54. J. Kaerst, *Geschichte des hellenistischen Zeitalters* II.1, 1909, pp. 118f., 120.

55. Julian, *Or.* 6, 201D. Cf. ibid., 188B, 189Aff., 192A, 198D; *Or.* 7, 214BC.

56. Crates, *Epp.* 6; 13; 15; 16; Diog., *Epp.* 30; 37.

57. On the pride of the misanthropic Cynic, see Gerhard, *Phoinix*, pp. 67ff.

58. Gerhard, *Phoinix*, pp. 65f., is unconvincing in his assertion that the use of the first person plural in Teles points to such an identification. Socrates, *Ep.* 23.2, '. . . we do not have such great wisdom, but only enough not to harm people in our association with them', is a *captatio benevolentiae*.

59. The letters of recommendation on behalf of political officials (Socrates *Epp.* 3; 4) are designed to illustrate his support of good men.

60. See Abraham J. Malherbe, 'Gentle as a Nurse', *NovT* 12, 1970, pp. 210ff., and 'Medical Imagery'.

61. For the criticism of resident philosophers in the context of harsh wandering preachers, see Dio Chrysostom 32.8ff., and cf. Malherbe, 'Gentle as a Nurse', pp. 205f.

62. For the Cynic's divine commission, cf. Dio Chrysostom 13.9, on which see J. L. Moles, 'The Career and Conversion of Dio Chrysostom', *JHS* 98, 1978, pp. 79–100, esp. 98f., and 32.12, on which see E. Wilmes,

Beiträge zur Alexandrinerrede (or. 32) *des Dion Chrysostomos,* 1970, pp. 8–17.

63. See Socrates, *Epp.* 1.2f.; 2; 4; 6. 8ff.; 15.2; 19; 21; 22.1; 28.2; 29.4.

64. See Obens, *Qua aetate Socratis,* pp. 11–13, for a catalogue of references to the theme.

65. E.g. Socrates, *Epp.* 9.4; 14.5f.; 22.1.

66. Cf. Socrates, *Epp.* 12; 29.5. For the seriousness with which the various types of literature are viewed, see *Epp.* 15.2f.; 18.2; 22.2. The literary dialogues are rejected, *memorabilia* are acceptable, but letters are preferred.

67. See A. Swift Riginos, *Platonica,* pp. 111–17, 148f., for Diogenes, and pp. 98–100 for Antisthenes.

68. Represented by Gomperz, *Greek Thinkers* II, p. 164; S. Dill, *Roman Society from Nero to Marcus Aurelius,* 1905²; W. Capelle, *Epiktet, Teles und Musonius,* 1948, pp. 15, 212f.

69. Represented by J. Bernays, *Lucian und die Kyniker,* 1879; H. Rahn, 'Die Frömmigkeit der Kyniker', *Paideuma* 7, 1960, pp. 280–92, who is dependent on Julian and Themistius.

70. Gerhard, *Phoinix,* pp. 79–83, 165–76, and 'Zur Legende', pp. 394ff.

71. See Lucian, *Demon.* 11, 23, 27, 34, 37, and cf. Dudley, *A History of Cynicism,* p. 178.

72. For his harshness, see Lucian, *Demon.* 21; *Peregrinus* 17, 18, 19.

73. See Malherbe, 'Pseudo Heraclitus, Epistle 4', pp. 45–51, which does not, however, do justice to the evidence of the Socratic epistles.

74. Note also Socrates, *Ep.* 34.3 and for the modesty with which the assertion is made, cf. Julian, *Or.* 7, 235 CD.

75. For a similar apologetic use of the Pythia, see Julian, *Or.* 7, 211Df., and cf. H. Niehues-Pröbsting, *Der Kynismus des Diogenes und der Begriff des Zynismus,* 1979, pp. 77–81.

76. D.L. 6.104. Cf. Mejer, *Diogenes Laertius,* pp. 3f., 6.

77. On his personality, see G. W. Bowersock, *Julian the Apostate,* 1978, pp. 13–20, and on his attacks on the pseudo-Cynics, W. J. Malley, *Hellenism and Christianity,* 1978, pp. 144–55.

78. Julian, *Or.* 6, 199A; *Or.* 7, 290ABC, 210D–211B. See notes 62 and 75 for the divine commission.

79. Julian, *Or.* 6, 181A, 202D.

80. Ibid., 201BC. The characteristics of his models, Diogenes and Crates, differ from those of the letters attributed to them, and have much in common with Lucian's description of Demonax.

81. Julian, *Or.* 7, 210C.

82. Ibid., 224C–226D.

83. On Sallustius, see K. Praechter, 'Salustios', *PW* 2nd series, IB, 1920, cols. 1967–70.

4. *Self-Definition in Later Platonism*

1. See on this the chapter '*Platonici, Academici*', pp. 206–25 of John Glucker's recent book, *Antiochus and the Late Academy,* 1978.

2. Glucker, *Antiochus*, esp. pp. 64–88.

3. Cicero, *Luc.* 18; Sextus Empiricus, *Pyrrh.* 1.235.

4. Much later, in the second century CE, the Anonymous Theaetetus Commentary still raises the question as to whether Plato is dogmatizing or not in this work (cf. Hermann Diels, Wilhelm Schubart, *Anonymer Kommentar zu Platons Theatet (papyrus 9782) nebst drei Bruchstücken philosophischen Inhalts*, 1905, cols. 54, 38ff.), though the author feels that he is.

5. Fr. 210, Plasberg (Teubner edition of *Academica*): *Ait enim (Cicero) illis morem fuisse occultandi sententiam suam nec eam cuiquam nisi qui secum ad senectutem usque vixissent aperire consuesse.*

6. Cicero, *Luc.* 139.

7. Glucker, *Antiochus*, pp. 15–17.

8. Slightly revised from H. Rackham, *Cicero: De Finibus bonorum et malorum*, 1914 (repr. 1967), pp. 397–9.

9. See on this Paul Moraux, *Der Aristotelismus bei den Griechen: von Andronikos bis Alexander von Aphrodisias* I, 1973, pp. 3–94.

10. Slightly revised from H. Rackham, *De Finibus*, p. 303.

11. Cf. Moraux, *Der Aristotelismus* I, pp. 181–93.

12. Cf. J. M. Dillon, *The Middle Platonists*, 1977, pp. 124f.

13. See the summary by Arius Didymus of Eudorus's ethical doctrine in Stobaeus, *Ecl.* 2.42.7ff.: *Eklogai Joannis Stobaei anthologium* II (ed. C. Wachsmuth), 1974³, p. 42.7ff.

14. On the murky origins of these documents, see W. Burkert, 'Hellenistische Pseudopythagorica'.

15. Cf. *Middle Platonists*, pp. 114–35.

16. C. G. Zumpt, *Über den Bestand der philosophischen Schulen in Athen und die Succession der Scholarchen*, APAW 1844, pp. 27–119.

17. J. Lynch, *Aristotle's School*, 1972, pp. 54–67, and 177–89.

18. See above, n. 1.

19. See Dillon, *Middle Platonists*, pp. 247–57. The fragments of Atticus, quoted by Eusebius in his *Praeparatio evangelica*, are collected in the Budé ed. of Baudry (Paris 1931), and now in a new edition from Édouard Des Places, in the same series (1980).

20. Plutarch, *An. proc.* 1, 2, *Mor.* 1012B, 1013AB.

21. On Favorinus, see now the excellent discussion of Glucker, *Antiochus*, pp. 280–93. I mention Favorinus only because Phillip De Lacy, in a review of *The Middle Platonists* in the *Southern Journal of Philosophy*, 1980, takes me to task for not recognizing the continuance of the sceptical tradition in Platonism after Antiochus, in such figures as Cicero, Plutarch and Favorinus. I simply do not see these figures adding up to a tradition, nor can I see in the 'scepticism' of Cicero or Plutarch more than an affectation, which does not touch their deepest convictions. The sceptical tradition continued outside Platonism, with Aenesidemus, Agrippa and Sextus Empiricus.

22. Cf. Numenius, frr. 23–8, ed. É. Des Places.

23. Numenius, fr. 23.

24. Numenius, fr. 25, lines 75–83.

25. Sextus Empiricus, *Pyrrh.* 1.234, trs. R. G. Bury, LCL I.

26. E.g. Plutarch, *Mor.* 102D, 621F, 791A, 1120C, 1122A.

27. Academics: Lucian, *Pisc.* 43; *Bis Acc.* 15; *VH* 2.18; Platonists, id., *Herm.* 16; *Eun.* 3; *Icar.* 29; *Nigr.* 2.

28. Aulus Gellius, *NA* 11.5.6–8; 15.2.1; 17.15.1; 17.21.48.

29. Origen, *Contra Celsum*, ed. and trs. H. Chadwick, 1953, p. 12.

30. In an Arabic version of his lost work *On Hippocrates' Anatomy*, written between 162 and 166 CE, collected by Richard Walzer in *Galen on Jews and Christians*, 1949, pp. 10f.

31. Plotinus, *Enn.*. 2.9.6, trs. Armstrong, LCL II, p. 247.

32. Julian, *Adv. Galil.* 96Cff., LCL III, pp. 328ff.

33. Plotinus, *Enn.* 2.9.18, LCL II, p. 297.

34. The only complete edition of the *Platonic Theology* of Proclus is still that of Aemilius Portus (1618), but this is now being superseded by the excellent Budé text of Saffrey and Westerink, which has so far reached Vol. III (of six). I quote from their edition.

35. Proclus, 1.1. 12–15 (ed. Saffrey and Westerink).

36. Plutarch, *Is. et Os.* 77, *Def. or.* 23, *Quaest. conviv.* 8.2 (*Mor.* 382D, 422E, 718CD).

37. Albinus, *Didask.*, ed. Hermann, p. 182.7ff.

38. Theon of Smyrna, *Expos.*, ed. Hiller, pp. 14.17–16.2.

5. Hairesis and Heresy

1. Galen, *De libris propriis* 1 (*Scr. Min.* II, p. 93 Müller, henceforth M).

2. G. Bergsträsser, *Ḥunain ibn Isḥāq, Über die syrischen und arabischen Galenübersetzungen*, 1925, pp. 4f.

3. Cf. O. Temkin, 'Studies on late Alexandrian Medicine I', *Bulletin of the Institute of the History of Medicine* 3, 1935, pp. 405–30.

4. Galen starts out with a more traditional bipartite division (Empiricist vs Rationalist or Dogmatist; see below), but by ch. 6 (*Scr. Min.* III, p. 12 Helmreich, henceforth H) he has added the Methodists as a third major *hairesis*. See also the Galenic and pseudo-Galenic texts mentioned in nn. 5–6.

5. Cf. e.g. Galen, *De optima secta* 7 (I, pp. 117ff. Kühn, henceforth K); ps.-Galen, *Definitiones medicae* 14 (XIX, p. 353 K); ps.-Galen, *Introductio sive medicus* 3 (XIV, p. 678 K). In ps.-Galen, *Def.* 14, the possibility of a fourth *hairesis* – the Pneumatists – is hesitantly admitted.

6. *Libr. propr.* 1 (*Scr. Min.* II, p. 94 M).

7. Cf. Temkin, 'Studies', pp. 405–30; I. von Müller, 'Über die dem Galen zugeschriebene Abhandlung 'Peri tēsaristēs haireseōs', *SBAW* 1898.1, pp. 53–162; F. Kudlien, 'Dogmatische Ärzte', *PW* Suppl. X, 1965, cols. 179f.

8. Cf. Anonymus Londinensis, *Supplementum Aristotelicum* III (1893), ed. H. Diels; M. Wellmann, *Hermes* 57, 1922, 396ff.

9. Ps.-Galen, *Introd.* 4 (XIV, p. 683 K); K. Deichgräber, *Die griechische Empirikerschule*, 1965², p. 41.

10. Ibid.

11. Erotian, *Vocum Hippocraticarum collectio*, p. 5 Nachmanson.

12. Ps.-Galen, *Introd.* 4; Deichgräber, *Empiriker*, p. 41.

13. Galen, *De libr. propr.* 9 (*Scr. Min.* II, p. 115 M); Caelius Aurelianus, *De morbis acutis* 2.6.32 (=fr. 144 Deichgräber).

14. Caelius Aurelianus, ibid.

15. Galen, *De libr. propr.* 9.

16. Galen, *De pulsuum differentiis* 4.10 (VIII, pp. 746f. K).

17. Ibid.

18. Celsus, prooem. 10: *rationalis disciplina* vs *ex ipsa professione se empiricos appellaverunt*; cf. also 13ff. (*ii, qui rationalem medicinam profitentur. . .*) vs 27ff. (*ii, qui se Empiricos ab experientia nominant*).

19. It is conceivable that *hairesis* was used as a philosophical group referent as early as the third century BCE, but the evidence is not conclusive. Polystratus, a pupil of Epicurus, used the word more than once, but his reference to the *hairesis* of the *apatheis* and the *kynikoi* (ed. K. Wilke, p. 20) as adversaries could well be a reference to their 'thoughts' or 'doctrinal choices', without clear implications of 'school'. The passage in A. Vogliano, *Epicuri et Epicureorum scripta*, 1928, fr. 3, col. IIa, 13–15, is even less conclusive. The Stoic Chrysippus's book *Hairesis, addressed to Gorgippides* (Diogenes Laertius [henceforth D.L.] 7.191) also does not represent conclusive or even persuasive evidence that philosophers used *hairesis* for 'school' as early as the third century BCE; 'choosing' is a good philosophical subject.

20. Antipater of Tarsus, a Stoic philosopher of the second century BCE, wrote a treatise *Against the haireseis* (SVF III, no. 67, p. 257). Since *hairesis* remained a central concept in Stoic ethics – as it had been in Aristotelian ethics – for individual moral or intellectual 'inclination' or 'choice', as opposed to *phygē* or avoidance, it is conceivable that Antipater meant something other than 'school' when he used *hairesis* (e.g., 'choices' he opposed).

21. Polybius 5.93.8.

22. Dionysius of Halicarnassus, *Comp. verb.* 2 (*Opusc.* II, p. 7 Usener and Radermacher); *Ep. ad Ammaeum* 7 (*Opusc.* I, p. 266), following the long quotation from Aristotle's *Rhetoric* 1.2, 1356A35–B21. Cf. also *Comp. verb.* 19 (*Opusc.* II, p. 87): 'The hairesis of Isocrates and his acquaintances'.

23. Diodorus Siculus 2.29.6. Cf. Strabo 13.4.3 (Apollodorus's 'school' or rhetorical *hairesis*), 14.6.3 (Zeno was *archēgetēs* of the Stoic *hairesis*), and 17.3.22 (Cyrenaic *hairesis*).

24. Cicero, *Epp. fam.* 15.16.3. Cf. also Varro, *Saturae Menippeae*, no. 71 *Peri haireseōn*, no. 40 *Peri archaireseōn* (pp. 191f., 207–09 Riese).

25. Cf. D.L. 1.18: 'In ethics there have been ten *haireseis*: the Academic, Cyrenaic, Elian, Megarian, Cynic, Eretrian, Dialectic, Peripatetic, Stoic, and Epicurean'; 1.19; 'But Hippobotus says in his *On haireseis* that there are nine *haireseis* and *agōgai* . . .'. See also D.L. 1.21 et passim. Sextus Empiricus also illustrates the increasingly common tendency to call philosophical schools *haireseis*; cf. *Pyrrh.* 1.16f., 34, 185; *Adv. math.* 2.25; 7.27, 141, 190, 276, 331f.; 8.348, 350, 443. Sextus also uses it of medical *haireseis*: ibid., 1.237, 241.

26. Cf. e.g. already in the first century BCE Josephus, *Vita* 10, 12, 191; *AJ* 13.171 and 20.199; *BJ* 2.118f. See also IV below.

27. Cf. e.g. Apollonius Citiensis, *In Hippocratis De articulis comm.* 1–3 (*Corpus medicorum Graecorum* [*CMG*] XI.1.1, pp. 10, 38, 64 Kollesch/ Kudlien).

28. For further details, see Deichgräber, *Empiriker*, especially pp. 269ff.

29. Cf. von Staden, 'Experiment and Experience in Hellenistic Medicine', *Bulletin of the Institute of Classical Studies* 22, 1975, pp. 188–93; Deichgräber, *Empiriker*, pp. 121–30, 44–51, 65–80, 90–96; R. Walzer (ed.), *Galen on Medical Experience*, 1944, passim.

30. See n. 18.

31. Galen, *De sectis* 5 (*Scr. Min.* III, p. 11 H).

32. Cf. von Müller, esp. pp. 57ff.

33. The stage metaphor is commensurate with Galen's admittedly polemical accounts; cf. *Methodus medendi* 1.1–4 (X, pp. 1ff.K).

34. Celsus, prooem. 57.

35. Ibid.

36. Cf. Galen, *Meth. med.* 1.1 (X, pp. 5–7 K).

37. Cf. H. Diller, 'Thessalos', *PW* VIA, 1936, cols. 168–82; L. Edelstein, 'Methodiker', *PW* Suppl. VI, 1935, cols. 358–73.

38. Cf. Celsus, prooem. 10 (see n. 18).

39. Cf. Celsus, prooem. 57: . . . quasi viam quandam quam *methodon* nominant . . .; ibid. 62ff.

40. Cf. Diller, Edelstein, locc. citt.

41. Galen, *Meth. med.* 1.2 (X, p. 7 K).

42. Ibid., 1.1, p. 5 K.

43. Ibid., 1.1–4, pp. 4–39 K.

44. Sextus Empiricus, *Pyrrh.* 1.236–41.

45. Galen, *De sectis* 6 (*Scr. Min.* III, pp. 12ff. H).

46. Ibid.: 'Those who are called "Methodists" – for this is what they call themselves . . .'

47. Id., *Meth. med.* 1.2 (X, p. 8 K), quoting from Thessalus's letter to Nero: 'I have founded a *hairesis* that is new and is the only true one, on account of the fact that all physicians of earlier generations transmitted nothing useful – neither toward the preservation of health nor toward the remission of diseases.'

48. Id., *De sectis* 9, p. 23 H; cf. *Meth. med.* 1.4 (X, p. 35 K).

49. *Meth. med.* 1.1–4, passim.

50. Most of the arguments in sections II.3 and III of this analysis are presented in greater detail in ch. X of my forthcoming book, *The Art of Medicine in Ptolemaic Alexandria: Herophilus and his School* (Cambridge University Press).

51. For a discussion of the relevant evidence concerning Herophilus, see von Staden, *Art of Medicine*, ch. VI (A. *Introduction*). Among Herophilus's followers only Andreas, who commented on the relation of marrow and bone (Cassius Iatrosophista, *Problemata* 58, in *Physici et medici Graeci minores*, ed. Ideler, vol. I, p. 161), and Hegetor, who defended anatomy as essential to the discovery of correct surgical procedures (cf.

Apollonius Citiensis, *In Hp. De articulis* 3, CMG XI.1.1, pp. 78–80, 94), displayed an active interest in anatomy. Whether Hegetor actually practised dissection, as has recently been claimed, remains uncertain; cf. P. M. Fraser, *Ptolemaic Alexandria* I, p. 364. All Hegetor says to support this view is, however: 'But if they had understood the cause *on the basis of anatomy* . . .' – a flimsy basis for the assertion that 'Hegetor certainly did (practise) human dissection'.

52. This argument is developed in von Staden, 'Experiment and Experience', especially III (pp. 186–93).

53. Cf. von Staden, *Art of Medicine*, chs. VI–VII.

54. This is a composite description of Herophilus's view, culled from Galen, *De pulsuum differentiis* 4.2–3 (VIII, pp. 702–24 K) and 4.12 (p. 754 K), *De pulsuum usu* 4 (V, pp. 163f. K), *De dignoscendis pulsibus* 1.1 (VIII, p. 771 K) and 1.3 (pp. 786–88 K), *On Medical Experience* 13.6 (pp. 109f. Walzer).

55. Galen, *De pulsuum differentiis* 4.6 (VIII, pp. 732f. K); Marcellinus, *De pulsibus* 3 (p. 457 Schöne).

56. Galen, *Puls. diff.* 4.10 (VIII, pp. 748f. K).

57. Ibid. 4.8 (VIII, pp. 736–41 K).

58. Ibid. 4.8–10 (pp. 741–43 K).

59. Ibid. 4.4 (pp. 725–27 K).

60. *Puls. diff.* 4.10 (pp. 743–45 K); Marcellinus, *De pulsibus* 3 (p. 457 Schöne).

61. Galen, *Puls. diff.* 4.7 (VIII, pp. 734f. K).

62. Ibid. 4.4f. (pp. 726–32 K).

63. Although the Empiricists did engage in anatomical observation when the opportunity afforded itself (cf. Deichgräber, *Empiriker*, fr. 66–70), they rejected dissection. Similarly, at least some later Empiricists, notably Heraclides of Tarentum (first century BCE), were willing to offer empirical descriptions – but not definitions – of the pulse in terms of 'beat', but not to acknowledge the validity of concepts such as 'diastole' and 'systole', nor to allow the introduction of physiological principles to explain the pulse or to grant great diagnostic significance to pulse theory; cf. Deichgräber, fr. 71–77.

64. Ps.–Galen, *Introd.* 9 (XIV, pp. 698–99 K); Galen, *De dignoscendis pulsibus* 2.3 (VIII, p. 870 K); id., *Hipp. et Plat.* 8.5 (p. 688 Müller); Celsus, *Medicina* 1, prohoem. 14–15 (CML I, p. 19 Marx); ps.-Galen, *In 'Hippocratis' De alimento commentarius* 3.21 (XV, p. 346 K).

65. Cf. for example Galen, *De usu partium* 10.12 (*Scr. Min.* II, p. 93 H), *De locis affectis* 3.14 (VIII, p. 212 K), *Anat. admin.* 9.9 (pp. 9f. Duckworth), *In Hippocratis Epidemiarum* 2 comm. 4 (CMG V.10.1, p. 330), *De libris propriis* 3 (*Scr. Min.* II, p. 108 M), *De symptomatum causis* 1.2 (VII, pp. 88f. K); Rufus of Ephesus (?), *De anatomica partium hominis* 71–75 (pp. 184f. Daremberg/Ruelle); Calcidius, *In Platonis Timaeum comment.* (*Corpus Platonicum Medii Aevi: Plato Latinus* IV), pp. 256f. Waszink.

66. Aetius, *Plac.* 4.22.3 (*Dox. Gr.*, pp. 413f.; ps.- Plutarch, *Plac.* 4.22 (*Mor.* 903F–904B); ps.-Gal., *Hist. phil.* 103 (*Dox. Gr.*, p. 639).

67. Aetius, *Plac.* 5.2.3 (*Dox. Gr.*, p. 416); ps.-Plut., *Plac.* 5.2 (*Mor.* 904F; ps.–Galen, *Hist. phil.* 106 (*Dox. Gr.*, p. 640).

68. E.g. Galen, *Anat. admin.* 12.8 (p. 131 Duckworth), *De usu partium* 14.3 and 14.11 (*Scr. Min.* II, pp. 290, 321–3 H), *De semine* 1.15–16 (IV, pp. 565f., 582f. K), *De uteri dissectione* 3, 5, 7 and 9 (*CMG* V.2.1, pp. 38, 42–4, 46, 48 Nickel); Rufus of Ephesus, *De nominatione partium hominis* 184–86 (pp. 158f.); Soranus, *Gynaecia* 1.10.3; 1.12.2f.; 1.57.3f.; 3 prooem. 2–3.4 (*CMG* IV, pp. 8f., 42, 94f. Ilberg); Vindician, 'Brussels Fragment' *De semine*, in: W. Jaeger, *Diokles von Karystos*, 1938, pp. 191f. (For further details see von Staden, *Art of Medicine*, chs. VI.5 and VII.5f.)

69. Vindician, op. cit., p. 191; Oribasius, *Collectiones medicae*, lib. incert. 23.2f. (*CMG* VI.2.2 = vol. IV, p. 116 Raeder).

70. Anonymus Londinensis 24.27–35 (*Suppl. Aristot.* III.1, p. 44 Diels).

71. For full details see von Staden, *Art of Medicine*, especially chs. VII.7 and X.

72. Scribonius Largus, *Conpositiones*, praef. (p. 875 Deichgräber). Cf. Plutarch, *Quaest. conviv.* 4.1.3 (*Mor.* 663BC).

73. Cf. Pedanius Dioscurides, *De materia medica*, praef. 1 (I, p. 1 Wellmann). The twenty-five most important testimonia are assembled in von Staden, *Art of Medicine*, ch. XI (Testimonia: Andreas 18–44).

74. Cf. e.g. Galen, *De compositione medicamentorum per genera* 7.7 (XIII, p. 987 K); Pliny, *HN* 21.9.12 and 25.106.167f.

75. Cf. Galen, *De simplicium medicamentorum temperamentis et facultatibus* 1.29; 6 prooem. (XI, pp. 432, 794f. K), *Comp. med. per genera* 2.1; 2.5; 3.9; 4.7; 4.14 (XIII, pp. 462, 502, 642, 722, 751f. K), *De compositione medicamentorum secundum locos* 2.1; 6.8; 6.9; 7.13; 8.3 (XII, pp. 534, 972, 989; XIII, pp. 13, 162f. K); Soranus, *Gynaecia* 3.4.29 (*CMG* IV, p. 112 Ilberg).

76. Cf. Galen, *Comp. med. per genera* 2.1 and 2.5 (XIII, pp. 462, 502 K), *Comp. med. sec. locos* 6.9 (XII, p. 989 K).

77. Cf. Galen, *Comp. med. per genera* (XIII, pp. 362–1058 K) vs. *Comp. med. sec. locos* (XII, pp. 378–1007; XIII, pp. 1–36 K).

78. Pliny, *HN* 22.32.71; Gal., *Comp. med. sec. locos* 9.2 (XIII, pp. 243f. K).

79. E.g. Galen, ibid. 1.8; 2.1; 2.2; 3.1; 3.3; 5.1; 5.5; 6.8; 6.9 (XII, pp. 475–82, 502–4, 509f., 514f., 519–33, 582, 611–19, 646–55, 658f., 662–64, 686–88, 814–16, 858f., 864f., 979–83, 995–1000 K).

80. Ibid. 5.3 (XII, p. 843 K); Gal., *Comp. med. per genera* 5.15 (XIII, pp. 855 f. K).

81. Cf. Deichgräber, *Empiriker*, fr. 136–9, 157–66, 192–240, 252–5, 259, 262–4, 267–74.

82. For examples of Herophilean interest in surgery, cf. Galen's references to Andreas, *In Hp. De artic.* 1.18 and 4.47 (XVIII A, pp. 338f., 747 K); also Oribasius's extensive testimonia, *Coll. med.* 49.4.8–13, 19f., 45–50; 49–50; 49.5.1–5; 49.6 (*CMG* VI.2.2 = vol. IV, pp. 6, 7, 9, 10, 12 Raeder). On Hippocratic exegesis, see below.

83. Erotian, *Vocum Hippocraticarum collectio*, praef. and fr. 33 (pp. 4, 108 Nachmanson); Galen, *In Hippocratis Epidemiarum* 6.1.4 comment. 1.5 (*CMG* V.10.2.2, p. 21W).

84. The texts are collected in von Staden, *Art of Medicine*, ch. XIV (see especially Bacchius 12–76).

85. The first part of Bacchius's *Lexeis* contains glosses on words from the Hippocratic treatises *Prognostic, On the Sacred Disease, On Joints, Instruments of Reduction* and *Epidemics* 1 and 6. In Book 2 Bacchius explains Hippocratic words from the treatises *Prognostic, Prorrhetic* 1, *On Joints, In the Surgery, Instruments of Reduction, Regimen in Acute Diseases,* and *Epidemics* 2. Book 3 offers glosses on words from what later became known as *On the Nature of Bones,* from *On Fractures, On Joints, In the Surgery, On Places in Man,* and perhaps *Epidemics* 5. In addition, there are glosses which are not attributed to a specific book of Bacchius's *Lexeis*. These are on words from the Hippocratic treatises *Prognostic, Prorrhetic* 1, *On Fractures, On Joints, On Wounds in the Head, In the Surgery, Instruments of Reduction, On Diseases* 1, *On Places in Man, On the Use of Liquids, Aphorisms,* and *Epidemics* 1, 2, 3 and 5. The glosses concerning the *Aphorisms* and *Epidemics* 3 may also have been provided in Bacchius's commentary on, or edition of, these works. For further details and the evidence, see von Staden, *Art of Medicine,* ch. XIV.

86. Cf. Galen, *In Hp. Epid.* 2.2.20 comm. 2; 3.3.1 comm. 2.8; 6 comm. prooem. (*CMG* V. 10.1, p. 230 Pfaff; V.10.2.1, p. 87 Winkelbach; V.10.2.2, pp. 3f. W); *In Hp. De officina medici comm.* 1, praef. (XVIII B, pp. 631f. K); *In Hp. Aphorismos comm.* 7.70 (XVIII A, pp. 186f. K).

87. Erotian, *Voc. Hp.* α.103 (p. 23 N), κ.31 (p. 51 N); Galen (?), *Explanatio vocum Hippocratis,* s.v. *kammoron* (XIX, p. 108 K).

88. Galen, *In Hp. Epid.* 3.6–7 comm. 2.4, 2.8–9 (*CMG* V. 10.2.1, pp. 75–7, 86–94W).

89. Cf. Erotian, *Voc. Hp.,* praef. and 1.5 (pp. 5, 91 N).

90. Galen, *In Hp. Epid.* 2.2.20 comm. 2; 3.3.1 comm. 2.4; 6 comm. prooem.; 6.4.8 comm. 4.11; 6.4.20 comm. 4.27; 6.5.15 comm. 5.26; 6.6.14 comm. 6 (*CMG* V. 10.1, p. 230; V.10.2.1, p. 80; V.10.2.2, pp. 3–4, 212, 243, 304, 306, 378).

91. Erotian, *Voc. Hp.,* praef. (p. 5 N).

92. Cf. Deichgräber, *Empiriker,* fr. 309–65 and pp. 317–22.

93. Apollonius Citiensis, *In Hp. De artic.* 1 (*CMG* XI.1, 1, p. 10 Kollesch/ Kudlien): 'I see, King Ptolemy, that *you* are well disposed toward medicine, while *you* see that *I* eagerly execute your orders . . . [and I have explicated the inventions of the most divine Hippocrates concerning instruments for helping men], which you ordered me to communicate to you at present.' The same king is likewise addressed in the prefaces to Books 2 and 3 of Apollonius's commentary (pp. 38, 64 Kollesch/Kudlien).

94. Cf. Deichgräber, *Empiriker,* p. 206; Apollonius's floruit is roughly 70 BCE.

95. Fraser, *Ptolemaic Alexandria* I, p. 312.

96. Soranus, *Gynaecia* 1.27.2f. (*CMG* IV, p. 17 Ilberg).

97. Athenaeus, *Deipnosophistae* 7.312E; Scholium on Nicander, *Theriaca* line 823 (p. 198 Bussemaker).

98. Galen, *De pulsuum differentiis* 4.10 (VIII, pp. 746f. K).

99. Callimachus and Demetrius of Apamea both dealt explicitly with

signs; Demetrius wrote a book entitled *Signs* or *Semiotics*. Cf. Caelius Aurelianus, *Tardae passiones* 5.9.89, *Celeres vel acutae passiones* 3.18.178–79; Soranus, *Gynaecia* 2.55 (*CMG* IV, p. 91 Ilberg); Rufus of Ephesus, *Quaestiones medicinales* 3.21 (pp. 5f. Gärtner).

100. Cf. Galen, *In Hp. Epid.* 6.1.4 comm. 1.5 (*CMG* V.10.2.2, p. 21 W); ps.-Gal., *Introductio* 4 (XIV, p. 683 K); Deichgräber, *Empiriker*, fr. 6, fr. 351.

101. Among the targets of Aristoxenus's censure are his fellow-Herophileans Bacchius, Zeno, Chrysermus, Apollonius Mys, and Heraclides of Erythrae. Cf. Galen, *Puls. diff.* 4.7–10 (VIII, pp. 734–47 K), *De dignoscendis pulsibus* 4.3 (VIII, p. 955 K).

102. The evidence is presented in von Staden, *Art of Medicine*, ch. XXVIII, where the roughly forty testimonia and fragments of Demosthenes Philalethes are enumerated.

103. Cf. Galen, *In Hp. Epid.* 6.4.7 comm. 4.10 (*CMG* V.10.2.2, p. 203 W).

104. Cf. Athenaeus, *Deipnosophistae* 4.184BC (based on an account by historian Menecles of Barca, who perhaps was a victim of the expulsion order).

105. Strabo 12.8.20 (580C).

106. Cf. Epicurus, fr. 19.2 Arrighetti (= fr. 50 Usener); Plato, *Lg.* 764C8; Thucydides 7.29.5; Hyperides, *In Defence of Euxenippus* 22 (col. 17); Aeschines, *Against Timarchus* 9. But cf. also Antiphon, *On the Choreutes* 11: of a training room or practice room fitted out by the choregus in his own house. Galen almost never refers to the Herophilean and Erasistratean 'schools' as *didaskaleia*.

107. Cf. Strabo 17.1.8 (793–94C): 'The [Alexandrian] Museum is also part of the royal quarters; it has a covered walk (*peripatos*), an arcade (*exedra*), and a large house, in which the common meal of the men of learning (*philologoi*) who share the Museum [is provided]. In this association there exist common funds and a priest supervising the Museum, who in those days was appointed by the kings [sc. Ptolemies], but now by Caesar.' See also Müller-Graupa, *PW* XVI, 1935, cols. 801–21, *s.v.* 'Mouseion'; M. Rostovtzeff, *The Social and Economic History of the Hellenistic World*, 2nd impression, 1953, vol. I, pp. 1084f., vol. II, p. 1596 n. 39.

108. On Ephesus see J. Keil, 'Ärzteinschriften aus Ephesos', *Jahreshefte des österreichischen archäologischen Instituts* 8, 1905, pp. 128f.; P. Wolters, ibid. 9, 1906, pp. 295ff. On the Mouseion in Smyrna see L. Robert, *Études anatoliennes*, 1937, pp. 146–48. The evidence concerning the Mouseion in Athens remains controversial; cf. J. D. Oliver, 'The Mouseion in late Attic inscriptions', *Hesperia* 3, 1934, pp. 191–96, vs P. Graindor, 'Le nom de l'université d'Athenès sous l'Empire', *Revue belge de philologie et d'histoire* 17, 1938, pp. 207–212. Cf. also the general discussion in Fraser, *Ptolemaic Alexandria* I, pp. 312ff.

109. Cf. R. Herzog, 'Urkunden zur Hochschulpolitik der römischen Kaiser', *SPAW* 1935.32, pp. 967–1019 (also, id., pp. 1005f, on Mouseia outside Alexandria).

110. J. Benedum, 'Zeuxis Philalethes und die Schule der Herophileer

in Menos Kome', *Gesnerus* 31, 1974, pp. 221–34, especially 231ff. On the earthquake see Tacitus, *Ann.* 14.27. An earlier earthquake at Laodicea, in the reign of Tiberius, is reported by Suetonius, *Tiberius* 8. Cf. also W. M. Ramsay, *The Cities and Bishoprics of Phyrgia* I, 1895, p. 38; and *Oracula Sibyllina* 4.106.

111. Acts 24.5.
112. Acts 24.14.
113. Acts 28.22. Cf. also 5.17 (Sadducees), 15.5 and 26.5 (Pharisees).
114. Josephus, *Vita* 10.
115. *BJ* 2.119. See n. 26 above for further examples from Josephus. For examples of Philo's somewhat different uses see *Plant.* 151 and *Vit. contempl.* 29. On the rabbinical uses of *hairesis* cf. Schlier (see n. 117).
116. Eusebius, *HE* 8.17.6.
117. H. Schlier, 'Hairesis', *TDNT* I, 1964, p. 183.
118. Clement of Alexandria, *Strom.* 7.15.92.3. Cf. a similar use in the Edict of Milan, in Eusebius *HE* 10.5.2.
119. Clement, ibid., 7.15.89.3.
120. Ibid., 1.19.95.7; cf. also 7.17.108.1f.
121. It is possible that Jews used *hairesis* in roughly this sense of the Christians; cf. Justin Martyr, *Dial.* 108.2 (*PG* 6.725C).
122. Ignatius, *Ep. ad Trallianos* 6 (p. 92 Bihlmeyer; *PG* 5. 680A).
123. Cf. Origen, *CC* 2.3 (GCS I, p. 130); Justin, *Apol.* 1.26 (*PG* 6.368); Hegesippus, fr. 3 (*PG* 5.1317C); Basil, *Ep.* 188, canonica 1 (*PG* 32.665A), etc.
124. Philinus, the Empiricist, admittedly 'cut himself off' (*apotemomenos*) from the *hairesis* of Herophilus, and his polemics might have enhanced the Herophileans' sense of a 'school' identity, but the Herophileans did not require his apostasy to qualify as a *hairesis,* as little as apostasy from Herophilus was a necessary condition for the Empiricists' being a *hairesis*. Cf. Deichgräber, *Empiriker*, fr. 6 (a late testimonium).
125. Cf. Justin Martyr, *Dial.* 80.4 (*PG* 6.665A); this text suggests that similar use was made of *hairesis* with reference to the question who is a 'true Jew' (as opposed to Jewish and Jewish-Christian sects, whose members only are 'so-called Jews').
126. Basil, *Ep.* 188, can. 1 (*PG* 32.665A–B).
127. Clement, *Strom.* 7.17.108.1f. For further useful discussion of 'heresy' in these Christian contexts cf. Schlier, *TDNT* I, pp. 183f.; E. Wolf, *RCG* III, s.v., 'Häresie', pp. 13–15, and H. Köster, ibid., s.v., 'Häretiker im Urchristentum', pp. 17–21; W. Bauer, *Orthodoxy and Heresy in Earliest Christianity*, ET of 2nd edition, ed. R. A. Kraft and G. Krodel, 1971.
128. I Cor. 11.18–19.
129. Gal. 5.20.
130. Tit. 3.9. For the use of *hairetikos* in the early church cf. Irenaeus 3.3.4; Clement, *Strom.* 1.19.95.4; *Didasc.* 23, etc.
131. II Peter 2.1.
132. Schlier, op. cit., p. 183.
133. Cicero, *Epp. fam.* 15.16.3.

6. Sarapis and Isis

1. S. Morenz, *Egyptian Religion*, ET 1973, p. 268: from a list of the gods compiled by Dr Muller-Kriesel.

2. Tacitus, *Hist.* 4.80–84; Plutarch, *Is. et Os.* 27f., *Mor.* 361E–362B; Clement of Alexandria, *Protr.* 4.48.1–6, are our best sources for Sarapis's 'genesis'. Nevertheless Tacitus (c. 105 CE), Plutarch (c. 115 CE) and Clement (at the beginning of the third century) mention only various versions of the god's arrival at Alexandria without giving preference to any of them. The vagueness of the coming of Sarapis from a far-off country (Sinope, Pontus or Seleucia), the divine will manifested in a theophany, would be a mythical glaze which the priests of the Sarapeum of Rhacotis intentionally held up as a halo around their 'hybrid god'.

3. Cf. recently G. Mussies, 'Some Notes on the Name of Sarapis', *Hommages à M. J. Vermaseren* (*EPRO* 68), 1978, II, pp. 821–32.

4. For the widespread influence of the cult of Sarapis and Isis in Hellenistic and Roman eras, see among others Th. A. Brady, 'The Reception of the Egyptian Cults by the Greeks', *The University of Missouri Studies* 10, 1935, pp. 1–86 = *Sarapis and Isis, Collected Essays*, 1978, pp. 1–88; P. M. Fraser, 'Two Studies on the Cult of Sarapis in the Hellenistic World', *OpAth* 3, 1960, pp. 1–54; L. Vidman, *Isis und Sarapis bei den Griechen und Römern*, 1970; R. E. Witt, *Isis in the Greco-Roman World*, 1971; F. Dunand, *Le culte d'Isis dans le bassin oriental de la Méditerranée* (*EPRO* 26), I–III, 1973. Many of the monographs in this series deal with the expansion of the cult in the Western part of the Roman Empire. The inscriptions cited in this paper are from the *Sylloge Inscriptionum Religionis Isiacae et Sarapiacae* (*SIRIS*), 1969.

5. *Expositio totius mundi et gentium* 34.

6. Cf. S. Morenz, *Egyptian Religion*, pp. 52–4.

7. From the New Kingdom onwards, there was a tendency towards the universalism of Egyptian religion. Egyptian gods, as Amon-Re, Aton, extended their power to foreign peoples. But they were never considered as universal gods and the Egyptian religion never became a world religion. It may be said that before the Hellenistic era all the gods were national gods. Even Yahweh, who claimed to be the only God, nevertheless had special ties with Israel. Let us mention the miraculous healing of the Syrian Naaman (II Kings 5). By dipping seven times in the Jordan, he was healed of leprosy. He returned to the prophet Elisha and confessed that 'there is no god in all the earth but in Israel'. Then he asked the prophet's permission to take home two mules' burden of earth from the soil of Israel on which he might continue to worship Yahweh. From this story one may conclude that (*a*) while Yahweh was the god of the whole world, his true worship was only in Israel, (*b*) Yahweh was the god of Israel, he could be adored only on the soil of Israel and not on the soil where reigned another god. See for example J. Montgomery, *Kings*, repr. 1960, pp. 375f.

8. According to the 'imperialistic theory', the spread of Sarapis's cult outside Egypt was due to Ptolemaic political influence or propaganda.

On the contrary, I agree with P. M. Fraser, who argues against this thesis and proves that 'the cult of Sarapis spread outside Egypt in the main through private action, by traders, mercenaries, priests and travellers who had acquired a personal interest in the cult, primarily in Egypt' ('Two Studies', p. 49). Cf. also Fraser, *Ptolemaic Alexandria* I, pp. 275f.

9. See n. 4 above. After F. Cumont's excellent synthesis (*The Oriental Religions in Roman Paganism*, ET 1911), very few attempts at synthesis were made by modern scholars. L. Vidman (*Isis and Sarapis*) is more attentive to the evidence of epigraphical documents; R. E. Witt (*Isis in the Greco-Roman World*) lays stress on the phenomenon of the syncretism of Isis in the Roman era; F. Solmsen (*Isis among the Greeks and Romans*, 1979) underlines the close contacts of Isis with the traditions of classical civilizations. New archaeological, epigraphical and iconographical data provided by systematic and exhaustive research may lead to a more accurate synthesis.

10. The Isis self-definition in the formulation '*Ego eimi*' is very characteristic of the well-known aretalogies of Isis. See R. Harder, *Karpocrates von Chalcis und die memphitische Isispropaganda*, 1944; W. Peek, *Der Isishymnus von Andros und verwandte Texte*, 1950; D. Müller, *Aegypten und die griechischen Isis-Aretalogien*, 1961; J. Bergman, *Ich bin Isis. Studien zum memphitischen Hintergrund der griechischen Isis-Aretalogien*, 1968.

The problem of archetype (Egyptian or Greek) divides modern scholars: Harder and Bergman favour an Egyptian original from Memphis; A. D. Nock (in *Gnomon* 21, 1949, p. 221; *Essays* II, p. 703) and A. J. Festugière ('À propos des arétalogies d'Isis', *HTR* 42, 1949, pp. 209–34 = *Études de religion grecque et hellénistique*, 1972, pp. 138–63) favour a Greek original made in Egypt for Greeks and Hellenized Egyptians. For recent discussion, see Y. Grandjean, *Une nouvelle arétalogie d'Isis à Maronée*, 1975, pp. 8–15.

11. Apuleius, *Metam*. 11.5.1 (I have borrowed J. G. Griffith's translation in *The Isis-Book* [*EPRO* 39], 1975).

12. Medinet Madi, Hymn I, cf. V. F. Vanderlip, *The Four Greek Hymns of Isidorus and the Cult of Isis* (American Studies in Papyrology 12), 1972, pp. 17f. and 37–51; see also Bibliography, ibid.

13. Hymn I, 23–24; see Vanderlip's commentary, pp. 28–31.

14. For the inscription from Capua 'TE TIBI UNA QUAE ES OMNIA DEA ISIS', see my commentary in *Le culte des divinités orientales en Campanie* (*EPRO* 27), 1972, pp. 77 and 199–234. On the henotheistic acclamations in honour of Sarapis, cf. E. Peterson, *Eis Theos*, pp. 227–40; *SIRIS*, nos. 363, 364, 389, 751, 769.

15. I make a distinction between 'aretalogy' and 'prayer', even if these two forms of religious expression are sometimes blended. The aretalogy exalts the divine powers (*aretē, virtus*) in general or the miracles made by the divinity in specific circumstances. By 'prayers', I mean here all other forms of communion with the god as act of adoration – *proskynēma* – thanksgiving, liturgical or public hymn, litany. As the prayers are often the expression of the faith (*lex orandi lex credendi*), we may consider them as a source of religious understanding. The *litany of Oxyrhynchus* (*POxy*

XI.1380), the prayer of Lucius (in Apuleius, *Metam*. 11.25) or the hymns of Medinet Madi for instance are the true compendium of Isiac Credo.

16. *POxy* XI.1380, lines 174–9, 215.

17. On the commentary on this formula in Isis-Aretalogy, cf. Müller, *Aegypten*, pp. 74–85.

18. Apuleius, *Metam*. 11.6.

19. Julian, *Or*. 4, 135 D. Cf. Th. Hopfner, *Fontes historiae religionis aegyptiacae*, 1922–25, p. 538.

20. *SIRIS*, no. 389. See also F. Cumont, *Les religions orientales dans le paganisme romain*, 1929⁴, p. 79 fig. 5; Vidman, *Isis und Sarapis*, pp. 147–51.

21. *SIRIS*, nos. 459, 460, 461, 462, 778.

22. Cf. P. Roussel, *Les cultes égyptiens à Délos*, 1916, Doc. I, lines 30–34, p. 72; H. Engelmann, *The Delian Aretalogy of Sarapis* (*EPRO* 44), 1975, p. 27. (Isis is referred to as 'sharing the bed' [*homeunos*] of Sarapis.)

23. Cf. Grandjean, *Une nouvelle arétalogie*, p. 17 and commentary p. 55 and n. 108. F. Solmsen argues that '*sunoikos*' in the aretalogy of Maroneia 'hardly means more than "sharer of the temple" ' and refuses the argument of Grandjean in favour of "*sunoikos*" as "*compagnon*" ' (cf. Solmsen, *Isis among the Greeks and Romans*, p. 127 n. 4, and Grandjean, p. 55 n. 108).

24. *SIRIS*, no. 88.

25. See especially P. M. Fraser, 'Two Studies', p. 41.

26. Roussel, *Les cultes égyptiens*, Doc. I, lines 21–26, p. 72.

27. Cf. *SIRIS*, p. 354. Index, formulae imperativae.

28. Tibullus 1.3.27f. (Hopfner, *Fontes*, p. 147).

29. Ovid, *Amor*. 2.13.5–25 (Hopfner, *Fontes*, p. 150).

30. D.L. 5.76 (Hopfner, *Fontes*, pp. 58f.).

31. Aretalogy of Maronea, lines 6–11; cf. Grandjean, *Une nouvelle arétalogie*, pp. 17 and 24–34.

32. Aelius Aristides, *Or*. 45.34.

33. Medinet Madi, Hymn I, 32–34; cf. Vanderlip, *Four Greek Hymns*, pp. 33f.

34. Juvenal, *Sat*. 6.522.

35. Plutarch, *Is. et Os*. 27, *Mor*. 361D.

36. *IG* XII.5.739, 11f.

37. Apuleius, *Metam*. 11.23.7. For the discussion on the rites and the meaning of the initiation, cf. e. g. R. Reitzenstein, *Die hellenistischen Mysterienreligionen nach ihren Grundgedanken und Wirkungen*, 1927³, pp. 220–34; F. Dunand, 'Les mystères égyptiens aux époques hellénistiques et romaines', *Mystères et Syncrétismes*, 1975, pp. 11–62; Griffiths, *The Isis-Book*, pp. 286–308.

38. Apuleius 11.15.

39. Ibid.

40. Conversion means a radical change. 'By conversion we mean the reorientation of the soul of an individual, his deliberate turning from indifference or from an earlier form of piety to another, a turning which implies a consciousness that a great change is involved, that the old was wrong and the new is right' (A. D. Nock, *Conversion*, 1961, p. 7).

On the mystic conversion of Lucius, cf. P. Scazzoso, *Le metamorfosi di*

Apuleio, 1951, pp. 91–147; A. J. Festugière, *Personal Religion among the Greeks*, 1954, p. 72.

41. Apuleius 11.24.

42. Lucius's spiritual experience and emotions are well described by A. J. Festugière, *Personal Religion*, pp. 68–84.

43. More than once, Apuleius describes the 'opening ceremonies of the temple by dawn' (11.20) and the 'morning sacrifice' (11.22), or the 'morning salutations to the goddess' (11.27). These ceremonies were made in the presence of devotees 'who greeted the light of dawn and with raised voices announced the first hour of the day' (11.20). Griffiths compares this account by Apuleius with the description of the opening of the temple of Sarapis given by Porphyry, *Abst.* 4.9. Tibullus mentions how his Delia 'all clad in linen, would twice a day chant the praises conspicuous in the Egyptian throng' (Tibullus 1.3.23–32). We do not know if the faithful devotees had to attend religious offices daily, but it is certain that their presence was more frequent than generally in Graeco-Roman religion. The frescoes from Herculaneum may represent, according to some scholars, the morning and evening ceremonies with the numerous assembly of people, men, women and children (cf. Tran tam Tinh, *Isis à Pompéi*, 1964, pp. 101–3, pl. XXIII, XXIV; Tinh, *Le culte des divinités orientales à Herculanum* (*EPRO* 17), 1971, pp. 29–49, pl. XXVII, XXVIII). Cf. also Cumont, *Religions orientales*, pp. 80 and 241f. (cf. ET of 1st ed., pp. 85f. and 235–7).

44. Cf. among the most recent iconographical studies on Sarapis, W. Hornbostel, *Sarapis* (*EPRO* 32), 1973; L. Castiglione, 'Nouvelles données archéologiques concernant la genèse du culte de Sarapis', in *Mélanges M. J. Vermaseren* I, 1978, pp. 208–32; Tran tam Tinh, 'Sarapis debout: un problème iconographique', *Acts of the first International Congress of Egyptology*, 1979, pp. 645–9, pl. LXXXVII–LXXXIX.

45. The studies of Isis iconography are numerous but few are systematic. The first attempt of comprehensiveness on the theme of Isis as 'lady of the sea' is made by Ph. Bruneau in *BCH* 85, 1961, pp. 435–46; 87, 1963, pp. 301–8; 98, 1974, pp. 333–81. See also some of my iconographical essays: 'Isis et Sérapis se regardant', *RA* 1, 1970, pp 55–80; 'A propos d'un vase à reliefs du musée de Toronto', *RA* 2, 1972, pp. 321–40; *Isis lactans* (*EPRO* 37), 1973; 'De nouveau Isis lactans', *Hommages à M. J. Vermaseren* III, pp. 1231–68; 'Isis–Nymphe de Laodicée', *Mélanges d'études anciennes offerts à Maurice Lebel*, 1980, pp. 339–61; 'État des études iconographiques relatives à Isis, Sérapis et sunnaoi theoi', *ANRW* II.17.3 (in press).

46. On the problem of analogy between Christianity and Isaicism, cf. e.g. S. Morenz, *Egyptian Religion*, pp. 235–57; A. D. Nock, *Conversion*, pp. 167–71; H. Rahner, *Greek Myths and Christian Mystery*, 1971; A. Benoit, 'Les mystères païens et le christianisme', in *Mystères et syncrétisme*, 1975, pp. 73–92.

47. Apuleius, *Metam.* 11.26.

7. *Self-Definition in the Asclepius Cult*

1. Alfred Schutz and Thomas Luckmann, *The Structures of the Life-World*, 1973; Alfred Schutz, *On Phenomonology and Social Relations* (ed. H. R. Wagner), 1970; Peter Berger, *The Sacred Canopy*, 1967.

2. *Iliad* 2.728–33, ET Richmond Lattimore, 1951. Machaon is also mentioned as son of Asclepius in 4.193.

3. Correctly noted by C. Kerényi, *Asklepios: Archetypal Image of the Physician's Existence*, 1959, pp. xiv–xv.

4. Pindar, *Pyth.* 3.6f. (trs. Sandys, LCL, 1915, p. 185).

5. Ibid., 3.40–45.

6. Ibid., 3.46–53.

7. Aristophanes, *Plutus* 653–747 (Act II, Scene 2).

8. Ibid., 716–41.

9. Strabo and Livy, for example, mention the temple of Asclepius, located near Epidaurus, in which were still to be found in their time fragments of votive tablets containing testimony to the god's healing power. Strabo (*Geographica* 8.6.15) describes the sanctuary as 'the place of epiphany of Asclepius', while Livy recalls the rich offerings that once filled the place as expressions of gratitude to the god for the restoration of health.

10. Pausanias, *Description of Greece* 2.26.1ff.

11. Ibid., 2.26.7.

12. A comprehensive report of the excavations and an interpretation of the results were published by A. Defrasse and H. Lechat, *Épidaure: restauration et description des principaux monuments du sanctuaire d'Asclepios*, 1895. These texts have been transcribed and translated (into German) by Rudolf Herzog, *Die Wunderheilungen von Epidaurus*, *Philologus*, Suppl. 22, Heft 3, 1931, pp. 8–35.

13. Herzog, *Wunderheilungen*, p. 46.

14. Ibid., p. 58.

15. Ibid., p. 59.

16. Alison Burford, *The Greek Temple Builders at Epidauros*, 1969, p. 54.

17. Defrasse and Lechat, *Épidaure*, pp. 95–105. Confirmed by Burford, *Temple*, pp. 66f.

18. Pausanias, e.g., Athens (1.21.4), Pellona (3.21.2), Cyphanta (3.24.2), Corrone (4.34.5), Cyparissae (4.36.7), Cyrus (7.27.11), Olympia (5.11.11), Megalopolis (7.31.1).

19. Burford, *Temple*, p. 67. Also Walter A. Jayne, *The Healing Gods of Ancient Civilizations*, 1925, pp. 262–3.

20. Defrasse, *Épidaure*, p. 91.

21. From *Asclepius: Testimonies* I, ed. E. J. L. and L. Edelstein, 1945, pp. 258f. The Edelsteins' suggested date is second/first century BCE.

22. Nos. 47 and 55 in Herzog's numeration.

23. Burford, *Temple*, p. 17. *Contra* Herzog, *Wunderheilungen*.

24. Plato, *Protagoras* 311B.

25. Hippocrates, ed. W. H. S. Jones, LCL I, 1923, pp. xlivf.

26. On this see Kerényi, *Asklepios*, pp. 47–53, where it is stated flatly,

'When medical science was at its height at Kos, there was no temple of Asklepios but rather a state hospital, where citizens received medical attention free of charge' (p. 151).

27. The poet was mentioned by Diodorus Siculus (12.12f.), but the poem was found only in the late nineteenth century. See R. Herzog, *Koische Forschungen und Funde*, 1899, pp. 202–4.

28. Livy 10.47.

29. Livy Summary of Book 11.

30. Ovid, *Metamorphoses* 15.625–744.

31. Pausanias 2.27.6.

32. Defrasse and Lechat, *Épidaure*, pp. 152f.

33. Text and German translation in R. Herzog, *Wunderheilungen*, pp. 43–5.

34. M. Rostovtzeff, *Social and Economic History of the Roman Empire*, 1966², esp. pp. 130ff.; cit. from p. 121.

35. G. W. Bowersock, *Greek Sophists in the Roman Empire*, 1969, p. 1.

36. Bowersock, *Sophists*, p. 27.

37. André Boulanger, *Aelius Aristide et la sophistique dans la province d'Asie au IIe siècle de notre ère*, 1923, p. 180.

38. Cf. D. L. Tiede, *The Charismatic Figure as Miracle Worker*, 1972.

39. Boulanger, *Aristide*, p. 181.

40. Details in C. A. Behr, *Aelius Aristides and the Sacred Tales*, 1968, pp. 8–12.

41. Behr, *Aelius Aristides*, p. 25. Cf. *Sacred Tales* 2.7 (ed. Behr), pp. 74–6.

42. *Sacred Tales* 2.71–73.

43. Nothing comparable to the medical equipment found at such sites as Cos, Cnidus, Rhodes and Cyrene – that is, levers and beams to raise and lower patients, knives and surgical instruments – was found at Epidaurus. Cf. Charles Diehl, *Excursions in Greece to Recently Excavated Sites of Classical Interest*, 1893, p. 340; also Behr, *Aelius Aristides*, pp. 36f. for the lack of surgical equipment in the shrine at Pergamum.

44. Aristides notes in *Sacred Tales* 2.35 that he resided with Asclepiades, a warden of the shrine of the god at Pergamum.

45. Summarized from Behr, *Aelius Aristides*, pp. 36–9.

46. Behr, *Aelius Aristides*, p. 42.

47. Among the Sarapis and Isis inscriptions published by L. Vidman (*SIRIS*), see nos. 161, 173.

48. Herzog, *Wunderheilungen*, p. 149, notes that the Pergamene healing tradition was not opposed to divine healing, as distinct from the medical arts, but was hostile towards magic; texts are adduced to support this assertion. Herzog distinguishes – in my view, correctly – between miracle as the direct action of the god and magic as an inherent quality of an object, or a reaction induced by ritual performance or formulaic repetition. The distinction may be blurred in specific instances, but it is useful nonetheless for interpreting evidence and for clarifying and specifying life-worlds.

49. Aristides, *In Defence of Oratory* 67–70, trs. Behr, LCL I, 1973, pp. 320ff.

50. Christian Habicht, *Die Inschriften des Asklepieions*, 1969, pp. 6f., 11f.

51. Ibid., pp. 9f.; inscriptions nos. 5–30; list of names in Index, pp. 192–4.

52. Ibid., pp. 15.f; inscriptions nos. 31–43.

53. Ibid., inscriptions nos. 77, 90, 117, 127.

54. Ibid., p. 14; especially in inscription no. 161, the *lex sacra*, with text, translation and notes, pp. 167–90.

55. Ibid., p. 14; blood-letting is mentioned in inscription no. 139.

56. Ibid., p. 14; representations of the healed parts of the body are referred to in inscriptions nos. 89, 91, 115b, 116.

57. Ibid., pp. 6, 16f.

58. Kerényi, *Asklepios*, pp. 98, 100.

59. H. Idris Bell, *Cults and Creeds in Graeco-Roman Egypt*, 1953, p. 68.

60. Herzog, *Wunderheilungen*, pp. 65f.

61. Ibid., pp. 70–3.

62. In A. J. Brock, Introduction to *Galen: On the Natural Faculties* (LCL), 1916, p. xii.

63. Herzog, *Wunderheilungen*, p. 145.

8. Changing Dionysiac Identities

1. Z. Stewart in *La società ellenistica* (Storia e civiltà dei Greci 8, ed. R. B.Bandinelli), 1977, p. 538. (I quote from the unpublished English version with the author's permission.)

2. R. S. Kraemer, 'Ecstasy and Possession: Women of Ancient Greece and the Cult of Dionysus', in *Unspoken Worlds: Women's Religious Lives in non-Western Cultures* (ed. N. A. Falk and R. M. Gross), 1980, pp. 53–69. The author discusses her sociological view of maenadism (below, under I.2) at greater length in 'Ecstasy and Possession: The Attraction of Women to the Cult of Dionysus', *HTR* 72, 1979, pp. 55–80. Both articles contain misleading errors of fact but raise interesting questions about maenadic 'possession' and 'sociobiological roles'.

3. The classical formulation of this view is Xenophon, *Oec.* 7.22ff. Cf. K. J. Dover, *Greek Popular Morality in the Time of Plato and Aristotle*, 1974, pp. 95–102.

4. W. Burkert, *Griechische Religion der archaischen und klassischen Epoche*, 1977, pp. 333ff.

5. By the late fourth century BCE the Greeks were fully conscious of these differences. The earliest Greek comments on Egyptian animal-cults can be found in Herodotus (2.65ff., an objective report) and in fourth-century Attic comedy, of which Anaxandrides, *CAF* II, fr. 39, is typical, 'You pay homage to the bull (Apis), I sacrifice it to the gods. . . . You worship the dog (Anubis), I beat it'. Hecataeus of Abdera was the first Greek writer who recognized Jewish religion and the prohibition on making images of the Jewish god (*FGrH* 264 F 6; Strabo 16.2.35; Tacitus, *Hist.* 5.5.4).

6. Euripides, *Ba.* 170ff. (Teiresias and Kadmos), 827–846, 912ff. (Pentheus). See below, nn. 97, 200, 203.

7. *AP* 7.329, 7.353, 7.384, 7.455–457, 11.409; cf. n. 13. Epigrams which describe maenads and their ritual activities contain no references to wine-drinking (*AP* 6.134, 6.172, 7.485, 9.603). In *AP* 6.165 the woman acquired her addiction to wine *after* her retirement as a maenad.

8. Standard treatments of Dionysus as wine-god pay no attention to the different roles of the sexes and to the exclusion of women from Dionysus's gift. Cf. W. F. Otto, *Dionysus: Myth and Cult*, ET 1965, pp. 143–51 (German ed., pp. 133–41); M. P. Nilsson, *Geschichte der griechischen Religion* I, 1955², pp. 585–90; H. Jeanmaire, *Dionysos. Histoire du culte de Bacchus*, 1951, pp. 22–35; H. G. Horn, *Mysteriensymbolik auf dem Kölner Dionysosmosaik*, 1972, pp. 93–9.

9. Ennius, *Frag. scaen.* 124 Vahlen, *Lyaeus, vitis inventor sacrae*; Horace, *Od.* 1.18.1, *sacra vite*; Euripides, *TGF* (N), fr. 765, *ton hieron botryn*.

10. Henrichs, 'Die beiden Gaben des Dionysos', *ZPE* 16, 1975, pp. 139–44, esp. 141f.

11. Euripides, *Ba.* 274ff.; Henrichs, 'Prodicus on Religion', *HSCP* 79, 1975, pp. 107–23, esp. 109–11; 'The Sophists and Hellenistic Religion: Prodicus as the Spiritual Father of the Isis Aretalogies', in *Acts of the VIIth Congress of the Federation of Classical Studies, 1979* (forthcoming).

12. The recipients of the wine are called *brotoi* (Homer, *Il.* 14.325; Euripides, *Ba.* 280, 651), *thnētoi* (*Comica Adespota* 106.2, *CAF* III p. 423; Astydamas, *TGF* I, 60 F 6 Snell; P Fackelmann 5.8 ed. B. Kramer, *ZPE* 34, 1979, pp. 1ff.), *andres* (as opposed to the gods, Hesiod, fr. 239.1, Solon fr. 26.2 West), *thnētoi anthrōpoi* (Cypria fr. 10 Kinkel = fr. 13 Allen), or simply *anthrōpoi* (Plato, *Lg.* 2.672D; Diodorus Siculus 4.2.5, cf. 3.63.4).

13. Aelian, *VH* 2.38, Athenaeus 10.33 p. 429AB, 10.56 p. 441AB; H. Blümner, *Die griechischen Privatalterthümer*, 1882³, p. 70; M. Durry, 'Les femmes et le vin', *REL* 33, 1955, pp. 108–13; G. Piccaluga, 'Bona Dea' *SMSR* 35, 1964, pp. 202–23; S. B. Pomeroy, *Goddesses, Whores, Wives and Slaves: Women in Classical Antiquity*, 1975, pp. 143 and 153f. By contrast, drunken women were a stock joke in Attic comedy: H. G. Oeri, *Der Typ der komischen Alten in der griechischen Komödie, seine Nachwirkungen und seine Herkunft*, 1948, pp. 13–18, 39–46. Although we lack exact statistics, my impression is that even *hetairai* on archaic and classical vases are more often shown entertaining men at the symposium than drinking wine themselves.

14. Archilochus, fr. 120 West.

15. *SEG* XIV 604 (inscription on 'Nestor's Cup', c. 700 BCE); Solon fr. 26 West; Anacreon fr. 357 (12) Page.

16. W. J. Slater, 'Symposium at Sea', *HSCP* 80, 1976, pp. 161–70.

17. Aristophanes, *Ach.* 1071–1149, *Pax* 1127–1190.

18. Escape through wine: J. Roux, *Euripide, Les Bacchantes, II, Commentaire*, 1972, p. 346 on *Ba.* 279–283. The 'liberating' effect of Dionysus as wine-god is of course a commonplace; see e.g. Pindar, fr. 124.5f., Horace, *Od.* 1.18.3ff., Tibullus 1.7.39–42. Wine and hetairiai: J. Trumpf, *ZPE* 12, 1973, pp. 139–60. Scores of Hellenistic monarchs, including Philip II

(Demosthenes 2.18ff.) and Ptolemy IV (below, nn. 44 and 202), continued the upper-class custom of the symposium.

19. B. A. Sparkes, 'Treading the Grapes', *Bulletin van de Vereeniging tot Bevordering der Kennis van de antieke Beschaving te's Gravenhage* 51, 1976, pp. 47–56 (with plates).

20. Pictures and discussions of vintage scenes in various media (notably terracotta, mosaics and sarcophagi) can be found in many books. I know of no comprehensive treatment. Cf. H. von Rohden and H. Winnfeld, *Architektonische römische Tonreliefs der Kaiserzeit*, 1911, pp. 65ff. and 299f. with pls. 125.1 and 126.2; F. Matz, 'Vindemia. Zu vier bakchischen Sarkophagen', *Marburger Winckelmann-Programm* 1949, pp. 19–26, esp. 20f. (with pls.); R. Turcan, *Les sarcophages romains à représentations dionysiaques. Essai de chronologie et d'histoire religieuse*, 1966, pp. 559–67; F. Matz, *Die dionysischen Sarkophage* I–IV, 1968–1975, I (1968) nos. 8–11A, 13, 16–25, III (1969) no. 178; K. M. Dunbabin, *The Mosaics of Roman North Africa: Studies in Iconography and Patronage*, 1978, pp. 115–18, 185, 220, with pl. D and figs. 102–108, 184; E. R. Goodenough, *Jewish Symbols in the Greco-Roman Period, Vol. 6: Fish, Bread and Wine* II, 1956, pp. 46–53, with figs. 216–23, 225–27, 238; K. D. White, *Roman Farming*, 1970, pp. 46 and 229–46, with pls. 53, 55–7, 59–60; M. J. Vermaseren, *Liber in Deum. L'apoteosi di un iniziato dionisiaco*, 1976, pp. 22–7, with pls. VIII, XIX, XXI–XXII. The maenads acting as grape-pickers who appear on some Roman sarcophagi are exceptional; cf. Matz, *Die dionysischen Sarkophage* I, pp. 89ff., III, pp. 327f.

21. *Anacreontea* 59.5f. (*monon arsenes patousin/staphylēn*); *Gp.* 6.11. Female grape-pickers existed in fifth-century BCE Athens, but they were normally not of citizen status (Demosthenes 57.45, whence Pollux, *Onom.* 7.141). The ancient evidence for the personnel of the vintage is discussed in T. Keppel, 'Die Weinlese der alten Römer', *Programm der königl. Studienanstalt zu Schweinfurt für das Schuljahr 1873/74*, 1874, pp. 19–23, and M. Schuster, 'Vindemia', 'Vinitor', *PW* IXA, 1961, cols. 17–24, 121f.

22 Propertius 3.17.13–18. Ancient authorities on viticulture ignore women (Hesiod, *Op.* 609–14; Cato, *RR* 23–26; Varro, *RR* 1.54; Vergil, *Geor.* 2.226–419; Columella, *RR* 5.4–7; 10.423–32; 11.67–71; *Gp.* Books 4–8).

23. Longus 2.1–2 and 2.36.

24. Homer, *Il.* 18.567f.; *Anacreontea*, 59.3.

25. Otto, *Dionysus*, pp. 149–51 (German ed., pp. 138–41); Henrichs, 'Greek and Roman Glimpses of Dionysos', *Dionysos and His Circle: Ancient through Modern* (ed. C. Houser), 1979, pp. 1–11.

26. Wine as a 'drug' (*pharmakon*; cf. W. Artelt, *Studien zur Geschichte der Begriffe 'Heilmittel' und 'Gift'*, 1937): causing madness (Herodotus 1.212.2; cf. Philo, *Plant.* 148); dual power, good or bad (*Comica Adespota*, fr. 106/107, *CAF* III, pp. 423f.; Plutarch, *Quaest. conviv.* 3.7.1., *Mor.* 655E; cf. Hesiod, fr. 239 M.-W., Theognis 837–40, 873–6 West); causing pleasure (Alcaeus, fr. 335 L.-P.; Ion of Chios, fr. 26 West; Euripides, *Ba.* 283); cure against old age (Plato, *Lg.* 2.666B, cf. 2.672D). See L. Deubner, *Attische Feste*, 1932, p. 94; R. Merkelbach, 'Eine Notiz zu Kallimachos Fr. 178, 20',

ZPE 5, 1970, p. 90; R. Scodel, 'Wine, Water, and the Anthesteria in Callimachus Fr. 178 Pfeiffer.', *ZPE* 39, 1980, pp. 37–40.

27. An exceptional, small draught of neat wine (*akratos*) was in order during the 'liminal' period after dinner and before the symposium 'Philochorus, *FGrH* 328 F 5). See K. Kirchner, *Die sakrale Bedeutung des Weines im Altertum*, 1910, pp. 14f., 24ff., 38f.; P. von der Mühll, *Ausgewählte kleine Schriften*, 1975, pp. 488–90. A personification of unmixed wine (Akratos, Akratopotēs) was worshipped in Athens (Pausanias 1.2.5; Athenaeus 2.9 p. 39C = Polemo Historicus, fr. 40 Preller).

28. Plato, *Lg.* 6.775B, cf. 2.636E–637E, 666B, 673E–674C, *Smp.* 176A–E.

29. For Athens, see [Apollodorus] *Bibl.* 3.14 (mythical introduction of viticulture), Phanodemus, *FGrH* 325 F 1 (first mixing of wine, cf. Philochorus, *FGrH* 328 F 5), Plutarch, *Quaest. conviv.* 3.7.1 and 8.10.3, *Mor.* 655E and 735E ('new wine', *neos oinos*, broached at Pithoigia, 'Cask-Opening', the first day of the Anthesteria). Cf. C. Kerényi, *Dionysos: Archetypal Image of Indestructible Life*, ET, 1976, pp. 129–75 (German ed., pp. 115–48); Henrichs, 'Glimpses', pp. 5f.

30. Otto, *Dionysus*, pp. 97ff. (German ed., pp. 91ff.); M. P. Nilsson, *Griechische Feste von religiöser Bedeutung mit Ausschluss der attischen*, 1906, pp. 277, 279f., 292f., *Gesch. d. griech. Religion* I², pp. 589f.; cf. M. Smith, 'On the Wine God in Palestine (Gen. 18, Jn. 2, and Achilles Tatius)', *Salo Wittmayer Baron Jubilee Volume*, 1975, pp. 815–29. Actual wine-drinking in connection with wine-miracles is mentioned by Sophocles, *TGF* IV, fr. 255.8 Radt (Euboea, mixed wine), schol. T. Homer, *Il.* 13.21 III 400.1f. Erbse (Agrai, unmixed wine), and schol. D (A, B) Homer, *Il.* 13.21 = Euphorio fr. 118 Scheidweiler = *Collect. Alex.* fr. 100; Propertius 3.17.27f. (Naxos, unmixed wine).

31. But see below, under IV.2.

32. Deubner, *Attische Feste*, pp. 93–123; A. Pickard-Cambridge, *The Dramatic Festivals of Athens*, 1968², pp. 1–25; W. Burkert, *Homo Necans. Interpretationen altgriechischer Opferriten und Mythen*, 1972, pp. 236–69; *Griechische Religion*, pp. 358–64; H. W. Parke, *Festivals of the Athenians*, 1977, pp. 107–20 (who ignored Burkert's innovative synthesis).

33. R. Pfeiffer on Callimachus, fr. 178.1 (slaves); Aristophanes, *Ach.* 1085ff., 1198ff., and Antigonus Carystius ap. Athenaeus 10.50, 437E (*hetairai*); Philostratus, *Her.* 12.2 (Athenian boys; cf. n. 36); M. P. Nilsson, *Eranos* 15, 1915, pp. 184f. = *Opusc. Sel.* I, 1951, pp 149f.

34. Burkert, *Homo Necans*, p. 243 ('wohl ohne Frauen'). On the role of the priestess(es) who ladled, mixed and distributed the new wine, and on the controversial 'Lenaia vases', see Deubner, *Attische Feste*, pp. 127–30; Pickard-Cambridge, *Dramatic Festivals*, pp. 30–4; Burkert, *Homo Necans*, pp. 260–3; Henrichs, 'Greek Maenadism', pp. 153f.

35. Callimachus, fr. 178 (Pollis in Egypt); Possis, *FGrH* 480 F 1 (Themistocles in Magnesia ad Maeandrum).

36. Members of the Dionysiac association of the Iobakchoi were required to make a donation of wine in celebration of important landmarks in their lives such as 'marriage, birth, Pitchers (*choes*), ephebia', etc. (*IG* II/III², I.2, 1916, no. 1368.130). A boy's first celebration of the

Choes marked the end of infancy (*IG* III.2,1882,1342 = Kaibel, *Epigrammata Graeca* no. 157; Deubner, *Attische Feste*, pl. 16.1).

37. F. Poland, *Geschichte des griechischen Vereinswesens*, 1909.

38. Poland, *Vereinswesen*, pp. 196–203; A. Vogliano and F. Cumont, 'The Bacchic Inscription in the Metropolitan Museum', *AJA* 37, 1933, pp. 215–70; A. Bruhl, *Liber Pater*, pp. 268–308; M. P. Nilsson, *The Dionysiac Mysteries of the Hellenistic and Roman Age*, 1957, pp. 45–66; Nilsson, *Geschichte der griechischen Religion* II, 1961, pp. 358–67; Kerényi, *Dionysos*, pp. 349–88 (German ed., pp. 277–306).

39. Poland, *Vereinswesen*, pp. 262–4; Nilsson, *Dionysiac Mysteries*, pp. 61–4, 145. But among the dozens of cult-titles borne by members of Dionysiac groups, there is only one which relates to wine-drinking; the 'master of the mixing bowl' (*kratēriarchos*) in an imperial inscription from Apollonia in Thrace (*CIG* 2052).

40. *IG* II/III² 1368; *Syll.*³ 1109; L. Ziehen, *Leges Graecorum Sacrae* II 1, 1906, pp. 132–47 no. 46 (best commentary); F. Sokolowski, *Lois sacrées des cités grecques* (= *LSCG*), 1969, pp. 95–101 no. 51 (includes further bibliography); *Inscr. Graecae Urbis Romae*, ed. L. Moretti, I, 1968, no. 160.

41. *IG* II/III² 1368.37f., 57f., 113f., 119f., 127ff., 157f., 159ff. (this last passage prescribes wine-drinking at the funeral of a deceased Iobakchos); Poland, *Vereinswesen*, p. 266.

42. See below, under III 2.

43. *IG* II/III² 1368.8 ('for the honour and glory of the Bakcheion'), 15f. ('Stability and good order to the Bakcheion!'), 26f. ('Now we are the first of all the Bakcheia!'), 37, 101, 148; at 43f., *Bakcheia* refers to Dionysiac festivals. Like the Latin *bac(ch)anal* (*CIL* I² 581), *bakcheion* was also used to designate the club house of Dionysiac associations. Cf. Poland, *Vereinswesen*, pp. 68 and 197; Nilsson, *Dionysiac Mysteries*, p. 63.

44. *IG* II/III² 1368.48, 52, 63, 70, 112, 114, 152; Theocritus 7.67ff., 131ff. (rustic *stibades* in country setting); Athenaeus 7.276B (dining couches replaced by *stibades* at the 'Feast of the Flagons' given by Ptolemy IV); Philostratus, *VS* 2.3 (the Athenians celebrated the Dionysia on *stibades* of ivy in the 2nd century CE); Ziehen, *Leges Graecorum Sacrae* II 1, pp. 138f. (collection of evidence); L. Gernet, *REG* 41, 1928, pp. 315–17, 325–7 = *Anthropologie de la Grèce antique*, 1968, pp. 23–6, 31–3 (on 'fêtes de campagne' featuring 'tents' [*skēnai*] and *stibades*); Nilsson, *Dionysiac Mysteries*, pp. 63f. (on Dionysiac *stibades* as permanent installations); W. Burkert, *Structure and History in Greek Mythology and Ritual*, 1979, p. 44 (preparation of *stibades* seen as an appeasement ritual, a view which carries the analogy with animal behaviour too far).

45. S. Wide, 'Inschrift der Iobakchen', *Athenische Mitteilungen* 19, 1894, p. 248. But see K. Kourouniotes, '*Anaskaphai kai ereunai en Chiōi*', *Arch Delt.* 1, 1915, pp. 64–93; p. 92, fig. 37, for a partially identical design (a feline on either side of a drinking cup with two handles) on a dedication to Kore from Chios of imperial date.

46. *IG* II/III² 1368.64–95, 136–146 (in T. Robinson's unpublished translation, which I use with his permission): 'In the *stibas* no one is allowed to sing, cheer, or clap' (63f.) . . . 'Let a sergeant at arms (*eukosmos*) be

chosen or appointed by the priest. He will lay upon the disorderly or uproarious person the god's staff (*ton thyrson tou theou*). Whomever the staff is placed beside, if the priest or archibakchos so decide, let him depart from the banquet hall. If he refuses to go, bouncers (lit. 'horses', *hippoi*) who will be appointed by the priest shall eject him outside the vestibule, and he shall be liable to the fines imposed on those found fighting' (136–46).

47. *IG* II/III² 1368.113ff.; Nilsson, *Gesch. d. griech. Religion* II², pp. 380f. Ziehen, *Leges Graecorum Sacrae* II 1, p. 140 n. 33 took *theologia* to refer to the script for the sacred play.

48. *IG* II/III² 1368.121ff.; Nilsson, *Gesch. d. griech. Religion* II², pp. 361, 368, *Dionysiac Mysteries*, pp. 60f.; Burkert, *Homo Necans*, pp. 219–21 (Palaimon); Ziehen, *Leges Graecorum Sacrae* II 1, p. 142 (Proteurythmos).

49. Otto, *Dionysus*, pp. 86–91 (German ed., pp. 81–6); Kerényi, *Dionysos*, pp. 273–348 (German ed., pp. 218–77); F. R. Adrados, *Festival, Comedy and Tragedy. The Greek Origins of Theatre*, 1975.

50. Pickard-Cambridge, *Dramatic Festivals*, pp. 279–305.

51. The title of ch. III in E. R. Dodds, *The Greeks and the Irrational*. Dodds, whose paper of 1940 made 'maenadism' a household word (see n. 52; 'Mänadentum' and 'ménadisme' are equivalent modern abstractions, whereas *bakcheia* is the closest Greek analogue), did more than any other scholar, including his predecessor E. Rohde, to make the maenads of antiquity intelligible to the modern mind. Dodds's theory of maenadism is not only indebted to Rohde, especially for the fundamental concept of 'the Dionysiac psychology' (Dodds [*Euripides, Bacchae*, 1960², p. xi n. 2], actually echoing F. Nietzsche's language, 'the psychology of the Dionysian state' and 'the psychology of orgiasm', in a famous passage of *Götzen-Dämmerung*, x, 4–5, written in 1888), but also to Nietzsche's *Die Geburt der Tragödie* (below, n. 134), to J. Harrison for the sacramental interpretation of maenadic omophagy (below, nn. 207–16) as well as for the notion of ritual as prior to myth and that of 'collective emotion' (compare *Irrational*, p. 69, with Harrison, *Themis. A Study of the Social Origins of Greek Religion*, 1927², pp. 45–8), and finally, in a much less specific way, to the heritage of S. Freud.

52. E. Rohde, *Psyche. The Cult of Souls and Belief in Immortality among the Greeks*, ET, 1925, pp. 255–89 (2nd German ed., 1898, II, pp. 4–55); J. Harrison, *Prolegomena to the Study of Greek Religion*, 1922³, pp. 388–400; U. von Wilamowitz-Moellendorff, *Der Glaube der Hellenen* (henceforth *GdH*) II, pp. 67–70; Otto, *Dionysus*, pp. 103–19, 171–80 (German ed., pp. 96–112; 159–67); E. R. Dodds, 'Maenadism in the *Bacchae*', *HTR* 33, 1940, pp. 155–76, repr. in part (pp. 155–66) as an appendix to *The Greeks and the Irrational*, pp. 270–82; Dodds, *Euripides, Bacchae*, esp. pp. xi–xxv; Jeanmaire, *Dionysos*, pp. 157–219; Nilsson, *Gesch. d. griech. Religion* I², pp. 569–78; Henrichs, 'Greek Maenadism from Olympias to Messalina', *HSCP* 82, 1978, pp. 121–60.

53. The problem of maenadic origins, and of their reflection in maenadic myth and ritual, is unsolved, and conceivably incapable of any convincing solution by scholarly methods of inquiry. Scholarly study of maenadism

began in 1872, the year of Nietzsche's *Birth of Tragedy* (where satyrs become existential symbols while maenads are mentioned just thrice, in Sections, 5, 8, and 12, and merely as evocative literary images), when A. Rapp, without having a single maenadic inscription at his disposal, recognized mythical and cultic maenads as two distinct phenomena, the one 'ideal' and the other 'real' ('Die Mänade im griechischen Cultus, in der Kunst und Poesie', *RhM* 27, 1872, pp. 1–22, 562–611). The conspicuous differences between the two, and their subtle connections, have occupied scholars ever since. For the past one hundred years, mythical maenads and their wild actions of 'tearing apart' and 'eating raw' have tempted German and British scholars, respective heirs to historicism and the evolutionist quest for ritual primitivism, to posit an 'original' maenadic ritual, with actual *sparagmos* and omophagy, for the distant Greek past. Rapp himself saw historical maenadism as a 'faint trace' of an earlier, wilder rite (pp. 607–11). E. Rohde interpreted it mistakenly as the 'Hellenization' of the savage Thracian cult of Dionysus (*Psyche*, pp. 282ff., German ed. II, pp. 38ff.). For Jane Harrison, mythical maenads were *a priori* 'women-worshippers' and ritual 'mothers' of the 'holy child' Dionysus, and she took it for granted that mythical omophagy was a direct reflection of, and testimony for, cultic omophagy in prehistoric Greece if not in classical Athens (*Prolegomena*, pp. 395f., 482–91; *Themis*, pp. 38f., 423). According to Dodds, ritual maenadism was the institutionalization of a more primitive and spontaneous mass seizure which had swept through Greece in the archaic period (below, n. 86). Nilsson assumed that the maenads practised omophagy in 'the early stage of the Dionysiac movement', which he called the 'old orgia' (*Gesch. d. griech. Religion* I, pp. 156f., 569f., 576; *Dionysiac Mysteries*, pp. 4–7). I myself suggested once, but am less confident now, that maenadic myth 'preserves the memory of ancient tribal savagery' ('Greek Maenadism', p. 147). French scholars, methodologically committed to social anthropology and structuralism, tend to see maenadism in its crudest mythical formulation as a persistent expression of a savage impulse which survived unabated into the classical age in deviance from established social custom, or in pronounced opposition to sacrificial practice (Jeanmaire, *Dionysos*, pp. 85–8, 169f., 180f., 255ff., 265f.; M. Detienne, *Dionysos Slain*, ET, 1979, pp. 62–4, French ed., 1977, pp. 150–3; M. Daraki, 'Aspects du sacrifice dionysiaque', *RHR* 197, 1980, pp. 131–57). In vigorous defiance of established scholarly opinion, W. F. Otto insisted on the absolute priority of the manifest 'reality of deity', including Dionysus, and of a holistic Greek conception of the god's eternal essence, of which myth is the most direct and valid conceptualization and ritual the active expression. On Otto's theory, maenadic myth and maenadic ritual are twin brothers 'born of the same spirit', who represent different religious dispositions but join forces to recreate the total religious experience projected by Dionysus (*Dionysus*, pp. 7–46, 103–19; German ed., pp. 11–46; 96–112). For a recent but uneven analysis of modern approaches to Dionysus from Rohde to Nilsson, Dodds and, surprisingly, Guthrie (Jeanmaire is strangely excluded), and of their place in modern intellectual history, see P. McGinty, *Interpretation and Dionysos: Method in the Study of a God*, 1978.

54. Ultimately based on Euripides's *Bacchae*, the 'romantic' view of maenadism was first formulated by Rohde (*Psyche*, pp. 257f., German ed. II, pp. 9f., 15–8), refined by Dodds, and reiterated, with minor modifications, by *tout le monde* ('Maenads', *Oxford Classical Dictionary*, 1970², p. 636 is typical).

55. Maenadic rites were *trieterides* (Euripides, *Ba.* 133; Diodorus Siculus 4.3.3; Pausanias 10.4.3). Public *trieterides* with participation of *pasa polis*, including men, are attested for several Greek cities (to the list in Dodds, *The Greeks and the Irrational*, p. 278 n. 2, add the Hellenistic inscription from Scepsis published by Z. Taşlıklıoğlu and P. Frisch, *ZPE* 17, 1975, p. 107, line 16).

56. Henrichs, 'Greek Maenadism', pp. 123–55; for the Peloponnesus, see Nilsson, *Griechische Feste*, pp. 291f., 297f.

57. Sixteen Dionysiac 'holy women' in Elis (Plutarch, *Mul. virt.* 15, *Mor.* 251E; Nilsson, *Griechische Feste*, pp. 291f.); Delphic and Attic Thyiads (Nilsson, *Gesch. d. griech. Religion* I, p. 573); perhaps the fourteen *gerairai* who officiated at the Athenian Anthesteria (Burkert, *Homo Necans*, pp. 257ff.). These congregations reflect ancient clan structures. In Hellenistic Miletus, initiations into maenadic *thiasoi* required a permit which had to be purchased (Henrichs, 'Die Maenaden von Milet', *ZPE* 4, 1969, pp. 235ff.; 'Greek Maenadism', pp. 149f.).

58. Plutarch, *Mul. virt.* 13, *Mor.* 249EF; 'Greek Maenadism', p. 136.

59. Plutarch, *Prim. frig.* 18, *Mor.* 953CD.

60. 'Greek Maenadism', pp. 124, 130 n. 25, 148f.

61. Pausanias talked to the Delphic maenads (Thyiads), but to no great avail (10.4.2f.).

62. Diodorus Siculus 4.3.2–3; 'Greek Maenadism', pp. 144ff.

63. 'Greek Maenadism', pp. 137, 152ff.

64. 'Greek Maenadism', pp. 143–52, 155f.

65. 'Greek Maenadism', pp. 150–2; Nilsson, *Dionysiac Mysteries*, p. 7 ('The raw meal . . . has become a mere portion of raw flesh, laid down somewhere, and presumably understood as an offering'); Wilamowitz, *GdH* II, p. 372 n. 2 ('Die Bissen werden in Milet den Gläubigen nicht mehr widerlich gewesen sein. Die *hostia* war zur Hostie geworden'). See below, under IV.2.

66. Sokolowski, *LSCG* no. 18, A 44–51, Δ 33–40; G. Daux, *BCH* 87, 1963, pp. 603–34, esp. 628, 630f.; S. Dow, *BCH* 89, 1965, pp. 208–10; M. Detienne in *La cuisine du sacrifice en pays grec*, 1979, pp. 188f.; Henrichs, 'Greek Maenadism', pp. 147ff., 153f. (on sacrifices performed by Hellenistic maenads and on Athenian maenads). Semele and Dionysus are often associated in cult, occasionally in connection with ritual maenadism (Otto, *Dionysus*, pp. 67f.; Gow on Theocritus 26.6; J. Roux on Euripides, *Ba.* 998; Sokolowski on *LSCG* no. 96).

67. It is unknown which, if any, animal skins were worn by Greek maenads in the Hellenistic period.

68. Maenads carrying knives, daggers or short swords are common in

late classical and Hellenistic art ('Greek Maenadism', p. 151 n. 97), and walked in the Dionysiac procession of Ptolemy II (Athenaeus 5.198E = Callixenus of Rhodes, *FGrH* 627 F 2, p. 169.29). This is another indication of the conflation of mythical *sparagmos* with regular forms of animal sacrifice (*thysia*).

69. Burkert, *Structure and History*, pp. 36f., 45–58. Wilamowitz, *GdH* I, pp. 12f. differentiates between 'Religion der Gemeinschaft' (the official cult of the *polis* and private cults) and 'Religion des Herzens' (personal piety which did not find cultic expression). Maenadism in all its manifestations belongs clearly to the former category.

70. Plato's term in the *Phaedrus*, put in modern perspective by Dodds, *The Greeks and the Irrational*, pp. 75–7.

71. Euripides, *Ba.* 686ff.; Rohde, *Psyche*, p. 267 n. 6 (German ed. II, p. 6 n. 2); Wilamowitz, *GdH* II, p. 69; Dodds, *Bacchae*, p. xiii. W. K. C. Guthrie (*The Greeks and their Gods*, 1954, pp. 148f.) disagrees.

72. Detienne, *Dionysos Slain*, pp. 62f., 90f.; French ed., pp. 150f., 201 (on omophagy as a negation of the accepted diet); F. Graf, 'Milch, Honig und Wein. Zum Verständnis der Libation im griechischen Ritual', in *Perennitas. Studi in onore di Angelo Brelich*, 1980, pp. 209–21 (on mixed wine in 'Ausnahmesituationen').

73. Dodds, 'Maenadism in the *Bacchae*', pp. 155–66 = *The Greeks and the Irrational*, pp. 270–82; Jeanmaire, *Dionysos*, pp. 119–31, 259–62; I. M. Lewis, *Ecstatic Religion. An Anthropological Study of Spirit Possession and Shamanism*, 1971, pp. 90, 101, caption for pl. 1a opposite p. 112; B. Simon, *Mind and Madness. The Classical Roots of Modern Psychiatry*, 1978, pp. 251–7.

74. Dodds, *The Greeks and the Irrational*, p. 77, and 'Maenadism', pp. 157f., 160f. = *Irrational*, pp. 271f., 274 = Euripides, *Bacchae*, pp. xiv–xvi; Simon, *Mind and Madness*, p. 252.

75. Dodds, *Irrational*, pp. 76f.

76. Lewis, *Ecstatic Religion*; Simon, *Mind and Madness*, pp. 252–5; Kraemer, 'Ecstasy and Possession', 1979, pp. 20ff., 1980, pp. 64ff.

77. Burkert, *Griechische Religion*, pp. 254 and 435.

78. Kraemer, 'Ecstasy and Possession', 1980, pp. 60ff.; cf. Burkert, *Griechische Religion*, p. 256 ('die Mutterrolle verkehrt sich ins furchtbare Gegenteil', first emphasized by Otto, *Dionysus*, pp. 105ff.; German ed., pp. 97ff.); Simon, *Mind and Madness*, p. 252 (Euripides's Bacchae 'take on male functions and male powers, particularly those of warriors').

79. Nietzsche, *Werke: Kritische Gesamtausgabe* III 3, 1978, p. 15 frs. 1 [33–34] written in the fall of 1869, and *Die Geburt der Tragödie* (1872) section 1 (*Werke: Krit. Gesamtausgabe* III 1, pp. 25.5ff.; *Werke in drei Bänden* I, 1954–56, p. 24); Rohde, *Psyche*, pp. 283f. (German ed. II, pp. 42f., although Nietzsche's *Geburt der Tragödie* is nowhere mentioned in *Psyche*); Wilamowitz, *GdH* II, p. 72, who is here completely under the spell of Rohde (rightly stressed by Otto, *Dionysus*, p. 125); Dodds, 'Maenadism', pp. 157f. = *Irrational*, pp. 271f. = Euripides, *Bacchae*, pp. xiv–xvi. Again it is obvious that Nietzsche set an important trend in the modern interpretation of Dionysus (see nn. 51 and 134).

80. Dodds, 'Maenadism', pp. 160f. = *Irrational*, pp. 273f.; Simon, *Mind and Madness*, pp. 251f. A visit to any contemporary discotheque will further confirm the symptoms if not the alleged cause.

81. Dodds, 'Maenadism', p. 163 = *Irrational*, pp. 275f.; Guthrie, *The Greeks and their Gods*, p. 148 n. 2.

82. J. G. Frazer, *The Golden Bough* Part V, vol. I, 1912³, pp. 21f.; F. Cumont, *Les religions orientales dans le paganisme romain*, p. 310 n. 57; R. Eisler, 'Nachleben dionysischer Mysterienriten?', *Archiv für Religionswissenschaft* 27, 1929, pp. 172–83; Dodds, 'Maenadism', p. 164 = *Irrational*, p. 276; Jeanmaire, *Dionysos*, pp. 258–67 (apparently written without knowledge that he had predecessors); Kerényi, *Dionysos*, p. 85 (German ed., p. 82). Against Dodds's view, see H. S. Versnel, 'Pentheus en Dionysus', *Lampas 9*, 1976, pp. 24f.

83. This misleading adaptation of Euripides's poetic metaphor (*Ba.* 778 *hōste pyr hyphaptetai*) goes back to Rohde (*Psyche*, p. 305 n. 8, German ed. II, p. 42 n. 3), was taken over by Frazer (*Golden Bough* V 1, p. 3) and Dodds ('Maenadism', p. 158 = *Irrational*, p. 272 = *Euripides, Bacchae* p. xv), and has been reiterated ever since (for instance by Wilamowitz, *GdH* II, p. 72 'wie eine epidemische Krankheit', also inspired by Rohde; Nilsson, *Gesch. d. griech. Religion* I, p. 157; and most recently Burkert, *Griechische Religion*, p. 252: 'ein Massen-Phänomen, das fast ansteckend um sich greift').

84. Seriously proposed by Simon, *Mind and Madness*, p. 257.

85. Kraemer, 'Ecstasy and Possession', 1979, p. 20 = 1980, p. 68; cf. Jeanmaire, *Dionysos*, p. 169 (maenadism as 'une forme de libération de la pression sociale'). Contrast R. P. Winnington-Ingram, *Euripides and Dionysus. An Interpretation of the Bacchae*, 1948, p. 150: 'A rite so constituted may have been a rich experience for the performers, but it can hardly be said to have served an important social function, when these performers were a small company of consecrated women.' Separate cults for men and women were common in Greek religion and not limited to the particular sphere of Dionysus. But women actively engaging in animal sacrifice were rare outside maenadism; see Detienne in *La cuisine du sacrifice*, pp. 183–214.

86. Dodds, 'Maenadism', p. 159 = *Irrational*, p. 272 = *Euripides, Bacchae*, p. xvi, cf. xiv: 'There must have been a time when the maenads . . . became for a few hours or days what their name implies – wild women whose human personality has been temporarily replaced by another.' See above, n. 53.

87. K. Meuli, *Gesammelte Schriften*, 1975, pp. 1018–21; Otto, *Dionysus*, pp. 74–8 (German ed., pp. 71ff.); Dodds, *Euripides, Bacchae*, pp. xxv–xxviii; Guthrie, *The Greeks and their Gods*, pp. 165–73; H. S. Versnel, *Triumphus. An Inquiry into the Origin, Development and Meaning of the Roman Triumph*, 1970, pp. 240–3; Burkert, *Griechische Religion*, pp. 252f.; M. Detienne in *Dictionnaire des mythologies*, 1980, s.v. 'Dionysos'. The ultimate source for the historicizing interpretation of Dionysiac resistance myths is Rohde, *Psyche*, pp. 282f. (German ed. II, pp. 40f.).

88. Above, n. 53.

89. *Hom. h. Cer.* 386 (cf. Homer, *Il.* 22.460; *Il.* 6.132: 'mad' [*mainomenos*] Dionysus is found in the company of female attendants called 'nurses'); Aeschylus, *TGF*(N), fr. 382; Sophocles, *OT* 212; Euripides, *Ion* 552; Aristophanes, *Lys.* 1283; Dionysus as 'Lord of the maenads' (*mainadōn ana*, cf. Euripides, *Ba.* 601) in an Hellenistic verse inscription from Thasos (Roux, *Euripide, Les Bacchantes* II, p. 633). Cf. A. Rapp, 'Mainaden', in W. H. Roscher, *Lexikon der griech. und römischen Mythologie* II.2, 1894–97, col. 2243; Harrison, *Prolegomena*, pp. 388ff., 396.

90. G. S. Kirk (*The Bacchae by Euripides*, 1979, on *Ba.* 1295) observes that *mainomai* is used pejoratively throughout the Bacchae (of Pentheus and his like at 326, 359, 399, 887 and 999; but of drunken people at 301 and of satyrs at 130). It is used critically also in the one instance in which it refers to the Theban women whose madness was a punishment inflicted on them by Dionysus (1295). The technical term *mainas* was apparently used with similar discrimination. Of nineteen occurrences in the *Bacchae*, fifteen refer to the Theban maenads (52, 224, 829, 956, 981, 984, 1023, 1052, 1060, 1062, 1075, 1107, 1143, 1192, and 1226), three to maenads in general (103, 570, and the emphatic 'wearing the outfit of a mad bacchante-woman', 915 *skeuēn gynaikos mainados bakchēs echōn*, of Pentheus), but only one to the chorus of Asiatic maenads (601).

91. Miletus, epigram for a dead maenad, c. 200 BCE, ed. T. Wiegand, 'Die Ausgrabungen . . . zu Milet', *SPAW* 1905, 547; Torre Nova (Latium), Agrippinilla inscription, eds. Cumont and Vogliano in 'The Bacchic Inscription in the Metropolitan Museum,' *AJA* 37, 1933, pp. 215ff., esp. 256f. and 260–62; Diodorus Siculus 3.65.2f.; 4.5.1. Strabo 10.3.10 gives the following list of generic names for maenads: Bakchai, Lēnai (earliest occurrence in Heraclitus 22 B 14 Diels-Kranz, if genuine; cf. Henrichs, 'Die Maenaden', p. 224 n. 4), Thyiai (cf. Thyiades), and Mimallones (cf. R. Pfeiffer on Callimachus, fr. 503). 'Mainades' is not on Strabo's list, which reflects cult rather than literature. According to Philo (*Plant.* 148) 'mainades' constitutes a pejorative nickname of the 'Bakchai' (because wine makes 'mad'; above n. 26). Whereas *bakchoi* and *mystai* (the masculine forms) occur in close collocation in Heraclitus (B 14), Euripides (*TGF*(N), fr. 472 = *Cretans* fr. 79 Austin) and the gold plate from Hipponion (below, n. 152), maenadic rites are never called *mystēria* in classical or Hellenistic texts, although they are occasionally said to involve 'initiation' (*teletē*).

92. *IMagn.* 215 (c. 200 BCE); Diodorus 4.3.3 explicitly differentiates between the Bacchae of Hellenistic cult and the mythical *mainades* whom they imitate.

93. *IG* IX 1².3.670 (Physkos, imperial period); cf. Henrichs, 'Greek Maenadism', pp. 155f.

94. Pausanias 10.4.2; 10.6.4 (cf. 2.7.5); 10.32.7; cf. Plutarch, *Mul. virt.* 13, *Mor.* 249E (who associates the 'madness' of the Delphic Thyiads with their loss of the sense of time and place and with their physical exhaustion). For the connection of maenadic 'madness' and mountain-dancing, see also *Hom. h. Cer.* 386 and Sophocles, *Ant.* 1151f.

95. Euripides, *Ba.* 66f. (*ponon hēdyn kamaton t' eukamaton*), from a

passage of the parodos which describes the Bacchic mountain rites as 'cathartic' (76f.), i.e. as a religious group experience which 'merges the individual consciousness in a group consciousness' (Dodds, *Euripides, Bacchae*, p. xx; below, n. 134) and which translates physical exhaustion into spiritual well-being (75 *thiaseutai psychān*). A. J. Festugière, 'La signification religieuse de la Parodos des Bacchantes', *Eranos* 54, 1956, pp. 72–86 = *Études de religion grecque et hellénistique*, pp. 66–80, interprets the parodos as a maenadic 'gospel' whose message is 'happiness', *eudaimonia*, or a better world, for the followers of Dionysus who 'know the secret ritual' (*Ba.* 73 *teletas . . . eidōs*).

96. Detienne, *Dionysos mis à mort*, p. 216 (ET p. 117) n. 138, who echoes Gernet, *REG* 66, 1953, p. 383 = *Anthropologie*, p. 72; Wilamowitz, *GdH* II, pp. 67, 70; Nilsson, *Opusc. Sel.* II, 1952, pp. 526f.

97. Kadmos, Teiresias and Pentheus in Euripides's *Bacchae* dress as maenads for *dramatic* reasons (above, n. 6). Too much has been made of Pentheus's 'ritual dressing', most recently by B. Seidensticker, 'Sacrificial Ritual in the *Bacchae*', in *Arktouros. Hellenic Studies presented to B. M. W. Knox*, 1979, pp. 181–90, esp. 182f. An Attic black-figure pyxis (Eleusis 1212) from the mid-sixth century BCE shows a tragic chorus of men dressed as maenads (A. W. Pickard-Cambridge, *Dithyramb, Tragedy and Comedy*, 1962[2], pp. 80, 303 no. 20, pl. VIa). Equally inspired by theatrical convention, this time that of the satyr-play, is the Attic red-figure cylix from Corinth of the late fifth century BCE which shows a female figure wearing a shaggy loincloth with an attached phallus and dancing before Dionysus (S. B. Luce, *AJA* 34, 1930, p. 340, with fig. 4, who misinterpreted her as a 'hermaphrodite faun'; J. D. Beazley, *Attic Red-figure Vase-painters*, 1963[2], p. 1519; Pickard-Cambridge, *Dithyramb, Tragedy and Comedy*, pp. 115 and 313 no. 98; E. Langlotz, 'Filialen griechischer Töpfer in Italien?', *Gymnasium* 84, 1977, pp. 423–37, with plate XXI 2; Simon, *Mind and Madness*, plate opposite p. 252, unaware of the theatrical background, suggests a Freudian interpretation, 'a concrete representation of the fantasy of the maenad as phallic woman'). A fragment of a Hellenistic *lex sacra* from Tlos which mentions a ritual collection of money and men dressed in women's clothes must not be assigned to the cult of Dionysus (*pace* F. Kolb, *ZPE* 22, 1976, pp. 228–30) but to Cybele.

98. Dodds, 'Maenadism', p. 170, excludes men from maenadic rites (above, n. 96), with the exception of 'male officials of the cult', especially 'one male celebrant who is identified with the god' (also Dodds, on Euripides, *Ba.* 115, 135, 136). In support of his view, Dodds referred to *Ba.* 135ff., lines which have been interpreted differently and more plausibly in J. Roux's commentary, and to the male 'climber of Mount Mimas' (*mimantobatēs*) in an Erythraean inscription of the imperial period (H. Engelmann and R. Merkelbach, *Die Inschriften von Erythrai und Klazomenai* I, 1972, no. 64.6, who follow Dodds's 'maenadic' interpretation of *mimantobatēs*; but Dodds himself admitted, 'Maenadism', p. 156 n. 5, 'That the title is Dionysiac is not certain'.). Cf. Henrichs, 'Greek Maenadism', p. 133 n. 40 (against male participation in maenadic rites). Burkert (*Griech. Religion*, pp. 434f.) and Kraemer ('Ecstasy and Posses-

sion', 1979, pp. 15–8) resurrect Dodd's 'male celebrant'. Dionysus's presence at maenadic rites (Diodorus 4.3.3) was imagined by the maenads (and to that extent it was a real religious experience), but not re-enacted by a male substitute.

99. Herodotus, 4.78–80 (initiation of the Scythian King Skyles in Greek Olbia, c. 450 BCE); Burkert, *Griech. Religion*, pp. 432ff. *Bacchantes et furentes* ('raving mad') was still a proper description of male participants in orgiastic cults of Dionysus in late antiquity (Augustine, *Ep.* 17.4). 'Raving' (*lyssātās*) Euphron participates in biennial rites for Dionysus in an Hellenistic epigram (Aristodikos, *AP* 7.473, c. 250 BCE).

100. Cumont, *Les religions orientales*, pp. 195–204, 303–12; Wilamowitz, *GdH* II, pp; 370–86; A. J. Festugière, 'Les Mystères de Dionysos', *RB* 44, 1935, pp. 366–96 = *Études de religion grecque et hellénistique*, pp. 13–62; Kerényi, *Dionysos*, pp. 349–88.

101. Euripides, *Ba.* 465ff.; Burkert, *Griech. Religion*, pp. 434f.; H. S. Versnel, 'Pentheus en Dionysos', pp. 31–3 (in Dutch).

102. Inscription of 276/275 BCE ed. T. Wiegand, *Sechster vorläufiger Bericht über Ausgrabungen in Milet und Didyma*, APAW 1908, Anhang 1, pp. 22ff. = Sokolowski, *Lois sacrées de l'Asie Mineure*, 1955, no. 48; Henrichs, 'Greek Maenadism', pp. 149f.

103. *IMagn.*, no. 215; 'Greek Maenadism', pp. 133f.

104. Euripides, *Ba.* 221ff., 686ff., *Ion* 550ff.; Livy 30.8.6 (*vinum, nox* and *mixti feminis mares*; below, n. 151). Wine and sex orgies were also imputed to the early Christians by their detractors; cf. Henrichs in *Kyriakon. Festschrift J. Quasten* I, 1970, pp. 18–35, and *Die Phoinikika des Lollianos*, 1972, pp. 34ff. (on the charges against the Christians), pp. 44–7 (on the Roman Bacchanalia).

105. Emphasized by Kerényi, *Dionysos*, pp. 285–90 (German ed., pp. 226–31). Nietzsche, *Götzen-Dämmerung*, pp. x, 4 (above n. 51), though vague on Dionysiac 'mysteries', is illuminating on the phallus and on reproduction in connection with his vitalistic conception of Dionysus.

106. Aristotle, *Ath.* 3.5; [Demosthenes] 59.73, 76; Burkert, *Homo Necans*, pp. 255ff., *Griechische Religion*, pp. 361f.

107. On 'phallos-bearers' (*phallophoroi*) in Dionysiac processions see Nilsson, *Gesch. d. griech. Religion* I, pp. 590ff.; Burkert, *Griechische Religion*, p. 171; below, n. 142. On the connection of *phallophoroi* with ritual abuse (Semus of Delos, *FGrH* 396 F 24), see J. S. Rusten, *HSCP* 81, 1977, pp. 157ff., esp. 161.

108. T. B. L. Webster, *Greece and Rome* 13, 1966, pp. 22–31.

109. Occasionally young boys are shown before the *liknon* which contains the phallus, but unlike their female counterparts, they have their heads veiled. Cf. Cumont, 'Bacchic Inscription', pp. 250–3; Nilsson, *Dionysiac Mysteries*, pp. 30–7, 66–98; F. Matz, DIONYSIAKĒ TELETĒ. *Archäologische Untersuchungen zum Dionysoskult in hellenistischer und römischer Zeit*, Abh. Akad. Mainz, Geistes- u. sozialwiss. Klasse, 1963.15, pp. 1400ff. (with numerous pls.); P. Boyancé, 'Dionysiaca. À propos d'une étude récente sur l'initiation dionysiaque', *REA* 68, 1966, pp. 33–

60, esp. 35f., 42–5 (an instructive critique of Matz); Horn, *Mysteriensymbolik*, pp. 58–62, with figs. 33 and 56; Kerényi, *Dionysos*, pp. 273, 376f. (German ed., pp. 218f., 298) with fig. 72 and p. 359 (German ed., p. 285) with fig. 110D (Pompeii, Villa dei Misteri).

110. Henrichs, 'Glimpses' (see n. 25), p. 9; compare the nude Dionysus and half-nude maenads on the mid-fourth century BCE Derveni bronze krater, published by E. Giouri, *Ho kratēras tou Derbeniou*, 1978, esp. pls. A, B, E, 22, 26f., 32 and 35.

111. Roux, *Euripide, Les Bacchantes* II, pp. 342–4 on *Ba.* 276; Horn, *Mysteriensymbolik*, pp. 70–2; Graf, *Eleusis und die orphische Dichtung Athens in vorhellenistischer Zeit*, 1974, pp. 65f. (on cultic association of Demeter and Dionysus). Dodds on *Ba.* 402–16; Horn, *Mysteriensymbolik*, pp. 100f.

112. Henrichs, *Die Phoinikika des Lollianos*, p. 46 n. 9.

113. Nilsson, *Dionysiac Mysteries*, p. 131; Horn, *Mysteriensymbolik*, pp. 103–7.

114. Pickard-Cambridge, *Dramatic Festivals*, pp. 1–25, and Deubner, *Attische Feste*, pp. 103ff., 149f. (Anthesteria); Deubner, op. cit., pp. 135f. on Plutarch, *Cup. div.* 8, *Mor.* 52D (rural Dionysia).

115. Miletus epigram (above, n. 91), line 4; Henrichs, 'Greek Maenadism', pp. 148f.

116. 'Greek Maenadism', pp. 145f.

117. Inscription from Miletus of 276/75 (above, n. 102), lines 21–4; Callixenus of Rhodes, *FGrH* 627 F 2 p. 169.24; Cumont, 'Bacchic Inscription', pp. 240–3;

118. Henrichs, 'Die Maenaden', pp. 233f., 237f.

119. Burkert, *Griechische Religion*, pp. 254ff.

120. Euripides, *Ba.* 206–9; Dodds on *Ba.* 421–3; Tibullus 1.7.41f.

121. Cumont, 'Bacchic Inscription', p. 234.

122. The age of young boys who died as Dionysiac initiates is occasionally indicated in funerary inscriptions (Nilsson, *Dionysiac Mysteries*, pp. 106ff.; Horn, *Mysteriensymbolik*, pp. 90f.; Merkelbach, *ZPE* 7, 1971, p. 280). An unpublished inscription from Ankyra Sidera in Phrygia of perhaps the third century CE mentions a twelve-year old Flavios who was a *bukolos* (literally 'oxherd') in the thiasos of Dionysos Dithyrambos and who was killed when a wall in the precinct of the god collapsed during an earthquake. (I owe this reference to T. Drew-Bear.)

123. Burkert, *Griechische Religion*, pp. 390–5.

124. Euripides, *Ba.* 694, with the notes of Dodds and J. Roux; cf. Euripides, *Ph.* 655f.

125. Diodorus 4.3.3; Jeanmaire, *Dionysos*, pp. 171ff.; Burkert, *Griechische Religion*, p. 436.

126. Nilsson, *Dionysiac Mysteries*, pp. 95, 106–15; Horn, *Mysteriensymbolik*, pp. 88–92.

127. H. Herter, 'Das Kind im Zeitalter des Hellenismus', *Bonner Jahrbücher* 132, 1927, pp. 250–8; 'Das Leben ein Kinderspiel', *Bonner Jahrbücher* 161, 1961, pp. 73–84, esp. 74f. = *Kleine Schriften*, 1975, pp. 584–97, esp. 586f.; 'Das unschuldige Kind', *JbAC* 4, 1961, pp. 146–62 = *Kleine Schriften*, pp. 598–619.

128. Deubner, *Attische Feste*, pp. 114ff., 238ff.; G. van Hoorn, *Choes and Anthesteria*, 1951; Pickard-Cambridge, *Dramatic Festivals*, pp. 9–11; above, nn. 32–33, 36.

129. Sophocles, *TGF* IV, fr. 959 Radt; Diodorus 3.64.5f., 4.2.3f.; Ovid, *Metam.* 3.314f.; Nonnus, *Dion.* 9.25–131; M. P. Nilsson, *The Minoan-Mycenaean Religion and its Survival in Greek Religion*, 1950², pp. 564ff.; Henrichs, 'Greek Maenadism', pp. 140f.; G. M. A. Hanfmann and C. Moore, 'Hermes and Dionysos: A "Neo-Attic" Relief', *Fogg Art Museum Acquisitions*, 1969–70, pp. 41–9.

130. Dunbabin, *The Mosaics of Roman North Africa*, pp. 174–81; Horn, *Mysteriensymbolik*, p. 90 n. 16.

131. Turcan, *Les sarcophages romains à représentations dionysiaques*, pp. 405–40; N. Himmelmann-Wildschütz, *Marburger Winckelmann-Programm*, 1959; Horn, *Mysteriensymbolik*, pp. 105f.

132. Burkert, *Structure and History*, p. 49.

133. Private dedications to Dionysus are usually from the Hellenistic period, are often written in verse and invoke the god's blessings in personal matters (for instance *IG* II/III² 2948 and an unpublished iambic epigram from Thasos quoted by J. Roux, *Euripide, Les Bacchantes* II, pp. 633f.).

134. Dodds, *Euripides, Bacchae*, p. xx. Here and elsewhere essential elements in Dodds's interpretation of Dionysus derive from Nietzsche's *The Birth of Tragedy*. But Nietzsche is given credit only for the 'impressive antithesis' of the 'rational' religion of Apollo and the 'irrational' religion of Dionysus, a dubious dualism which Dodds rejects (*The Greeks and the Irrational*, pp. 68f.; Dodds was widely read in Nietzsche, cf. his *Missing Persons: An Autobiography*, 1977, pp. 19f.). Nietzsche based his existentialist aesthetics on the notion of the 'shattering of the individual and his fusion with primal being', which he found exemplified in the 'annihilation' of one's personal identity through identification with the satyric chorus as experienced by the spectator of Attic tragedy (*Die Geburt der Tragödie*, esp. sections 7–8, here quoted in the Kaufmann translation). Reduced to its anthropological core, Nietzsche's influential insight into the role of Dionysus as fosterer of a collective religious identity was first reformulated by J. Harrison (above, n. 51), who, unlike Dodds, acknowledged her positive debt to Nietzsche explicitly (*Prolegomena*, p. 445 n. 4). While there can be no doubt that the interpretation of Dionysiac cult as a liberating group experience isolates one of its most pervasive aspects, one does well to remember the intellectual conditions which favoured its rediscovery and modern formulation in the late nineteenth century.

135. From classical to late antiquity, followers of Dionysus impersonated various members of the mythical entourage of Dionysus at wine festivals and other informal Dionysiac occasions: Plato, *Lg.* 815C (nymphs, Pans, sileni, satyrs); Vergil, *Ecl.* 5.73 (satyrs); Plutarch, *Ant.* 24 (people of Ephesus dress as *bakchai*, satyrs and Pans for Mark Antony's arrival in 42/41 BCE); Lucian, *Salt.* 79 (Titans, Corybants, satyrs and *boukoloi* as stock characters in 'Bacchic dances', *Bakchikē orchēsis*); Longus 2.36–37 (vintage scenes; Pan and Syrinx); Philostratus, *VA* 4.21 (Horai,

nymphs and *bakchai* impersonated at Athenian Anthesteria). On the liberating ('cathartic') effect of Bacchic dances and music see Aristides Quintilianus, *Mus.* 3.25, with the comments of P. Boyancé, 'Dionysiaca', pp. 33f.

136. See p. 151 below.

137. Plato, *Phd.* 69C = *Orph. Frr.* 5 and 235. I suspect that Plato was drawing a distinction between ritual maenadism (typified by the thyrsus), which would not guarantee a preferred place in the underworld, and esoteric Bacchic initiation which conferred a special status.

138. Henrichs, 'Die Maenaden', p. 230 n. 24; 'Greek Maenadism', pp. 134 n. 41, 148f.

139. 'Greek Maenadism', pp. 125f. (seniority); *IG* II/III² 1368.37–41, 55–58 (family ties emphasized in the statutes of the Iobakchoi; above, nn. 40ff.); Horn, *Mysteriensymbolik*, pp. 88f. (family ties). The Agrippinilla inscription (Metropolitan Museum of Art, Acc. No. 26.60.70a; cf. nn. 91, 142, and at nn. 157–158) illustrates the connection between social rank and high office in a Dionysiac *thiasos* run by a distinguished Greek family of the second century CE.

140. A. D. Nock, *JHS* 48, 1928, pp. 29–37 = *Essays on Religion and the Ancient World*, pp. 144–52. Below, n. 190.

141. Athenaeus 5.197C–201E = Callixenus of Rhodes, *FGrH* 627 F 2.27–33; P. M. Fraser, *Ptolemaic Alexandria* I, pp. 202f. Verbatim quotations from Athenaeus are from C. B. Gulick, LCL II, pp. 395–411.

142. Agrippinilla inscription (above, nn. 91 and 139); *IGBulg.* 1517; R. Merkelbach, 'Die ephesischen Dionysosmysten vor der Stadt', *ZPE* 36, 1979, pp. 151–6. Cf. M. Guarducci, *Epigrafia greca* IV, 1978, pp. 183–9, with figs. 49–50.

143. Nilsson, *Dionysiac Mysteries*, pp. 49f.; Bruhl, *Liber Pater*, pp. 280ff.; F. Poland, 'speira', *PW* IIIa, 1929, col. 1591; for *systēma*, see Diodorus 4.3.3 and *systēmarchēs* in *IG Bulg.* 1517.

144. Poland, *Vereinswesen*, pp. 77, 84, 201f.

145. Jeanmaire, *Dionysos*, pp. 273f.

146. E. Schmidt, *Kultübertragungen*, 1909, p. 89 n. 1 (on the arrival by sea of a crude wooden image of Dionysus on Lesbos, cf. Pausanias 10.19.3) and p. 105 (on the myths of arrival); A. D. Nock, *Conversion*, pp. 71–3 (on the Roman Bacchanalia) and pp. 193f. (on Euripides's *Bacchae*).

147. Words of the root *'phan'* which describe the 'appearance' of Dionysus occur frequently in the Homeric Hymn to Dionysus and the prologue to the *Bacchae*. Diodorus (4.3.2) mentions Dionysus's 'epiphanies' (*epiphaneiai*) as regular events.

148. Henrichs, 'Greek Maenadism', pp. 152f.

149. *IMagn.* 215 (above, n. 92); Henrichs, 'Greek Maenadism', pp. 123–37; J. Fontenrose, *The Delphic Oracle. Its Responses and Operations*, 1978, p. 410 no. 171. Fontenrose, who classifies *IMagn.* 215 as a 'legendary response' as if it had no verifiably historical content, ignores the second foundation of Magnesia in 400/399 BCE, which is mentioned in the oracle; he fails to discuss the postcript, which describes the implementation of

the oracle at Magnesia; and finally, he deems the names of the three maenads (Koskō, Baubō and Thettalē) 'patently mythical', as if such names could not have existed in cult or ordinary life.

150. Above, n. 103; Burkert, ch. 1 above, pp. 6–8.: 'Family Organization'.

151. Livy 39.8–19; *CIL* I² 581 (Senatus consultum de Bacchanalibus); Nock, *Conversion*, pp. 71ff.; Jeanmaire, *Dionysos*, pp. 454ff.; Bruhl, *Liber Pater*, pp. 82ff.; Nilsson, *Dionysiac Mysteries*, pp. 14ff.; Henrichs, *Die Phoinikika des Lollianos*, pp. 44ff. and 'Greek Maenadism', pp. 134f.; J. A. North, *PCPS* n.s. 25, 1979, pp. 85–103.

152. G. Zuntz, *Persephone. Three Essays on Religion and Thought in Magna Graecia*, 1971, pp. 275–393; G. Pugliese-Carratelli, *PP* 29, 1974, pp. 108–26 (Hipponion tablet); G. Colli, *La sapienza greca* I, 1977, pp. 172–93, 399–405 (text of all fourteen plates published up to 1974, with Italian translation and notes); J. Breslin, *A Greek Prayer*, 1977, the editio princeps of the second tablet from Thessaly (now in the J. Paul Getty Museum at Malibu, California), reprinted at *ZPE* 25, 1977, p. 276. In recent years, W. Burkert has illuminated the background of the tablets on several occasions: *Gnomon* 46, 1974, pp. 326–8 (review of Zuntz); 'Le laminette auree: da Orfeo a Lampone', in *Orfismo in Magna Grecia. Atti del Quattordicesimo Convegno di Studi sulla Magna Grecia*, 1975, pp. 81–104; 'Orphism and Bacchic Mysteries: New Evidence and Old Problems', pp. 1–8 and 31ff.; *Griechische Religion*, pp. 436f.; and finally, in his unpublished Gray Lectures delivered at Cambridge University in March, 1979.

153. Colli, *La sapienza greca*, pp. 404f.: The tablets from Crete 'testify to the wide diffusion of the Orphic movement, and to the unity of its inspiration'.

154. The additional line ('But my race is from heaven') and the variant reading (the 'white' cypress) which make the Thessalian tablet in the Getty Museum different from the Cretan tablets, whose text is otherwise the same, are both paralleled in the Petelia tablet. West, 'Goldplättchen', pp. 129–36, reconstructed an 'archetype' for the longer tablets from Hipponion, Petelia, and Pharsalos, and a 'stemma' for the shorter Cretan tablets. The publication of the Getty specimen serves as a reminder that religious texts of this nature were in a constant state of flux, and that the shorter versions borrowed freely from the longer ones.

155. Written reproduction from memory best explains some of the textual errors and variants found on the plates (Burkert in his Gray Lectures). On practitioners of Orphic rites as religious craftsmen, see Burkert's contribution to this volume; on the gold plates, see his n. 2.

156. Burkert, 'Le laminette auree', p. 86; S. G. Cole, 'New Evidence for the Mysteries of Dionysos', *GRBS* 21, 1980, pp. 223–38.

157. Above, nn. 91, 139, 142.

158. Nilsson, *Opusc. Sel.* II, p. 541; R. Merkelbach, *Roman und Mysterium in der Antike*, 1962, pp. 193f.

159. Winnington-Ingram, *Euripides and Dionysos*, p. 155: 'The group is bound together . . . by outward symbols: by a common dress, consisting of fawnskin, headdress and wand, and by a common rallying-cry of Evoe

– by a uniform and a slogan.' Well said. But the ritual dress of Bacchic worshippers in the Hellenistic and imperial period remains a vexatious subject, on which see P. Boyancé, 'Dionysiaca', pp. 45–55. It is difficult to imagine that the maenadic wardrobe of the imperial period regularly included fawnskins and girdles made from snake-hides (so Boyancé), which were hardly available in sufficient quantity.

160. By W. Burkert at this Symposium.

161. Colli, *La sapienza greca* I, pp. 52–71, a collection of passages, mostly from fifth-century BCE sources, which bear on Dionysiac cult, is of little use. The only existing corpus of Dionysiac inscriptions is limited to Asia Minor and completely out of date (W. Quandt, *De Baccho ab Alexandri aetate in Asia Minore culto*, Diss. Philologicae Halenses, XXI 2, 1913).

162. *Hieros logos* is an ambiguous word whose meaning ranges from 'secret explanation' of ritual practices (W. Burkert, *Lore and Science in Ancient Pythagoreanism*, pp. 219f., on Herodotus 2.81) to 'sacred text' (so presumably in the Dionysiac edict ascribed to Ptolemy IV Philopator; see Fraser, *Ptolemaic Alexandria* II, p. 345 n. 114 for references). On the term *hieros logos* in general, see Henrichs, *Die Phoinikika des Lollianos*, p. 61 n. 27. The papyrus roll held by a boy on the Dionysiac wall painting in the Pompeian Villa of the Mysteries suggests a sacred book.

163. Nietzsche, *Die Geburt der Tragödie*, section 4 ('even in piercing shrieks', in the Kaufmann translation); Rohde, *Psyche*, p. 257 (German ed. II, p. 9): 'Excited by this wild music, the chorus of worshippers dance with shrill crying and jubilation. We hear nothing about singing: the violence of the dance left no breath for regular songs.' Cf. Harrison, *Prolegomena*, p. 413 ('such cries . . . are particularly exciting to the religious emotions'); and on Dionysiac exclamations in general, Versnel, *Triumphus*, pp. 27–38.

164. For instance in Eupolis, fr. 84 (*CAF* I, p. 278: *euai sabai*); Aristophanes, *Lys.* 1294 (*euoi euoi, euai euai*); Euripides, *Ba.* 141 (*euoi*); Philodamus of Scarphea, *Delphic Paean to Dionysus*, lines 5, 18, 31, 57 etc. (*Collect. Alex.* pp. 166f.: *euoi ō Iobakche*); Demosthenes, 18.260 (*euoi saboi*); Pausanias, 4.31.4 (*euoi*). Compare the derivatives Euios (of Dionysus, e.g. Euripides *Ba.* 157), *euazō* (e.g. Sophocles, *Ant.* 1134; Euripides, *Ba.* 68; Diodorus, 4.3.3), *euastērios* (in an inscription from Thasos; above, n. 89), and others.

165. German summary of the Russian publications by F. Tinnefeld, *ZPE* 38, 1980, pp. 67–71, esp. 70f.; Burkert, *Informationen zum altsprachlichen Unterricht* 2, 1980, p. 38.

166. Euripides, *Ba.* 116, 165 and 986 (each time a word indicating motion is followed by *eis oros eis oros*, a repetition which is characteristic of ritual formulae; tentatively identified as a ritual cry by Dodds, *The Greeks and the Irrational*, p. 278 n. 3); Hellenistic epigram from Miletus (above, n. 91) honouring a maenad who 'led you to the mountain (*eis oros*)' (the same phrase, *agein eis oros*, as *Ba.* 116); in the Physkos inscription (above, n. 93), *boukoloi* and *mainades* are fined unless they join the other club members *eis oros*.

167. Above, nn. 152 and 154.

168. Euripides *Ba.* 471–6; cf. above, n. 101.

169. Firmicus Maternus, *Err. prof. relig.* 18.1 (cf. 20.1. and 21.1) uses both terms as synonyms in connection with pagan cults. The Greek for *signum* is *sēmeion*, in the sense of 'verbal proof'; cf. R. Merkelbach, *ZPE* 6, 1970, pp. 245f.

170. Plautus, *Miles* 1016 (*cedo signum si harunc Baccharum es*, immediately followed by the password); cf. Nilsson, *Dionysiac Mysteries*, pp. 12–4.

171. Plutarch, *Cons. ad uxorem* 10, *Mor.* 611D ('mystical symbols of Dionysiac rites' known only to the initiate), interpreted as 'verbal formulas' by A. D. Nock, *Essays* II, p. 616 n. 35. PGurob 1.23 (R. A. Pack, *The Greek and Latin Literary Texts from Greco-Roman Egypt*, 1965², 2464; *Orph. Fr.* 31), a papyrus of the third century BCE, has the tantalizing sequence of words *heis Dionysos symbola*.

172. The password in Plautus, *Miles* 1016, is of course a comic distortion, not the real thing; the Dionysiac *symbolum* quoted by Firmicus Maternus, *Err. prof. relig.* 21.1, is corrupt and not necessarily authentic.

173. Apuleius, *Apol.* 55.8 (*signa et monumenta*), 56.1 (*sacrorum crepundia*, 'religious tokens of recognition'), 56.8 (*signa et memoracula*); Clement of Alexandria, *Protr.* 2.18.1 (*symbola*). By contrast, Ovid's *insignia Bacchi* (*Metam.* 6.598) refers to the accoutrements of a mythical maenad.

174. Apuleius, *Apol.* 55.8 trans. A. D. Nock, *Conversion*, p. 114: 'In Greece I took part in very many initiations. I keep carefully certain symbols and memorials (*quaedam signa et monumenta*) of them handed to me by the priests. What I say is nothing unusual or unknown. Those of you present who are initiated in the rites only of Father Liber, for instance, know what you keep concealed at home and worship far from all profane persons.'

175. P. Boyancé ('Dionysiaca', pp. 37–45), whose argument is based on the unlikely assumption that *crepundia* in Apuleius, *Apol.* 56.1 (above, n. 173) does not mean 'tokens of recognition' (*gnōrismata*) but specifically 'playthings' (*paignia*).

176. Clement of Alexandria, *Protr.* 2.22; cf. Henrichs, 'Die Maenaden', pp. 227–31.

177. On the mosaics see Dunbabin, *The Mosaics of Roman North Africa*, pp. 173–87.

178. The ivy-leaf was considered an 'emblem' of Dionysus (3 Macc. 2.29 *parasēmon Dionysou*), ivy-berries his 'token' (Philostratus, *Im.* 1.15 *gnōrisma*), felines and drinking vessels his 'symbols' (ibid., the panther as *tou theou symbolon*; Porph, *Antr.* 13, kraters and amphorae as *Dionysou symbola*).

179. Horn, *Mysteriensymbolik* (an eminently instructive book, despite its bias) represents the extreme pan-symbolic (in the religious sense) approach to Dionysiac iconography. By contrast, more recent studies of Dionysiac art are less speculative, and more methodological; see Dunbabin, *Mosaics* (above, n. 177), and especially A. Geyer, *Das Problem des Realitätsbezuges in der dionysischen Bildkunst der Kaiserzeit*, 1977, a rigorous attempt to differentiate between mythical and cultic, or 'real', elements

in Dionysiac representations. (Geyer's equation of 'cultic' and 'real' ignores the role of myth in Dionysiac cult.)

180. Dunbabin, *The Mosaics of Roman North Africa*, pp. 170f., 205 n. 42; H. Hommel, 'Das Datum der Munatier-Grabstätte in Portus Traiani und die "hederae distinguentes" ', *ZPE* 5, 1970, pp. 293–303, esp. 300ff., and the addendum *ZPE* 6, 1970, p. 287. 'Hederae distinguentes' is the name for ivy-leaves used in inscriptions to separate words.

181. Bruhl, *Liber Pater*, pp. 8 and 55; Horn, *Mysteriensymbolik*, pp. 85f.

182. *Etymologicum Genuinum* A and B (= *Etym. Magnum*) s.v. *gallos*; P. Perdrizet, 'Le fragment de Satyros sur les dèmes d'Alexandrie', *REA* 12, 1910, pp. 217–47, esp. 236–8; F. J. Dölger, 'Die Gottesweihe durch Brandmarkung oder Tätowierung im ägyptischen Dionysoskult der Ptolemäerzeit, *Antike und Christentum* 2, 1930, pp. 100–6; J. Tondriau, 'Tatouage, lierre et syncrétismes', *Aegyptus* 30, 1950, pp. 57–66; Fraser, *Ptolemaic Alexandria* II, pp. 347f. n. 118. According to Plutarch (*Quo. adul.* 12, *Mor.* 56E), tympana and 'lilies' (lotus flowers?) were also used as tattoo marks by Ptolemy IV (cf. C. A. Lobeck, *Aglaophamus*, 1829, pp. 657f.; Dölger, 'Die Gottesweihe', pp. 104f.; Wilamowitz, *GdH* II, p. 378 n. 1).

183. Perdrizet, 'Fragment de Satyros', pp. 236f. n. 2; Harrison, *Prolegomena*, p. 463, *Themis*, pp. 132f.; Dölger, 'Zur Frage der religiösen Tätowierung im thrakischen Dionysoskult. "*Bromio signatae mystides*" in einer Grabinschrift des 3. Jh. n. Chr.', *Antike und Christentum* 2, 1930, pp. 107–16, esp. 112ff. with pls. 9–10; J. W. B. Barns and H. Lloyd-Jones, *Studi italiani di filologia classica* n.s. 35, 1963, p. 222 (on Phanocles fr. 1.25f., *Collect. Alex.* p. 107).

184. A metrical tomb inscription of the third century CE from Philippi, Macedonia, mentions, in connection with satyrs and nymphs, *Bromio signatae mystides* who are joined by the deceased boy on the Elysian fields (F. Bücheler, *Carmina latina epigraphica* II, 1897, no. 1233.17). Cf. Perdrizet, 'Fragment de Satyros', p. 237; Dölger, 'Zur Frage der religiösen Tätowierung' (above, n. 183) p. 116, who sees in the female initiates with the Dionysiac *signum* mere mythical maenads; Wilamowitz, *GdH* II, p. 380.

185. It is noteworthy that the leaf points upward and the stem downward, whereas *hederae distinguentes* (above, n. 180) invariably point downward in inscriptions, including some from Erythrai.

186. H. Engelmann and R. Merkelbach, *Die Inschriften von Erythrai und Klazomenai* II, 1973, nos. 345 (second century BCE) and 357 ('Grabplatte', no date); Wilamowitz, *GdH* II, p. 378.

187. Cf. Matz, DIONYSIAKĒ TELETĒ, pls. 2, 4–13, 15–17; Horn, *Mysteriensymbolik*, figs. 55–56; Kerényi, *Dionysos*, figs. 71–72, 110A–E, 133, 135–136.

188. Of particular interest, apart from the ubiquitous maenads and satyrs, are such roles as that of 'Silenus' (the title for ushers and bouncers in Dionysiac associations, cf. Cumont, 'Bacchic Inscription', pp. 244–6), 'Daddy' (*appas*, *IMagn.* 117, imperial period) and 'nurse' (*hypotrophos*, ibid.), which show how vital biological and social functions were interpreted in terms of traditional mythical figures.

189. On Dionysiac cult-titles related to animals, see Nilsson, *Opusc. Sel.* II, pp. 535f., who considers them the product of 'the bucolic and archaizing taste' typical of the Hellenistic and early imperial age. But the fact remains that the 'Tier im Menschen', especially in Dionysiac men, was never fully tamed.

190. Ptolemy II staged his Dionysiac 'trionfo' (above, pp. 150f. and n. 141); Ptolemy IV was tattooed with an ivy-leaf (above, p. 157 and n. 182) and gave Dionysiac drinking parties (below, p. 158 and n. 202); the Roman consul Marius reportedly drank from a *kantharos* 'in imitation of Dionysus' after his victory over the Cimbri in 101 BCE (Pliny, *HN* 33.11.150; Valerius Maximus 3.3.6); Mark Antony (above, n. 135) wined under a Dionysiac canopy on the Athenian acropolis in 39 BCE (Athenaeus 4.148BC = Socrates of Rhodes, *FGrH* 192 F 2), dressed as Dionysus for his Alexandrian triumph in 34 (Velleius Paterculus 2.82.4), and was ultimately deserted by Dionysus in 31 (Plutarch, *Ant.* 75.4ff., a telling piece of Augustan anti-propaganda); Caligula, called 'Neos Dionysos', donned 'Dionysiac dress' while administering justice (Athenaeus 4.148D). In general see J. Tondriau, 'Dionysos, Dieu royal', *Annuaire de l'Institut de Philologie et d'Histoire Orientales et Slaves* 12, 1952, pp. 441–466; Versnel, *Triumphus*, pp. 250–4.

191. Nock, 'Neos Dionysos', in 'Notes on Ruler-Cult', *Essays* I, pp. 144–52, esp. 148.

192. F. Nietzsche, *Die Geburt der Tragödie*, end of section 1 ('under the charm of Dionysus' man 'feels himself a god', in the Kaufmann translation); Rohde, *Psyche*, p. 262, German ed. II, p. 26 ('the impulse to union with god, the extinction of the individual in the divine'); more recently Burkert, *Griechische Religion*, p. 252 ('Verschmelzung' of worshippers and god). Contrast Boyancé, 'Dionysiaca', p. 52: 'Il ne s'agit pas, selon nous, d'une identification mystique de l'initié à son dieu, mais du fait que l'un est le modèle parfait de l'autre.'

193. Otto, *Dionysus*, p. 176 (German ed., pp. 163f.); Dodds, *Euripides, Bacchae*, pp. 133f.; *Orph. Hymn.* 42.4 (*arsena kai thēlyn*); Lydus, *Mens.* 4.160; F. Jacoby on Philochorus, *FGrH* 328 F 7a.

194. Diodorus 4.5.2; Cornutus, *Theologia Graeca* 30. On the joint representation of a young and a bearded Dionysus, *both* of the effeminate type, on Roman sarcophagi see Matz, *DIONYSIAKĒ TELETĒ*, pp. 1420–7, a response to R. Turcan, 'Dionysos Dimorphos', *Mélanges d'Archéologie et d'Histoire*, 1958, pp. 243–93; J. Collins-Clinton, *A Late Antique Shrine of Liber Pater at Cosa*, 1977, pp. 42f. (with additional bibliography); Turcan, *Les sarcophages romains à représentations dionysiaques*, pp. 391–3, 516, 524f., 533 n. 7.

195. 'War/Peace' (*Eirēnē Polemos*) next to the name of Dionysus on Orphic bone carvings from Olbia (Burkert in ch. 1, n. 2 above and in *Informationen zum altsprachlichen Unterricht* 2, 1980, pp. 36–8; F. Tinnefeld, *ZPE* 38, 1980, pp. 67ff.); Horace, *Od.* 2.19; Aristides, *Or.* 41.5; cf. Plutarch, *Ant.* 24.4; *Demetr.* 2.3; *Coh. ira* 13, *Mor.* 462B.

196. 'Life/Death' (*Bios Thanatos*) on Orphic bone carvings from Olbia (preceding note); Olympiodorus, *In Phd.* p. 38.13f. Norvin (Dionysus as

'steward of life and death'); cf. Heraclitus 22 B 15 Diels-Kranz (identity of Hades and Dionysus).

197. J. Roux, *Euripide, Les Bacchantes* II, pp. 307f. on *Ba.*, 187f.

198. Above, n. 18.

199. Aristides, *Or.* 41.9; Philostratus, *Im.* 1.2.5.

200. Deubner, *Attische Feste*, p. 133 n. 2; Dodds, *Euripides, Bacchae*, p. 181 on *Ba.* 854f. ('probably a reflection of ritual'; but see my nn. 97 and 203); C. Gallini, 'Il travestimento rituale di Penteo', *Studi e materiali di storia delle religioni* 34, 1963, pp. 211–28, esp. 215–18; W. J. Slater, 'Artemon and Anacreon', *Phoenix* 32, 1978, pp. 185–94, esp. 190f.

201. The evidence (both written and pictorial) has been collected by Slater, 'Artemon', pp. 188ff.; Nilsson, *Opusc. Sel.* III, 1960, pp. 81–4; Kerényi, *Dionysos*, p. 340 (German ed., p. 269), with figs. 104f.

202. Lucian, *Cal.* 16. 'Ptolemy Dionysus' has been identified as Ptolemy IV (above, p. 157 and n. 182) by Fraser, *Ptolemaic Alexandria* II, pp. 345 n. 112, 715f. n. 140.

203. Most prominently Pentheus dressed as a maenad in Euripides, *Ba.* 820ff., 912ff., a scene often claimed to reflect ritual (although ritual maenadism excluded males; see I.2 above), for instance by Gallini (above, n. 200) and Seidensticker (above, n. 97). In Athens in the second century CE, men apparently acted out 'effeminate dances' in the theatre during the Anthesteria (Philostratus, *VA* 4.21; above, n. 135).

204. Deubner, *Attische Feste*, p. 142f. This change of sexual roles for ritual purposes is a survival of initiatory coming-of-age rites; see A. Rutgers van der Loeff, *Mnem.* n.s. 43, 1915, p. 414; P. Vidal-Naquet, *PCPS* 14, 1968, pp. 57–60; F. Graf, *MH* 36, 1979, pp. 15 n. 117 and 17f.; C. Calame, *Les choeurs de jeunes filles en Grèce archaïque* I, 1977, pp. 258f.; cf. Burkert, *Structure and History*, pp. 29f.

205. [Apollodorus] *Bibl.* 3.4(28).3; Seneca, *Oed.* 418ff. Dionysus's disguise was a precaution against Hera's anger, a motif which is not primarily ritualistic. Yet it has been argued, on the analogy of Achilles's upbringing as a girl on Scyros, that the female disguise in both cases reflects archaic rites of passage (J. Bremmer, *Studi storico-religiosi* 2, 1978, p. 7, and in *Antike Welt* [forthcoming]; above, n. 204).

206. Dodds, *Euripides, Bacchae*, p. xiv (maenads), p. 181 (Pentheus], *Irrational*, p. 77 ('profound alteration of personality' as a possible effect of Dionysiac cult).

207. This is the Cambridge School version of Lev. 17.11 (so quoted by Harrison, *Prolegomena*, p. 483, and by Dodds at n. 209); cf. Gen. 9.4 and Deut. 12.23. The concept is central to W. Robertson Smith's sacramental theory of sacrifice as developed in chs. VIII and IX of his *Lectures on the Religion of the Semites*, 1894². Typically, G. Murray rendered Euripides, *Cretans, TGF*(N) fr. 472 = fr. 79 Austin, line 11 ōmophagous daitas as 'his red and bleeding feasts', a translation adopted by Harrison, *Prolegomena*, p. 481 and *Themis*, p. 118.

208. Dodds, while referring to Frazer's *The Golden Bough* (Part V, *Spirits of the Corn and the Wild* II, 1912³, pp. 138–68, entitled 'The Homoeopathic Magic of a Flesh Diet'), seems to echo Harrison, *Prolegomena*, p. 486 ('The

idea that by eating an animal you absorb its qualities is too obvious a piece of savage logic to need detailed illustration'). 'Simple savage' and 'savage logic' are Frazer's terms (ibid., pp. 138 and 202).

209. Dodds, 'Maenadism', p. 165 = *Irrational*, p. 277 = *Euripides, Bacchae*, pp. xviif.

210. John 6.56. Harrison's discussions of omophagy are tinged with Christian vocabulary (e.g. *Prolegomena*, pp. 452f., 'the sacramental mystery of life and nutrition' realized in the 'breaking of bread' and the 'drinking of wine'). Wilamowitz too, though resisting the sacramental interpretation (below, n. 214), compared the Milesian *omophagion* to the eucharist (above, n. 65).

211. Above, n. 207. On Harrison's use of Robertson Smith and of the notorious camel of St Nilus see McGinty, *Interpretation and Dionysos*, p. 78.

212. The sacramental interpretation of maenadic omophagy is much less prominent in Frazer's *Golden Bough* (1st ed., 1890, II, p. 43 = 3rd ed., Part V 2, p. 16; cf. 3rd ed., V 1, pp. 17f.) than in Harrison's work (following note).

213. Harrison, *Themis*, pp. 118–57 (quotation on p. 119), a supplement to, and modification of (along totemistic lines), *Prolegomena*, pp. 478–88.

214. E.g. Wilamowitz, *GdH* II, p. 68 (see above, n. 210); Otto, *Dionysus*, pp. 107, 130–32 (German ed., pp. 99f., 121ff.); Jeanmaire, *Dionysos*, p. 267; Festugière, *RB* 44, 1935, pp. 196 and 206 = *Études*, pp. 17 and 27; Winnington-Ingram, *Euripides and Dionysus*, p. 156 n. 1. Rohde (cf. above, n. 192) considered omophagy the result of the exalted Dionysiac state, and not the vehicle for it.

215. O. Gruppe, *Griechische Mythologie und Religionsgeschichte*, 1906, pp. 729–37 (who refers to both Robertson Smith and the eucharist); L. R. Farnell, *The Cults of the Greek States* V, 1909, pp. 161–68; F. Schwenn, *Die Menschenopfer bei den Griechen und Römern*, 1915, pp. 71–5 (based on Robertson Smith); Cumont, *Les religions orientales*, p. 201, and *After-Life in Roman Paganism*, 1922, p. 120; J. Schmidt, *PW* XVIII, 1939, *s.v.* 'Omophagie', cols. 380–2.

216. Above, n. 209. It is inexcusable that Dodds, while expressing a debt to 'Gruppe's view' (preceding note) of sacramental omophagy ('Maenadism', p. 166 = *Irrational*, p. 277), nowhere revealed the full extent of his indebtedness to Jane Harrison (above, n. 51). Instead, he advised his readers that her *Prolegomena* 'should be used with caution' (*Euripides, Bacchae*, pp. xif. n. 2).

217. I once succumbed to temptation myself (*Die Phoinikika des Lollianos*, p. 78). Nock and Nilsson also modified their views on this issue. Compare their early sacramental phase (Nock, *Essays* I, pp. 108f.; Nilsson, *Griechische Feste*, pp. 260, 308) with their later reservations (Nock, *Essays* II, pp. 819f.; Nilsson, *Greek Piety*, 1948, pp. 21f. and *Gesch. d. griech. Religion* I, pp. 576f.).

218. See I 2 above.

219. Above, n. 11.

220. Dodds, *Euripides, Bacchae*, p. xiii. Cf. Dodds on Euripides, *Ba.*

284f.; A. S. Pease on Cicero, *ND* 3.16.41 (Cicero rejects the idea of sacramental wine-drinking, thereby confirming its existence if not its currency); Kirchner, *Die sakrale Bedeutung des Weines*, pp. 87–90; Frazer, *Golden Bough*, Part V 2, p. 167.

221. Turcan, *Les sarcophages romains à représentations dionysiaques*, pp. 532–4; Henrichs, *Die Phoinikika des Lollianos*, pp. 74–7.

222. R. Eisler, *Orphisch-dionysische Mysteriengedanken in der christlichen Antike* II, 1925, pp. 198–217; Horn, *Mysteriensymbolik*, pp. 93–9.

223. The 'Orphic' gold plates of the late classical and Hellenistic period are the most eloquent written evidence for Bacchic eschatology (above, nn. 152 and 154). For the Hellenistic period, I note the phrase 'who knows her share of the good life' (*kalōn moiran epistamenē*) which concludes the commemorative epigram for a Milesian maenad (above, n. 91; cf. R. Merkelbach, 'Milesische Bakchen', *ZPE* 9, 1972, pp. 77–83, esp. 79ff.). According to Plutarch (*Cons. ad ux.* 10, *Mor.* 611D), in the first century CE, initiates of Dionysiac mysteries share the knowledge that there will be rewards and punishments after death. A Latin inscription of imperial date gives a poetic description of the Dionysiac Elysium (above, n. 184).

224. F. Cumont, *Recherches sur le symbolisme funéraire des Romains*, 1942; Bruhl, *Liber Pater*, pp. 309–31; Nilsson, *Dionysiac Mysteries*, pp. 116–32; Horn, *Mysteriensymbolik* (see above, n. 179).

225. Matz, *Die dionysischen Sarkophage* I, pp. 86–8.

226. H. R. W. Smith, *Funerary Symbolism in Apulian Vase-Painting*, 1976; M. Schmidt, A. D. Trendall, A. Cambitoglou, *Eine Gruppe apulischer Grabvasen in Basel*, 1976.

227. Bruhl, *Liber Pater*, pp. 77f. with pl. II; Horn, *Mysteriensymbolik*, fig. 50.

228. G. Precht, *Das Grabmal des L. Poblicius*, 1975, pls. 4–5 (Pan with hare and pedum, and another Pan with a syrinx, each next to a tree surrounded by a snake; decorative mask and winged eros in a higher register) and pl. 14 (dancing maenad carrying the rear half of a dissected fawn).

229. Turcan, *Les sarcophages romains à représentations dionysiaques*, pp. 9f., 369–71, 468–72 (triumph of Dionysus), 502–4 (banquet), 521–23 and 531f. (Dionysus and Ariadne), 568–92 (erotes), 615–17 (Seasons personified). I am indebted to Dr J. N. Bremmer (Center for Hellenic Studies, Washington, D.C., and University of Utrecht) and to Dr F. Graf (University of Zurich) for several corrections and for valuable suggestions.

9. *The Formation of Authoritative Tradition in the Greek Magical Papyri*

1. See above, pp. 1–22.

2. For the marks of a magician see Morton Smith, *Jesus the Magician*, 1978, pp. 81–93. Informative in this respect is also the autobiographical

account of the magician Thessalos, for which see especially Jonathan Z. Smith, 'The Temple and the Magician', in *Map is not Territory*, 1978, pp. 172–89.

3. See the discussion in Smith, *Map is not Territory*, 191ff.

4. For a general survey see Arthur Darby Nock, 'Greek Magical Papyri' (1929), reprinted in his *Essays on Religion and the Ancient World* I, pp. 176–94. By implication the question of self-definition is treated also in my paper 'Fragments from a Catabasis Ritual in a Greek Magical Papyrus', *History of Religions* 19, 1980, pp. 287–95.

5. *Papyri Graecae Magicae. Die griechischen Zauberpapyri*, ed. with GT K. Preisendanz; 2nd ed., A. Henrichs, 2 vols., 1973–4. The papyri are cited according to this edition by numbers and lines.

6. Origen, *Contra Celsum*, trs. H. Chadwick, pp. 23f.

7. For the use of *mageia* see also IV. 2319, 2449, 2453; *magikē empei[ria]* I. 331.

8. See Hesiod, *fr.* 272; Plato, *Resp.* 364C. For further references see H. D. Betz, *Galatians*, ET 1979, p. 55 n. 108. Cf. also *PGM* XII. 26: *peithein ton Erōta*.

9. This concept seems to be due to Neoplatonist influence. Cf. Iamblichus, *Myst.* 6.6; 3.7. See also *PGM* IV. 1762, 1780, 1807. See Th. Hopfner, 'Theurgie', *PW* 6a, 1937, cols. 258–70, esp. 267f.

10. IV. 476, 723; V. 110; XII. 331, 333.

11. IV. 794; I. 131.

12. IV. 2592.

13. XIII. 128.

14. XIX. a. 52.

15. XII. 322.

16. IV. 2477.

17. See IV. 2254; also I. 127; IV. 172, 744; XIII. 57, 428.

18. See IV. 172, 476ff., 733ff. (discussed below).

19. I am indebted here to the yet unpublished paper by William C. Grese, 'The Transformation of a Magic Text: Magic and Hermeticism in *PGM* III. 494–611'.

20. III. 591–601; translation is mine. For the parallel version in the Nag Hammadi texts see *The Nag Hammadi Library in English* (ed. James M. Robinson and Marvin W. Meyer), 1977, pp. 298f.

21. See II. 128; III. 159; IV. 1266; XII. 93. It should be noted that Neoplatonist philosophy was interested in this phenomenon because of its implications for the philosophy of language. See on this Maurus Hirschle, *Sprachphilosophie und Namenmagie im Neuplatonismus. Mit einem Exkurs zu 'Demokrit' B 142*, 1979.

22. See III. 412; IV. 2108.

23. See, e.g., I. 79; III. 326, 345, 368.

24. For the connection between Hermeticism and magic see the yet unpublished paper by William C. Grese, 'New Hermetic Texts and the Greek Magical Papyri'.

25. V. 286–302, trs. Morton Smith.

26. See for further reterences Theodor Hopfner, *Griechisch-ägyptischer Offenbarungszauber* II, 1924, pp. 1ff.

27. William Brashear, 'Ein Berliner Zauberpapyrus', *ZPE* 33, 1979, pp. 261–278.

28. For Aphrodite see also IV. 1265, 3209, 3249; VII. 215. See Wolfgang Speyer, *Bücherfunde in der Glaubenswerbung der Antike*, 1970, pp. 72ff.

29. See, e.g. IV. 452, 792, 804.

30. Translation is mine.

31. Cf. Albrecht Dieterich, *Abraxas*, 1891, pp. 165f. See also XIII. 947; VII. 451.

32. See Karl Preisendanz, 'Pitys 3', *PW* XX, 1950, cols. 1882f.; idem, 'Ostanes', *PW* XVIII, 1942, cols. 1610–42.

33. See V. 96–171; VII. 619–27; XIII. 1–3, 21, 343f., 724, 731f., 970, 1057, 1077.

34. See I. 39f.; 191; IV. 499ff.

35. See XIII. 56f., 380, 428.

36. IV. 733–750, ET Marvin W. Meyer, *The 'Mithras Liturgy,'* 1976.

37. I. 193; IV. 2512, 2518f.; XIII. 742, 755.

38. See also I. 41, 130, 146.

39. See esp. I. 217; IV. 1610; XII. 237, 240; XIII. 742, 763; XXII. b. 20; LVII. 13.

40. VII. 339; XI. c. 1.

41. I. 46, 52; III. 424; VII. 249, 863; XIII. 3, 15f. and often.

42. On the importance of the letter form in the *PGM* see Johannes Sykutris, 'Epistolographie', *PW* Suppl. V, 1931, col. 207.

43. See also V. 51; XII. 407; XXIV a. 2.

44. See also IV. 1167, 3249, 3252; V. 96; VIII. 42.

45. See IV. 885ff.; XII. 276; XIII. 81ff., 149ff., 457ff., 593ff.

46. XII. 401–7, my translation. Cf. 'The Discourse on the Eighth and the Ninth' (Nag Hammadi Codex VI, 6), in *The Nag Hammadi Library in English*, pp. 296f. For the concept of *lysis* see Gudeman, 'Lyseis', *PW* XIII, 1927, cols. 2511–29.

47. See e.g. I. 97–130, 172–93; III. 162–4. The term 'aretalogical' has been intentionally used to describe this section.

48. I. 126–30, ET Edward N. O'Neil.

49. K. Preisendanz, *Papyrusfunde und Papyrusforschung*, 1933, pp. 91–5.

50. Collecting ancient literature seems to have preoccupied the philosphers of the time. See Marinus, *Vita Procli*, especially chs. 26, 27, 33, 38.

10. *The Imperial Cult: Perceptions and Persistence*

1. On benefactor cults, see above all A. D. Nock, '*Soter* and *Euergetes*', in *The Joy of Study*, 1951; also G. W. Bowersock, *Augustus and the Greek World*, 1965.

2. Tacitus, *Ann.* 6.18 (of Theophanes of Mytilene).

3. Cicero, *Att.* 5.21.7, Shackleton Bailey, *Cicero's Letters to Atticus*, no. 114 (vol. III, 1968, p. 68): *statuas, fana, tethrippa prohibeo.*

4. Cf. the references in Bowersock, *Augustus*, pp. 150f.

5. C. Marcius Censorinus, cos. 8 BC, was the last Roman governor to receive a cult in his own province (*SEG* II, 549, cf. J. and L. Robert, *Bull. épig.*, 1979, #457), and Cn. Vergilius Capito the last to receive a cult anywhere, cf. L. Robert, 'Le Culte de Caligula à Milet et la province d'Asie', *Hellenica 7*, 1949, p. 209. A contemporary of Capito was probably the eponym of the Balbilleia at Ephesus, but it is by no means clear who this Balbillus, presumably Ti. Claudius Balbillus, was. Among the possibilities is a procurator in Asia and a prefect of Egypt. If we knew more, therefore, a Balbillus might have to be added to the list of ultimate magistrates with benefactor cults outside of the imperial house. On the Balbilli: H.-G. Pflaum, *Les carrières procuratoriennes équestres* I, 1960, pp. 34–41.

6. See A. Stein, 'Zur sozialen Stellung der provinzialen Oberpriester', *Epitymbion Swoboda*, 1927, pp. 300ff.

7. Note especially Nock's remarks in *CAH* 10, 1934, p. 481, and his articles 'The Roman Army and the Roman Religious Year', *HTR* 45, 1952 and 'Deification and Julian', *JRS* 47, 1957.

8. E.g., *MAMA* 6.370; *IGRom.* 4.93 and 1273.

9. In reconsidering Nock's argument, den Boer lays stress on Vespasian's miracles as reported by Tacitus, *Hist.* 4.81, 'Heerscultus en ex-votos in het Romeinse Keizerrijk', *MNAW.L* 36.4, 1973; cf. A. Henrichs, 'Vespasian's Visit to Alexandria', *ZPE* 3, 1968, especially pp. 65ff.

10. See G. W. Bowersock, 'Greek Intellectuals and the Imperial Cult in the Second Century A.D.', *Le culte des souverains dans l'empire romain*, 1973, esp. pp. 195–200.

11. A. H. M. Jones, *Augustus*, 1970, p. 150: 'The Greek inhabitants of the eastern provinces were used to worshipping kings, and when they came under the republican rule of Rome worshipped proconsuls, expensive though it was to build a temple every year.' This statement is erroneous in more ways than one.

12. Cf. Nock, 'The Roman Army', pp. 237f. (*Essays* II, p. 778).

13. See L. Robert, 'Sur des inscriptions d'Ephèse: fêtes, athlètes, empereurs, épigrammes', *RPh* 41, 1967, pp. 7–84.

14. Observe the lively discussion by K. Hopkins, 'Divine Emperors or the Symbolic Unity of the Roman Empire' in his *Conquerors and Slaves*, 1978, esp. pp. 219ff.

15. On the last item cf. H. W. Pleket, 'An Aspect of the Emperor Cult: Imperial Mysteries', *HTR* 58, 1965, pp. 331ff.

16. See L. Robert, 'Deux poètes grecs à l'époque impériale', *Stele. Festschrift N. Kontoleon*, 1977, pp. 10ff.; 'Fêtes, musiciens et athlètes', in his *Études épigraphiques et philologiques*, 1938, pp. 45ff.

17. Hopkins, 'Divine Emperors', pp. 221ff., emphasizes the importance of the statue.

18. Cf. E. Schürer, *The History of the Jewish People in the Age of Jesus Christ*, ET, vol. I, 1973, pp. 378–81. In the early empire at Augustus's initiative the Jews offered regular sacrifices to the Most High God in the

temple on behalf of the emperor and the Roman nation – at Augustus's
expense according to Philo (*Legat.* 317, cf. 157).

19. *Dig.* 27.1.15.6 and 50.2.3.3.
20. Pliny, *Ep.* 10.96.
21. See J. Beaujeu, 'Les apologètes et le culte du souverain', *Le culte des souverains dans l'empire romain*, 1973.
22. Beaujeu, 'Les apologètes', pp. 109 and 114. The passage ascribed to Melito, if it is indeed by him, is far more explicit: J. B. Pitra, *Spicilegium Solesmense* II, 1855, XXXVIII–LIII (Syriac).
23. Tertullian, *Apol.* 32–33. The quotation is from 33.
24. See W. Eck, 'Christen im höheren Reichsdienst im 2. und 3. Jahrhundert?', *Chiron* 9, 1979, pp. 450ff., and his refutation of Klauser in the matter of an exemption from the oath for Christians from the time of Marcus Aurelius.
25. TAZ 5.1; pAZ 3.1 (42b); bAZ 40b–41a. I am deeply grateful to Dr Harry Fox for his careful, detailed analysis of these texts and for translations which I have, for the most part, used here. Discussion of the Talmudic evidence at the McMaster symposium was helpful. Morton Smith raised the interesting point that the Mishnah text might not in the first instance allude to imperial statues, as everyone has hitherto assumed. On the Talmudic evidence for the imperial cult see especially E. E. Urbach, 'The Rabbinical Laws of Idolatry in the Second and Third Centuries in the Light of Archaeological and Historical Facts', *IEJ* 9, 1959 (pp. 238ff. for the texts cited here). See also M. Hadas-Lebel, 'Le paganisme à travers les sources rabbiniques des IIe et IIIe siècles', *ANRW* II.19.2, 1979, pp. 422ff., 'Les symboles du pouvoir et la question du culte impérial'.
26. PAZ 3.1 (42b) It seems reasonable to render *shultanot* as 'governors'.
27. Ibid.: 'And why was he called Nahum, man of holy of holies? Because he did not look at the image of a coin all his days.' Cf. Urbach, 'The Rabbinical Laws', p. 241, 'In addition to the ideological reasons for their opposition. . . ., (the Jews) sensed that the glittering splendour of the outward display of imperial power was for Jews fraught with the danger of social and national assimilation.'
28. L. Koep, 'Die Konsekrationsmünzen Kaiser Konstantins und ihre religionspolitische Bedeutung', *JbAC* 1, 1958, pp. 94–104; cf. S. Calderone, 'Teologia politica, successione dinastica e consecratio in età costantiniana', *Le culte des souverains dans l'empire romain*, 1973, esp. pp. 249 and 256.
29. Eusebius, *Vit. Const.* 4.73.
30. J. H. Eckhel, *Doctrina numorum veterum*, 1798, 8.473; O. Hirschfeld, 'Zur Geschichte des römischen Kaiserkultes', *SPAW* 35, 1888, pp. 833–62; E. Beurlier, *Le culte impérial*, 1891, p. 286.
31. *ILS* 705.
32. *Cod. Theod.* 16.10.2 (ET Pharr). This measure is wrongly ascribed to Constantine II by Calderone, 'Teologia politica', p. 267.
33. Eusebius, *Vit. Const.* 4.25.
34. Calderone, 'Teologia politica'; for an example of what is being

attacked here, see P. **Bruun,** 'The Consecration Coins of Constantine the Greek', *Arctos* n.s. 1, 1954, notably p. 27: 'In fact, the sun chariot turns out to be a reminiscence of the ascent of Elijah in the eyes of Christians.'

35. *ILS* 694 (arch: *instinctu divinitatis*); *Pan. Lat.* 12(9), 2.5 (*habes profecto aliquod cum illa mente divina, Constantine, secretum*) and 16.2 (*divina mens*); 4(10), 12.1 (*divinitus armis tuis deditum*), 14.2 (*divinitus missos*). In the arch inscription it occurs to me to ask whether the *mentis* in the phrase *mentis magnitudine* may not be the *divina mens*, as in the panegyrics, rather than Constantine's great mind, as usually assumed.

36. For pagan opinions, see the citations to follow (from panegyrics). For Christians, Eusebius, *HE* 8.17 *ad fin.*; Lactantius, *de mort. persecut.* 20; Eusebius, *Vit. Const.* 1.16f. (the most rapturous account of Constantius).

37. *Pan. Lat.* 7(6), 14.3.

38. *Pan. Lat.* 6(7), 8.2.

39. Ibid., 7.3. Koep, 'Die Konsekrationsmünzen Kaiser Konstantins', p. 519, wrongly ascribes this passage to the panegyric of 313.

40. Cohen 5, p. 554 no. 11 (2nd ed., vol. 7, p. 61 no. 28).

41. See, most recently, K. Weitzmann, *Age of Spirituality*, 1979, pp. 522f. Two of the horses are missing. See also O. Perler, *Die Mosaiken der Juliergruft im Vatikan*, 1953; J. Toynbee and J. B. Ward-Perkins, *The Shrine of St Peter and the Vatican Excavations*, 1956, pp. 72–4. I am deeply grateful to Katherine Dunbabin for guiding and correcting my thinking about this mosaic.

42. Eusebius, *Vit. Const.* 4.73.

43. *Cod. Theod.* 15.4.1 (ET Pharr).

44. See M. P. Charlesworth, 'The Refusal of Divine Honours', *PBSR* 15, 1939, pp. 1ff.

45. Tacitus, *Ann.* 4.38.

46. Dio Cassius 52.35: *pasai de poleis naoi, pantes de anthrōpoi agalmata (en gar tais gnōmais autōn aei met' eudoxias enidrythēsēi).*

47. *CIL* 11.258; G.B. de Rossi, *Inscriptiones Christianae urbis Romae* I, 1857ff., 767; *Cod. Iust.* 5.17.9.

48. *CIL* 8.10516.

49. Libanius, *Or.* 18.304.

50. Nock, 'Deification and Julian'.

51. *RAC*, s.v. 'Constantinus der Grosse', col. 371.

52. Philostorgius, *Kirchengeschichte* 3.1 (GCS), 1972, p. 28: . . . *tēn Kōnstantinou eikona, tēn epi tou porphyrou kionos histamenēn, thysiais te hilaskesthai kai lychnokaiais kai thymiamasi timan, kai euchas prosagein hōs theōi.*

53. Eusebius, *Vit. Const.* 4.71.

54. *Pan. Lat.*: Pacatus 6.4.

55. Chr. Habicht, *Le culte des souverains dans l'empire romain*, 1973, pp. 264f.

POSTSCRIPT: While this article has been in the press, S. G. MacCormack's *Art and Ceremony in Late Antiquity*, 1981, has given us a valuable treatment of the consecrations of Constantius and Constantine.

Bibliography

I. TEXTS, EDITIONS AND TRANSLATIONS
cited in the notes

Albinus, *Didaskalos, Platonis Dialogi* VI, ed. C. F. Hermann, Leipzig 1853, repr. 1936, pp. 152–89.

Anonymus Londinensis, *Supplementum Aristotelicum* III, ed. H. Diels, Berlin 1893.

Apollonius Citiensis, *In Hippocratis De articulis commentarius*, ed. J. Kollesch and F. Kudlien (*CMG* XI.1.1), Berlin 1965.

Apostolischen Väter, Die, I, ed. K. Bihlmeyer, Tübingen 1924.

Aristides, Aelius, *In Defence of Oratory*, ET C. A. Behr (LCL I), London/Cambridge, Mass. 1973.

— *Orationes* 16–53, ed. B. Keil, *Quae supersunt omnia* II, Berlin 1898.

— *Orations* 16–53, ET C. A. Behr, *Complete Works* II, Leiden 1981.

Asclepius. A Collection and Interpretation of the Testimonies, ed. E. J. L. and L. Edelstein, 2 vols., Baltimore 1945.

Athenaeus, *The Deipnosophists*, ET C. B. Gulick (LCL), 7 vols., London 1927–41.

Atticus, *Fragments*, ed. É. Des Places, Paris 1980.

Calcidius, *In Platonis Timaeum commentarius*, ed. J. H. Waszink (Corpus Platonicum Medii Aevi: Plato Latinus IV), London and Leiden 1962.

Callimachus, ed. R. Pfeiffer, Bonn 1923.

Carmina latina epigraphica II, ed. F. Bücheler, Leipzig 1897.

Cassius Iatrosophista, *Problemata*, in *Physici et medici Graeci minores* I, ed. J. L. Ideler, Berlin 1841.

Celsus, *Medicina*, I, ed. F. Marx (*CML* I), Leipzig 1915.

Cicero, *Academica*, ed. O. Plasberg, Leipzig 1922.

— *Letters to Atticus*, ed. and trs. D. R. Shackleton Bailey, 7 vols.. Cambridge 1965–70.

— *De finibus bonorum et malorum*, ed. H. Rackham (LCL), London 1914 (repr. 1967).

— *De natura deorum libri* III, ed. A. S. Pease, Cambridge, Mass. 1955.

Clement of Alexandria, ed. O. Stählin (GCS), 3 vols., Leipzig 1905–9.

Collectanea Alexandrina, ed. J. U. Powell, Oxford 1925.

Comicorum Atticorum Fragmenta, ed. T. Kock, 3 vols., Leipzig 1880–88.

Cynic Epistles, The: A Study Edition, ed. Abraham J. Malherbe, Missoula 1977.

242

Bibliography

Cypria, ed. T. W. Allen (*Homeri Opera* 5), Oxford 1912.

Demosthenes, *Orationes*, ed. S. H. Butcher and W. Rennie (Oxford Classical Texts), 3 vols., 1903–21.

Didascalia apostolorum, Syriac version, trs. R. H. Connolly, Oxford 1929.

Diogenes of Oenoanda: The Fragments, ed. C. W. Chilton, Oxford 1971.

Dionysius of Halicarnassus, *Opuscula*, ed. H. Usener and L. Radermacher, 2 vols., Leipzig 1909.

Doxographi Graeci, ed. H. Diels, Berlin 1879.

Ennius, *Ennianae poesis reliquiae*, ed. J. Vahlen, Leipzig² 1903.

Epicurus, ed. H. Usener, Leipzig 1887.

Epigrammata Graeca, ed. G.Kaibel, Berlin 1878.

Epistolographi Graeci, ed. R. Hercher, Paris 1873 (repr. 1965).

Erotian, *Vocum Hippocraticarum collectio*, ed. E. Nachmanson, Uppsala 1918.

Euripides, *Bacchae*, ed. E. R. Dodds, Oxford² 1960.

— *The Bacchae*, ET G. S. Kirk, Cambridge² 1979.

— *Hippolytos*, ed. W. S. Barrett, Oxford 1964.

Eusebius, *Praeparatio evangelica*, ed. and trs. E. H. Gifford, 5 vols., Oxford 1903.

Fragmente der Vorsokratiker, ed. H. Diels and W. Kranz, Berlin⁵ 1934.

Fronto, *Epistulae*, ed. S. A. Naber, Leipzig 1867.

Galen, *Opera Omnia*, ed. C. G. Kuhn, 20 vols., Leipzig 1821–33 (repr. 1964–5).

— *In Hippocratis Epidemiarum*, ed. E. Wenkebach and F. Pfaff, *CMG* V.lo, Leipzig 1955–60.

— *On Anatomical Procedures*, ET W. L. H. Duckworth, Cambridge 1962.

— *On the Natural Faculties*, ed. A. J. Brock (LCL), London 1916.

— *Scripta Minora* I, ed. J. Marquardt, II, ed. I. Müller, III, ed. G. Helmreich, Leipzig 1884–93.

— *De placitis Hippocratis et Platonis*, ed. I. Müller, Leipzig 1874.

Hesiod, *Fragmenta*, ed. R. Merkelbach and M. L. West, Oxford 1961.

Hippocrates, ed. W. H. S. Jones (LCL), 4 vols., London 1923–31.

Homer, *Iliad*, ET Richmond Lattimore, Chicago 1951.

Iambi et elegi Graeci ante Alexandrum cantati, ed. M. L. West, 2 vols., Oxford 1971–2.

Iamblichi Chalcidensis in Platonis Dialogos commentariorum fragmenta, ed. J. M. Dillon, Leiden 1973.

Iamblichus, *De communi mathematica scientia liber*, ed. N. Festa, Leipzig 1891.

— *De vita Pythagorica*, ed. L. Deubner, Leipzig 1937; 2nd ed. by U. Klein, Leipzig 1975.

Iustinus, *Epitoma historiarum Philippicarum Pompei Trogi*, ed. O. Seel, Leipzig 1935.

Julian, ed. W. C. Wright (LCL), 3 vols., London 1913–23.

Leges Graecorum Sacrae II, ed. J. de Prott and L. Ziehen, Leipzig 1906.

Marcellinus, *De pulsibus*, ed. H. Schöne (*Festschrift zur 49. Versammlung deutscher Philologen und Schulmänner*), Basel 1907.

Bibliography

The 'Mithras Liturgy', ET Marvin Meyer (Texts and Translations: Graeco-Roman Religion 2), Missoula 1976.

The Nag Hammadi Library in English, ed. James M. Robinson and Marvin W. Meyer, Leiden 1977.

Numenius Apamensis, Fragments, ed. É. Des Places (Budé), Paris 1973.

Olympiodorus, In Platonis Phaedonem commentaria, ed. W. Norvin, Leipzig 1913.

Oribasius, ed. J. Raeder (CMG VI), Leipzig and Berlin 1926–33.

Origen, Contra Celsum, ET H. Chadwick, Cambridge 1953.

Origenes Werke (GCS), 12 vols. Leipzig 1897 –

Orphicorum Fragmenta, ed. O. Kern, Berlin 1922.

XII Panegyrici Latini, ed. R. A. B. Mynors (Oxford Classical Texts), 1964.

Papyri Graecae Magicae. Die griechischen Zauberpapyri, ed. with GT K. Preisendanz, 2 vols., Leipzig 1928–31; 2nd ed., A. Henrichs, 2 vols., Stuttgart 1973–4.

Pedanius Dioscurides, De materia medica, ed. M. Wellmann, Berlin 1906–14.

Philodemus, Peri parrēsias, ed. A. Olivieri, Leipzig 1914.

— Peri poiēmatōn, ed. A. Hausrath, Jahrbücher für klassische Philologie Suppl. 17, 1889, p. 211.

Philostorgius, Kirchengeschichte, ed. J. Bidez, rev. ed. F. Winckelmann (GCS), Berlin 1972.

Pindar, Odes, ed. Sir John Sandys (LCL), London 1915.

Plato, Dialogi, ed. C. F. Hermann, 6 vols., Leipzig 1851–53, often reprinted.

Plotinus, ed. A. H. Armstrong (LCL), 3 vols., London 1966–67.

Poetae melici Graeci, ed. D. L. Page, Oxford 1962.

Poetarum Lesbiorum Fragmenta, ed. E.Lobel and D. L. Page, Oxford 1955.

Polemon, Fragmenta, ed. L. Preller, Amsterdam 1964.

Polystratus, ed. C. Wilke, Leipzig 1905.

Posidonius, I: The Fragments, ed. L. Edelstein and I. G. Kidd, Cambridge 1972.

Proclus, Théologie platonicienne, ed. with FT H. G. Saffrey and L. G. Westerink (Budé), 6 vols., Paris 1968 –

Rufus of Ephesus, Works, ed. C. Daremberg and C. E. Ruelle, Paris 1879.

— Die Fragen des Arztes an den Kranken, ed. with GT H. Gärtner, Berlin 1962.

Scholia in Euripidem, ed. E. Schwartz, 2 vols., Berlin 1887, 1891.

Scholia in Lucianum, ed. H. Rabe, Leipzig 1906.

Die Schule des Aristoteles, Texte und Kommentar, ed. F. Wehrli, 8 vols., Basel² 1967–69.

Sextus Empiricus, ed. R. G. Bury (LCL), 4 vols., London 1933–49.

Soranus, ed. J. Ilberg (CMG IV), Leipzig 1927.

Stobaeus, Joannes, Anthologium, ed. C. Wachsmuth and O. Hense, 5 vols., Berlin 1884–1912; Zurich³ 1974.

Stoicorum Veterum Fragmenta, ed. H. von Arnim, 4 vols., Leipzig 1903–24.

Sylloge Inscriptionum Religionis Isiacae et Sarapiacae, (ed. L. Vidman, Berlin 1969; cited as SIRIS).

244

Bibliography

Theodosian Code, The, ed. and trs. C. Pharr, Princeton 1952.
Theon of Smyrna, *Expositio Rerum Mathematicarum ad Legendum Platonem Utilium,* ed. E. Hiller, Leipzig 1878.
Tragicorum Graecorum Fragmenta, ed. A. Nauck, Leipzig² 1889; cited as TGF(N).
Tragicorum Graecorum Fragmenta I, ed. B. Snell, Göttingen 1971, IV, ed. S. Radt, Göttingen 1977.
Varro, Marcus Terentius, *Saturarum Menippearum reliquiae,* ed. A. Riese, Leipzig 1865.

II. SECONDARY LITERATURE

Adrados, F. R., *Festival, Comedy and Tragedy. The Greek Origins of Theatre,* Leiden 1975.
Africa, T. W., 'The Opium Addiction of Marcus Aurelius', *JHI* 22, 1961, pp. 97–102.
Alföldi, A., 'Redeunt Saturnia regna VII: Frugifer-Triptolemos im ptolemäischen Herrscherkult', *Chiron* 9, 1979, pp. 553–606.
Amand, D., *Fatalisme et liberté dans l'antiquité grecque,* Louvain 1945.
Ammann, A. N., *-ikos bei Platon,* Freiburg 1953.
Andresen, C., *Die Kirchen der alten Christenheit.* Stuttgart 1971.
Artelt, W., *Studien zur Geschichte der Begriffe 'Heilmittel' und 'Gift'* (Studien zur Geschichte der Medizin 23), Leipzig 1937.
Barns, J. W. B., and H. Lloyd-Jones, 'Un nuovo frammento papiraceo dell'elegia ellenistica', *Studi italiani di filologia classica* n.s. 35, 1963, pp. 205–27.
Bauer, W., *Orthodoxy and Heresy in Earliest Christianity,* ET of 2nd ed. (ed. R. A. Kraft and G. Krodel), Philadelphia 1971.
Beaujeu, J., 'Les apologètes et le culte du souverain', *Le culte des souverains dans l'empire romain* (Entretiens Hardt 19), Geneva 1973, pp. 103–42.
Beazley, J. D., *Attic Red-figure Vase-painters,* Oxford² 1963.
Behr, C. A., *Aelius Aristides and the Sacred Tales,* Amsterdam 1968.
Bell, H. Idris, *Cults and Creeds in Graeco-Roman Egypt,* Liverpool and New York 1953.
Benedum, J., 'Zeuxis Philalethes und die Schule der Herophileer in Menos Kome', *Gesnerus* 31, 1974, pp. 221–34.
Benoit, A., 'Les mystères païens et le christianisme', *Mystères et syncrétisme* (eds. M. Philonenko and M. Simon), Paris 1975, pp. 73–92.
Berger, Peter, *The Sacred Canopy,* New York 1967.
Bergman, J., *Ich bin Isis. Studien zum memphitischen Hintergrund der griechischen Isisaretalogien* (Acta Universitatis Upsaliensis, Historia religionum 3), Uppsala 1968.
Bergsträsser, G., *Ḥunain ibn Isḥāq. Über die syrischen und arabischen Galenübersetzungen,* Leipzig 1925.
Bernays, J., *Lucian und die Kyniker,* Berlin 1879.

Bertram, F., *Die Timonlegende*, Heidelberg 1906.

Betz, H. D., 'Fragments from a Catabasis Ritual in a Greek Magical Papyrus', *History of Religions* 19, 1980, pp. 287–95.

— *Galatians*, Hermeneia, ET Philadelphia 1979.

Beurlier, E., *Le culte impérial*, Paris 1891.

Billerbeck, M., *Epiktet: Von Kynismus*, Leiden 1978.

Blümner, H., *Die griechischen Privatalterthümer*, Freiburg/Tübingen³ 1882.

Boas, F., *The Religion of the Kwakiutl* II, New York 1930.

Boehm, F., *De symbolis Pythagoreis*, Diss. Berlin 1905.

Boer, W. den, 'Heersercultus en ex-votos in het Romeinse Keizerrijk', *MNAW.L*, N.R. 36.4, 1973, pp. 99–115.

Bonhoeffer, A., *Epictet und die Stoa*, Stuttgart 1890.

— *Die Ethik des Stoikers Epictet*, Stuttgart 1894.

Borger, R., *Handbuch der Keilschriftliteratur* III, Berlin 1975.

Boulanger, André, *Aelius Aristide et la sophistique dans la province d'Asie au IIᵉ siècle de notre ère*, Paris 1923.

Bowersock, G. W., *Augustus and the Greek World*, Oxford 1965 (pp. 112–21 repr. with revisions and in German translation as 'Augustus und der Kaiserkult im Osten', in *Römischer Kaiserkult*, ed. A. Wlosok, Darmstadt 1978, pp. 389–402).

— 'Greek Intellectuals and the Imperial Cult in the Second Century A.D.', *Le culte des souverains dans l'empire romain* (Entretiens Hardt 19), Geneva 1973, pp. 180–212.

— *Greek Sophists in the Roman Empire*, Oxford 1969.

— *Julian the Apostate*, Cambridge, Mass. 1978.

Boyancé, P., 'Dionysiaca. À propos d'une étude récente sur l'initiation dionysiaque', *REA* 68, 1966, pp. 33–60.

— 'Remarques sur le papyrus de Dervéni', *REG* 87, 1974, pp. 91–110.

— 'Sur la vie pythagoricienne', *REG* 52, 1939, pp. 36–50.

Brady, Th. A., 'The Reception of the Egyptian Cults by the Greeks', *The University of Missouri Studies* 10, 1935, pp. 1–86, repr. in *Sarapis and Isis, Collected Essays* (ed. F. Mitchel), Chicago 1978.

Brashear, William, 'Ein Berliner Zauberpapyrus', *ZPE* 33, 1979, pp. 261–78

Bremmer, Jan, 'Heroes, Rituals and the Trojan War', *Studi storico-religiosi* 2, 1978, pp. 5–38.

Breslin, J., *A Greek Prayer*, Pasadena, California 1977.

Bruhl, A., *Liber Pater. Origine et expansion du culte dionysiaque à Rome et dans le monde romain*, Paris 1953.

Bruneau, Ph., 'Existe-t-il des statues d'Isis Pélagia?' *BCH* 98, 1974, pp. 333–81.

— 'Isis Pélagia à Délos', *BCH* 85, 1961, pp. 435–46.

— 'Isis Pélagia à Délos' (Compléments), *BCH* 87, 1963, pp. 301–8.

Brunt, P. A., 'Marcus Aurelius and the Christians', *Studies in Latin Literature and Roman History*, ed. C. Deroux, II (Collection Latomus 168), Brussels 1980, pp. 483–520.

— 'Marcus Aurelius in his *Meditations*', *JRS* 64, 1974, pp. 1–20.

Bibliography

Bruun, P., 'The Consecration Coins of Constantine the Great', *Arctos* n.s. 1, 1954, pp. 19–31.

Burford, A., *Craftsmen in Greek and Roman Society*, London 1972.

— *The Greek Temple Builders at Epidauros*, Liverpool 1969.

Burkert, W., *Griechische Religion der archaischen und klassischen Epoche*, Stuttgart 1977.

— 'Hellenistische Pseudopythagorica', *Philologus* 105, 1961, pp. 16–43, 226–46.

— *Homo Necans. Interpretationen altgriechischer Opferriten und Mythen* (*RGVV* 32), Berlin/New York 1972.

— 'Le laminette auree: da Orfeo a Lampone', in *Orfismo in Magna Grecia*, Atti del Quattordicesimo Convegno di Studi sulla Magna Grecia, Naples 1975, pp. 81–104.

— 'Die Leistung eines Kreophylos. Kreophyleer, Homeriden und die archäische Heraklesepik', *MH* 29, 1973, pp. 74–85.

— *Lore and Science in Ancient Pythagoreanism*, ET Cambridge, Mass. 1972.

— 'Neue Funde zur Orphik', *Informationen zum altsprachlichen Unterricht*, Arbeitsgemeinschaft Klassischer Philologen beim Landesschulrat für Steiermark, 2, 1980, pp. 27–42.

— 'Orpheus und die Vorsokratiker. Bemerkungen zum Derveni-Papyrus und zur pythagoreischen Zahlenlehre', *Antike und Abendland* 14, 1968, pp. 93–114.

— 'Orphism and Bacchic Mysteries: New Evidence and Old Problems of Interpretation', *Protocol of the 28th Colloquy of the Center for Hermeneutical Studies in Hellenistic and Modern Culture* (ed. W. Wuellner), Berkeley 1977.

— Review of G. Zuntz, *Persephone, Gnomon* 46, 1974, pp. 321–8.

— *Structure and History in Greek Mythology and Ritual*, Berkeley/London 1979.

Calame, C., *Les choeurs de jeunes filles en Grèce archaïque*, 2 vols., Rome 1977.

Calderone, S., 'Teologia politica, successione dinastica e consecratio in età costantiniana', *Le culte des souverains dans l'empire romain* (Entretiens Hardt 19), Geneva 1973, pp. 215–69.

Capelle, W., *Epiktet, Teles und Musonius*, Zurich 1948.

Castellino, G. R., *Testi Sumerici e Accadici*, Turin 1977.

Caster, M., *Lucien et la pensée religieuse de son temps*, Paris 1937.

Castiglione, L., 'Nouvelles données archéologiques concernant la genèse du culte de Sarapis', *Hommages à M. J. Vermaseren* (ed. M. B. de Boer and T. A. Edridge; EPRO 68), Leiden 1978, I, pp. 208–32.

Charlesworth, M. P., 'The Refusal of Divine Honours', *PBSR* 15, 1939, pp. 1–10.

Clinton, K., *The sacred officials of the Eleusinian Mysteries*, Philadelphia 1974.

Cohen, Henry (ed.), *Description historique de monnaies frappées sous l'empire romain*, 7 vols., Paris 1859–68; 2nd ed., 8 vols., 1880–92.

Cole, S. G., 'New Evidence for the Mysteries of Dionysos', *GRBS* 21, 1980, pp. 223–38.

Bibliography

Colli, G., *La sapienza greca* I, Milan 1977.

Collins-Clinton, J., *A Late Antique Shrine of Liber Pater at Cosa* (EPRO 64), Leiden 1977.

Cumont, F., *Afterlife in Roman Paganism*, New Haven 1922.

— *Recherches sur le symbolisme funéraire des Romains* (Haut-Commissariat de l'État français en Syrie et au Liban, Service des Antiquités, Bibliothèque archéologique et historique, fasc. 35), Paris 1942.

— *Les religions orientales dans le paganisme romain*, Paris⁴ 1929, repr. 1963; ET of 1st ed., *The Oriental Religions in Roman Paganism*, Chicago 1911.

— and A. Vogliano, 'The Bacchic Inscription in the Metropolitan Museum', *AJA* 37, 1933, pp. 215–70.

Daraki, M., 'Aspects du sacrifice dionysiaque', *RHR* 197, 1980, pp. 131–57.

Daux, G., 'La grande démarche: un nouveau calendrier sacrificiel d'Attique (Erchia)', *BCH* 87, 1963, pp. 603–34.

Deichgräber, K., *Die griechische Empirikerschule*, Berlin/Zurich² 1965.

De Lacy, P., 'Lucretius and the History of Epicureanism', *TAPA* 79, 1948, pp. 12–23.

— Review of J. Dillon, *The Middle Platonists*, *Southern Journal of Philosophy* 18, 1980.

Delatte, A., *La vie de Pythagore de Diogène Laerce*, Brussels 1922.

Defrasse, A. and H. Lechat, *Epidaure: restauration et description des principaux monuments du sanctuaire d'Asclépios*, Paris 1895.

Detienne, Marcel, 'Les chemins de la déviance: Orphisme, Dionysisme et Pythagorisme', in *Orfismo in Magna Grecia*, Atti del Quattordicesimo Convegno di Studi sulla Magna Grecia, Naples 1975 (cited as *Taranto*).

— *La cuisine du sacrifice grec*, Paris 1979.

— 'Dionysos', *Dictionnaire des mythologies*, Paris 1980.

— *Dionysos mis à mort*, Paris 1977; ET *Dionysos Slain*, Baltimore 1979.

— 'Pratiques culinaires et esprit de sacrifice', *La cuisine du sacrifice en pays grec* (ed. M. Detienne and J.-P. Vernant), Paris 1979, pp. 7–31.

— 'Violentes "eugénies". En Pleines Thesmophories: des femmes couvertes de sang', *La cuisine du sacrifice*, pp. 183–214.

Deubner, L., *Attische Feste*, Berlin 1932.

de Vogel, C. J., *Pythagoras and Early Pythagoreanism*, Assen 1966.

DeWitt, N. W., *Epicurus and his Philosophy*, Minneapolis 1954.

— 'Organization and Procedure in Epicurean Groups', *CP* 31, 1936, pp. 205–11.

— *St Paul and Epicurus*, Minneapolis 1954.

Diehl, Charles, *Excursions in Greece to Recently Excavated Sites of Classical Interest*, London 1893.

Diels, Hermann and Wilhelm Schubart, *Anonymer Kommentar zu Platons Theatet (papyrus 9782) nebst drei Bruchstücken philosophischen Inhalts*, Berlin 1905.

Dietrich, Albrecht, *Abraxas*, Leipzig 1891.

Dill, S., *Roman Society from Nero to Marcus Aurelius*, London² 1905.

Diller, H., 'Thessalos', *PW* VIA, 1936, cols. 163–82.

Dillon, J. M., *The Middle Platonists*, London and Ithaca 1977.

Bibliography

Dodds, E. R., *The Greeks and the Irrational*, Berkeley 1951.
— 'Maenadism in the *Bacchae*', *HTR* 33, 1940, pp. 155–76.
— *Missing Persons: An Autobiography*, Oxford 1977.
— *Pagan and Christian in an Age of Anxiety*, Cambridge 1965.
Dölger, F. J., 'Zur Frage der religiösen Tätowierung im thrakischen Dionysoskult. "*Bromio signatae mystides*" in einer Grabinschrift des 3. Jh. n. Chr.', *Antike und Christentum* 2, 1930, pp. 107–16.
— 'Die Gottesweihe durch Brandmarkung oder Tätowierung im ägyptischen Dionysoskult der Ptolemäerzeit', *Antike und Christentum* 2, 1930, pp. 100–6.
Döring, I., *Exemplum Socratis*, Wiesbaden 1979.
Dörrie, H., 'Emanation – ein unphilosophisches Wort im spätantiken Denken', *Parusia. Studien zur Philosophie Platons und zur Problemgeschichte des Platonismus. Festgabe für J. Hirschberger* (ed. K. von Flasch), Frankfurt 1965, pp. 119–141.
Dover, K. H., *Greek Popular Morality in the Time of Plato and Aristotle*, Oxford 1974.
Dow, S., 'The Great Demarkhia of Erkhia', *BCH* 89, 1965, pp. 180–213.
Dudley, D. R., *A History of Cynicism*, London 1937.
Dunand, F., *Le culte d'Isis dans le bassin oriental de la Mediterranée* (*EPRO* 26), 3 vols., Leiden 1973.
— 'Les mystères égyptiens aux époques hellénistiques et romaines', *Mystères et Syncrétismes* (ed. M. Philonenko and M. Simon), Paris 1975, pp. 11–62.
Dunbabin, K. M., *The Mosaics of Roman North Africa: Studies in Iconography and Patronage*, Oxford 1978.
Durry, M., 'Les femmes et le vin', *REL* 33, 1955, pp. 108–13.
Ebeling, E., *Tod und Leben nach den Vorstellungen der Babylonier* I, Berlin 1931.
Eck, W., 'Christen im höheren Reichsdienst im 2. und 3. Jahrhundert?', *Chiron* 9, 1979, pp. 449–64.
Eckhel, J. H. *Doctrina numorum veterum*, 8 vols., Vienna 1792–98.
Edelstein, L., *Ancient Medicine*, Baltimore 1967.
— 'Methodiker', *PW* Suppl. VI, 1935, cols. 358–73.
Eisler, R., 'Nachleben dionysicher Mysterienriten', *ARW* 27, 1929, pp. 172–83.
— *Orphisch-dionysische Mysteriengedanken in der christlichen Antike* (Vorträge der Bibliothek Warburg 2, 1922–23), Leipzig/Berlin 1925.
Emeljanow, V., 'A Note on the Cynic Short Cut to Happiness', *Mnem.* n.s. 18/2, 1965, pp. 182–84.
Engelmann, H., *The Delian Aretalogy of Sarapis* (*EPRO* 44), Leiden 1975.
— and R. Merkelbach, *Die Inschriften von Erythrai und Klazomenai*, 2 vols., Bonn 1972, 1973.
Erbse, H., 'Die Vorstellung von der Seele bei Marc Aurel', *Festschrift für F. Zucker zum 70. Geburtstage*, Berlin 1954, pp. 129–52.
Farnell, L. R., *The Cults of the Greek States* V, Oxford 1909.
Farquharson, A. S. L., *The Meditations of the Emperor Marcus Aurelius*, 2 vols., Oxford 1944.

Bibliography

Farrington, B., *The Faith of Epicurus*, New York 1967.

Fehrle, E., *Die kultische Keuschheit im Altertum*, Giessen 1910.

Festugière, A. J., *À propos des arétalogies d'Isis'*, *HTR* 42, 1949, pp. 209–34.

— *Epicurus and His Gods*, ET Oxford 1955, (orig. Paris 1946).

— *Études de philosophie grecque*, Paris 1971.

— *Études de religion grecque et hellénistique*, Paris 1972.

— 'Les Mystères de Dionysos', *RB* 44, 1935, pp. 366–96 (= *Études de religion grecque et hellénistique*, pp. 13–62).

— *Personal Religion among the Greeks*, Berkeley/Los Angeles 1954.

— 'La signification religieuse de la Parados des Bacchantes', *Eranos* 54, 1956, pp. 72–86 (= *Études de religion grecque et hellénistique*, pp. 66–80).

Fontenrose, J., *The Delphic Oracle. Its Responses and Operations*, Berkeley/London 1978.

Fraser, P. M., *Ptolemaic Alexandria*, 3 vols., Oxford 1972.

— 'Two Studies on the Cult of Sarapis in the Hellenistic World', *OpAth* 3, Skrifter utgivna av Svenska Institutet i Athen 7, 1960, pp. 1–54.

Frazer, J. G., *The Golden Bough. A Study in Comparative Religion*, 2 vols., London 1890.

— *The Golden Bough. A Study in Magic and Religion*, Part V: *Spirits of the Corn and of the Wild*, 2 vols., London[3] 1912.

Fritz, K. von, *Mathematiker und Akusmatiker bei den alten Pythagoreern*, SBAW 1960. 11.

— 'Pythagoras', *PW* XXIV, 1963, cols. 171–209.

— *Pythagorean Politics in Southern Italy*, New York 1940.

— 'Telauges', *PW* VA, 1934, cols. 194–96.

Funghi, M. S., 'Una cosmogonia orfica nel papiro di Derveni', *PP* 34, 1979, pp. 17–30.

Funk, K., 'Untersuchungen über die Lucianische Vita Demonactis', *Philologus* Suppl. 10, 1907, pp. 561–674.

Gallavotti, C., *Empedocle, Poema fisico e lustrale*, Milan 1975.

Gallini, C., 'Il travestimento rituale di Penteo', *SMSR* 34, 1963, pp. 211–28.

Georgi, D., *Die Gegner des Paulus im 2. Korintherbrief*, Wissenschaftliche Monographien zum Alten und Neuen Testament 11, Neukirchen-Vluyn 1964.

Gerhard, G. A., *Phoinix von Kolophon*, Leipzig/Berlin 1909.

— 'Zur Legende vom Kyniker Diogenes', *ARW* 15, 1912, pp. 388–408.

Gernet, L., 'Dionysos et la religion dionysiaque. Éléments hérités et traits originaux', *REG* 66, 1953, pp. 377–95 (= *Anthropologie de la Grèce antique*, Paris 1968, pp. 63–90).

— 'Frairies antiques', *REG* 41, 1928, pp. 313–59 (= *Anthropologie*, pp. 21–62).

— *Le génie grec dans la religion*, Paris 1932 (repr. 1970).

Geyer, A., *Das Problem des Realitätsbezuges in der dionysischen Bildkunst der Kaiserzeit* (Beiträge zur Archäologie 10), Würzburg 1977.

Bibliography

Giouri, E., *Ho Kratēras tou Derbeniou*, (Bibl. tis en Athinais Archaiol. Hetair. 89), Athens 1978.

Glucker, John, *Antiochus and the Late Academy*, Göttingen 1978.

Goldschmidt, V., *Le système stoicien et l'idée de temps*, Paris³ 1977.

Gomperz, T., *Greek Thinkers* II, New York 1908.

Goodenough, E. R., *Jewish Symbols in the Greco-Roman Period 6: Fish, Bread and Wine* II (Bollingen Series 37), New York 1956.

Graf, F., 'Apollon Delphinios', *MH* 36, 1979, pp. 2–22.

— *Eleusis und die orphische Dichtung Athens in vorhellenistischer Zeit* (RGVV 33), Berlin 1974.

— 'Milch, Honig und Wein. Zum Verständnis der Libation im griechischen Ritual', *Perennitas. Studi in onore di Angelo Brelich*, Rome 1980, pp. 209–21.

Graindor, P. 'Le nom de l'université d'Athènes sous l'Empire', *Revue belge de philologie et d'histoire* 17, 1938, pp. 207–12.

Grandjean, Y., *Une nouvelle arétalogie d'Isis à Maronée*, Leiden 1975.

Grese, William C., 'New Hermetic Texts and the Greek Magical Papyri', unpublished paper.

— 'The Transformation of a Magic Text: Magic and Hermeticism in *PMG* III. 494–611', unpublished paper.

Griffiths, J. G., *The Isis-Book*, ET (*EPRO* 39), Leiden 1975.

Gruppe, O., *Griechische Mythologie und Religionsgeschichte*, Munich 1906.

Guarducci, M., *Epigrafia greca IV: Epigrafi sacre pagane e cristiane*, Rome 1978.

Gudeman, A., 'Lyseis', *PW* XIII, 1927, cols. 2511–29.

Guthrie, W. K. C., *The Greeks and their Gods*, London 1950, Boston, Mass., 1951, repr. 1954.

— *A History of Greek Philosophy* I, Cambridge 1962.

— *Orpheus and Greek Religion*, Cambridge² 1952.

Habicht, Chr., 'Die augusteische Zeit und das erste Jahrhundert nach Christi Geburt', *Le culte des souverains dans l'empire romain* (Entretiens Hardt 19), Geneva 1973, pp. 41–99, 264–5.

— *Die Inschriften des Asklepieions* (= *Altertümer von Pergamon* VIII.3, Deutsches Archäologisches Institut), Berlin 1969.

Hadas-Lebel, M., 'Le paganisme à travers les sources rabbiniques des IIᵉ et IIIᵉ siècles', *ANRW* II. Principat. 19.1. *Religion (Judentum: Allgemeines; Palästinisches Judentum)*, Berlin 1979, pp. 397–485.

Hadot, I., *Seneca und die griechisch-römische Tradition der Seelenleitung*, Berlin 1969.

Hadot, P., 'Une clé des Pensées de Marc-Aurèle', *Les Études Philosophiques*, Jan.-March 1978, pp. 65–84.

— 'La physique comme exercice spirituel ou pessimisme et optimisme chez Marc-Aurèle', *RTP* 22, 1972, pp. 225–39.

Hanfmann, G. M. A., and C. Moore, 'Hermes and Dionysos: A "Neo-Attic" Relief', *Fogg Art Museum Acquisitions*, 1969–70, pp. 41–9.

Harder, R., *Karpocrates von Chalcis und die memphitische Isispropaganda*, Berlin 1944.

Harrison, J., *Prolegomena to the Study of Greek Religion*, Cambridge³ 1922.

Harrison, J., *Themis. A Study of the Social Origins of Greek Religion*, Cambridge² 1927.

Haussleiter, J., *Der Vegetarismus in der Antike*, Berlin 1935.

Helm, R., 'Lucian und die Philosophenschule', *NJA* 9, 1902, pp. 351–69.

Hengel, M., *Judaism and Hellenism*, ET, 2 vols., London/Philadelphia 1974.

Henrichs, A., 'Die beiden Gaben des Dionysos', *ZPE* 16, 1975, pp. 139–44.

— 'Greek and Roman Glimpses of Dionysos', *Dionysos and His Circle: Ancient through Modern* (ed. C. Houser; The Fogg Art Museum), Cambridge, Mass. 1979, pp. 1–11.

Henrichs, A., 'Greek maenadism from Olympias to Messalina', *HSCP* 82, 1978, pp. 121–60.

— 'Die Maenaden von Milet', *ZPE* 4, 1969, pp. 223–41.

— 'Pagan Ritual and the Alleged Crimes of the Early Christians', *Kyriakon. Festschrift J. Quasten* I (ed. P. Granfield and J. A. Jungmann), Münster 1970, pp. 18–35.

– 'Philodemos "De Pietate" als mythographische Quelle', *Cronache Ercolanesi* 5, 1975, pp. 5–38.

— *Die Phoinikika des Lollianos. Fragmente eines neuen griechischen Romans* (Papyrologische Texte und Abhandlungen 14), Bonn 1972.

— 'The Sophists and Hellenistic Religion: Prodicus as the Spiritual Father of the Isis Aretalogies', *Acts of the VIIth Congress of the Federation of Classical Studies, Budapest 1979* (forthcoming).

— 'Two Doxographical Notes: Democritus and Prodicus on Religion', *HSCP* 79, 1975, pp. 93–123.

— 'Vespasian's Visit to Alexandria', *ZPE* 3, 1968, pp. 51–80.

Hepding, H., 'Iamos', *PW* IX, 1916, cols. 685–89.

Herter, H., 'Das Kind im Zeitalter des Hellenismus', *Bonner Jahrbücher* 132, 1927, pp. 250–8.

— 'Das Leben ein Kinderspiel', *Bonner Jahrbücher* 161, 1961, pp. 73–84 (= *Kleine Schriften*, Munich 1975, pp. 584–97).

— 'Das unschuldige Kind', *JbAC* 4, 1961, pp. 146–62 (= *Kleine Schriften*, pp. 598–619).

Herzog, R., *Koische Forschungen und Funde*, Leipzig 1899.

— 'Urkunden zur Hochschulpolitik der römischen Kaiser', *SPAW* 1935. 32, pp. 967–1019.

— *Die Wunderheilungen von Epidaurus, Philologus*. Suppl. 22, Heft III, Leipzig 1931.

Himmelmann-Wildschütz, N., 'Fragment eines attischen Sarkophags', *Marburger Winckelmann-Programm*, 1959, pp. 25–50.

Hirschfeld, O., 'Zur Geschichte des römischen Kaiserkultes', *SPAW* 1888. 35, pp. 833–62.

Hirschle, Maurus, *Sprachphilosophie und Namenmagie im Neuplatonismus. Mit einem Exkurs zu 'Demokrit' B 142* (Beiträge zur Klassischen Philologie 96), Meisenheim am Glan 1979.

Hirzel, R., *Untersuchungen zu Cicero's philosophischen Schriften*, 2 vols., Leipzig 1881–82.

Bibliography

Hock, R., 'Simon the Shoemaker as an Ideal Cynic,' *GRBS* 17, 1976, pp. 48–52.

Hoistad, R., *Cynic Hero and Cynic King*, Uppsala 1948.

— 'Cynicism', *Dictionary of the History of Ideas* I, New York 1968, pp. 627–34.

Hommel, H., 'Das Datum der Munatier-Grabstätte in Portus Traini und die "hederae distinguentes"', *ZPE* 5, 1970, pp. 293–303.

Hoorn, G. van, *Choes and Anthesteria*, Leiden 1951.

Hopfner, Th., *Fontes historiae religionis aegyptiacae*, Bonn 1922–25.

— *Griechisch–ägyptischer Offenbarungszauber* II, Leipzig 1924.

— 'Theurgie', *PW* VIa, 1937, cols. 358–70.

Hopkins, Keith, 'Divine Emperors or the Symbolic Unity of the Roman Empire', in his *Conquerors and Slaves*, Cambridge 1978, pp. 197–242.

Horn, H. G., *Mysteriensymbolik auf dem Kölner Dionysosmosaik* (Beihefte der *Bonner Jahrbücher* 33), Bonn 1972.

Hornbostel, W., *Sarapis* (*EPRO* 32), Leiden 1973.

Hornsby, H. M., 'The Cynicism of Peregrinus Proteus', *Hermathena* 48, 1933, pp. 65–84.

Hoven, R., *Stoïcisme et Stoïciens face au problème de l'au-delà* (Bibliothèque de la Faculté de philosophie et lettres de l'Université de Liège 197), Paris 1971.

Ingenkamp, H. G., *Plutarchs Schriften über die Heilung der Seele*, Göttingen 1971.

Jaeger, W., *Diokles von Karystos*, Berlin 1938, repr. 1963.

— *The Theology of the Early Greek Philosophers*, Oxford 1947.

Jayne, Walter A., *The Healing Gods of Ancient Civilizations*, New Haven 1925.

Jeanmaire, H., *Dionysos. Histoire du culte de Bacchus*, Paris 1951.

Jones, A. H. M., *Augustus*, London 1970, New York 1971.

Jungkuntz, R., *Epicureanism and the Church Fathers*, PhD Diss., University of Wisconsin, Ann Arbor 1961.

— 'Fathers, Heretics and Epicureans', *JEH* 17, 1966, pp. 3–10.

Kaerst, J., *Geschichte der hellenistischen Zeitalter* II.1, Leipzig-Berlin 1909.

Kapsomenos, S. G., 'Ho Orphikos Papyros tēs Thessalonikēs', *ArchDelt* 19, 1964, pp. 17–25.

Keil, J., 'Ärzteinschriften aus Ephesos', *Jahreshefte des Österreichischen Archäologischen Instituts* 8, 1905, pp. 128–38.

Keppel, T., 'Die Weinlese der alten Römer', *Programm der königl. Studienanstalt zu Schweinfurt für das Schuljahr 1873/74*, Schweinfurt 1874.

Kerényi, C., *Asklepios: Archetypal Image of the Physician's Existence*, ET (Bollingen Series 65.3), New York 1959; German ed., Darmstadt² 1956.

— *Dionysos: Archetypal Image of Indestructible Life*, ET (Bollingen Series 65.2), Princeton/London 1976; German ed. Munich/Vienna 1976.

Kern, O., *Orpheus*, Berlin 1920.

Kett, P., *Prosopographie der historischen griechischen Manteis bis auf die Zeit Alexanders des Grossen*, Diss. Erlangen 1966.

Kindstrand, J. F., *Bion of Borysthenes*, Uppsala 1976.

Bibliography

Kirchner, K., *Die sakrale Bedeutung des Weines im Altertum* (RGVV 9.2), Giessen 1910.

Köhler, L., 'Die Briefe des Sokrates und die Sokratiker', *Philologus* Suppl. 20.2, 1928.

Koep, L., 'Die Konsekrationsmünzen Kaiser Konstantins und ihre religionspolitische Bedeutung', *JbAC* 1, 1958, pp. 94–104 (repr. in *Römischer Kaiserkult* ed. A. Wlosok, Darmstadt 1978, pp. 509–27).

Köster, H., 'Häretiker im Urchristentum', *RGG* III, Tübingen³ 1959, cols. 17–21.

Kolb, F., 'Zu einem "heiligen Gesetz" von Tlos', *ZPE* 22, 1976, pp. 228–30.

Kourouniotes, K., 'Anaskaphai kai ereunai en Chiōi', *ArchDelt* 1, 1915, pp. 64–93.

Kraemer, R. S., 'Ecstasy and Possession: The Attraction of Women to the Cult of Dionysus', *HTR* 72, 1979, pp. 55–80.

— 'Ecstasy and Possession: Women of Ancient Greece and the Cult of Dionysus', *Unspoken Worlds: Women's Religious Lives in non-Western Cultures* (ed. N. A. Falk and R. M. Gross), New York 1980, pp. 53–69.

Kramer, B., 'Zwei literarische Papyrusfragmente aus der Sammlung Fackelmann', *ZPE* 34, 1979, pp. 1–18.

Kudlien, F., 'Dogmatische Ärzte', *PW* Suppl. X, 1965, cols. 179–80.

Lambert, W. G. and A. R. Millard, *Atraḫasīs, The Babylonian Story of the Flood*, Oxford 1969.

Langlotz, E., 'Filialen griechischer Töpfer in Italien?', *Gymnasium* 84, 1977, pp. 423–37.

Larsen, B. D., *Jamblique de Chalcis*, Aarhus 1972.

Lévi-Strauss, C., *Structural Anthropology*, New York 1963.

Lévy, Isidore, *La légende de Pythagore de Grèce en Palestine*, Paris 1927.

— *Recherches esséniennes et pythagoriciennes*, Geneva 1965.

Lewis, I. M., *Ecstatic Religion. An Anthropological Study of Spirit Possession and Shamanism*, New York 1971.

Linforth, I. M., *The Arts of Orpheus*, Berkeley 1941.

Lloyd, G. E. R., *Magic, Reason and Experience*, Cambridge 1979.

Lobeck, C. A., *Aglaophamus sive de theologiae mysticae Graecorum causis*, 2 vols., Königsberg 1829.

Löffler, I., *Die Melampodie*, Meisenheim 1963.

Long, A. A., *Hellenistic Philosophy*, New York 1974.

— 'Heraclitus and Stoicism', *Philosophia* 5–6, 1975–76, pp. 123–56.

— 'The Stoic Concept of Evil', *PhilosQ* 18, 1968, pp. 329–43.

Luce, S. B., 'Attic red-figured vases and fragments at Corinth', *AJA* 34, 1930, pp. 334–43.

Lynch, J., *Aristotle's School*, Berkeley and Los Angeles 1972.

MacCormack, S. G., *Art and Ceremony in Late Antiquity*, Berkeley 1981.

Malherbe, Abraham J., 'Gentle as a Nurse', *NovT* 12, 1970, pp. 203–17.

— 'Hellenistic Moralists and the New Testament', *ANRW* II. *Principat.* 26. *Religion (Vorkonstantinisches Christentum: Neues Testament: Allgemeines*, ed. W. Haase), in press.

— 'Medical Imagery in the Pastoral Epistles', *Texts and Testaments: Critical*

Bibliography

Essays on the Bible and Early Church Fathers (ed. W. E. March), San Antonio 1980, pp. 19–35.

— 'Pseudo Heraclitus, Epistle 4: The Divinization of the Wise Man', *JbAC* 21, 1978, pp. 54–6.

Malley, W. J., *Hellenism and Christianity*, Rome 1978.

Matz, F., *Die dionysischen Sarkophage I–IV*, Berlin 1968–75.

— *DIONYSIAKĒ TELETĒ. Archäologische Untersuchungen zum Dionysoskult in hellenistischer und römischer Zeit* (Abh. Akad. Mainz, Geistes- u. sozialwiss. Klasse, 1963.15), Wiesbaden 1964.

— 'Vindemia. Zu vier bakchischen Sarkophagen', *Marburger Winkelmann-Programm*, 1949, pp. 19–26.

McGinty, P., *Interpretation and Dionysos: Method in the Study of a God*, The Hague/Paris/New York 1978.

Meissner, B., *Babylonien und Assyrien II*, Heidelberg 1925.

Mejer, J., *Diogenes Laertius and his Hellenistic Background*, Wiesbaden 1978.

Merkelbach, R., 'Dionysisches Grabepigramm aus Tusculum', *ZPE* 7, 1971, p. 280.

— 'Eine Notiz zu Kallimachos Fr. 178, 20', *ZPE* 5, 1970, p. 90.

— 'Die ephesischen Dionysosmysten vor der Stadt', *ZPE* 36, 1979, pp. 151–6.

— 'Milesische Bakchen', *ZPE* 9, 1972, pp. 77–83.

— 'Der orphische Papyrus von Derveni', *ZPE* 1, 1967, pp. 21–32.

— 'Ein neues "orphisches" Goldblättchen', *ZPE* 25, 1977, p. 276.

— *Roman und Mysterium in der Antike*, Munich, 1962.

— '*Sēmeion* im Liebesepigramm', *ZPE* 6, 1970, pp. 245f.

Meuli, K., *Griechische Opferbrauche*, Anhang 2, in *Gesammelte Schriften*, Basel 1975, pp. 1018–21.

Miller, D. E., 'Sectarianism and Secularization: The Work of Bryan Wilson', *RSR* 5, 1979, pp. 161–74.

Moles, J. L., 'The Career and Conversion of Dio Chrysostom', *JHS* 98, 1978, pp. 79–100.

Momigliano, A., 'The Social Structure of the Ancient City', *Anthropology and the Greeks* (ed. S. C. Humphreys), London 1978, pp. 177–93.

Montgomery, J., *A Critical and Exegetical Commentary on the Books of Kings* (ed. Henry Snyder Gehman; International Critical Commentary), Edinburgh and New York 1951 (repr. 1960).

Moraux, Paul, *Der Aristotelismus bei den Griechen: von Andronikos bis Alexander von Aphrodisias I*, Berlin 1973.

Morenz, S., *Egyptian Religion*, ET Ithaca 1973 (orig. Stuttgart 1960).

Moretti, L. (ed.), *Inscriptiones Graecae Urbis Romae*, 3 vols., Rome 1968–79.

Mühll, Peter von der, 'Das griechische Symposion', *Ausgewählte kleine Schriften* (Schweizerische Beiträge zur Altertumswissenschaft 12), Basel 1975.

Müller, D., *Aegypten und die griechischen Isis-Aretalogien*, Berlin 1961.

Müller, I. von, 'Peri tēs aristēs haireseōs', *SBAW* 1898. 1, pp. 53–162.

Müller, R., *Die epikureische Gesellschaftstheorie*, Berlin 1972.

Müller-Graupa, E., 'Museion', *PW* XVI, 1935, cols. 801–21.

Mussies, G., 'Some Notes on the Name of Sarapis', *Hommages à M. J.*

Bibliography

Vermaseren (ed. M. B. de Boer and T. A. Edridge; EPRO 68), Leiden 1978, II, pp. 821–32.

Nachov, I., 'Der Mensch in der Philosophie der Kyniker', *Der Mensch als Mass der Dinge* (ed. R. Müller), Berlin 1976.

Neuenschwander, R., *Marc Aurels Beziehungen zu Seneca und Poseidonios* (Noctes Romanae 3), Bern 1951.

Niehues-Pröbsting, H., *Der Kynismus des Diogenes und der Begriff des Kynismus*, Munich 1979.

Nietzsche, F., *Werke in drei Bänden* (ed. K. Schlechta), Munich 1954–56.

— *Werke: Kritische Gesamtausgabe* III: 1–4 (ed. G. Colli and M. Montinari), Berlin and New York 1972–78.

Nilsson, M. P., 'Die Anthesterien und die Aiora', *Eranos* 15, 1915, pp. 181–200 (= *Opusc. Sel.* I, Lund 1951, pp. 145–65).

— *The Dionysiac Mysteries of the Hellenistic and Roman Age*, Skrifter utg.av Svenska institutet i Athen, 8°, 5, Lund 1957.

— 'En marge de la grande inscription bacchique du Metropolitan Museum', *SMSR* 10, 1934, pp. 1–17 (= *Opusc. Sel.* II, Lund 1952, pp. 524–41).

— *Geschichte der griechischen Religion*, 2 vols., Munich² 1955 and 1961.

— *Greek Piety*, Oxford 1948.

— *Griechische Feste von religiöser Bedeutung mit Ausschluss der attischen*, Leipzig 1906.

— 'A Krater in the Cleveland Museum of Art with Men in Women's Attire', *Acta Archaeologica* 13, 1942, pp. 223–26 (= *Opusc. Sel.* III, Lund 1960, pp. 81–4).

— *The Minoan-Mycenaean Religion and its Survival in Greek Religion*, Lund² 1950.

Nock, A. D., *Conversion. The Old and New in Religion from Alexander the Great to Augustine of Hippo*, Oxford 1933, repr. 1961.

— 'Deification and Julian', *JRS* 47, 1957, pp. 115–23 (repr. in *Essays* II, pp. 833–46).

— *Essays on Religion and the Ancient World*, 2 vols. (ed. Z. Stewart), Oxford/ Cambridge, Mass. 1972 (cited as *Essays*).

— 'Greek Magical Papyri' (1929), *Essays* I, pp. 176–94.

— 'Notes on Ruler-Cult I–IV', *JHS* 48, 1928, pp. 21–42 (repr. in *Essays* I, pp. 134–59).

— 'Religious Developments from the close of the Republic to the Death of Nero', *CAH* 10, 1934, pp. 465–511.

— Review of R. Harder, *Karpokrates von Chalkis und die memphitische Isispropaganda*, *Gnomon* 21, 1949, pp. 221–8 (repr. in *Essays* II, pp. 703–11).

— 'The Roman Army and the Roman Religious Year', *HTR* 45, 1952, pp. 186–252 (repr. in *Essays* II, pp. 736–90).

— 'Soter and Euergetes', in *The Joy of Study, Festschrift F. C. Grant* (ed. S. E. Johnson), New York 1951, pp. 127–48 (repr. in *Essays* II, pp. 720–35).

Norden, E., 'Beiträge zur Geschichte der griechischen Philosophie', *JCPh* Suppl. 19, 1893, pp. 377–462.

North, J. A., 'Religious Toleration in Republican Rome', *PCPS* n.s. 25, 1979, pp. 85–103.

Bibliography

Obens, W., *Qua aetate Socratis et Socraticorum epistulae quae dicuntur scriptae sunt*, Münster 1912.

Oeri, H. G., *Der Typ der komischen Alten in der griechischen Komödie, seine Nachwirkungen und seine Herkunft*, Basel 1948.

Oliver, J. D., 'The Mouseion in late Attic inscriptions', *Hesperia* 3, 1934, pp. 191–96.

Otto, W. F., *Dionysus: Myth and Cult*, ET, Bloomington 1965; German ed. Frankfurt 1933.

Pack, R. A., *The Greek and Latin Literary Texts from Greco-Roman Egypt*, Ann Arbor² 1965.

Parke, H. W., *Festivals of the Athenians*, Ithaca/New York 1977.

— *The Oracles of Zeus*, Cambridge, Mass. 1967.

Peek, W., *Der Isishymnus von Andros und verwandte Texte*, Berlin 1950.

Perdrizet, P., 'Le fragment de Satyros sur les dèmes d'Alexandrie', *REA* 12, 1910, pp. 217–47.

Perler, O., *Die Mosaiken der Juliergruft im Vatikan*, Freiburg 1953.

Peterson, E., *Eis Theos. Epigraphische, formgeschichtliche und religions-geschichtliche Untersuchungen*, Forschungen zur Religion und Literatur des Alten und Neuen Testaments 41, Göttingen 1926.

Pfiffig, A., *Religio Etrusca*, Graz 1975.

Pflaum, H.-G., *Les carrières procuratoriennes équestres sous le haut empire romain* I, Paris 1960.

Piccaluga, G., 'Bona Dea. Due contributi all' interpretazione del suo culto', *SMSR* 35, 1964, pp. 202–23.

Pickard-Cambridge, A., *Dithyramb, Tragedy and Comedy* (ed. T. B. L. Webster), Oxford² 1962.

— *The Dramatic Festivals of Athens* (ed. J. Gould and D. M. Lewis), Oxford² 1968.

Pitra, J. B., *Spicilegium Solesmense* II, Paris 1855.

Pleket, H. W., 'An Aspect of the Emperor Cult: Imperial Mysteries', *HTR* 58, 1965, pp. 331–47.

Poehlmann, R. von, *Geschichte der sozialen Frage und des Sozialismus in der antiken Welt*, 2 vols., Munich³ 1925.

Poland, F., *Geschichte des griechischen Vereinswesens* (Preisschriften gekrönt u. herausgegeben von der Fürstlichen Jablonowskischen Gesellschaft zu Leipzig, Nr. XXIII der historisch-nationalökonomischen Sektion), Leipzig 1909.

— 'Speira', *PW* IIIA, 1929, cols. 1586–92.

Pomeroy, S. B., *Goddesses, Whores, Wives and Slaves: Women in Classical Antiquity*, New York 1975.

Praechter, K., *Die Philosophie des Altertums*, Berlin 1926.

— 'Salustios', *PW* 2nd Series, IB, 1920, cols. 1967–70.

Precht, G., *Das Grabmal des L. Poblicius*, Cologne 1975.

Preisendanz, Karl, 'Ostanes', *PW* XVIII, 1942, cols. 1610–42.

— *Papyrusfunde und Papyrusforschung*, Leipzig 1933.

— 'Pitys 3', *PW* XX, 1950, cols. 1882f.

Pugliese-Carratelli, G., and G. Foti, 'Un sepolcro di Hipponion e un nuovo testo orfico', *PP* 29, 1974, pp. 91–126.

Bibliography

Quandt, W., *De Baccho ab Alexandri aetate in Asia Minore culto*, Diss. Philologicae Halenses, XXI 2, Halle 1913.

Rabbow, P., *Seelenleitung*, Munich 1954.

Rahn, H., 'Die Frömmigkeit der Kyniker', *Paideuma* 7, 1960, pp. 280–92.

Rahner, H., *Greek Myths and Christian Mystery*, ET, New York 1971.

Ramsay, W. M., *The Cities and Bishoprics of Phrygia* I, Oxford 1895.

Rapp, A., 'Die Mänade im griechischen Cultus, in der Kunst und Poesie', *Rheinisches Museum* 27, 1872, pp. 1–22, 562–611.

— 'Mainaden', in W. H. Roscher (ed.) *Lexikon der griechischen und römischen Mythologie* II.2, Leipzig 1894–97, cols. 2243–83.

Reesor, M. E., 'The Stoic Categories', *AJP* 78, 1957, pp. 63–82.

Reinhardt, K., 'Poseidonios', *PW* XXII, 1953, cols. 558–826.

— *Poseidonios über Ursprung und Entartung*, Heidelberg 1928.

Reitzenstein, R., *Die hellenistischen Mysterienreligionen nach ihren Grundgedanken und Wirkungen*, Leipzig/Berlin 1927³ (repr. Darmstadt 1956).

Rengstorf, K., 'Apostolos', *TDNT* I, pp. 407–45.

Riginos, A. Swift, *Platonica*, Leiden 1976.

Rist, J. M., *Epicurus: An Introduction*, Cambridge 1972.

— 'The Heracliteanism of Aenesidemus', *Phoenix* 24, 1970, pp. 309–19.

— *Stoic Philosophy*, Cambridge 1969.

— 'Zeno and Stoic Consistency', *Phronesis* 22, 1977, pp. 161–74.

Robert, J. and L., *Bull. épig.* in *REG* 92, 1979, no. 457, p. 492.

Robert, L., 'Le culte de Caligula à Milet et la province d'Asie', *Hellenica* 7, 1949, pp. 206–38.

— 'Deux poètes grecs à l'époque imperiale', *Stele. Festschrift N. Kontoleon*, Athens 1977, pp. 1–20.

— *Études anatoliennes*, Paris 1937.

— 'Fêtes, musiciens et athlètes', *Études épigraphiques et philologiques*, Paris 1938, pp. 7–112.

— 'Sur des inscriptions d'Ephèse: fêtes, athlètes, empereurs, épigrammes', *RPh* 41, 1967, pp. 7–84.

Rösler, W., *Dichter und Gruppe*, Munich 1980.

Rohde, E., *Psyche*, 2 vols., Freiburg² 1898; ET, *Psyche. The Cult of Souls and Belief in Immortality among the Greeks*, London 1925.

— 'Die Quellen des Jamblichus in seiner Biographie des Pythagoras', *Kleine Schriften* II [ed. F. Schöll], Tübingen 1901, pp. 102–72 (repr. from *RhM* 26, 1871, pp. 554ff.; 27, 1872, pp. 23ff.).

Rohden, H. von, and H. Winnefeld, *Architektonische römische Tonreliefs der Kaiserzeit*, Berlin and Stuttgart 1911.

Rose, H. J., 'The grief of Persephone', *HTR* 36, 1943, pp. 247–50.

Rossi, G. B. de, *Inscriptiones Christianae urbis Romae*, I, Rome 1857ff.

Rostovtzeff, M., *The Social and Economic History of the Hellenistic World*, 3 vols., Oxford 1941, repr. 1953.

— *Social and Economic History of the Roman Empire*, 2 vols., Oxford² 1957, repr. New Haven 1966.

Roussel, P., *Les cultes égyptiens à Délos*, Paris/Nancy 1916.

Roux, J., *Euripide, Les Bacchantes, II, Commentaire*, Paris 1972.

Bibliography

Rudolph, K., 'Wesen und Struktur der Sekte', *Kairos* 21, 1979, pp. 241–54.

Rusajeva, A. S., 'Orfizm i kult Dionisa b Olbii', *Vestnik Drevnej Istorii* 143, 1978, pp. 87–104.

Rusten, J. S., '*Wasps* 1360–1369: Philokleon's *Tōthasmos*', *HSCP* 81, 1977, pp. 157–61.

Rutgers van der Loeff, A., 'De Oschophoriis', *Mnem.* n.s. 43, 1915, pp. 404–15.

Sartori, F., *Le eterie nella vita politica ateniese del VI e V sec. A. C.*, Rome 1957.

Scazzoso, P., *Le metamorfosi di Apuleio*, Milan 1951.

Schering, O., *Symbola ad Socratis et Socraticorum Epistulas Explicandas*, Greifswald 1917.

Schlier, H., 'Hairesis', *TDNT* I, Michigan/London 1964, pp. 180–85.

Schmid, W., 'Epikur', *RAC* V, 1962, cols. 681–819.

Schmidt, E., *Kultübertragungen* (RGGV 8.2), Giessen 1909.

Schmidt, J., 'Omophagie', *PW* XVIII, 1939, cols. 380–2.

Schmidt, M., A. D. Trendall and A. Cambitoglou, *Eine Gruppe apulischer Grabvasen in Basel*, Mainz 1976.

Schmithals, W., *The Office of Apostle in the Early Church*, ET Nashville 1969 (orig. 1961).

Schubart, W., 'Ptolemäus Philopator und Dionysos', *Amtliche Berichte der Preussischen Kunstsammlungen* 38, 1916–17, pp. 189–98.

Schürer, E., *The History of the Jewish People in the Age of Jesus Christ*, ET (rev. and ed. G. Vermes and F. Millar), Edinburgh, vol. I, 1973, vol. II, 1979 (orig. ET Edinburgh 1885ff.).

Schulz-Falkenthal, H., 'Kyniker – Zur inhaltlichen Deutung des Namens', *WZHalle* 26.2, 1977, pp. 41–9.

Schuster, M., 'Vindemia', *PW* IXA, 1961, cols. 17–24.

— 'Vinitor', *PW* IXA, 1961, cols. 121f.

Schutz, Alfred, *On Phenomenology and Social Relations* (ed. H. R. Wagner), Chicago 1970.

— and Thomas Luckmann, *The Structures of the Life-World*, Evanston 1973.

Schwabacher, W., 'Pythagoras auf griechischen Münzbildern', *Opuscula K. Kerényi dedicata*, Stockholm 1968, pp. 59–63.

Schwenn, F., *Die Menschenopfer bei den Griechen und Römern* (RGVV 15.3), Giessen 1915.

Scodel, R., 'Wine, Water, and the Anthesteria in Callimachus Fr. 178 Pfeiffer', *ZPE* 39, 1980, pp. 37–40.

Seidensticker, B., 'Sacrificial Ritual in the Bacchae', in *Arktouros. Hellenic Studies presented to B. M. W. Knox* (ed. G. W. Bowersock, W. Burkert and M. C. J. Putnam), Berlin/New York 1979, pp. 181–90.

Simon, B., *Mind and Madness. The Classical Roots of Modern Psychiatry*, Ithaca/London 1978.

Simpson, A. D., 'Epicureans, Christians, Atheists in the Second Century', *TAPA* 72, 1941, pp. 372–81.

Slater, W. J., 'Artemon and Anacreon', *Phoenix* 32, 1978, pp. 185–94.

— 'Symposium at Sea', *HSCP* 80, 1976, pp. 161–70.

Bibliography

Smith, H. R. W., *Funerary Symbolism in Apulian Vase-Painting* (University of California Publications: Classical Studies 12), Berkeley/Los Angeles/London 1976.

Smith, Jonathan Z., 'The Temple and the Magician', in *Map is not Territory. Studies in the History of Religions* (Studies in Judaism in Late Antiquity 23), Leiden 1978, pp. 172–89.

Smith, Morton, *Jesus the Magician*, San Francisco 1978.

— 'More New Fragments of Diogenes of Oenoanda', *Études sur l'Epicurisme antique* (eds. J. Bollack and A. Laks), Lille 1976, pp. 279–318.

— 'On the Wine God in Palestine (Gen. 18, Jn. 2, and Achilles Tatius)', *Salo Wittmayer Baron Jubilee Volume* (ed. S. Lieberman; American Academy for Jewish Research), Jerusalem 1975, pp. 815–29.

Smith, W. Robertson, *Lectures on the Religion of the Semites*, London² 1894.

Sokolowski, F., *Lois sacrées de l'Asie Mineure* (École française d'Athènes, Travaux et Mémoires 9), Paris 1955.

— *Lois sacrées des cités grecques* (École française d'Athènes, Travaux et Mémoires 18), Paris 1969 (cited as *LSCG*).

Solmsen, F., *Isis among the Greeks and Romans*, Cambridge, Mass. 1979.

Sparkes, B. A., 'Treading the Grapes', *Bulletin van de Vereeniging tot Bevordering der Kennis van de Antieke Beschaving te's Gravenhage* 51, 1976, pp. 47–56.

Speyer, Wolfgang, *Bücherfunde in der Glaubenswerbung der Antike*, Göttingen 1970.

Stanton, G. R., 'The cosmopolitan ideas of Epictetus and Marcus Aurelius', *Phronesis* 13, 1968, pp. 183–95.

Steckel, H., 'Epikuros', *PW* Suppl. XI, 1968, cols. 579–652.

Stein, A., 'Zur sozialen Stellung der provinzialen Oberpriester', *Epitymbion H. Swoboda*, Reichenberg 1927, pp. 300–11.

Stewart, Z., 'La religione', in *La società ellenistica. Economia, diritto, religione* (Storia e Civiltà dei Greci 8, ed. R. Bianchi Bandinelli), Milan 1977, pp. 503–616.

Sykutris, J., *Die Briefe des Sokrates und die Sokratiker*, Paderborn 1933.

— 'Epistolographie', *PW* Suppl. V, 1931, cols. 186–220.

— 'Sokratikerbriefe', *PW* Suppl. V, 1931, cols. 981–87.

Tannery, P., 'Orphica fr. 208 Abel.', *RPh* 23, 1899, pp. 126–29.

Taşlıklıoğlu, Z. and P. Frisch, 'New Inscriptions from the Troad', *ZPE* 17, 1975, pp. 101–14.

Temkin, O., 'Studies on late Alexandrian Medicine I', *Bulletin of the Institute of the History of Medicine* 3, 1935, pp. 405–30.

Thesleff, H., ed., *The Pythagorean Texts of the Hellenistic Period*, Aabo 1965.

Thulin, C. O., *Die etruskische Disziplin II: Die Haruspizin*, Goeteborg 1906, repr. Darmstadt 1968.

Tiede, D. L., *The Charismatic Figure as Miracle Worker*, Missoula 1972.

Tinh, Tran tam, 'À propos d'un vase à reliefs du musée de Toronto', *RA* 2, 1972, pp. 321–40.

— *Le culte des divinités orientales à Herculanum* (EPRO 17), Leiden 1971.

— *Le culte des divinités orientales en Campanie* (EPRO 27), Leiden 1972.

Bibliography

— 'De nouveau Isis lactans', *Hommages à M. J. Vermaseren* (ed. M. J. de Boer and T. A. Edridge; EPRO 68), Leiden 1978, III, pp. 1231–68.

— 'Etat des études iconographiques relatives à Isis, Sérapis et sunnaoi theoi', *ANRW* II. 17.3. *Religion (Heidentum: römische Götterkulte, orientalische Kulte in Der römische Welt)* (in press).

Tinh, Tran tam (ctd), *Isis à Pompéi*, Paris 1964.

— 'Isis—Nymphe de Laodicée', *Mélanges d'études anciennes offerts à Maurice Lebel*, Quebec 1980, pp. 339–61.

— 'Isis et Sérapis se regardant', *RA* 1, 1970, pp. 55–80.

— *Isis lactans (EPRO 37)*, Leiden 1973.

— 'Sarapis debout: un problème iconographique', *Acts of the First International Congress of Egyptology*, Berlin 1979, pp. 645–9.

Tinnefeld, F., 'Referat über zwei russische Aufsätze', *ZPE* 38, 1980, pp. 65–71.

Todd, R. B., *Alexander of Aphrodisias on Stoic Physics* (Philosophia Antiqua 28), Leiden 1976.

Tondriau, J., 'Dionysos, Dieu royal', *Annuaire de l'Institut de Philologie et d'Histoire Orientales et Slaves* 12, 1952, pp. 441–55.

— 'Tatouage, lierre et syncrétismes', *Aegyptus* 30, 1950, pp. 57–66.

Toynbee, A. J., *A Study of History* I, Oxford² 1935; V, Oxford 1939.

Toynbee, J., and J. B. Ward-Perkins, *The Shrine of St Peter and the Vatican Excavations*, London 1956.

Trumpf, J., 'Über das Trinken in der Poesie des Alkaios', *ZPE* 12, 1973, pp. 139–60.

Turcan, R., 'Dionysos Dimorphos', *Mélanges d'Archéologie et d'Histoire* (École française de Rome 70), Paris 1958, pp. 243–93.

— *Les sarcophages romains à représéntations dionysiaques. Essai de chronologie et d'histoire religieuse* (Bibliothèque des Écoles françaises d'Athènes et de Rome 210), Paris 1966.

Urbach, E. E., 'The Rabbinical Laws of Idolatry in the Second and Third Centuries in the Light of Archaeological and Historical Facts', *IEJ* 9, 1959, pp. 149–65, 229–45.

Vanderlip, V. F., *The Four Greek Hymns of Isidorus and the Cult of Isis* (American Studies in Papyrology 12), Toronto 1972.

Verbeke, G., *L'évolution de la doctrine du Pneuma du Stoicisme à S. Augustin*, Paris/Louvain 1945.

Vermaseren, M. J., *Liber in Deum. L'apoteosi di un iniziato dionisiaco (EPRO 53)*, Leiden 1976.

Versnel, H. S., 'Pentheus en Dionysos. Religieuze achtergronden en perspectieven', *Lampas* 9, 1976, pp. 8–41.

— *Triumphus. An Inquiry into the Origin, Development and Meaning of the Roman Triumph*, Leiden 1970.

Vidal-Naquet, P., 'The Black Hunter and the Origin of the Athenian Ephebeia', *PCPS* n.s. 14, 1968, pp. 49–64.

Vidman, L, *Isis und Sarapis bei den Griechen und Römern*, Berlin 1970.

Vogliano, A., *Epicuri et Epicureorum scripta*, Berlin 1928.

Bibliography

Vogt, J., *Von der Gleichwertigkeit der Geschlechter in der bürgerlichen Gesell-schaft der Griechen*, Abh. Mainz 1960.

von Soden, W., 'Die erste Tafel des altbabylonischen Atramhasis-My-thus', *Zeitschrift für Assyriologie* 68, 1978, pp. 50–94.

von Staden, H., *The Art of Medicine in Ptolemaic Alexandria: Herophilus and his School*, Cambridge (forthcoming).

— 'Experiment and Experience in Hellenistic Medicine', *Bulletin of the Institute of Classical Studies* 22, 1975, pp. 188–93.

Walzer, Richard, *Galen on Jews and Christians*, Oxford 1949.

— ed., *Galen on Medical Experience*, Oxford 1944.

Webster, T. B. L., 'The Myth of Ariadne from Homer to Catullus', *Greece and Rome* 13, 1966, pp. 22–31.

Wehrli, F., ed., *Die Schule des Aristoteles*, 8 vols., Basel² 1967–69.

Weitzmann, K., ed., *Age of Spirituality*, New York 1979.

Wellmann, M., 'Der Verfasser des Anonymus Londinensis', *Hermes* 57, 1922, pp. 396–429.

West, M. L., 'Notes on newly-discovered fragments of Greek authors', *Maia* 20, 1968, pp. 195–205.

— 'Zum neuen Goldplättchen aus Hipponion', *ZPE* 18, 1975, pp. 229–36.

White, K. D., *Roman Farming*, London 1970.

Whitehorne, J. E. G., 'Was Marcus Aurelius a hypochondriac?', *Latomus* 36, 1977, pp. 413–21.

Wide, S., 'Inschrift der Iobakchen', *Athenische Mitteilungen* 19, 1894, pp. 248–82.

Wiegand, T., 'Vierter vorläufigen Bericht über die Ausgrabungen der Königlichen Museen zu Milet', *SPAW* 1905. 25, pp. 533–48.
Sechster vorläufiger Bericht über Ausgrabungen im Milet und Didyma. APAW 1908, Anhang 1.

Wilamowitz-Moellendorff, U. von, *Der Glaube der Hellenen* (cited as *GdH*) II, Berlin 1932.

Wilken R. L., 'Collegia, Philosophical Schools, and Theology', *The Catacombs and the Colosseum* (ed. S. Benko and J. J. O'Rourke), Valley Forge, Pa. 1971, pp. 268–91.

Wilmes, E., *Beiträge zur Alexandrinerrede (or. 32) des Dion Chrysostomos*, Bonn 1970.

Wilson, B. R., *Religious Sects*, London 1970.

— *Sects and Society*, London 1961.

Winnington-Ingram, R. P., *Euripides and Dionysus. An Interpretation of the Bacchae*, Cambridge 1948.

Witke, C., 'Marcus Aurelius and Mandragora', *CP* 60, 1965, pp. 23f.

Witt, R. E., *Isis in the Greco-Roman World*, New York 1971.

Wolf, E., 'Häresie', *RGG* III, Tübingen³ 1959, cols. 13–15.

Wolff, H. J., *Das Problem der Konkurrenz von Rechtsordnungen in der Antike*, SHAW 1979.5.

Wolters, P., 'Archiatros to d'', *Jahreshefte des österreichischen archäolo-gischen Instituts* 9, 1906, pp. 295–7.

Zeller, Eduard, *Die Philosophie der Griechen* III 2, Leipzig⁴ 1902.

Bibliography

Ziegler, K., 'Orpheus', *PW* XVIII, 1939–42, cols. 1200–1316, 1341–1417.

Zimmern, H., *Beiträge zur Kenntnis der Babylonischen Religion* II, Leipzig 1901.

Zumpt, Carl Gottlob, *Über den Bestand der philosophischen Schulen in Athen und die Succession der Scholarchen*, APAW 1844, pp. 27–119.

Zuntz, G., 'Die Goldlamelle von Hipponion', *WS* 89, 1976, pp. 129–51.

— 'Once more the so-called Edict of Philopator on the Dionysiac mysteries', *Hermes* 91, 1963, pp. 228–39, 384.

— *Persephone. Three Essays on Religion and Thought in Magna Graecia*, Oxford 1971.

Index of Names

Abaris, 10, 15, 185 n. 21
Achilles, 234 n. 205
Achilles Tatius, 4
Adrados, F. R., 218 n. 49
Aenesidemus, 191 n. 106, 198 n. 21
Aeschines, 7, 10, 185 n. 29
Aeschylus, 130
Africa, T. W., 34, 191 n. 40
Agathe Tyche, 106
Agathodaimon, 106, 115
Agrippa, 198 n. 21
Agrippinilla, 154
Albinus, 61, 66, 70, 74
Alcinous, 70
Alexander of Abonuteichos, 189 n. 105
Alexander of Aphrodisias, 44, 69
Alexander (of Cilician Seleucia), 24, 36
Alexander the Great, 13, 26, 47, 131f.
Alexander Philalethes, 87f., 95
Alföldi, A., 185 n. 26
Amand, D., 193 n. 21
Ambrose, 182
Ammann, A. N., 187 n. 53
Ammonius, 66
Amphiaraos, 7
Anaxilaus of Larissa, 189 n. 105
Andreas, 88, 92, 94, 201 n. 51, 203 n. 82
Andresen, C., 184 n. 9
Andronicus, 64
Anonymus Londinensis, 79
Antiochus of Ascalon, 62–8, 74, 198 n. 21
Antipater of Tarsus, 200 n. 20
Antisthenes, 52, 57, 197 n. 67
Antoninus Pius, 35, 40, 134
Antony of Egypt, 13
Antony, Mark, 227 n. 135, 233 n. 190
Anubis, 213 n. 5

Apellas, Julius, 126f
Aphrodite, 105f., 116, 142, 148, 165, 238 n. 28
Apis, 101, 108, 213 n. 5
Apollo, 10, 106, 120, 122, 125f., 131, 134, 139, 227 n. 134
Apollo Hyperboreios, 10, 16, 19
Apollodorus of Athens, 3
Apollodorus of Pergamum, 200 n. 23
Apollonius of Chalcedon, 24
Apollonius of Citium, 91, 204 nn. 93, 94
Apollonius of Delos, 102, 104, 110
Apollonius of Delos II, 102, 111
Apollonius Mys, 79, 89, 92, 94, 205 n. 101
Apollonius of Tyana, 166, 187 n. 58, 189 n. 105
Apuleius, 106f., 109, 112f., 117, 157, 210 n. 43
Arcesilaus, 61–64, 68
Archilochus, 140
Ariadne, 148, 236 n. 229
Aristides, Aelius, 108, 112, 118, 127–36, 212 n. 44
Aristippus, 51f., 57, 195 n. 40
Aristobulus, 21
Ariston, 23, 65
Aristonicus, 65
Aristophanes, 121
Aristotle, 13, 16, 20, 22, 60–62, 64f., 79, 81, 162, 189 n. 98
Aristoxenus, 13–16, 18, 21, 79, 87, 92f., 95, 187 nn. 56, 62, 205 n. 101
Arius Didymus, 198 n. 13
Armstrong, A. H., 199 n. 31
Arsinoë II, 103 f.
Artelt, W., 215 n. 26
Artemis, 105f., 116, 120, 139
Asclepiades of Bithynia, 81

265

Index of Names

266

Index of Names

Claudius Maximus, 24
Cleanthes, 36
Clement of Alexandria, 27, 30, 44, 97f., 101, 157, 191 n. 29, 207 n. 2
Clinton, K., 185 n. 26
Clitomachus, 63, 67
Cole, S. G., 229 n. 156
Colli, G., 229 nn. 152, 153, 230 n. 161
Collins-Clinton, J., 233 n. 194
Constantine, 13, 97, 174, 176–82, 240 nn. 32, 35, 241 n. 39, P.S.
Constantius, 177–79, 241 n. 36, P.S.
Coronis, 120, 122
Crantor, 64
Crates, 51, 53, 62, 197 n. 80
Cratippus, 65
Cratylus, 37
Cronius, 72
Cumont, F., 208 n. 9, 209 n. 20, 210 n. 43, 217 n. 38, 222 n. 82, 225 nn. 100, 109, 226 nn. 117, 121, 232 n. 188, 235 n. 215, 236 n. 224
Cybele, 105, 224 n. 97
Cydias, 91

Damascius, 69
Damon, 16
Daraki, M., 219 n. 53
Dardanos, 166
Daux, G., 220 n. 66
Defrasse, A., 123, 126, 211 nn. 12, 17, 20, 212 n. 32
Deichgräber K., 199 n. 9, 200 n. 12, 201 nn. 28, 29, 202 n. 63, 203 n. 81, 204 nn. 92, 94, 205 n. 100
De Lacy, P. H., 193 n. 8, 198 n. 21
Delatte, A., 188 n. 82, 189 n. 93
Demeter, 105f., 139f., 148, 226 n. 111
Demetrius, 48, 89, 94
Demetrius of Apamea, 204 n. 99
Demetrius of Phaleron, 26, 111
Democritus, 166
Demonax, 49–52, 56, 58, 197 n. 80
Demosthenes, 11, 130
Demosthenes Philalethes, 86f., 89, 93, 95, 205 n. 102
Des Places, É., 198 nn. 19, 22
Detienne, Marcel, 2, 184 nn. 5, 7, 186 n. 47, 219 n. 53, 220 n. 66, 221 n. 72, 222 nn. 85, 87, 224 n. 96
Deubner, L., 215 n. 26, 216 nn. 32,

34, 217 n. 36, 226 n. 114, 227 n. 128, 234 nn. 200, 204
DeWitt, N. W., 192 nn. 3, 4, 193 nn. 11, 12, 13, 14
Diehl, C., 212 n. 43
Diels, H., 198 n. 4
Dietrich, A., 238 n. 31
Dill, S., 197 n. 68
Diller, H., 201 nn. 37, 40
Dillon, J. M., 46, 187 n. 58, 198 nn. 12, 15, 19
Dio Cassius, 180
Dio Chrysostom, 30, 48
Diocles of Carystus, 81
Diocles of Cnidus, 68
Diodorus Cronus, 28
Diodorus Siculus, 13, 15, 80f., 90, 144, 149, 228 n. 147
Diogenes, 188 n. 78, 194 n. 24, 197 nn. 67, 80
Diogenes Antonius, 188 nn. 73, 75
Diogenes of Apollonia, 79
Diogenes of Babylon, 184 n. 19
Diogenes Laertius, 13, 36, 49, 58, 62, 193 n. 19
Diogenes of Oenoanda, 48, 51, 53f., 57–9, 190 n. 47
Dion of Syracuse, 24, 65
Dionysius I, 17
Dionysius II, 16
Dionysius of Halicarnassus, 80f.
Dionysus, 2, 4f., 7f., 12, 101, 106, 134, 137–60, 214 nn. 8, 18, 219 n. 53, 220 n. 66, 221 n. 79, 222 n. 85, 223 nn. 89, 90, 224 nn. 95, 97, 98, 225 nn. 99, 105, 226 nn. 110, 111, 227 nn. 133, 134, 135, 228 nn. 146, 147, 230 n. 164, 231 n. 178, 233 nn. 190, 192, 194, 195, 196, 234 n. 205, 236 n. 229
Dioscurides Phacas, 94
Dodds, E. R., 33–5, 146, 159, 184 n. 14, 191 n. 38, 192 n. 49, 218 nn. 51, 52, 219 n. 53, 220 nn. 54, 55, 221 nn. 70, 71, 73, 74, 75, 79, 222 nn. 80, 81, 82, 83, 86, 87, 224 nn. 95, 98, 226 nn. 111, 120, 124, 227 n. 134, 230 n. 166, 233 n. 193, 234 nn. 200, 206, 207, 208, 235 nn. 209, 216, 220
Dölger, F. J., 232 nn. 182, 183, 184
Döring, K., 195 n. 28
Dörrie, H., 191 n. 27

267

Index of Names

Habicht, C., 182, 213 nn. 50, 51, 52, 53, 54, 55, 56, 57, 241 n. 55
Hadas-Lebel, M., 240 n. 25
Hades, 101, 108, 115, 233 n. 196
Hadot, I., 193 n. 12
Hadot, P., 190 n. 2
Hadrian, 26, 33, 35, 41, 134, 166
Hanfmann, G. M. A., 227 n. 129
Harder, R., 208 n. 10
Harpocrates, 109, 116
Harrison, Jane, 159, 218 nn, 51, 52, 219 n. 53, 227 n. 134, 230 n. 163, 232 n. 183, 234 nn. 207, 208, 235 nn. 210, 211, 212, 213, 216
Haussleiter, J., 186 n. 47, 188 n. 63
Hecataeus of Abdera, 213 n. 5
Hecate, 105
Hegesippus, 97
Hegetor, 86, 94, 201 n. 51
Heinimann, F., 185 n. 28
Helios, 101, 115, 165
Helm, R., 195 n. 29
Helvidius Priscus, 24, 27
Hengel, M., 189 n. 101
Henrichs, A. 1, 184 n. 11, 185 n. 27, 214 nn. 10, 11, 215 n. 25, 216 nn. 29, 34, 218 n. 52, 220 nn. 56, 57, 66, 223 nn. 91, 93, 224 n. 98, 225 nn. 102, 104, 226 nn. 110, 112, 115, 118, 227 n. 129, 228 nn. 138, 148, 149, 229 n. 151, 230 n. 162, 231 n. 176, 236 n. 221, 239 n. 9.
Hepding, H., 185 n. 25
Hephaestus, 139
Hera, 139
Heracleius, 58
Heracles, 51, 106, 115, 172
Heraclides of Erythrae, 79, 87, 91f., 94, 205 n. 101
Heraclides of Tarentum, 79, 90f., 202 n. 63
Heraclitus, 30, 36f., 39, 53, 59, 223 n. 91
Hercher, R., 193 n. 18
Hermes, 106f.,
Herodotus, 7, 104, 213 n. 5
Herondas, 125
Herophilus, 78, 81f., 85–90, 92f., 95, 201 n. 51, 202 n. 54, 206 n. 124
Herter, H., 226 n. 127
Herzog, R., 122, 135, 205 n. 109, 211 nn. 12, 13, 14, 15, 22, 23, 212 nn. 27, 33, 48, 213 nn. 60, 61, 63

Hesiod, 9, 73
Himmelmann-Wildschütz, N., 227 n. 131
Hipparchus, 18
Hippasus, 21
Hippobotus, 193 n. 19, 200 n. 25
Hippocrates, 7, 53, 80–82, 90, 94, 123–5, 204 n. 93
Hippolytus, 11
Hirschfeld, O., 176, 240 n. 30
Hirschle, M., 237 n. 21
Hirzel, R., 191 n. 44
Hock, R. F., 195 n. 40
Hoistad, R., 193 n. 20, 195 n. 31, 196 n. 53
Holl, K., 187 n. 59
Homer, 7, 73, 166
Hommel, H., 232 n. 180
Hoorn, G. van, 227 n. 128
Hopfner, Th., 209 nn. 19, 28, 29, 30, 237 n. 9, 238 n. 26
Hopkins, K., 239 nn. 14, 17
Horn, H. G., 214 n. 8, 226 nn. 109, 111, 113, 122, 126, 227 nn. 130, 131, 228 n. 139, 231 n. 179, 232 nn. 181, 187, 236 nn. 222, 224
Hornbostel, W., 210 n. 44
Hornsby, H. M., 193 n. 23
Hoven, R., 191 n. 36
Hunain ibn Isḥāq, 77
Hygieia, 106, 126

Iamblichus, 13, 16, 18, 20f., 69, 75, 187 nn. 58, 59, 189 n. 90
Ieu, 167
Ignatius, 97
Ingenkamp, H. G., 193 n. 12
Irenaeus, 97
Isidorus of Medinet Madi, 106, 112
Isis, 101–9, 111–17, 138, 165, 207 n. 4, 208 nn. 9, 10, 210 n. 45, 212 n. 47
Isocrates, 7
Iustinus, 13

Jacob, 166
Jacoby, F., 233 n. 193
Jaeger, W., 184 n. 4, 203 n. 68
Jayne, W. A., 211 n. 19
Jeanmaire, H., 214 n. 8, 218 n. 52, 219 n. 53, 221 n. 73, 222 nn. 82, 85, 226 n. 125, 228 n. 145, 229 n. 151, 235 n. 214
Jesus Christ, 97, 116

Index of Names

Jones, A. H. M., 173, 239 n. 11
Jones, W. H. S., 125
Josephus, 96, 206 n. 115
Julian the Apostate, 49f., 54, 58f., 69, 71, 73, 108, 180–82, 193 n. 19, 195 n. 32, 197 n. 69
Jungkuntz, R., 193 n. 5
Juppiter, 178f.
Justin Martyr, 97, 175
Justinian, 66

Kadmos, 224 n. 97
Kaerst, J., 196 n. 54
Kapsomenos, S. G., 183 n. 1
Keil, J., 205 n. 108
Keppel, T., 215 n. 21
Kerényi, C., 119, 134, 211 nn. 3, 26, 213 n. 58, 216 n. 29, 217 n. 38, 218 n. 49, 222 n. 82, 225 nn. 100, 105, 226 n. 109, 232 n. 187, 234 n. 201
Kern, O., 183 n. 4
Keryx, 163
Kett, P., 185 nn. 25, 29
Kindstrand, J. F., 195 n. 31
Kirchner, K., 216 n. 27, 236 n. 220
Kirk, G. S., 223 n. 90
Köhler, L., 194 n. 28
Koep, L., 240 n. 28, 241 n. 39
Köster, H., 206 n. 127
Kore, 105, 139, 142, 185 n. 21, 217 n. 45
Kourouniotes, K., 217 n. 45
Kraemer, R. S., 213 n. 2, 221 nn. 76, 78, 222 n. 85, 224 n. 98
Kramer, B., 214 n. 12
Kudlien, F., 199 n. 7

Lambert, W. G., 186 nn. 37, 39
Larsen, B. D., 187 n. 58
Lechat, H., 123, 126, 211 nn. 12, 17, 212 n. 32
Lévi-Strauss, C., 10, 119, 186 n. 46
Lévy, Isidore, 21, 189 n. 103
Lewis, I. M., 221 nn. 73, 76
Libanius, 180
Linforth, I. M., 183 n. 4
Livy, 125, 211 n. 9
Lloyd, G. E. R., 185 n. 23
Lloyd-Jones, H., 232 n. 183
Lobeck, C. A., 232 n. 182
Löffler, I., 185 n. 25
Long, A. A., 36, 190 n. 11, 191 n. 43, 193 n. 6

Longus, 140, 154
Luce, S. B., 224 n. 97
Lucian of Samosata, 47, 49–52, 56, 69, 127, 195 n. 33, 196 n. 43, 197 n. 80
Lucius, 67, 112–14, 117, 209 nn. 15, 40, 210 n. 42
Luckmann, T., 211 n. 1.
Lucullus, 63f.
Lycus, 90
Lynch, J., 66, 198 n. 17
Lysis, 18, 189n. 96

MacCormack, S. G., 241, P.S.
Machaon, 211 n. 2
Malherbe, A. J., 192 n. 1, 194 n. 27, 195 n. 37, 196 nn. 47, 60, 61, 197 n. 73
Malley, W. J., 197 n. 77
Manetho, 165f.
Mannsperger, D., 187 n. 55
Mantias, 89f., 94
Marcion, 98
Marcus Aurelius, 23–44, 69, 73, 130, 154, 190 nn. 15, 18, 191 nn. 30, 39, 43, 192 nn. 52, 56, 59, 240 n. 24
Marcus Brutus, 24
Matz, F., 215 n. 20, 225 n. 109, 232 n. 187, 233 n. 194, 236 n. 225
Maximus of Ephesus, 73
Maximus of Tyre, 50, 70
McGinty, P., 220 n. 53, 235 n. 211
Meir, Rabbi, 175f.
Meissner, B., 185 n. 24
Mejer, J., 193 n. 19, 197 n. 76
Melampus, 7
Melito, 175, 240 n. 22
Menecles of Barca, 205 n. 104
Merkelbach, R., 183 n. 1, 215 n. 26, 224 n. 98, 226 n. 122, 228 n. 142, 229 n. 158, 231 n. 169, 232 n. 186, 236 n. 223
Metrodorus, 63
Meuli, K., 222 n. 87
Millard, A. R., 186 nn. 37, 39
Miller, D. E., 184 n. 8
Mithras, 172
Moderatus of Gades, 189 n. 105
Moles, J. L., 196 n. 62
Momigliano, A., 3, 184 n. 8
Montgomery, J., 207 n. 7
Moore, C., 227 n. 129
Moraux, P., 198 nn. 9, 11
Morenz, S., 207 nn. 1, 6, 210 n. 46

Index of Names

Moretti, L., 217 n. 40
Moses, 71f., 166
Mühll, P. von der, 216 n. 27
Müller, D., 208 n. 10, 209 n. 17
Müller, I. von, 199 n. 7, 201 n. 32
Müller, R., 193 n. 9
Müller-Graupa, E., 205 n. 107
Murray, G., 234 n. 207
Musaeus, 4, 8
Musonius Rufus, 48
Mussies, G., 207 n. 3

Nachov, I., 195 n. 39
Neanthes, 17, 21
Neoclides, 121
Nephotes, 166f.
Nero, 32, 84, 95, 201 n. 47
Neuenschwander, R., 191 n. 30
Nicomachus, 13, 15, 187 n. 58, 189
  nn. 90, 105
Nicostratus, 67
Niehues-Pröbsting, H., 197 n. 75
Nietzsche, F., 156, 218 n. 51, 219 n..
  53, 221 n. 79, 225 n. 105, 227 n.
  134, 230 n. 163, 233 n. 192
Nigidius Figulus, 189 n. 105
Nike, 106, 116
Nilsson, M. P., 154, 184 n. 4, 214 n.
  8, 216 nn. 30, 33, 217 nn. 38, 39,
  43, 44, 218 nn, 47, 48, 52, 219 n.
  53, 220 nn. 56, 57, 65, 222 n. 83,
  224 n. 96, 225 nn. 107, 109, 226 nn.
  113, 122, 126, 227 n. 129, 228 n.
  143, 229 nn. 151, 158, 231 n. 170,
  233 n. 189, 234 n. 201, 235 n. 217,
  236 n. 224
Nock, A. D., 172, 181, 208 n. 10, 209
  n. 40, 210 n. 46, 228 nn. 140, 146,
  229 n. 151, 231 nn. 171, 174, 233 n.
  191, 235 n. 217, 237 n. 4, 238 n. 1,
  239 nn. 7, 9, 12, 241 n. 50
Norden, E., 195 n. 28
North, J. A., 229 n. 151
Numenius, 48, 68f., 71f., 74

Obens, W., 195 n. 28, 197 n. 64
Oeri, H. G., 214 n. 13
Oenomaus of Gadara, 49, 51, 58, 195
  n. 32
Oliver, J. D., 205 n. 108
Oribasius, 203 n. 82
Origen, 69, 97, 162
Orpheus, 1f., 4f., 8, 10–12, 73, 166,
  185 n. 21

Osiris, 101, 106, 108f., 113–15, 165
Ostanes, 166
Otto, W. F., 214 n. 8, 215 n. 25, 216
  n. 30, 218 nn. 49, 52, 219 n. 53,
  220 n. 66, 221 nn. 78, 79, 222 n.
  87, 233 n. 193, 235 n. 214
Ovid, 125f.

Pacatus, 181
Pachrates, 166
Panaetius, 33
Parke, H. W., 185, n. 22, 216 n. 32
Paul, 96, 99, 194 n. 27
Pausanias, 122 f., 126, 144, 146
Pease, A. S., 189 n. 93, 236 n. 220
Peek, W., 208 n. 10
Pentheus, 223 n. 90, 224 n. 97, 234
  nn. 203, 206
Perdrizet, P., 232 nn. 182, 183, 184
Peregrinus Proteus, 49–51, 56, 58f.,
  194 n. 23, 195 n. 32
Peripatos, 61, 64, 67, 77
Perler, O., 241 n. 41
Persephone, 9, 116
Peter, 99
Peterson, E., 208 n. 14
Pfeiffer, R., 216 n. 33, 223 n. 91
Pfiffig, A., 185 n. 34
Pflaum, H.-G., 239 n. 5.
Phalaris, 32
Philinus of Cos, 78, 90f., 206 n. 124,
  214 n. 18
Philip of Macedon, 26
Philo of Alexandria, 66, 74, 206 n.
  115, 223 n. 91
Philo of Larissa, 61–4, 67f.
Philostorgius, 181f.
Philostratus, 128
Phintias, 17
Pibechis, 166
Piccaluga, G., 214 n. 13
Pickard-Cambridge, A. W., 216 nn.
  32, 34, 218 n. 50, 224 n. 97, 226 n.
  114, 227 n. 128
Pindar, 9, 120f.
Piso, 64
Pitra, J. B., 240 n. 22
Pitys, 164, 166f.
Plato, 4f., 8, 10, 14, 16, 31, 33, 39,
  51, 57, 60, 62–4, 67f., 70–5, 81,
  124f., 130, 133, 195 n. 40, 196 n.
  51, 198 n. 4, 221 n. 70, 228 n. 137
Plautus, 156

271

Index of Names

Pleket, H. W., 239 n. 15
Pliny, 174 f.
Plotinus, 65–7, 69–74
Plutarch, 24, 28, 61, 66f., 69, 74f., 101, 112, 144, 156, 198 n. 21, 207 n. 2, 232 n. 182, 236 n. 223
Pluto, 101, 106, 108, 115
Plutus, 121
Pnouthis, 163, 166–8
Poehlmann, R. von, 188 n. 66
Poland, F., 217 nn. 37, 38, 39, 41, 43, 228 n. 143, 144
Polemainetos, 7
Polemon, 25, 62, 64f.
Polybius, 79f.
Polycrates, 20
Polystratus, 200 n. 19
Pomeroy, S. B., 214 n. 13
Pompeius Trogus, 13
Pompey, 36, 171
Porphyry, 13, 66, 68–70, 74, 187 n. 59
Posidonius, 31f., 191 n. 29, 192 n. 53
Praechter, K., 193 n. 23, 194 n. 25, 195 n. 34, 197 n. 83
Praxogoras, 78, 81f.
Precht, G., 236 n. 228
Preisendanz, K., 162, 169, 238 nn. 32, 49
Proclus, 69, 73–5, 184 n. 34
Prytanis, 80
Psammetichos, 164, 166
Ptolemy II Philadelphus, 110, 150f., 221 n. 68, 233 n. 190
Ptolemy IV Philopator, 7, 157, 215 n. 18, 217 n. 44, 230 n. 162, 232 n. 182, 233 n. 190, 234 n. 202
Pugliese Carratelli, G., 183 n. 2, 229 n. 152
Pythagoras, 2, 12–21, 36, 70, 166, 187 n. 55, 188 n. 79, 189 nn. 95, 96

Quandt, W., 230 n. 161
de Quincey, T., 34

Rabbow, P., 193 n. 12
Rackham, H., 198 n. 8
Rahn, H., 197 n. 69
Rahner, H., 210 n. 46
Ramsay, W. M., 206 n. 110
Rapp, A., 219 n. 53, 223 n. 89
Reesor, M. E., 190 n. 23
Reinhardt, K., 184 n. 18

Reitzenstein, R., 187 n. 59, 209 n. 37
Rengstorf, K., 194 n. 27
Riginos, A. Swift, 195 n. 40, 197 n. 67
Rist, J. M., 190 nn. 1, 10, 191 nn. 29, 31, 34, 45, 192 n. 48, 193 n. 17
Robert, J., 239 n. 5
Robert, L., 205 n. 108, 239 nn. 5, 13, 16
Robinson, T., 217 n. 46
Rösler, W., 187 n. 61
Rohde, E., 156, 183 n. 4, 185 n. 19, 187 n. 58, 218 nn. 51, 52, 219 n. 53, 220 n. 54, 221 nn. 71, 79, 222 nn. 83, 87, 230 n. 163, 233 n. 192, 235 n. 214
Rohden, H. von, 215 n. 20
Rose, H. J., 186 n. 41
Rostovtzeff, M., 127, 205 n. 107, 212 n. 34
Roussel, P., 209 nn. 22, 26
Roux, J., 214 n. 18, 220 n. 66, 223 n. 89, 224 n. 98, 226 nn. 111, 124, 227 n. 133, 234 n. 197
Rudolph, K., 184 n. 8
Rusajeva, A. S., 183 n. 2
Rusten, J. S., 225 n. 107
Rusticus, Junius, 24, 27
Rutgers van der Loeff, A., 234 n. 204

Sallustius, 59, 73, 197 n. 83
Sarapis, 101–12, 114–17, 128, 131, 138, 207 nn. 2, 4, 8, 208 n. 14, 209 n. 22, 210 nn. 43, 44, 212 n. 47
Sartori, F., 187 n. 61
Scaevola, Q. Mucius, 171
Scazzoso, P., 209 n. 40
Schering, O., 195 n. 28
Schlier, H., 206 nn. 117, 127, 132
Schmid, W., 192 n. 5, 193 nn. 6, 17
Schmidt, E., 228 n. 146
Schmidt, J., 235 n. 215
Schmidt, M., 236 n. 226
Schmithals, W., 194 n. 27
Schubart, W., 185 n. 30, 198 n. 4
Schürer, E., 239 n. 18
Schulz-Falkenthal, H., 195 n. 39
Schuster, M., 215 n. 21
Schutz, A., 211 n. 1
Schwabacher, W., 187 n. 55
Schwenn, F., 235 n. 215
Scodel, R., 216 n. 26
Seeck, O., 178

272

Index of Names

273

Index of Names

von Soden, W., 186 n. 39
von Staden, H., 184 n. 8, 201 nn. 29, 51, 202 nn. 52, 53, 203 nn. 68, 71, 73, 204 nn. 84, 85, 205 n. 102

Walzer, R., 199 n. 30, 201 n. 29
Ward-Perkins, J. B., 241 n. 41
Webster, T. B. L., 225 n. 108
Weitzmann, K., 241 n. 41
Wellmann, M., 199 n. 8
Wesley, J., 83
West, M. L., 183 n. 2, 186 n. 42, 229 n. 154
White, K. D., 215 n. 20
Whitehorne, J. E. G., 191 n. 39
Wide, S., 217 n. 45
Wilamowitz-Moellendorff, U. von, 3, 5, 183 n. 4, 184 nn. 10, 16, 218 n. 52, 220 n. 65, 221 nn. 69, 71, 79, 222 n. 83, 224 n. 96, 225 n. 100, 232 nn. 182, 184, 186, 235 nn. 210, 214
Wilken, R. L., 192 n. 2
Wilmes, E., 196 n. 62
Wilson, B., 3, 184 n. 8
Winnefeld, H., 215 n. 20
Winnington-Ingram, R. P., 222 n. 85, 229 n. 159, 235 n. 214
Witke, C., 191 n. 40

Witt, R. E., 207 n. 4, 208 n. 9
Wolf, E., 206 n. 127
Wolff, H. J., 185 n. 28
Wolters, P., 205 n. 108

Xenocrates, 60, 64f.
Xenophon, 57f.

Zeller, E., 189 n. 102
Zeno the Stoic, 23, 25, 43, 64, 200 n. 23
Zeno the Physician, 87, 89, 91, 94, 205 n. 101
Zeno of Sidon, 193 n. 6
Zeno of Tarsus, 110
Zeus 32, 39, 101, 106f., 115f., 129, 131f., 134, 172
Zeuxis Philalethes, 94f.
Ziegler, K., 183 n. 4
Ziehen, L., 217 nn. 40, 44, 218 nn. 47, 48
Zimmern, H., 186 n. 35
Zoilos, 110
Zopyrus of Alexandria, 90
Zoroaster, 166
Zumpt, C. G., 66, 198 n. 16
Zuntz, G., 183 nn. 2, 4, 185 nn. 22, 30, 229 n. 152

Index of Passages

Index of Passages

Index of Passages

Index of Passages

Index of Passages

Index of Passages

JEWISH AUTHORS AND WORKS

CHRISTIAN AUTHORS AND WORKS

Index of Passages